THE DESPERATE HOURS

THE
DESPERATE
HOURS

ONE HOSPITAL'S FIGHT TO
SAVE A CITY ON THE PANDEMIC'S
FRONT LINES

MARIE BRENNER

FLATIRON
BOOKS
NEW YORK

www.flatironbooks.com

Title page image by bookzv/Shutterstock.com

Designed by Donna Sinisgalli Noetzel

The Library of Congress Cataloging-in-Publication Data is available
upon request.

ISBN 978-1-250-80573-7 (hardcover)
ISBN 978-1-250-83193-4 (ebook)

Our books may be purchased in bulk for promotional, educational,
or business use. Please contact your local bookseller or the Macmillan
Corporate and Premium Sales Department at 1-800-221-7945, extension
5442, or by email at MacmillanSpecialMarkets@macmillan.com.

First Edition: 2022

10 9 8 7 6 5 4 3 2 1

For Dash—born in the first days of the pandemic—and Lucy, and Milo.

And for Nathan and Rachel, Kiev, Louise and Shepard, Ainsley and Adeline, Freedom and Madiba, Isabella and Sophia, Daphne, Francesca, Bruns and Emme, Chase, Juliette, Gemma, Jade, Liran, Jonah, Mateo, Talia, Colette, Nicolas, Eric, Ellis Rose, and all the children and grand-children of NewYork-Presbyterian's front lines who will someday learn of their parents' and grandparents' roles in the saving of lives.

Emergencies are crucibles that contain and reveal the daily, slower-burning problems of medicine and beyond—our vulnerabilities; our trouble grappling with uncertainty, how we die, how we prioritize and divide what is most precious and vital and limited; even our biases and blindnesses.

—SHERI FINK, *FIVE DAYS AT MEMORIAL*

New York was my country. There was something about New York: We will rise to this occasion. There was a determination, a grittiness. This is our city. We are going to get through.

—RICK EVANS, NEWYORK-PRESBYTERIAN

Cast of Characters

NewYork-Presbyterian Administration

Steven Corwin	president and chief executive officer
Laura Forese	executive vice president and chief operating officer
Daniel Barchi	group senior vice president and chief information officer
Peter M. Fleischut	senior vice president and chief transformation officer
Yoko Furuya	chief epidemiologist, director of infection prevention and control
Frank Bennack	former chairman of the board
Jerry Speyer	chairman of the board
Joe Ienuso	group senior vice president, facilities and real estate
Anand Joshi	vice president, procurement and strategic sourcing
Scott McClintock	manager, warehouse and logistics, health-care technology management
Rick Evans	senior vice president and chief experience officer
Lauren Wasson	vice president, office of graduate medical education

Randy Subramany	director of supply chain
Emme Deland	senior vice president of strategy, senior adviser to the Dalio Center for Health Justice
Nathan Stern	chief medical technology officer
Julia Iyasere	executive director, Dalio Center for Health Justice

NewYork-Presbyterian/Weill Cornell Medical Center

Augustine Choi	dean of Weill Cornell Medicine
Kate Heilpern	group senior vice president and COO
Arthur "Art" Evans	chief of hospital medicine
Rosanne Raso	vice president and chief nursing officer
Anthony Hollenberg	chair of medicine
Chris Belardi	emergency medicine physician and COVID patient
Fernando Martinez	chief of pulmonary and critical care and vice chair of medicine
Roy Gulick	chief of the division of infectious diseases
Nathaniel Hupert	internal medicine physician, public health researcher, and emergency response modeler
Matt McCarthy	physician/scientist, author, head of COVID treatment planning
Rudy Tassy	physician assistant
Kirana Gudi	vice chair of education, pulmonary critical-care specialist
Rae-Jean Hemway	director of nursing, pediatric services
Kerry Kennedy Meltzer	first-year internal medicine resident
Rahul Sharma	chair of emergency medicine
JoAnn Difede	director of program for anxiety and traumatic stress studies
Karen Bacon	pediatric nurse and COVID patient

Joseph Fins	chief of the division of medical ethics
David Berlin	medical director for critical-care services
Fernando Fernandez	security guard

5 South/medical ICU at Weill Cornell

Lindsay Lief	director of medical intensive care unit
Judith Cherry	pulmonary critical-care nurse
Kapil Rajwani	pulmonary critical-care specialist
Kelly Griffin	director of medical intensive care unit night program
Hasina Outtz Reed	researcher and critical-care physician
Alexandra Racanelli	pulmonologist
Ben-Gary Harvey	pulmonary and critical-care specialist
Geraldine Epping	nurse
Bradley Hayward	pulmonary critical-care and palliative-care physician
Elyse LaFond	second-year pulmonary fellow
Denise "Mama Deb" Inacay	nurse
Marjorie Walcott	housekeeper
Anthony Sabatino	nursing director

NewYork-Presbyterian/Columbia University Irving Medical Center

Laureen Hill	group senior vice president, chief operating officer
Mary D'Alton	chair of obstetrics and gynecology
Elizabeth "Lizzy" Oelsner	assistant professor of medicine
Allan Schwartz	chief, division of cardiology
Veronica Roye	outpatient liver-transplant coordinator
Tomoaki Kato	director of adult and pediatric liver and intestinal transplantation and COVID patient

Angela Mills	chair of emergency medicine services
Mark Apfelbaum	associate clinical professor of medicine
Daniel Brodie	director of medical ICUs
Steven Miller	codirector of non-operating-room anesthesiology
Oliver Panzer	anesthesiologist
David Wang	anesthesiologist
Beth Hochman	trauma surgeon and surgical SWAT team leader
Cleavon Gilman	emergency medicine physician
Gregg Rosner	associate professor of medicine
Peter Liou	abdominal transplant fellow and surgical SWAT team member
Kenneth Prager	chair of the medical ethics committee and director of clinical ethics
Jessica Forman	physician assistant
Craig Smith	surgeon in chief
Katherine Fischkoff	general surgeon and bioethicist
Kevin Roth	pathologist in chief
Dusty Carpenter	liver-transplant fellow
Andrew Knapp	anesthesiology resident
Gabrielle Clarke	head of transport
Victor Holness	morgue attendant
Jeffrey Shaman	infectious disease modeler and epidemiologist

NewYork-Presbyterian Lawrence Hospital

Michael Fosina	president
Xenia Frisby	associate chief quality officer
Andrew Amaranto	emergency medicine physician
Laurie Ann Walsh	chief nursing officer
Anthony Pucillo	interventional cardiologist

NewYork-Presbyterian Allen Hospital

Lorna Breen	emergency department director
Sofia Tam	chief resident and surgical SWAT team leader
Anna Podolanczuk	pulmonary critical-care physician

NewYork-Presbyterian Queens

Jaclyn Mucaria	president
Amir Jaffer	chief medical officer
Manish Sharma	chair of emergency medicine
Suzanne Pugh	director of emergency services
Pierre Saldinger	chairman of the department of surgery, surgeon in chief
Joseph Cooke	chair of medicine

NewYork-Presbyterian Brooklyn Methodist Hospital

Robert Guimento	hospital president
Felix Khusid	administrative director of respiratory therapy and pulmonary physiology center
Perry Cook	hematology/oncology specialist

NewYork-Presbyterian Lower Manhattan Hospital

Harjot Singh	epidemiologist
David Scales	internal medicine physician
David Weir	pulmonary intensivist

The Experts

Jay Varma	epidemiologist and senior adviser for public health and COVID-19 to Mayor Bill de Blasio and director of Cornell Center for Pandemic Prevention and Response

Ken Raske   president and chief executive officer of
                             Greater New York Hospital Association

The Patients and Their Families

Lawrence Garbuz   lawyer, patient at NewYork-
                            Presbyterian Lawrence
Adina Lewis   wife of Lawrence Garbuz
Susie Bibi   wife and mother, patient at Weill Cornell
Reuben Bibi   husband of Susie Bibi
Jeanne Rizzuto   New York City public school teacher
Chris Kampel   IT tech, patient at Weill Cornell
Sam Sportiello   Chris Kampel's fiancée
Robert Kampel   Chris Kampel's father
Mary Kampel   Chris Kampel's mother

The Community

Kang Liu   microbiologist with family in Wuhan
Richard Belsky   Kang Liu's husband
Donald G. McNeil Jr.   *New York Times* correspondent
Sarah Maslin Nir   *New York Times* correspondent
Li Wenliang   ophthalmologist, whistleblower in
                            Wuhan
Oxiris Barbot   NYC health commissioner
Maeve Kennedy McKean   executive director, Global Health
                            Initiative, sister of Kerry Kennedy
                            Meltzer
Lisa Stoia   medical-supply company owner
Bill de Blasio   mayor of New York City
Andrew Cuomo   governor of New York
Michael Schmidt   head of the New York State Task Force
Jim Malatras   Empire State College president
                            (SUNY chancellor August 2020 to
                            December 2021)

Introduction

A commonplace of writing advice is to explore what you are most afraid of: Find your fear, and there is your story. Like most people, I dread going into hospitals. I fear infection and the sense of looming decay. Hospitals, we know too well, can be the portal to death but also a place of miracles and cures. Still, the fear of hospitals is very real. Who hasn't heard a family member or friend plead, "Whatever you do, don't put me in a hospital"? Who hasn't experienced the worry that wafts from the waiting rooms or seen the looks of dread and glazed eyes in the coffee-cup-filled lounges?

In June 2020, when I heard of the possibility of reporting and writing this book, I didn't hesitate for a second. I would be able to penetrate one of the world's greatest hospital systems, in New York, and interview those who had lived and led the city through a once-in-a-lifetime pandemic. What these medical professionals did and what they learned, the mistakes they made, the breakthroughs they discovered and the triumphs they experienced, would come to set a template for the entire country. I needed to understand the fear that overcame everyone who stayed in New York throughout the surge of March and April as hospitals in the city were overwhelmed—and to understand those whose lives are lived as a calling to save every life they can. I would discover that many of my questions would not have an easy answer: What draws people to fight for the common good in a crisis? How can people expose themselves to so much risk?

In March 2020, as tents reminiscent of the Civil War overtook the grounds of hospitals throughout New York City, gallant descriptions of past wars were used again and again to rally the city of dreams. The governor of New York had his finest moment, using his rhetorical flourishes to swing for the big leagues of leadership, indicating we would fight as was done on the beaches of Normandy, meet the enemy as the Union had at Gettysburg, endure the hardships as the residents of Stalingrad had when under siege. All of it was meant to comfort as the unfathomable scenes cascaded: of refrigerated trucks, now temporary morgues, parked on Lexington Avenue and on the driveways of NewYork-Presbyterian's premier teaching hospitals—Weill Cornell Medical Center on Manhattan's Upper East Side and Columbia University Irving Medical Center in Washington Heights.

That spring, night after night, New Yorkers gathered at their windows at 7:00 p.m. and cheered for the doctors and nurses and respiratory therapists and physician assistants and transporters inside every hospital in the city who showed up every day to try to save lives. New Yorkers banged pots, they yelled, they drove in the streets honking horns. They waved to their neighbors and sometimes sat outside on their stoops and called to each other across the street. They sang arias as people had in the hot spots of Italy earlier that spring. The evening applause became the soundtrack of a city in crisis, and it went on for months. But the banging of the pots, the pans, the calls for glory could not camouflage reality: New York and its hospitals were completely unprepared, even at NewYork-Presbyterian, the Mount Olympus of health-care systems. They were so unprepared that academic chairs of the medical schools affiliated with the hospital were deployed as volunteers to help sort and fold six hundred thousand pairs of scrubs the hospital ordered in haste to protect thirty thousand employees. The scrubs arrived separately, tops and bottoms, and all had to be matched for size. And in the end, unlike after wars or massive terrorist events, the hospitals erected no enduring stone memorials to all those who died in service to save lives. Photos on the bulletin boards of nurses and respiratory therapists and doctors who had died vanished, as if a collective corporate decision had been made not to tarnish the brand. When I asked about this later, I was told there were "privacy concerns." The shame of silence haunted many who desperately wanted to honor the dead.

The COVID pandemic started in Wuhan, China, a city that few in the United States had ever heard of, and ended up devastating nearly every corner of America. But if there was one city that had to be saved, it was New York, because if the virus truly went out of control there, it might have spread with such ferocity that the death toll in the United States could have been in the millions. New York was the fort that had to be held, and it was, at profound cost: Thirty-five employees of NewYork-Presbyterian—doctors, nurses, transporters, cleaners—and more than thirty thousand residents of the city died. In addition, there were untold thousands of survivors burdened with mysterious long-term side effects of the disease and uncountable men, women, and children who lost loved ones. And while the blight that spread across the country would kill more than one million Americans by April 2022, had NewYork-Presbyterian crumbled, the damage to the nation and the world would have been many times worse than what we did experience.

At the beginning of the pandemic, there were three things that many at NewYork-Presbyterian assumed—three things that turned out to be wrong. The first was that they had what they needed to handle it. The second was that people across America would come together and cooperate to win the war against COVID. The third was that the vaccine would be the end of the pandemic. December 14, 2020, the day the vaccine arrived, did turn out to be thrilling—and, as we know now, heartbreaking. But it's easy—too easy—to assert that because COVID has persisted in an increasingly contagious (if also increasingly harmless-to-the-vaccinated) form, nothing done during that first year really mattered. When historians look back at the first year of the pandemic, they will recognize not only the immeasurable heartbreak but also that New York held on, and that made the difference.

The doctors in my own family were treated with reverence, as high priests from another culture. One cousin spoke often of her training at the Mayo Clinic during World War II, when the first doses of sulfa powder came to her unit and saved the lives of dying children. One of the few women at Mayo in that era, she projected the formality of a character in an Edith Wharton novel, occasionally calling her husband, a prominent surgeon, "Dr. Fischer" at the few family gatherings they found the time to attend. The fact that their patients came first was never questioned. Many of the doctors I met in my months of reporting shared the same belief.

As I discovered in the course of reporting this book, the span of NewYork-Presbyterian is massive, and so was the pandemic's impact on it. It has 4,066 beds, and campuses that extend through every borough except Staten Island and up into Westchester County and the Hudson Valley. In 2021, there were 1.2 million separate interpreter sessions in 216 languages, most frequently in Spanish, Mandarin, Cantonese, Russian, Korean, Arabic, Bengali, Fuzhou, Haitian Creole, and Polish. Across the campuses, there are sixty-two pastoral-care employees. The hospital system uses 120,000 surgical masks a day. At the height of the New York surge, NewYork-Presbyterian employees were given 40,000 rides a week, 3,000 hotel rooms a night, and 34,000 meals a day. The hospital ran out of disposable thermometers and stethoscopes and cleaning supplies and hand sanitizer; it had to rely on sanitizer manufactured in the New York State prison system. Two football field–size warehouses were opened to accommodate the massive lend lease–style operations that transferred equipment to and from the hospital sites dozens of times per day. The number of isolation gowns used for PPE jumped from 15,000 a day to 115,000 a day; N95s from 2,500 a day to 16,000 a day. The hospital more than doubled its ICU capacity—and its ventilator supply—as 1,000 clinicians and nurses arrived to assist from the hospital systems of the Mayo Clinic, Rochester, Pittsburgh, Cayuga, and UCSF, among many others. In an ordinary year, there are 700,000 emergency department visits and 5 million ambulatory visits. But nothing about March 2020 and the months that followed was in any way ordinary—or planned for.

Through more than eighteen months of reporting on ten campuses of NewYork-Presbyterian, I interviewed nearly two hundred doctors, nurses, transporters, porters, and aides who worked at every level of the hospital system, from the morgue to the research labs. Many of them had never spoken about their experiences to anyone on the outside, including their families. They had one common feature: a belief that walking away from what they did was not an option. I heard over and over again variations of: *I didn't think about it. I had to be at the hospital the next day.* The doctors and nurses worked themselves to tears and exhaustion, and some of them did not make it. But there was also a flowering of ingenuity and creativity, of improvisation and invention. They tightrope walked and they juggled a thousand and one objects and they leaped into space, hoping a trapeze was on its way. This was their moment, and they seized it, at great cost but with no choice in the matter. "The rapture of action," the renowned heart surgeon Craig Smith called it. They were not divine, but they did divine things. What follows are their stories.

1

Long after the god-awful New York City pandemic spring of 2020, Dr. Lindsay Lief would remember the excruciating morning the alternate universe came calling. Death was everywhere. It was April 3—a Friday, and one of the worst days at the height of the surge. The *New York Times'* banner headline ran the width of the front page: "Unrivaled Job Losses Accelerate Across US." Underneath, a travel map of the United States was mottled with coronavirus red.

At dawn, Lief rushed through the beige halls of the fifth floor of the billion-dollar Greenberg Pavilion at New York's Weill Cornell Medical Center and pushed through the swinging doors of her ICU to find a message relayed from Steven Corwin, the president and CEO of NewYork-Presbyterian. Lief tried to process the gist of an e-mail sent to all the ICUs and their nursing supervisors: "Corwin wants to do video rounds with you later if you are around."

Everything about that sentence had been unimaginable to her just weeks before. It was almost unheard of for the CEO of the hospital to reach out and down to critical-care teams; it was like—well, it was hard to think what it was like. The head of NASA asking to sit in on the weekly meeting of a high-school astronomy club? The boss of a Hollywood studio calling a theater in Fargo and asking to speak with the manager at a concession stand? Before the pandemic hit New York, Lief had only the faintest sense of Corwin's background;

he was at the helm of the hospital mother ship, far removed from patient care. Over the years, they had met briefly at hospital dinners when Lief was being handed yet another award, but her seat was definitely not at his table.

Lief is the director of the medical intensive care unit on 5 South, one of six ICUs at NewYork-Presbyterian/Weill Cornell. The original hospital was created by royal charter in 1771, and it is still considered the Emerald City of medical care in the great metropolis. She oversees a team of eleven critical-care physicians (the attendings) and dozens of highly trained nurses, respiratory therapists, pharmacists, X-ray techs, and housekeepers ("environmental services," in hospital-speak), all of whose task is to help heal the sickest of the sick, to conjure miracles amid the breakdown of the body's systems.

On a normal day, back before all of this, Lief would have awakened and taken her children from their home in Greenpoint (the northernmost neighborhood in Brooklyn) to school in Williamsburg, joining the throng of hip Brooklyn moms and clusters of heder boys in their yarmulkes and *payos* navigating for space on the sidewalks, before going to work. Now her normal days involved waking up when it was still dark, after far too little sleep. She was often the only person on the road as she crossed the deserted Queensboro Bridge. She would reach Weill Cornell at 6:00 a.m. The atmosphere inside the hospital was surreal. The marble entrance halls, once jammed with crowds of visitors, were desolate; the gift shop shuttered; the Au Bon Pain in the lobby, where in the old days she'd bought croissants for her team, completely dark. Lief could hear the deafening noise from the jerry-rigged HEPA filter systems a few floors away, and as she headed to her office she saw her colleagues and the scurrying shadows of doctors and nurses and respiratory therapists and accountants working as patient transporters rushing up and down the stairs wearing frayed N95s and plastic shields or scuba goggles retrieved from their childhood basements, not waiting for an elevator for fear of the very air they might breathe.

Video rounds? What could Steve Corwin possibly see on his iPad? He couldn't see the fear on the faces of the nurses who worked in rooms where aerosolized droplets escaped from clogged ventilator tubes but who had to wear masks they had used for days, long after they should have been discarded and replaced, as there were no replacements. The iPad would show, but not show, Weill Cornell's beloved emergency department doctor Chris Belardi struggling for his life on a vent after the first weeks of frontline duty. Same with two close friends who had contracted COVID at a party; the entertainer who had just had a birthday and seemed unlikely to make it to his next birthday; the critically ill twenty-eight-year-old months away from his wedding; and on and on and on. Lief had already decided that she didn't care about the "no visitors during COVID" rule— she would allow the twenty-eight-year-old's fiancée to be by his side when he died.

The truth was that you had to be there on 5 South—had to have been there—to understand what was going on, and yet Corwin, because of the hospital's legal policies, was forced to resort to a brief FaceTime tour of the floor. Corwin felt caught between the fierce tug of his calling as a doctor and his responsibilities as head of the hospital. For years, he had been a cardiologist most at home in the ICU and had run ICUs at Columbia-Presbyterian.

In a blur, Lief heard Anthony Sabatino, her nurse manager, announce, "Lindsay, Steve wants to hear from you."

And then there he was on her iPad, the head of the hospital speaking to her from his apartment a few blocks from the hospital, himself ordered into quarantine by the board of trustees, who had been worried about his health, since someone in the corporate office had tested positive.

Though few on 5 South knew it, for weeks Corwin had been on Zoom call after Zoom call, from dawn to midnight, trying to get new equipment, parts for broken machines, and, especially, masks—one million of them—battling with the state and FEMA and the White House and the suppliers they had long relied on.

All night Corwin and his wife, Ellen, a former ICU nurse he'd met when he was a resident, listened to the endless sirens of the ambulances screaming up and down the FDR Drive. He would get updated on the number of admissions, intubations, and deaths and try to deal with the fact that at its lowest point, his hospital system—number one among New York City hospitals in the *U.S. News & World Report* ratings—was down to two days' worth of the personal protective equipment (PPE) without which doctors, nurses, and staff could not function. The hospital had gone from one COVID patient on March 3 to twenty-five hundred on March 31, and the rate was increasing. He often closed his eyes as he tried to absorb it all, overwhelmed and exhausted.

"Lindsay," Corwin said now. "What can I do for you? How can I be helpful?"

Lief suddenly heard herself sobbing. "Dr. Corwin, we are not okay," she replied. "We are breaking down. I am desperately worried about my staff. We are the ones who are having to make the ethical decisions about beds and ventilators, and we are putting our nurses in danger."

Corwin took it in. He let her cry. "Whatever you decide, you have my full backing and the backing of the hospital," he said. He added some general reassurance, but mostly he just listened.

Bradley Hayward, one of 5 South's critical-care attendings, interrupted Lief—a patient was coding; the tubes of yet another garbage ventilator from the state had clogged with the horrible COVID mucus that congealed as hard as old chewing gum.

End of video rounds for Lief; she was on the run again.

For a moment, her fury evaporated, erased by the immediate urgency, the snap of tunneled focus that made her such a brilliant ICU doctor. Lief felt strangely reassured—they were proceeding the best they could in wartime conditions; 5 South was on it.

But there were only so many machines that worked, and there were so, so many patients, some with better chances than others. Day after day, hour after hour, as scores of desperately ill people rushed to the hospital, there were often three or four patients who needed ventilators at the same time and, on several occasions, only one or two that seemed to be available. *Yes,* Lief and Hayward would be told, as would the doctors in the other ICUs and in the emergency department, *we have more somewhere, in this storage area or auxiliary hospital.* Lief would be told constantly: *They are going to show up.* But when and how? And how to keep someone alive until they did? And so the calls to hospital ethicists and the agony of the need for triage decisions out of corporate lines with no state-sanctioned crisis rules in place. *What am I going to do,* Lief thought, *write in the chart that Corwin says it is okay for the patient to die in the ICU?*

Later, reflecting on Corwin's outreach, Lief thought that, despite his empathic tone, Corwin was saying something between the lines. *Oh, we are getting the policy*—that they should trust the credo of William Osler, by many measures the father of modern medicine, who'd preached the need for Olympian detachment: Sometimes you had to cut your losses and move on.

Osler, who'd practiced in the late nineteenth and early twentieth centuries, had revolutionized medical training by taking his students into the public wards. Treatment options were limited then, so his instructions both allocated resources and reinforced the power of the doctor by virtue of distance. Emotions would be seen as revealing uncertainty, and for their own good, patients had to think of their doctors as rational and certain. Lief, however, was of a generation that believed in the need for radical transparency. She had long since stopped caring if a patient's family saw her break down and cry.

Looking at the computer screen, she saw that one hundred ventilators were set to arrive—a miracle—but then saw that sixty of them were broken. They were potentially usable, but refurbishing them—finding parts; testing them, fingers crossed—would result in an immeasurable delay. One hundred ventilators in Lief's new reality actually meant forty. And because of the hastily drawn-up rules of engagement, they would likely go to all the other pop-up ICUs and the emergency departments, or EDs. So she was left with the hard facts: Under New York State law, if she instructed her attendings not to try to resuscitate COVID patients, she could be accused of murder.

Hayward told her, "It's hard to say to the head of the hospital, 'This is all very nice, but from a practical point of view, when I am called to court a year from now, do I say that you would support us? Where are you?' What are we going to say when we fill out the forms about the reason of death? 'Corwin said it was okay to not put the patient on a vent'? Is Corwin going to testify in court for you?"

Beyond the ethical and legal complications, the younger attendings were enraged that Corwin, once a "real doctor," was not walking the halls in his PPE as they were but was instead at home, with all the comforts a large New York apartment provided. That he might have been sleepless too, that he might have been working frantically to help them in the ways that he could—well, when you were falling asleep in your chair or at a small table in a crowded break room, the idea of Corwin in a big bed with clean sheets seemed like a betrayal.

On 5 South, they could not see the effort being put in by Corwin and the hospital's chief operating officer, Laura Forese. Her responsibilities were endless: How would she get enough equipment for the hospital when the governor insisted eighteen thousand ventilators would be needed by the state that very week? How would the hospital get thirty-seven thousand meals delivered to its employees four times a day? Forese and Corwin had to come up with solutions. Corwin understood that the cool blond former pediatric orthopedic surgeon—the only female resident in her class—hid the strain she was under with an imperiousness that could alienate staff. He considered it unfair that, even now, the few women running corporations in America were judged by outdated boys' club standards; it was as if, to be allowed to succeed, they had to hide their at times fierce executive command.

Forese presided over her daily hospital briefings with anchorwoman detachment, a tone that, as the crisis grew, struck many as at odds with their reality. The more pressure that was on her, the more she tried to control every aspect of corporate communication. At the height of the surge, the CEO of one of the city's most prestigious medical centers, Mount Sinai Hospital, decamped for Palm Beach, a story that broke in the tabloids and sent a frisson of fear through NewYork-Presbyterian. Was their corporate leadership, many wondered, similarly out of touch?

Lief's own view was more nuanced: This is our job as well as our calling. Wasn't that the whole point of spending years and years studying and training and going without sleep so you could study and train some more? Could Corwin help? Yes, he could, and yes, he should—the ice beneath 5 South was cracking. But when it seemed like your system was buckling, when it seemed clear that if the plague wasn't halted in your city, the world itself would be ravaged, you just heeded the call as best you could.

Indeed, the day before Corwin tried to buck up Lief's spirits, the son-in-law of the president of the United States, Jared Kushner, was busy infuriating every governor and hospital head in America by proclaiming that "the notion of the federal stockpile was, it's supposed to be our stockpile, it's not supposed to be the states' stockpiles that they then use." On a conference call later that week, Corwin tried to explain to Kushner how dire the situation was inside NewYork-Presbyterian, which provided 20 percent of all New York City's hospital care. "Don't give me anecdotes," Kushner snapped at Corwin. "I just want facts." Clearly revved up by his father-in-law's public accusation that the New York hospitals "were selling masks out the back door," Kushner challenged Corwin: "How can you use that many masks?"

"Are you kidding?" Corwin snapped back. "Do you have any idea how bad this is? Why don't you come and see? No one is selling masks out the back door of my place. And the board members are not jumping the line to get into the ICU."

Most of the board had shunned Donald Trump and his son-in-law for years, even before Trump became president, but now, however galling, they were in desperate need. That was the end of the outburst; Corwin knew the best way to deal with the arrogance of Jared Kushner was to fall silent, to try to win the match by losing the point.

Few who heard the story found it remarkable that Corwin could easily contact Kushner or, for that matter, the president; New York's best nonprofit hospitals, with budgets in the billions and boards made up of Wall Street titans and the heads of tech and media companies, were implicitly, if not explicitly, linked to those in power. Corwin was paid many millions of dollars each year for not only his stellar managerial skills but also his ability to leverage the Favor Bank in New York City, the hardball capital of the world from the days of Tammany Hall to the halls of modern medicine.

Lief knew none of this—there hadn't been even a moment to step back and wonder what was going on outside her wards. For her, the outside world had vanished; the only evidence of its existence was what seemed like a ceaseless avalanche of dying patients, all of them desperately hoping the Amazing Place would live up to its nickname.

Begin here, on Manhattan's Upper East Side, with the nearby East River and its parade of tugs and barges. Its filigree of streets are lined with town houses and apartment buildings, its avenues are clotted with restaurants, grocery stores, and boutiques. This is the neighborhood where today's NewYork-Presbyterian/Weill Cornell Medical Center—the behemoth originally organized for the elite of the city and known for more than two centuries as New York Hospital—has resided for almost a hundred years. Its facilities and researchers have drawn presidents, prime ministers, and luminaries, from Jacqueline Kennedy Onassis to the shah of Iran, all seeking what has long been considered the best care in New York. It was, for many in the city, the cornerstone of NewYork-Presbyterian, created when New York Hospital and Presbyterian Hospital merged—managerially but not geographically—forming a sprawling, nine-billion-dollar ten-hospital empire with each affiliated Ivy League institution keeping its hallowed medical school as a separate fiefdom; the acquisition of Columbia gave NewYork-Presbyterian its deep-bench research cachet. (NewYork-Presbyterian is partnered with the medical schools of Columbia and Cornell, two Ivy League institutions, both located in New York State.) Some New Yorkers simply refer to the Upper East Side cornerstone as Cornell or Weill Cornell and to the uptown hospital renowned for its research as Columbia. The merger had not changed old habits.

If you look down from a helicopter flying over Manhattan, you can see the span of the hospital empire from south to north. NewYork-Presbyterian brackets Manhattan, from the Lower Manhattan campus on William Street near Chinatown all the way north to the

Allen at 220th Street; it extends to Queens, Brooklyn, and three hospitals in Westchester. The ten hospital campuses require a team of over two thousand employees to maintain the hundreds of acres of real estate. All of those acres—as well as three million square feet of interiors.

The Lower Manhattan campus serves much of the Asian American population in a neighborhood near Chinatown that was badly damaged by the 9/11 terrorist attacks. To the north, on the East River close to Sixty-Eighth Street, is NewYork-Presbyterian/ Weill Cornell and the medical school, in the same location since the 1930s. Hopscotch one hundred blocks north and a bit west and you are at the sprawl of NewYork-Presbyterian/Columbia University Irving Medical Center and its medical school, called "P and S." Officially, it's named Vagelos College of Physicians and Surgeons, an impossible mouthful of a name many in the city choose to ignore. That campus includes the Morgan Stanley Children's Hospital and the Sloane Hospital for Women.

At Weill Cornell, in the Edwardian era, when it was still called New York Hospital, there were Persian carpets in the private rooms and daily deliveries of flowers. There was an in-house hair salon, a barber, and a cleaner—some New Yorkers even arranged to live there full-time, as paying guests. (No longer, although the view of the river from the VIP suites remains splendid.) Well endowed by local billionaires, NewYork-Presbyterian is a nonprofit system, garnering billions of dollars in tax benefits. In exchange for its nonprofit status, the system does not turn away anyone—not asylum seekers, or the undocumented, or the homeless. All through the city, there are bus-stop ads with crimson billboards announcing THE AMAZING PLACE: #1 IN NEW YORK CITY. But the hospital isn't just *in* New York City; it *is* New York City. Walk into the clamor of the crowd in the entry pavilion off East Sixty-Eighth Street and hear a babble of Hindi and Urdu, Farsi and Mandarin, Spanish and Russian. There are often knots of families sitting on low benches talking after seeing loved ones or waiting for taxis and Ubers to take them back to the land of the well. Standing in the entrance, they look toward Rockefeller University, hidden behind high walls. For decades, Nobel laureates and postdocs have strolled through its Philosophers Garden and around its sixteen private acres, landmark Founder's Hall, and iconic geodesic dome. It was the first biomedical research center in America, funded by a Rockefeller who had lost a grandchild to scarlet fever at the turn of the century; the first to identify a virus as the cause of the Spanish flu. It was a true enclave of scientific academic privilege, and research doctors from the hospital would dash back and forth to its labs, but it was otherwise closed to the world outside its gates.

At Weill Cornell, Lief's small, windowless office is on the fifth floor, just off a corridor at the entrance of 5 South, the medical intensive care unit. There are twenty spacious beige patient rooms, glassed in for germ control, with state-of-the-art equipment. The cubicles circle a long island of desks for residents, nurses, respiratory therapists, and physician assistants. The building was constructed in the 1980s in a brutalist style, and many visitors wonder how the attendings put up with the tiny, airless shared cubicles, shoebox conference rooms, and cramped lounge, where, during the day, research scientists struggle to prop their laptops on a wobbly glass table, and those treating patients catch quick naps if they were on call the previous night. Not that long ago, they had battled to save the call room, where there were actual beds for the on-call physicians. That one they'd lost.

Five South team members refer to themselves as family—they attend each other's weddings and children's birthday parties, nurture colleagues who break up with loved ones, and all day long hover in one another's cubicles discussing every aspect of patient care. However much they complain about their offices, many in the 5 South family say they would never dream of working anywhere else.

Lief herself had never questioned the profession she'd chosen. In medical school, she had fallen in love with the wonders and mysteries of the lungs. All these years later, the facts continued to astonish her. There were those who assessed that people take twenty thousand breaths a day; over the course of their lives, they inhale five hundred million times. The estimates varied widely, but however many breaths a person took, the vitalizing journey filled Lief with wonder. Each bit of air flows through a cavern of sinuses before it reaches the trachea and bronchi, which are lined with cilia, tiny waving hairs that filter out large particles of pollen and smoke and dust. From there, air goes to the bronchioles, and then, finally, to the alveoli, where oxygen is absorbed into the bloodstream. Like everything in the human body, the lungs are a miracle, but unlike, say, a kidney or an appendix, they are a miracle that you have some control over. In and out, in and out—researchers have calculated that every breath you take contains a molecule from the breath of every person who has ever lived, and these molecules will in turn be passed to future generations. As Lief walked the halls of the hospital, the breath of Joan of Arc, Cleopatra, Virginia Woolf, Harriet Tubman, FDR, all four of the Beatles (and, yes, Yoko), and billions of others from the dawn of man until that moment joined her. And for months of the pandemic, a handful of those molecules would be the only physical contact she had with her children.

Lief, a forty-three-year-old mother of two, has cascading silver-blond hair and an almost encyclopedic recall of the patients who passed through her twenty-bed unit during the spring of 2020, even the ones who weren't under her direct care. There were the patients who could be saved even after months on a ventilator and the patients she thought could be saved but who, it turned out, could not.

In one of our first conversations, I asked her about which patients she remembered. "I remember every patient," she said crisply. "And how long they were with us—and what we tried to do." Then her voice broke.

As an intern at Weill Cornell, Lief had loved the time she spent in the MICU—the medical intensive care unit—with its hourly calibrations of everything that was happening in the body. Later, as an attending, Lief would intoxicate her residents with her all-heart, take-no-prisoners approach to what she called "real medicine"— what mattered most of all was the human connection. There wasn't a day when she did not think about the six-year-old battling leukemia whom she'd met during her training. He had a feeding tube, but his only wish was for a slice of pizza, forbidden by everything in his treatment plan. Endless debate ensued: Was giving him the pizza wise? How would his digestive tract react? "Get him the fucking pizza," Lief said, then she pumped him with painkillers for the possible agony to follow the meal. Was this medicine or something else? A few months later, she saw the boy on the pediatric floor. "And what about the day you had the pizza?" she asked, feeling guilty about breaking the rule. Had she made the right choice? "It was the best day ever," he told her. "The last time I ate anything." A few weeks later, he was gone. So maybe it was medicine after all.

Back in March 2020, 5 South had been the first unit at Weill Cornell to admit a COVID patient, and the team had been treating them ever since. And since COVID went after the lungs, 5 South had been the funnel through which nearly every victim passed until ICUs took over the entire hospital. But now, more than a year later, a great amnesia had begun to sweep the city. Had everyone forgotten what it was like a year ago, when patients were dying everywhere?

Lief hadn't—and neither had anyone she worked with. Lief felt compelled to remember it all, concerned that everything they had experienced would vanish into a ghost universe or become shards of memory that could be blandly repurposed as "lessons learned," one of the most infuriating of all hospital corporate-messaging terms used to wall off feelings.

There had been so much of that—spin, cheerful encouragement, back-patting—and not just during the pandemic. Lief had learned in her first years as a pulmonary intensivist that you did not go to meetings and say there was a problem—you were not allowed to have "problems," only "challenges that you have a creative, multidisciplinary approach for." The art was to try to navigate actual emotions, to chirp the buzzwords of the suits and leave quickly. At meetings, Lief would be greeted with "Thanks, everyone, for your continuing hard work and leadership, and we're overcoming the challenges as they appear." She'd listen because she knew she had to and then she'd return to her office. Behind her desk she had a Ruth Bader Ginsburg action figure, a wedding picture of her and her husband, and several photos of her boys. There, in her T-shirt and cargo pants—the harried-Brooklyn-mom ensemble—and her white coat, she'd try not to break down, and after a moment she'd go back to work, because people were dying all around her.

Early on in Lief's career, she had learned what it took to rise in the politics of the hospital system. She was a chief resident—an experience that gave her a bracing education on the power struggles of running a hospital—and also clocked time in a lab, where she'd believed at first that "science was very pure and without bias." That perception was quickly shattered. At her first lab meeting, after Lief presented her preliminary research plan, she was told she had to have a list of funders before she was allowed to continue. At the next meeting, she was told that her research list was all wrong. "I didn't cite the five guys who were going to review my eventual manuscript. And if I didn't cite them, then I wouldn't get published. And that was lab meeting number two."

Like many in critical care, Lief rarely spoke of her work to people who weren't in medicine. It was hard to explain the heartache you felt when a patient flatlined; it was even hard to explain the explosion of joy she would get when she and her team were able to save a patient thanks to knowledge and procedures that had not even existed a few years before. Normally—whatever *normally* meant in an intensive care unit—half of 5 South's patients would be on ventilators, and all of them would be trying to recover from various life-threatening events: complications of stem cell transplants, suicide attempts, bacterial infections, blood clots, gastrointestinal bleeds. Now, recalled one of the 5 South pulmonologists, you had the surreal experience of seeing every patient in the entire emergency department and the hospital suffering from the exact same disease. In every room in the ICU on 5 South, as well as on every floor, there were patients on ventilators with hastily placed HEPA filter machines to clean the air. The noise level was overwhelming. The ventilators beeped with alarm after alarm; respiratory therapists suctioned breathing tubes and raced from floor to floor to find machines that actually worked. That too was part of the immense grief and anger that Lief and her team now lived with.

As always in the vaudeville show of New York City, the tabloids set the scene. For days, horror had piled on horror. "Bedlam: No Room to Breathe—Video Reveals Virus Patients Packed into Queens Hospital"; "Treated Like Trash: Mount Sinai Nurses Wearing Garbage Bags as Coronavirus Supplies Run Dry"; "Terrible Toll: Virus Dead Forklifted into Trucks Outside Brooklyn Hospital." Front pages were clotted with puns and gloom. "Fever Pitch," "Field Hospital in Central Park," "1 Dies Every 14 Minutes Over 24 Hours in NYC," bannered the *New York Post*—the most popular paper by far among the NewYork-Presbyterian staff, its headlines closely attended to—on March 30, 2020, when the white tents of a field hospital appeared in the East Meadow. And that was before the peak.

In an early all-hospital briefing, Corwin had addressed thousands of NewYork-Presbyterian employees. His tone was somber: "We are in this together—the cavalry isn't coming." The next day, the city would announce that in the month of March, a thousand New Yorkers had died of COVID-19.

But Corwin was wrong. The cavalry rushed in from every department in the hospital. Accountants worked as transporters, wheeling the dying and the dead. At the height of the surge, Corwin got authorization to pay for three thousand hotel rooms around the city, food for the extended families of all employees who needed help, day care, and transportation—a billion-dollar outlay. In one call, he snapped, "I don't give a damn what it costs." He insisted on an unlimited line of credit to fund the hiring of doctors and nurses and former air force pararescue medics and to make sure that the hospital had a field hospital and oxygen farms. He all but scoured sofas for lost coins and hunted for equipment stashed in forgotten places. *I found 200 N95s in a storage cabinet*, a Goldman Sachs partner texted Corwin. *We will take them*, the CEO replied. Two hundred masks could mean two hundred lives saved, and at that moment the hospital had only enough masks for the next forty-eight hours. Cosmetics companies and gourmet markets delivered crates of skin creams and delicacies for everyone working on the front lines. Surgeons, urologists, medical students, cardiologists, retired NewYork-Presbyterian internists fanned out through the corridors of the system's ten hospitals, emptying trash cans and relearning how to titrate medicines in the ICU—a skill many of the older doctors had not used since medical school.

COVID would reveal everything—the pressure that made some crumble but also the valor that meant confronting the fragility of the big-business hospital system, with its marble halls and gleaming towers paid for by New York titans. The Weill in Weill Cornell was in honor of financier Sanford Weill and his wife, Joan, a thank-you

for their one-hundred-million-dollar donation. All of these complexities had to be navigated by Corwin, an amateur historian and
voracious reader who used literature as a personal tuning fork. In the
first weeks of the pandemic, he would decide that it was crucial that
everything they were going through be documented. In his own way,
he was as much of a truth teller as Lindsay Lief.

And then there were the entitled rich. The New York-Presbyterian
mother ship was close to the 10021 zip code, the gold coast of the
city. While the hospital struggled to get equipment and staff, only
blocks away there were those who tried to acquire their own ventilators and purchase their way to a last resort. At a dinner on Park
Avenue in early March 2020, one woman took her guests to a closet
and showed them four ventilators she had recently purchased, God
knows how, for twenty thousand dollars each. Amazon sold out of
eight-hundred-dollar oxygen-bar machines. People bought oxygen-
facial kits, believing, without evidence, that a pinch of oxygen might
save them. Among those who lived in buildings without doormen
or elevators, there was a brisk business in tubes of Nuun, electro-
lyte tablets used by runners. Lists circulated of home necessities suggested by ED doctors in Seattle, who had seen the first onslaught of
patients. In hardware stores, boxes of N95 masks that had sold for
twenty dollars in February were going for two hundred dollars in the
first week of March, after which they vanished completely. Grocery
shelves were stripped.

As always, the working-class residents of the outer boroughs
were hit fastest and hardest. When COVID cascaded through New
York, it decimated areas of Queens and Brooklyn served in large part
by public hospitals but also by New York-Presbyterian institutions
in Brooklyn and Queens and Lower Manhattan and Inwood, just
north of Washington Heights.

Before they begin practicing medicine, doctors take an oath that's often shorthanded as *First, do no harm.* The pandemic revealed the trapdoor of that declaration: Harm to whom? In the first weeks of chaos, with thousands of useless and damaged tests in circulation from the CDC, the state-of-the-art testing machine—one of the few in the city—remained shut off at Columbia Medical Center, waiting for a paralyzed state and federal government to okay the tortuous regulations that controlled whether and how they could be used. COVID patients who couldn't wait flocked to emergency departments; doctors screamed for hours at the New York State Department of Health trying to get their failing patients tested; no one wanted to wait, but almost everyone *had* to wait, sometimes too long. When the state finally got on the bandwagon, it demanded everyone process tests in a lab in Albany, slowing things down even more. Throughout the hospital, there was an anxious refrain: *We cannot get ahead of the state and the CDC. They will take away our license to operate.* For many inside the hospital, the idea that New York State would shut down its premier hospital system in the middle of a pandemic was preposterous, and there were those who believed that the New York nonprofit hospitals' failure to break ranks, to instead remain silent about the policy failures, inconsistencies, and incompetence of various agencies, was outright corporate cowardice, a grievous sin of both commission and omission. But inside the corporate offices of NewYork-Presbyterian, there was a genuine belief that Andrew Cuomo, the governor of New York, was so vindictive that to risk his wrath was to jeopardize any chance of aid the state could have helped provide.

The madness coming from 1600 Pennsylvania Avenue was a handicap no hospital had ever faced, and NewYork-Presbyterian was facing it along with every hospital in America. How to proceed with a moribund federal response that pitted hospitals and states against each other to bid for outmoded ventilators and broken masks only to have their supplies hijacked by FEMA for the government's use? And with a president who so disrespected his public health officials that he exiled them and surrounded himself with a surreal cast of unqualified "experts"? That had not been on the curriculum of any medical school or the focus of any residency. The best and the brightest of the city's medical establishment were suddenly on their own, confronting the miasma of misinformation that hovered in the Oval Office—advisers like the radiologist Scott Atlas, a man with no pandemic experience who claimed that the best course of action to eradicate the threat was, more or less, *for everyone to get infected* and who said that masks had little effectiveness. But from the hospital, there was almost no public response pushing back. How many would die as a result of such misguided (to be charitable) advice and the silence or support it received from the hospitals?

By the summer of 2020 and in the later second surge, whether it was rational or not, staffers directed their anger at the hospital leadership for its clear lack of preparedness and its perceived deficit of courage. Rage oozed through the corridors and flared from nurses and residents in Zoom therapy sessions and one-on-one "wellness meetings" and in private consultations with the hastily constructed mass-therapy services. Spurred by another epidemic—the plague of violence and American inequality—doctors and frontline workers questioned their medical training and their privilege, or lack of it, in the hospital hierarchies.

Lief was deeply concerned about the state of mind of some of her youngest attendings, who openly discussed how nauseated they were by the hyperbole that tried to brand them as heroes. They knew that, like actual frontline soldiers, they could be viewed as collateral damage by a hospital administration always trying to cut costs and unable to defy state and federal regulations that were put in place before the pseudoscience and obfuscations of the White House were fully understood. They blurted out how much they hated the 7:00 p.m. banging of pots from all of the buildings of the city to support the frontline workers. Meanwhile, the critical-care teams were left in a sea of dying patients. Hopes and prayers, pots and pans—however well intentioned, the cacophony was a reminder of how unprepared they'd been, what Corwin would later call "a failure of imagination on our part."

But who could have imagined that a year later, in the relatively wild and carefree summer of 2021, Lief would still be trying to save those who refused to protect themselves and shrugged off the risk or embraced disinformation, and those who were double vaccinated but still managed to contract acute disease? If in 2020 there had been a near infinity of moments on 5 South when time was of the essence, now it almost seemed as if time were irrelevant. "It still feels like everyone is on a ventilator, sick, on dialysis," Lief reflected. "Everyone's in PPE and there's still new sick people getting intubated every day." In a wellness survey sent to thirty thousand employees of the NewYork-Presbyterian hospital system that summer, members of the 5 South team scored the lowest.

I spent months in the NewYork-Presbyterian system and interviewed many doctors and frontline workers. A lot of them were in various stages of post-traumatic stress and were reluctant to share their experiences for fear of returning to the trauma. Others were fearful of retribution should they stray from the PowerPoint vocabulary that the hospital's leadership insisted on. Soon after the first surge began, a draconian gag order was placed on everyone in the hospital. Heads of departments were threatened; expert doctors who regularly appeared on TV were shut down by gorgons of corporate communications worried about the truth chipping away at the hospital's brand. But in my first meeting with Lief, it was clear that she could no longer strictly adhere to the hospital's insistence on keeping it all in.

I was drawn to Lief from the first moment I saw her, in a video that had been recorded during the height of the COVID surge of March 2020. As a project for the historian Ron Suskind, Lief and Dr. Kelly Griffin, who ran the ICU at night, had spoken about their desperate attempts to save their patients. Lief wept. It is not clear just how many people saw the video, but undoubtedly the audience included Steven Corwin.

Over the years, Corwin had risen from a young virtuoso ICU doctor who smoked two packs a day and was teased for his thick curly hair to the CEO of one of America's largest health-care systems. He oversaw its employees (which, depending on who was included, ranged from twenty thousand to forty-seven thousand) and earned close to ten million dollars a year for his labors. While that salary was actually far less than what his cohorts at other hospital systems earned, he now counted billionaires among his friends (and, crucially, hospital donors), lived in a substantial New York City apartment, and had a second home in Long Island's tony Sag Harbor.

His own background was far more modest. Corwin's father, Leonard, had lost his dad at the age of six and was a latchkey kid through the Depression; he'd helped to support his mother from the time he was in high school. After the war, he went to Cornell and then Cornell Law School on the GI Bill, and although he could have joined a competitive white-shoe law firm in the city, he preferred a modest life in White Plains with his family, where his wife, Sylvia, who got her masters in education from Harvard, taught elementary school.

Steven Corwin received his medical degree from Northwestern and did his residency in internal medicine at Columbia-Presbyterian Medical Center, where he served as chief resident—one of the most prestigious residency positions in American medicine at one of America's most prestigious hospitals. He went on to do a fellowship in cardiology at the same hospital. Back then, Columbia-Presbyterian Medical Center and New York Hospital/Cornell competed for research grants and celebrated patients seeking the best medical care in the world. Now, thirty years later, even though the hospitals had merged, competition still churned among the academic chairs fighting for NewYork-Presbyterian funding as well as national and international funding. The competition was so fierce that there were even some instances when researchers wouldn't share their findings with colleagues studying similar problems at the rival hospital.

Corwin stood out from almost every other hospital chief in his passion for books. Recently, he'd been drawn to the works of W. G. Sebald, whose surgical understanding of the layers of reversals and chance occurrences mirrored his own inner life. At the peak of the pandemic, in his sleepless hours, Corwin took solace in Chilean author Roberto Bolaño's massive *2666*, a nine-hundred-page epic set in a fictional version of Juárez. Corwin was passionate about the life and works of Frederick Douglass, which he would return to in cycles. The pandemic took him away from the Metropolitan Opera House, the only place where he truly relaxed. Would he ever again be able to attend a performance? He didn't know. Nobody did.

The mobilization and prosecution of the fight to save New York was massive and often ad hoc. Improvisation became the order of the day. Hospital staff invented new machines to replace those that failed (an astonishing amount of machinery provided by the government had turned out to be unusable) or were insufficient for the deluge of patients. Gear that had been designed for a single use was jerry-rigged to work multiple times. At the height of the surge, hospital staff, assisted by former military medics, threw together a field hospital at the Columbia University soccer stadium in five days. And as part of that project, a separate oxygen supply was built outside. The stadium, at almost the tip of northern Manhattan, was adjacent to NewYork-Presbyterian Allen Hospital, where the emergency department was so overwhelmed patients were packed together on stretchers in the hall. All through the NewYork-Presbyterian systems, the halls of the pop-up ICUs had hoses in such a tangle they often tripped people transporting equipment or patients. Medical supplies were so short, NewYork-Presbyterian ran so low on dialysis solution the staff prepared to mix their own in basement labs; some doctors at Columbia started rationing the dialysate solution and there were reports of patients receiving only half their usual treatment. On the expansive Columbia University Irving Medical Center campus between 165th and 168th Streets, where Nobel Prize winners have their labs, weeks were spent experimenting on ventilators to see if a single machine could support more than one patient. Masks were kept in locked cabinets to prevent stealing; sometimes nurses treating COVID patients broke down because even they could not get the masks. Fights broke out when only doctors were issued scrubs. Day care was arranged as well as transportation while nurses sobbed, holding the hands of the dying saying goodbye to their families on FaceTime. Corwin frantically allocated and reallocated dwindling resources, begged government officials for help, and tried to rally his troops as best he could from his apartment. All this while NewYork-Presbyterian was undergoing a massive transformation of its electronic record-keeping, perhaps the worst-timed systems update in medical history.

For months, there were no medications to treat the disease. The doctors tried drugs never intended for anything like COVID—hydroxychloroquine and remdesivir—as well as over-the-counter standards Pepcid and Tylenol. Clinicians had frantic exchanges with colleagues around the world. At Columbia University Irving Medical Center, Dr. Mary D'Alton had "at least twenty calls a day from all over the world" from distressed doctors hoping her team had found something. "Every day I had first five hundred e-mails, then five thousand, from doctors around the world. They would range from 'Have you tried X?' to 'Where can we get dexamethasone?'" recalled Dr. Roy Gulick, the chief of infectious diseases at Weill Cornell. In his frequent briefings, Gulick often told the ICU heads, "I just spoke with Tony," referring to Anthony Fauci, with whom he had worked closely for decades.

Of course, a version of this happened at almost every hospital in America. But in New York, at the city's most elite hospital system, it happened before it happened anywhere else and with both greater velocity and catastrophe. "However bad you think it was, it was so much worse," Dr. Elizabeth Oelsner said. "The press did not get the half of it. People were wearing scuba gear and they were showing up and they were doing their best, and their best was not good enough. And you knew that the disease was so bad so many were going to die no matter how good you were."

Who wouldn't cry when they saw the image? In tears, the microbiologist Kang Liu Belsky passed her iPhone to her husband, Rick Belsky, a professor of Chinese history at Hunter College. Kang and Rick stared at the photo taken from the balcony of Kang's sister Chang's apartment building in Wuhan. Her nephew—they had never met—was a stolid and squat one-year-old in a raspberry wool sweater and cargo pants, and he stood leaning on the rail with his back to the camera. His view was of a distant universe of high-rises the color of butterscotch. Directly below the balcony, there was a vast parking lot where the few cars looked abandoned. Above, the sky was a pale winter blue. Not a single person was visible. Chang's WeChat text was bleak. *I feel fear and desperation. . . . I wish someone could take my baby to somewhere safe . . . but the city is in lockdown, no one can come in. . . . No one can leave.* It was January 23, 2020, and Wuhan had just announced it was under lockdown.

For weeks, Kang had been worried about her family. Known professionally as Kang Liu, she had lived in America for twenty-five years, ever since she qualified for a scholarship to study microbiology and immunology at Fordham; she had gone on to earn her doctorate at Rockefeller University. Kang had tried for years to convince her sister to enter her own field of research as Chang finished her doctorate in America. But Chang wanted to be close to their parents, both high-school teachers in Wuhan.

Kang's specialty was the immunity protection potential of dendritic cells (immune-system messengers) and how they could be used in vaccines. While getting her PhD, she worked in the lab of Ralph Steinman, whose research on immunology earned him a Nobel in 2011. Kang then went on to the lab of physician/scientist Ian Lipkin, the celebrated "master virus hunter" and director of Columbia's Center for Infection and Immunity, known for his prescient early understanding of the pathogens of West Nile disease, SARS, and HIV. Kang was now the head of a pharmaceutical research laboratory in Greenwich, Connecticut, not far from her home in Hastings-on-Hudson.

On December 31, 2019, slivers of information started to come out of China, and Rick texted Kang's father: *We heard about recent cases of pneumonia caused by unclear reason in Wuhan. Please protect yourselves.* On January 4, Kang's father responded: *We have heard about news of mysterious pneumonia in Wuhan since January 1st. The government's official report informed us and highlighted "no person-to-person transmission" and "no report of medical staff infected." . . . It was suspected to originate from a seafood market and it has been taken care of. There is no sign of emergency or chaos.*

Later, there were long explanations in every newspaper and magazine and web outlet with headlines like "What Is a Coronavirus?" and "What Is COVID-19?" The stories and alerts used language that could be understood by those who were not virologists: A coronavirus is a type of virus, many of which can cause disease. If you have a robust immune system, COVID, like the flu or the common cold, is relatively harmless. However, if the virus reaches the lower airway, it can severely damage the lungs; the air sacs fill with fluid, which limits their ability to take in oxygen, which in turn can lead to acute respiratory distress. In some cases, people need to be put on ventilators to stay alive.

But that was still unknown, even to Kang, as information from China was difficult to obtain.

On January 8, 2020, Donald G. McNeil Jr., the *New York Times'* science reporter who has written widely on epidemics, filed his first Wuhan-related report to the editors of the paper for review and then distribution to hundreds of reporters and editors around the world. Summarizing for readers, senior editor Steve Kenny said that McNeil and Sui-Lee Wee, the reporter working with him on the story, had explained that "researchers in China have identified a new virus that is behind a mysterious pneumonia-like illness that has caused a panic in the central Chinese region." Quoting from the article Kenny wrote, "'There's no evidence that the virus, a coronavirus, is readily spread by humans, and it has not been tied to any deaths. But health officials in China and internationally are watching it carefully, as it comes from the same region where the deadly SARS epidemic broke out in the early 2000s.'"

Later, the Chinese government's story changed. McNeil sent an update to Wee. State media officials now said that the pneumonias were thought to be caused by "a previously unknown coronavirus." McNeil also sent her the latest CDC travel advisory, which said that "there had been fifty-nine cases with no deaths and no reports of spread from person to person or to health-care workers." McNeil, who had reported from sixty countries and was celebrated for his prescient analyses of epidemics, later described the chaos of misinformation that was emanating from China in the early days as "a perfect example of the fog of war that envelops outbreaks of new pathogens." Suspecting that something worrisome was going on, the two reporters dug deeper.

It would take weeks for the CDC and the World Health Organization (WHO) to confirm what McNeil and Wee had by then already reported—that on New Year's Eve, the mayor of Wuhan had ordered the arrest of eight whistleblowers. But there was more—just before the end of December, Li Wenliang, a doctor in Wuhan, had sent a private message to colleagues warning them to protect themselves from what appeared to be a new and dangerous respiratory virus. Two days before McNeil sent his first report to the *Times,* Chinese authorities had forced Li to recant and confess that his comments were inaccurate and damaging to order. (About a month later, he would be dead of COVID.)

McNeil wrote later that on January 20, Dr. Zhong Nanshan, sometimes called "China's Fauci," said on state TV that "Wuhan had a disaster on its hands." On January 21, Kang's father texted Rick: *The plague is getting worse in Wuhan. The Xi and Li made the statement in CCTV news and the citizens started to be alert. Lots of pre-arranged celebration gathering and meetings were cancelled. Everyone wears mask when leaving home. Because of the baby, Chang and we are more nervous than ever.*

Two days later, the government ordered the city locked down. Chang was not even allowed to leave her apartment to get food for her baby; everything was dropped outside her door. Through WeChat, she let her sister know she was "terrified."

McNeil recalled, "At this point, nobody was thinking about it in New York. Everybody was like, 'Oh, this is a problem in China.' I'm going, 'If this is sustained human-to-human transmission, this could get here.' I'm the only one who is thinking this way right then. The foreign desk was worried about it as a problem in China, and flights were cut off from China by the Trump administration [on January 31]. There was a meeting where the editors were talking with the reporters in China about the economic effects of this. And at one of these meetings, I'm sitting there thinking, *You people don't understand*

this. You don't understand how serious this is. Finally, my editor turned
to me and said, 'Donald, you are sitting on something.' And I said,
'You guys don't understand the import of this. It's not just the flights
from China that are going to stop.' The business editor looked at me
and said, 'He's saying that flights from all over Asia might stop?' And
I said, 'Yeah, there and more. This is a transmissible virus.' . . . He just
let out a snort like he didn't believe me."

A few days later, while walking to the Hastings-on-Hudson train
station, Kang ran into a close friend, Xenia Frisby, who lived around
the corner. "Xenia, I am so worried about my sister," Kang blurted
out. "What are you hearing at the hospital? What are they saying?"

Frisby was the associate quality-control director of NewYork-
Presbyterian Lawrence, a branch of the NewYork-Presbyterian system
located in Bronxville, just outside New York City. From her office at
the hospital, she had been closely watching the reports from Wuhan
and following the hospital's early alerts and McNeil's reporting—all of
it deeply troubling but not yet at the push-the-panic-button level. She
tried to reassure Kang by saying that she was not delaying her family's
upcoming trip to Lisbon, where they would meet up with her oldest
daughter, Ariadne, who was teaching English in a Madrid school.

Kang knew Ariadne well. As a teenager, Ariadne had often baby-
sat Kang's children, and Kang's children now did the same for Xenia's
fourth child, who was seven. The two friends had helped start a book
club for their circle of scientists and professionals in Hastings, and
at one early gathering, Xenia had confided to Kang that she'd had
Ariadne when she was still in high school, back in Flagstaff, Arizona.
Her last name was Irish and her first name was Greek, but her family
had emigrated from Mexico. Feeling shunned by the Anglo girls in
her Catholic school for being "too Hispanic" and by the Hispanics
for being "too Anglo," Xenia spent long hours in the biology lab and

dreamed of being a doctor. When she learned she was pregnant, she debated whether to put the baby up for adoption, an idea that filled her with profound sadness. That week in morality class, the nuns showed a movie about an abortion. "It was propaganda," Xenia said. "But it terrified me and thank God I saw it. What would I have done if I hadn't had Ariadne?"

Keeping the baby meant Xenia's carefree high-school days were over. Ariadne's father made it clear he was not too interested in helping out, but his mother assisted Xenia as much as she could. Xenia resolved that no matter what, she would not give up her dream of medical school. Her parents, both high-school teachers, assured her they would support her.

Ariadne was still in diapers when Xenia won a scholarship to the University of Arizona. In four dizzying years, Xenia graduated with honors and then attended the University of North Carolina's medical school in Chapel Hill. There she met her future husband, Andy Bomback, a nephrologist who had grown up in Westchester, New York. When Bomback got a fellowship at Columbia Medical Center, the family headed north. In the first ten years of their marriage, they had three more children; their Hastings home was filled with toys and books. The house was just a few blocks from the high school and the train station, and Bronxville was only a twenty-minute drive away.

"Are you coming to book club?" Xenia asked Kang after trying to calm her down. The February book was *The Yellow House,* Sarah Broom's haunting memoir of her family's home in East New Orleans that—like most of the homes in this historically Black community— was swept away during Hurricane Katrina. (Later, Kang and Xenia— who went on to play a crucial role in NewYork-Presbyterian's attempt to save New York—both remarked on how strange it was that the group's February choice focused on a city dealing with a disaster.)

That week, Donald McNeil was on the subway when he learned that there were now ten thousand cases and two hundred deaths. "I was thinking, *Oh my God, this has gone from thirty-six cases with no deaths to five hundred cases with twelve deaths to ten thousand cases with two hundred deaths in China.* That's a two percent mortality rate and a very fast-moving pandemic. I thought to myself, *I'm pretty sure that's close to the figures of the 1918 pandemic.*

"I was at my girlfriend's house that night and looked up the mortality rates and said, 'Yeah, I am right.' I kept the piece of paper I wrote it down on. And when I came into the paper the next day, I told [the editor of the science section] Celia Dugger, 'This is going to be the big one. This is the big one we've been talking about.' She said, 'Donald, we can't write a story that says that just based on your map. You've got to call a dozen experts and speak to them and see what they think.' And so I did." McNeil's story, published February 2, was headlined "Wuhan Coronavirus Looks Increasingly Like a Pandemic, Experts Say."

Nathaniel Hupert often wondered what direction his life would have taken if President Bill Clinton had not read *The Cobra Event*, Richard Preston's 1997 thriller about a bioterrorist attack on New York City. One of Preston's earlier books, the nonfiction blockbuster *The Hot Zone*, had lodged itself in the American psyche with its harrowing descriptions of how Ebola could make a "face slide off like overcooked oatmeal," as the *Times* reviewer noted. Published three years later, *The Cobra Event* sometimes bogged down in inside-the-CDC details, but it also presented a plausible scenario of what could happen in New York City if a virus was weaponized. The reviewers weren't as smitten by *The Cobra Event* as they were by *The Hot Zone*, but Preston found a receptive audience in the Oval Office.

When *The Cobra Event* came out, Hupert was in his second year of residency at the University of Pittsburgh, focusing on medical ethics and how to treat the disabled. He was completely unaware of the book, but there was a heightened sense in certain intelligence circles that germ warfare attacks might become a new threat in the United States. In 1995, sarin gas had been released in the Tokyo subway, injuring thousands and killing thirteen people.

Bill Clinton was galvanized by *The Cobra Event*, and in early 1998, he started staging elaborate meetings at the White House that included, among others, William Haseltine, the noted scientist and entrepreneur perhaps best known for his seminal work on the human genome, and Richard Clarke, the administration's counterterrorism coordinator. Each participant was asked, "Is what Richard Preston wrote actually plausible?" Within months, fifty-one million dollars had been budgeted to begin the National Pharmaceutical Stockpile.

Hupert grew up in New York, the son of multimedia artist Margia Kramer, whose themes were often political. His father, David Hupert, at one time directed the education department at the Whitney Museum downtown. Hupert had been drawn to the mysteries of geometry in elementary school, and he got into Stuyvesant, a public high school for those gifted in math and science. He was, a colleague said of him, "a cosine in a sine world," an outlier polymath who had always wanted to be a doctor. (His grandmother often talked to him about seeing her mother collapse on the steps of their house in Brooklyn, a victim of the Spanish flu.) Hupert was a pure New Yorker who took the subway to school and between his parents' downtown apartments. Unsurprisingly, much of his childhood was spent in museums.

He took a leave from Harvard his sophomore year and went to Florence, where he found his way into an archive of fourteenth-century medical manuscripts. On his return, he found a rare-book room at Harvard that contained a stunning collection of incunabula (the earliest printed texts). In one, written in an almost indecipherable medieval Latin, Hupert—who spoke Italian and had studied Latin—saw glimmers of something that called out to him. An Italian physician influenced by the Oxford Calculators, a renowned group of medieval mathematicians, asked, "What does it mean for Christ's body to be infinitely divisible into the Eucharist?" which led them to all sorts of discussions about fractions and how to combine infinite theories, Hupert explained. "What the doctors were doing was taking these ideas about combining parts and trying to see if they could apply them to combining hot and cold parts of drugs." With his adviser, Hupert labored over a translation; it became the basis of his thesis and helped sail him into Harvard Medical School.

From the time he got to Harvard Medical School, Hupert had a ready answer for the inevitable question, "So, Nathaniel, why does modeling really matter?" He learned to say, "It matters because it is important to try to understand unfolding events." He could offer up more complex explanations that would quote Picasso's pronouncement on art: "A lie that makes us realize the truth, at least the truth that is given us to understand." But the simpler explanation was that Hupert, a mathematician, had the deepest faith in the power of numbers to reveal consequences—the "science of better," as it would be taught to him at Weill Cornell.

For Hupert, computer modeling started in a dorm at medical school when his colleague Mark Roberts introduced him to a system of decision analysis. Also at Harvard Medical School was the current head of the CDC, Rochelle Walensky, who was as well drawn to the puzzle box of mathematical probabilities to reveal solutions for public health crisis and disease. Roberts, like Walensky, would go on to a major role in public health at his lab at the University of Pittsburgh.

In August 2000, Hupert was hired by Weill Cornell. He was ecstatic—everyone in his world understood what it meant to be a part of Cornell Medical School. The previous year, the New York tabloids could not get enough of the Y2K bug, the computer flaw that some feared would lead to the ultimate doomsday. There were months of headlines and hysteria: *Everything will crash on January 1, 2000! There is no digital key to dealing with the year 2000! Computers are programmed only up to 1999!* Entire countries prepared emergency strategies to offset the absolute certitude that Y2K would shut down cities. Preppers—those who see catastrophe everywhere—stocked canned food and moved into caves.

Banks, transportation, health-care systems—all could come down, and if they did, what then? How would a major city be able to distribute the tens of millions of antibiotics in the National Pharmaceutical Stockpile (today known as the Strategic National Stockpile) if there was a biological attack? Almost no money had been allocated for the local hospitals and clinics that would have to contain an outbreak if a biological agent overcame the city.

That summer, a federal grant of $250,000 was offered to New York's hospitals to come up with a plan to deal with such vulnerabilities. In September 2000, one month after Hupert started at Weill Cornell, Alvin Mushlin, chair of the medical school's department of public health, asked, "Nathaniel, do you want to work on this?"

"I loved the idea and said, 'Why not?' It was all about discrete event simulation," Hupert said.

Weill Cornell's emergency physician in chief, Neal Flomenbaum, was a giant in the field of disaster response as well as a senior editor of *Goldfrank's Toxicologic Emergencies*, a standard reference for toxicology. Weill Cornell was the only hospital that applied for the grant.

For much of his first year as an attending, Hupert was part of a team developing and testing a plan to get emergency antibiotics to millions of New Yorkers in the event of a bioterrorism attack. That the project—known as Operation Tripod—was being run out of Weill Cornell was a sign that this was very real, and the most adept disaster experts had been called in to advise.

In preparation for Operation Tripod, hundreds of briefing books were stacked on the white steel files of the Office of Emergency

Management (OEM). Everything relies on accurate data, Hupert later said, and he was often in and out of the office, making sure that everything was correct. He ran his numbers and calculations again and again, checked and rechecked the data for his models. How could you give antibiotics to all of New York City in forty-eight hours? How quickly could you move a crowd of X through a hospital emergency department? How many antibiotics could you distribute to X number of people in an hour? You could fall into a loop; data and projections run through a supercomputer produced more data and projections . . .

The date for Operation Tripod had been determined months earlier. Hundreds of observers arrived in the city two days before. Joining OEM were members of the FBI and the Department of Justice and the Department of Health and Human Services; in years to come, Operation Tripod would be thought of as a shining moment in government when agencies and a major hospital worked together, a model for how the city and the federal government could unite to ensure that New York City would be prepared in case of a public health catastrophe.

Hupert and his partner, the philosopher Alice Crary, were living in Tribeca, a few blocks from where he had grown up. He had to take two trains to get to the hospital by 6:00 a.m. to see patients, but he liked living downtown, so that was that. Still, when there was a chance to sleep in, he wasn't one to waste it.

The original plan was for Hupert to meet two colleagues at the OEM office at 9:00 a.m. on Tuesday, the day before the exercise, and drive with them to Pier 92, an Operation Tripod staging area on the west side of Manhattan, but one of them—the future head of Philadelphia's emergency medicine response—had run into Hupert the day before and suggested that they not go in until 11:00 a.m. "Let's not worry about getting in so early," he said. "These are going to be very long days ahead."

The more Hubert thought about it, the more tempting that later arrival was. The exercise itself would take place in two days, on Wednesday, but between the next morning and the end of Operation Tripod, he would be lucky to get even a few hours of sleep. Just thinking about it, he felt tension and fatigue seep through his body, and not just because of the next two days. The following week he and Crary had invited friends to their commitment ceremony, and they still had vows to write. The extra hours of rest would be a gift.

On Monday night, Hupert and Crary stayed up late to work on their commitment vows. Exhausted, he was even more appreciative of his colleague's suggestion. Eleven o'clock had never sounded better.

Like any statistician, Hupert hoped to eliminate chance. It existed, of course—always would. But how could you look deep within data and recognize an initially invisible logic, a mathematical melody, cause and effect? That was the challenge: to find the narrative so you would be able to tell the story differently the next time. But sometimes chance was all that mattered. The OEM office was on the twenty-third floor of the North Tower of the World Trade Center. On that Tuesday morning, Hupert slept in, so he was home when the planes smashed into the Twin Towers. Making coffee at 8:46 a.m., he felt his building vibrate and his radio went to static. He looked out his window directly at the North Tower just after the first plane crashed into the side. Hupert went to his roof and set up his camera on a timer. From his one year of disaster preparation, he knew immediately that this was no accident. He ran to get Crary, and they got out the door, with their dog, both of them still believing that Crary's first day of teaching at the New School would go on as planned. As they rushed north toward the New School on West Eleventh Street, they saw the second plane hit and watched the crowds coming toward them, covered in ash. Operation Tripod, scheduled to start the next day, September 12, 2001, was delayed until the following May.

At that second go-round in the spring of 2002, Hupert met the man who'd created the National Pharmaceutical Stockpile. They hit it off, and for the next few years, he frequently traveled to a Center for Domestic Preparedness facility in Anniston, Alabama, where the first cohort of those who were organizing the bioterror response in each state and territory were being trained. Soon after, he was brought in as a special medical academic adviser for the CDC, a job he could do while he continued to see patients at Weill Cornell. "I got to know all the Waffle Houses between Atlanta and Anniston," Hupert said. The CDC had done a lot of early work on chemical munitions in Anniston, he learned. There was a small cemetery for all the animals who had died in experiments.

At a press conference in September 2005, President George W. Bush was asked what he had done on his summer vacation. Bush, according to author Michael Lewis, mentioned that he had read John Barry's sweeping *The Great Influenza: The Story of the Deadliest Pandemic in History*. Barry's account of the 1918 Spanish flu—a virus that killed more than fifty million people around the world—vividly portrayed the horror of what happened in America when over half a million lost their lives. Barry later learned that Stewart Simonson, a senior aide to Mike Leavitt, the newly appointed secretary of health and human services, had handed his boss the book and said, "When we have a pandemic, there's going to be a 9/11 report, and you are going to be the bad guy in it. So you'd better read this." Leavitt read it, bought fifty copies, and highlighted the important parts. One copy went to the president. "It was an inflection point," Simonson told Lewis. "Up till then there was no money for this. People would say, 'Oh, it's just the flu.'"

By the summer of 2005, Bush had become obsessed by America's lack of any kind of real planning for a pandemic. Hurricane Katrina would decimate New Orleans. That same year, a new coronavirus had moved from an animal—perhaps a masked palm civet—into humans. Globally, approximately eight thousand were infected, and eight hundred died. Thus prompted, the federal government tried to focus on what could happen if there were virus mutations that could produce another 1918 pandemic. Lewis reported that one plan, quickly generated by the Department of Health and Human Services, so enraged Bush that he said, "This is bullshit." The plan was too limited. Rajeev Venkayya, a staffer at Homeland Security who had a medical degree, noted the president's concern about public health. "We need a whole of society plan," Bush said. "What are you going to do about foreign borders? And travel? And commerce?" Venkayya remembered thinking: *And how were you going to stop hundreds of thousands of Americans from dying while they waited for a speeded-up vaccine?*

Venkayya had worked his way up from a White House fellowship to a unit in the Homeland Security Council called the Biodefense Directorate. That May he'd been named the unit's head. In one weekend, in the basement of his parents' house, he wrote a twelve-page proposal that, a month later, received $7.1 billion in funding, according to Lewis.

Among those who became part of the subculture of epidemiologists and modelers in the Bush White House's think tank was James Lawler, director of the Global Center for Health Security at the University of Nebraska. (Years later, in the spring of 2020, Lawler, in his white coat and trimmed salt-and-pepper beard, captivated viewers with his medical lectures on COVID-19 given in front of a large screen of ultra-blue squiggles and red crowned spheres. Using terms that few outside the field of microbiology have heard of—*Golgi apparatus, endoplasmic reticulum*—Lawler explained the incomprehensible with a droll spin that raised his COVID briefings to a must-watch.)

As a result of Operation Tripod and 9/11, Hupert became part of a largely unknown circle of pandemic modelers, a subset of the federal response team whose data analysis helped predict the trajectory of a global calamity. His focus was on hospitals and how pandemics— Ebola, SARS, cholera—affected patient loads and supplies needed. The fact that he was a clinician was uncommon in the modeling world; on a daily basis, he treated patients who needed to be intubated and read digital images of damaged lungs, and he had written exhaustively researched papers on communicating with patients and their families struggling with the unknowables and heartbreak of end-of-life issues. Thus, unlike many of his mathematically inclined cohort, he knew hospitals from the inside out.

Disaster modeling was a relatively new field in 2001; researchers relied on the capabilities of supercomputers, and, as is always the case with calculation, they required accurate information to make projections. "I knew a bunch of modelers because of my technical background and I reached out to them," Hupert recalled.

At Weill Cornell, Hupert joined a world of beautiful minds at an extraordinary moment, an orchestra of talents focused on the new and complex labyrinth of data accumulation and application to ensure international public health. In one memorable meeting, a mentor warned him, "Nathaniel, beware. If you want to become a modeler, there is almost no funding for this in America." Instead of giving up and going back to being "just" a doctor, Hupert chose to figure out how to pay his own way. He spent several years on the National Academy of Medicine's committee looking at evidence-based emergency preparedness. "All of the other people on the permanent committee were much more senior. Some I had known from my earliest days in the CDC. When we got to talking about funding, every single one of them said, 'Oh, there's no funding for this stuff. I would never tell a young scholar to go into this field. There's no pathway for academic success because there is no agent, no entity at the NIH that is devoted to this.'" Despite everyone's good intentions, to continue the research he thought was so crucial, he had to find the money himself.

More than a decade and a half later, Hupert, whose survival on 9/11 had been a matter of sheer luck, would again be running numbers, altering projections, modeling deviations of an apocalypse in an attempt to remove luck from the equation and figure out how to save New York—this time for real.

It was an almost impossible assignment: Peter Fleischut and his team at NewYork-Presbyterian had to get hundreds of doctors to sign off on the protocols central to the hospital's launch of Epic, the electronic medical records system. He had less than a year to train sixteen thousand employees of Columbia Medical Center, Lawrence Hospital in Bronxville, and the Allen, a few miles north of Columbia in Inwood, the northernmost point of Manhattan, in the maddeningly complicated new system. There was no wiggle room on the go-live date; this first launch was a warm-up for a second, even larger round that would bring tens of thousands of other employees into the system. Fleischut had not slept in months.

The tension around the Epic launch occupied all who were forced to take part in the training: *Here we go again. More Big Brother. More code after code to justify the ninety-eight-dollar charge for three Tylenol.* Everyone complained about having to deal with yet another electronic medical records system, about having to spend more time taking notes on a laptop while patients described their symptoms, the hour it took to record every aspect of a thirty-minute visit to fill the coffers of the nine-billion-dollar corporation, the annoying alerts that now went not to their work phones but their personal devices. And, of course, there was the endless documentation. But there was no getting away from it. Health care in America was big business, and NewYork-Presbyterian was big in that big business. Endowments were great, but if you didn't have enough money coming in from patients or their insurance companies, the lights went off. So an efficient and effective record system was basically the circulatory system of a hospital: If there was no oxygenation via income, the whole body would shut down.

Ironically, the finance team would later say that Epic wasn't for profit but to try to unite their far-flung institutions with one unified record. But few in the hospital who had to now deal with Epic's exhausting requirements cared what the reason was; it just made their lives as health-care providers more demanding.

There may have been no more poorly timed effort to revamp a hospital's electronic medical records system than there was at NewYork-Presbyterian just before the pandemic hit. The three-campus launch of Epic had been years in the planning. Fleischut, the hospital's chief transformation officer, had assembled an extraordinary team to manage the transition. The launch date was scheduled, and it was set in stone: January 31, 2020.

For over two years, Fleischut and Daniel Barchi, the hospital's chief information officer, had worked with a team of hundreds, including people from the company that made Epic, to hammer out all the details. The first hurdle: Seven hundred NewYork-Presbyterian doctors had to agree on best practices in their specialties for the new electronic medical records system. Disagreement was constant, and at times there were screaming sessions. What was the proper protocol to treat diabetes? To treat blood clots? How many liability concerns had to be addressed for a nurse to be able to give Tylenol to a patient? The data accumulation was at times almost overwhelming—twenty years of medicine, thousands of orders for thousands of patients. Anesthesiologists, pulmonologists, cardiologists, oncologists . . . it went on and on and on. Who was going to get this group to agree on anything? For instance, doses of insulin—each endocrinologist had his or her own standing protocol.

Fleischut has always been the tech junkie in any room. As a child, he fell in love with a PalmPilot and had his first Mac before he was eight. He went to medical school at Jefferson Medical College and did his anesthesiology residency at Weill Cornell, where he was shocked by how retro that hospital's data system was compared with Jefferson's electronic one. So he designed an app to make sure that every medication prescribed was entered in a meticulous database—a geek triumph, he later said, that got to 99 percent compliance throughout the hospital.

As a practicing anesthesiologist at Weill Cornell, he focused on updating the operating rooms, including quality issues such as how blood was administered. Fleischut was used to the constant pushback about the depersonalization of medicine, to doctors who raged that all they were now were billing systems. The harried residents who had to speed up their appointments—well, they were on the clock. Four minutes for an average hospitalist visit? That was the timing pushed at some for-profit hospitals, but not, Fleischut told those who asked him, at NewYork-Presbyterian.

Nevertheless, although NewYork-Presbyterian was indeed a not-for-profit hospital system, that didn't mean it didn't charge for its services—often a lot. Its rates for procedures were frequently the highest in the city, and administrators made no apology for that.

As anyone who has gone to a doctor in this millennium painfully realizes, there is a bill for nearly everything. Some of these charges are the equivalent of the Pentagon's legendary $640 toilet seat: Patients are billed for everything from Tylenol to Band-Aids. But more mystifying are the bills, printout after printout, page after page, code after code. Our broken medical system is virtually the only industry where technological advances have increased costs instead of lowering them. Not only do other rich countries (including our neighbor

Canada) have much cheaper health care, but that health care is often more efficient. In a huge 2013 *Time* magazine special report on American health care, investigative journalist Steven Brill focused much of his criticism on the excessive ordering of CT scans and MRIs. For example, England had 5.9 MRI machines per million people, while America had 31.5 per million. Assuming that Americans are not 500 percent more likely to need an MRI than their English counterparts, it was reasonable to ask who was benefiting from all those American MRI scans. As Brill showed, those who benefited most from all those scans were the hospitals and doctors who billed patients billions of dollars for imaging they might not have needed.

When confronted about some of the stratospheric bills sent to NewYork-Presbyterian patients, Corwin was unapologetic. What looked simple to a patient was usually anything but. Need a blood test? That required building and staffing an entire phlebotomy department. Those machines patients took for granted because they'd seen them on TV? Sometimes they cost many millions of dollars. Want access to the finest doctors in the world? Well, they didn't work for minimum wage. Plus, the hospital lost money on every Medicare patient and had to make it up to keep its high standard of care.

Corwin's training on Epic came in December 2019 at a private session with Allan Schwartz, the chief of Columbia's division of cardiology and Bill Clinton's cardiologist. Schwartz and Corwin did their residencies at what was then Columbia-Presbyterian. For Schwartz, that residency had felt like a kind of miracle, as the hospital, like many others, was in its last years of the silent judgment system, where a bright young resident would get the look of *Just how Jewish are you?* before being allowed into Columbia's doors. There was one Black resident out of sixty-eight: Carlton McGregor, who had attended Harvard Medical School. "It's hard to believe now, but 1980 was still a different world,"

McGregor said. "We did not dwell on race identity with each other. It was more subtle and complicated." Friendships were forged around treating patients. McGregor became a pulmonologist, but he and Corwin initially trained together, and Corwin, a cardiologist, later took care of a member of McGregor's family.

On the first morning of Epic training, Corwin asked Schwartz, "Are you getting this?"

"Are you kidding me?" Schwartz responded.

"We were like Abbott and Costello," Corwin said. But the pair was determined to master the Epic system, and over the next two days, they learned it. A few months later, in 5 South, Lindsay Lief and Bradley Hayward struggled with it as well. "The number of alerts I have to click through just to do one thing. The patients are like, 'I just want Tylenol. What's taking so long?' You should see what I have to do to get a tab of Tylenol. . . . You click in *acetaminophen*. Fifty orders might come up, every combination drug that has acetaminophen in it—the pediatric, the OB, the IV form . . . you have to scroll for five minutes to find the right one. Then you click it. Now, once you click it, there are a hundred more check boxes you have to do. . . . Do you want three twenty-five? Do you want six fifty? Do you want nine fifty? Do you want it PRN or standing? Q four, q six . . . right? When it was a paper chart, you just wrote what you wanted. Because it's a computer, it's algorithmic. It might be fifty clicks to get a Tylenol. And then you have to wait for a pharmacist to see the order, do something on their end, get the nurse to recognize it's on there, then scan a badge, type in a hundred things. . . . Then the patient has to swipe the medicine bar code. So it's a million clicks. And people are like, 'I just want Tylenol. . . . I had one in my purse,'" Lief said.

"You can never get away from it. The same phone that I have pictures of my kids on has Epic on it, so when I'm at home, it's alerting me to random things even though I'm not in charge of my patient. Or I click in my phone to do something else at home and it's staring at me."

It was understood by everyone who was training on the system that Epic was a part of the larger issues of a hospital corporation with thousands of ridiculous Medicare and private insurance billing rules. "They focus on things that are basically irrelevant to patient care but are required," Hayward said. "So you spend forty minutes with a patient who is very complicated; you look at their CT scans and you talk to their family. It's a complicated story and you would have to say that is a 'high-level' visit, but you can't say that, because if you did that review of systems, asked them all the questions required, even if they're irrelevant..." Completing the paperwork could take longer than the visit itself.

On the fourteenth floor of Columbia Medical Center, Veronica Roye, the outpatient liver-transplant coordinator, struggled with the new system. Roye, thirty-eight, upbeat with a ready smile and a self-assured manner, was the center of a close group of friends who had trained with her at Columbia's nursing school, and she had always relished a challenge, but mastering Epic was as difficult for her as it had been for Steve Corwin. Roye grew up in East Harlem. Her father, an entrepreneur who had emigrated from Jamaica, named his fish store after his oldest daughter. Coming home from school every day with her grandmother, Roye would walk under a large sign: MISS VEE'S FISH AND CHIPS. Her father also owned a small fleet of Cadillacs, which he'd rent out to limo drivers.

Up the street from Miss Vee's at 140th Street in West Harlem was a cluster of housing projects where two of her cousins lived. Roye felt safe biking around the block because everyone, from the owner of the hardware store next door to the barber, watched out for her. "Hi, Miss Vee," her father's customers would call to her when they came to order fish and chips or pick up the fresh fish her father took her to buy at the historic Fulton Fish Market.

Roye's father loved having his daughter with him in the store. To entertain her, he built a wooden loft and ladder over the freezer. In the loft were a chair, a small desk, pillows, and all kinds of books. When he had time, he read to her. Roye thought of her loft as her personal kingdom. Later, she used it as her quiet place to focus on school assignments. She attended P.S. 50, an elementary school in East Harlem. Occasionally during the school year, she worked the fish-and-chips window to help out, and always in the summer.

Roye thought she might become a teacher, but switched to nursing when she visited a friend who worked at a hospital. Her first nursing job was at Lincoln, a public hospital in the South Bronx. Most of her patients in the emergency department were Black. One day, before Roye's shift, a Jewish child arrived at the hospital after having had a seizure. When Roye got to work, the ED was filled with cops; she was stopped from going into the resuscitation room. They told her to talk to a rabbi standing nearby. "This was the first time I learned that if you have a Hasidic child, you have to speak to the rabbi—never the parents," Roye said. "It was a defining moment for me. I realized there was so much I did not know outside of my world." She set her sights on getting a job at NewYork-Presbyterian and bombarded the hospital's talent coordinator with applications.

Finally, a full-time position opened up in the pediatric ICU. Roye landed the job and began her nursing career at Weill Cornell in 2015. She also worked part-time at Columbia's liver-transplant department. Many of Roye's patients were battling cancer or had complications from transplants. A few years into her time at Weill Cornell, she could not help noticing that white nurses with far less experience than she had were getting the most challenging cases. During one shift in the PICU—pediatric ICU—as she was preparing medication for a baby, the infant's mother challenged her and said she did not know what she was doing. "You are going to kill my baby," she said. "I am going to sue the hospital." She began to scream: "I am reporting you to the department of health." There were four white babies in the unit; Veronica saw all the parents staring at her as if she were in the wrong. Suddenly, Roye felt like a pariah. She complained to her supervisor, who was also Black. "You know this is racism," she said. "Veronica, we all deal with it. Just try to ignore it," the supervisor said. It was clear to Roye that the supervisor wasn't going to do anything to defend Roye that might put her own job at risk.

But Roye couldn't ignore it. She later talked about her sense that she was disrespected and believed it affected how she felt about staying at Weill Cornell. One year later she quit, leaving, she said, blistering comments about the racism she'd suffered. She expected to hear from the hospital HR team. She never did.

Roye was determined to put her Weill Cornell experience behind her. She felt lucky she had kept her second job at Columbia's liver-transplant center. Working two jobs at once enabled her to save enough money for a down payment on a house, and when her son was ten years old, she moved to Maywood, New Jersey. Two years later, she was accepted at Columbia's nursing school for her doctorate. Roye had long ago learned to ignore all the frequent small annoyances of life—the taxis that wouldn't stop for her, the slights she perceived coming from her professors. Thoughtless comments about a Caribbean patient's diet nettled her, as did references to race as a "biological" construct, rather than a social one. Who did not understand that health was often directly related to having the money to pay for decent doctors and insurance?

Roye put off scheduling her Epic training as long as she could. She had been called in to consult on a complicated new case, the latest miracle operation of Tomoaki Kato. Of all the transplant surgeons

Roye worked with, she had a special affection for Kato. She appreciated his exquisite manners. He always stopped by the desks of the three outpatient nurses whose offices faced his suite down the hall; he wasn't talky, but there was always a smile, a comment about the day, the weather, and he would notice small details of their lives. She teased him about the marathons he ran but didn't train for. Roye felt he never even noticed her race. Kato operated on anyone who needed a transplant; the more impossible the procedure, the more he was drawn to it.

Kato had a long title: surgical director of adult and pediatric liver and intestinal transplantation. But that bureaucratic title—director—obscured what he really was, which was perhaps the finest transplant surgeon in the world.

In some ways, it seemed like Kato had been destined for a life of the most sophisticated manual labor. When he was a child in Tokyo, his slim, long fingers, delicate hands, and sensitive technique had so impressed his classical guitar teachers that they recorded his recitals and encouraged him to apply to a music conservatory. There was a sense of music to his work in the hospital theater too; each operation was a symphony within which were a series of movements (literally) with their own rhythm and melody.

Unlike most other department chiefs across the hospital, Kato had not gone to medical school in the United States. He'd studied and done his residency in his native Japan before coming to do a clinical fellowship in Miami in 1997. He moved up in the ranks to become the head of the liver and transplantations center at the University of Miami Hospital. As awareness of his brilliance at the operating table increased, it seemed only a matter of time before Columbia would try to bring him into the fold.

"We were recruiting a surgeon at the time," Jean Emond, the chief of transplantation services, recalled. He and Corwin reviewed a list of possible candidates, and Emond said, "Well, actually, the best surgeon is Tom Kato. He's in Florida . . . but I don't know if we can get him here."

Kato was far from unknown; he was already, in Corwin's words, "a virtuoso in the operating room. He can do operations—literally can do operations nobody else can do. He would do these procedures where he would spend twenty hours where he would take every organ out of the abdomen and scrape off the various tumors." Corwin said they should try to get him, and they got him. After twelve years of sun and the beach, Kato headed north, but not before performing a miracle procedure on a sixty-three-year-old in Miami, a fifteen-hour tour de force involving multiple organs being removed and then replaced that made the *New York Times*.

It was no exaggeration to say, as Corwin did, that Kato did operations that nobody else could do—in fact, some of what he did, nobody else had thought possible. Many saw the human body as ultimately unfathomable, but he saw it as a brainteaser. He successfully revived a failing liver by figuring out how to attach it to a portion of a healthy liver from a donor, and as mind-boggling as that was to his fellow surgeons, it was relatively straightforward compared with some of the other multiorgan shuffling he invented. Kato would swap and remove and connect multiple organs with extraordinary delicacy, timing, and creativity. He once figured out a way to transplant part of a bladder by also transplanting two kidneys connected by ureters—the tubes that carry urine from the kidneys to the bladder—to a section of a donor bladder. Nobody had ever successfully transplanted a partial human bladder before. And as if that sort of thing weren't enough, Kato once removed and reimplanted six organs to reach an otherwise inaccessible abdominal tumor. Terms like *jaw-dropping* and *cutting-edge* became standard for Kato's surgeries, and that as well as the more profound fact of the number of lives he saved brought a degree of celebrity to the quiet surgeon and the hospital where he worked. In the *New York Times* article, Emond labeled Kato "our Michael Jordan."

As is the case with any transplant operation, especially

unprecedented ones, not every story had a happy ending. Back in 2009, Kato had been forced to cut out two-thirds of a patient's stomach and sections of his intestines and pancreas in order to remove a massive, ten-pound tumor. The whole procedure took a total of forty-three hours—the longest operation Kato had ever done at the time—but four months later, the patient began to fail, and the death he'd postponed by undergoing the surgery came at last. But there were wonderful stories too. In 2012, Kato and his team saved the life of a four-year-old New Jersey girl at virtually the last minute under extreme circumstances: Hurricane Sandy was approaching New York, and the donated liver was in Nevada. Organs for transplant are viable for only a few hours after they leave the donor's body, so even without the storm, getting the liver to the little girl in time would have been difficult. Every charter company they went to declined to fly, given the weather and schedule, but Kato refused to give up. As Tod Brown, an organ procurement coordinator, recalled in the *New York Times,* "Dr. Kato knew he was going to get that organ, one way or another." Finally, they found a company that agreed to make the trip. The plane—with the precious donor organ—landed outside New York; an ambulance rushed the liver from there to Columbia; and the child's operation was a success. (That articles about his surgeries made it into the *New York Times* was further evidence of just how pioneering Kato's work could be.)

At times, Kato could be like his own hurricane, despite his calm demeanor. On any given week, he performed three complex twenty-hour surgeries. Often when he rushed down the hospital halls, he was followed by his residents and fellows, like photographers tracking a celebrity—which, in a way, they were. He was known as "the machine." To relax, he ran marathons.

———

Before she went to work with liver-transplant patients, Roye read everything she could about Kato and her new specialty, an effort made easier by the fact that he had been profiled in *Esquire*, and *New York Times* science reporter Denise Grady had been permitted to scrub in for Kato's surgery miracles on two separate occasions. In her research, Roye learned how difficult it was to get transplants for people of color, who lacked access to the sort of medical care that might lead them to a transplant surgeon, patients who desperately needed help but who would not have known that a miracle-maker like Kato even existed. Roye's dream was to be able to find those in need and bring them to Columbia.

Kato's special expertise was pediatric abdominal tumors. One seven-year-old, Heather McNamara, had a tumor that had wrapped itself around the major blood vessels to her spleen, liver, stomach, pancreas, and small intestines. Every major cancer surgeon told her parents that her condition was inoperable and that they should take her home and let her live out her last months in peace.

In Miami, Kato had performed several ex vivo (meaning "out of the body") surgeries, removing the diseased organs, scraping off the tumors, then replacing the organs. Meeting Heather and her family for the first time in 2008, Kato told the McNamaras he would try to save her; he gave her a fifty-fifty chance of surviving the procedure. Three surgical teams worked with Kato—it took twenty-three hours, but Heather survived. Two years later she filmed a commercial for NewYork-Presbyterian in which she recounted: "Dr. Kato said that he took all my organs out and put the ones I needed back in. And I was better, and I am just so happy to be better, and cancer-free." McNamara had just graduated from college.

And now, in December 2019, word circulated through Roye's department that Kato was taking on his most challenging surgery ever—a pair of conjoined twins, connected through a liver, a surgery of such rarity that Kato later told me, "If you are lucky, you get one surgery like this in a lifetime." This was his first.

As Epic training continued around Roye, the twins and their mother were flown in from Sierra Leone on an ambulance plane. Roye, sworn to secrecy because the hospital, she assumed, was trying to avoid media attention, sat in on the early training sessions describing what it would take to separate the twins, who shared a liver and part of the abdominal wall. The surgery preparation would take months, but it was scheduled for February 21, 2020. In the meantime, the family was staying secluded in a room at NewYork-Presbyterian's Morgan Stanley Children's Hospital.

As the pandemic infiltrated China in December and January, the intensity of Epic training took over the hospital. Writing in the *New Yorker*, Siddhartha Mukherjee, a biologist, physician at Columbia, and author (he won a Pulitzer Prize for his book *The Emperor of All Maladies*), decried the hijacking of clinical medicine as it morphed into an ever more complicated and medically counterproductive information system. If the Epic databases were trackable, the information would have been invaluable, Mukherjee noted, for finding ways to understand a pandemic. But it turned out to be impossible for patient information to be shared across departments—approvals would be needed from an institutional review board and permissions gotten for each and every patient. Mukherjee noted in the *New Yorker* a tweet by a cardiologist at Massachusetts General Hospital in Boston: "'Why are nearly all notes in Epic . . . basically *useless* to understand what's happening to patient during hospital course?'" Another doctor's reply: "'Because notes are used to bill, determine level of service, and document it rather than their intended purpose, which was to convey our observations, assessment, and plan. Our important work has been co-opted by billing.'"

Almost two years later, Corwin had no doubt that the launch of Epic had taken most of the time and attention of Fleischut's modeling group. "That turned out to be a problem—that is where our attention was," he confessed.

Not completely.

As the hospital prepared to roll out Epic, Fleischut's modeling team was trading COVID models with Nathaniel Hupert. "We were worried. We wanted to make sure that we had enough ventilators. We were trying to overlay this all with the modeling that was coming from the city."

Epic had pandemic modeling built into its electronic projections. In late January and early February, tabletop exercises were run at Columbia for all the department heads, reassuring Fleischut. The models were based on beds and, later, on the number of ventilators that might be required. But the number of N95 masks that the hospital used weekly was thought by the hospital supply team to be approximately four thousand—and N95 masks were left out of the modeling assumptions. Models projected future needs for hand sanitizers, but the hospital team deemed the current mask supply, including what was stored in the hospital's warehouse, more than enough. But the modelers were working off numbers they associated with a severe influenza outbreak, as was the CDC. This turned out to be a catastrophic miscalculation. By the third week of March, NewYork-Presbyterian would need ninety thousand masks (the sum total of all it had on hand and in the warehouse) *every day* to protect its front-line workers—and that was one of hundreds of hospital supplies that would be throttled by COVID-19's avalanche of supply-chain issues.

3

The first data about the emerging coronavirus came from lab researchers at the Shanghai Public Health Clinical Center, which had a partnership with a Wuhan hospital; they uploaded it onto a public website for medical investigators. On January 11, 2020, the Chinese government formally shared the genomic sequence of the virus with the World Health Organization and assessed with what would turn out to be wildly incompetent optimism that there would be no widespread transmission. But the release of the genomic sequence confirmed that the virus was a coronavirus, the type of virus that had caused SARS, possibly coming from bats. The genomic sequence allowed labs all over the world to develop tests to detect the virus, a way to identify and contain the spread.

Two days later, on January 13, Thailand reported the first case outside China: a woman from Wuhan who was visiting the country. On January 24, it was reported that the second case in the United States was a woman from Wuhan who lived in Chicago and had gone home to take care of her father. When she returned to Chicago, she had difficulty breathing. She was admitted to the hospital, and her husband also turned out to be infected. Reporting the case, the *New York Times* used the term "Wuhan coronavirus" and quoted the CDC's director of the National Center for Immunization and Respiratory Diseases, Nancy Messonnier, soon to occupy headlines around the world.

"The immediate risk to the American public is low at this time, but the situation continues to evolve rapidly," Messonnier said. On January 24, federal officials were monitoring sixty-three possible coronavirus cases in twenty-two states.

While the president obsessed about the House impeachment managers and the slate of witnesses called to testify about his election campaign's ties to Ukraine, a thirty-five-year-old man flew back to Seattle after visiting family in Wuhan. Arriving on January 15, he was unaware he had the virus. A few days later, he was taken to a hospital in Everett, a bedroom community of Seattle. At first, his symptoms seemed to indicate he had a severe flu. It would take five days for the White House to learn the true cause of his condition.

Inside China, public health officials held a series of secret meetings warning that the virus was on its way to becoming a pandemic. The fear was ratcheting up at NewYork-Presbyterian too—at least among some. Increasingly concerned by what she was hearing, Lizzy Oelsner sent a text to friends from her resident days at Columbia University Medical Center: *Have you gotten masks yet? Get them NOW.* Then: *Mask up. I am serious.* Oelsner, a research scientist who worked on lung diseases, kept texting her friends and family for the next weeks, sending pictures of masks—masks for the fashionable, masks that would operate like N95s. Later, she said, "I knew, as of January fifteenth, this was a catastrophe."

On January 22, NewYork-Presbyterian sent out its first all-hospital alert:

"An outbreak caused by a novel Coronavirus has been detected in Wuhan City, China. All persons presenting to the medical facility with fever and respiratory illness should be screened for travel to Wuhan City within the past 2 weeks. Persons with fever and lower respiratory illness who travelled to Wuhan, China, or came into close contact with an ill person under investigation is immediately given a mask, moved to a negative pressure room, isolated." (A negative-pressure environment is a room in which the pressure inside is lower than it is outside; this keeps contaminants—such as COVID-infected droplets—in the room.) "Routinely available tests do not detect it," the alert added ominously.

In 5 South, Lindsay Lief was not alarmed. "There were hospital-wide e-mails that went out at the end of January," recalled Lief. "We get alerts like this not that infrequently." She added, "I think it was 'Oh, okay, there's something from Wuhan; I'm sure we're going to see a lot of people from Wuhan.' I don't think we were as worried about it, clearly, as we should have been."

In January, at Columbia University's Mailman School of Public Health, the noted infectious-disease modeler Jeffrey Shaman had started to construct a COVID model based on how rapidly the virus was spreading in China. He had a growing fear, he would later say, that the scale of the coming COVID pandemic would approach that of the 1918 flu pandemic. Shaman's modeling group analyzed data from 375 Chinese cities to determine how many people could be infected via asymptomatic spread. His model was one of the first. *New York Times* reporter Jeneen Interlandi later wrote that Shaman's group was "horrified" by the result: 86 percent of cases in China were most likely not being reported. "We were looking at the maps of what's going on in China. And we were seeing how it spread so rapidly from its epicenter, all of those people hopping on airplanes and going to Thailand, Japan, Korea, and the United States." Shaman wondered, *How many of the infections are being documented? What fraction are not? And how contagious, per person, are those people who are never being identified?* Shaman did not share any of his early data findings with the medical side of the hospital.

"I don't interact with the hospital," Shaman said. "I've never talked to Steve Corwin. I'm at Columbia Medical Center." Instead, he drilled down with his team to complete the data studies that he presented at an influential conference of global epidemiologists on Valentine's Day, three weeks after NewYork-Presbyterian had put out its all-hospital alert. "That got us enormous buzz." The study came out in *Science* in March and was reported in the *New York Times* and on NPR. Asked about this later, Shaman bridled. "You would have to talk to [the hospital] about whether or not they read the paper. I don't remember specifically talking to them prior to April of 2020." Five years earlier, Shaman had approached the hospital about doing flu forecasting for them but received, he said, "little interest."

There are reasons. Disease modeling is taken very seriously in England but less so in the United States, where there is no formal structure to connect policy makers with respected modelers. Pandemic forecasting is even more challenging, despite the arrival of supercomputers. There are so many modelers and so many different databases; how do you assess who is correct about how humans will behave? "Why was it so hard for epidemiologists and public-health officials to get on the same page? Why did so many leaders fail to engage with the best evidence or even just the right experts?" Shaman asked Interlandi.

From his years at the CDC, Nathaniel Hupert had long been obsessed by the exact same question. Now, since the earliest days of January, when he wasn't on call at Lower Manhattan, he worked from his attic office in Princeton, New Jersey, where he had relocated. Hupert was focused on the mysterious virus.

He wasn't the only one. Almost as soon as the news from Wuhan broke, the University of Nebraska epidemiologist James Lawler reached out to him. Lawler's first query dropped in Hupert's in-box on January 8.

Nathaniel: Can you help me with some hospital projections?

Despite its brevity, the question was, for Hupert, a code red, an indication that this mysterious outbreak in Wuhan might just be the great pandemic that had long been predicted.

Or maybe not. In late January, as news of the COVID-19 outbreaks filtered from Iran and Lombardy, Hupert reached out to his former CDC colleagues who had helped model the 2014 Ebola outbreak and its possible effects on hospital capacity. In 2014, NewYork-Presbyterian committed five million dollars toward creating elaborate quarantine rooms and drills for doctors and nurses to protect themselves with PPE, almost all of which would go unused.

What hospitals prepared for was the arrival of scores of patients whose situation would be as acute an emergency as what happened to one New York doctor who became infected doing relief work in Africa.

In the autumn of 2014, thirty-three-year old Craig Spencer, a board-certified emergency medicine physician at Columbia Medical Center, returned from a humanitarian mission to Guinea with Doctors Without Borders. Although he had dressed in full protective gear, Spencer had no best-practice guidelines, a harbinger of what would happen in 2020.

Arriving home, he did not assume that he might be infected. He stayed with his fiancée, went bowling and out to dinner. A few days later he ran a high fever and wound up in quarantine at Bellevue Hospital, the largest public teaching hospital in the city and one of eight hospitals in the state designated to treat Ebola patients. Bellevue had dealt with New York City epidemics since the yellow fever outbreaks of the 1790s; it had special quarantine units for critically ill patients, and employees had begun drills as soon as Ebola was declared an "international health emergency." Spencer would become the fourth patient in the United States to be diagnosed with Ebola and—as the tabloids made defiantly clear—the man who "brought" Ebola to New York. His case enraged the city, including citizen Donald Trump, who accused him of a shameful lack of caution. At Bellevue, his condition deteriorated and he lost twenty pounds before the disease was arrested.

Spencer, now the director of global health and emergency medicine at Columbia Medical Center, was following closely the possible outbreak of coronavirus, as COVID was called in the first weeks of the year, on a cruise ship in Japan. Spencer saw his own history repeating on the *Diamond Princess*, quarantined off the coast of Yokohama, after the cruise director discovered that a passenger from Hong Kong who had previously been aboard had tested positive. The *Diamond Princess* carried more than 2,650 passengers in predictably close quarters now trapped in their rooms without fresh air as COVID spread rapidly through the ship. As the crisis unfolded, Spencer tried to warn the public about the coming threat by detailing to a *Time* magazine reporter his own harrowing experience. On February 4, *Time* ran the article by Melissa Chan with the headline "This Doctor Was Vilified After Contracting Ebola. Now He Sees History Repeating Itself with Coronavirus."

All through January, Lawler and Hupert e-mailed back and forth as they followed the growing crisis. Hupert was analyzing the modeling coming from Johns Hopkins on what little data was obtainable from Wuhan and Hubei Province, noticing discrepancies in the reported fatality rates depending on the local source. On January 30, Hupert received the first of hundreds of e-mails he would get as part of a semisecret group of modelers and epidemiologists; the e-mail chain was referred to as "Red Dawn," a reference to the 1984 movie in which a group of American teens fights a Soviet invasion.

By late January, Duane Caneva, the chief medical officer of the Department of Homeland Security, had become almost frantic that he could not get anyone in the White House to really pay attention to what was coming toward the United States. A Trump appointee, Caneva was a pandemic expert who had brought in as his deputy Melissa Harvey, who had put in years working on disaster preparedness. Harvey and Hupert had worked together during the Ebola crisis trying to understand the metrics. Now, in the Department of Homeland Security, Caneva and Harvey knew they had to create a semirogue, confidential gathering place for the world's top pandemic epidemiologists to share information about what they were seeing.

"I brought in Nathaniel on day one," Harvey said. "I e-mailed him and said, 'I need you on this.'" Harvey was already trying to understand the possible financial and economic havoc a pandemic similar to the 1918 flu pandemic could wreak on the country. She asked Hupert to reach out to the NewYork-Presbyterian/Weill Cornell leadership to see if anyone from Wall Street could advise.

It was February 3. Craig Spencer was already out with his warnings in *Time*—but he, like Jeffrey Shaman, would be largely ignored. Immediately, Hupert tried to alert the Weill Cornell leadership: "Do you know how I might . . . contact one or two of our board members to see what financial impact estimates are being made for coronavirus scenarios? I am being asked to do this by my contact at the DHS, who needs we believe to jump-start consideration of large-scale and economically disruptive measures for contact/reduction if and when the nCOV really hits our shores." Hupert e-mailed one department head and then another and another. All remained unanswered. What would a hospitalist at Lower Manhattan who had worked for the CDC possibly understand about what was coming that an academic dean didn't already get?

One of the first Red Dawn e-mails, a forwarded message from two days earlier, was from Carter Mecher, with whom Hupert had worked at the Bush White House and the CDC. Mecher had been one of the people who were most concerned by the data slipping out of China, and his concern was now amplified. Mecher would soon leap into national notoriety as a central figure in Michael Lewis's vivid 2021 pandemic history, *The Premonition*.

Incredibly, the scores of Red Dawn e-mails, with an ever expanding list of epidemiologists, would stay secret until a group of *New York Times* reporters broke the story of their existence on April 11, the day New York City recorded its 5,463rd COVID death.

January 28
6:04 p.m.

The chatter on the blogs is that WHO and CDC are behind the curve. I'm seeing comments from people asking why WHO and CDC seem to be downplaying this ... no matter how I look at this, it looks to be bad ... The projected size of the outbreak already seems hard to believe, but when I think of the actions being taken across China, that are reminiscent of 1918, Philadelphia, perhaps those numbers are correct ... And if we accept that level of transmissibility, the CFR [case fatality rate] is approaching the range of a severe flu epidemic. And if we assume the case ascertainment rate is even worse than 2009 H1N1, this is really going to be unbelievable (higher transmissibility than flu). Any way you cut it, this is going to be bad. You guys made fun of me screaming to close the schools. Now I am screaming, close the colleges and universities.

Is CDC monitoring the blogs? One thing I am checking for each day is availability of respirators on amazon and ebay (just curious since this is an indirect way of taking the temperature of the country).

From Omaha, Lawler wasted no time responding, in an e-mail that, months later, would be widely reported:

January 28, 2020
8:56 p.m.

Great Understatements in History:
Napoleon's retreat from Moscow—"just a little stroll gone
   bad."
Pompeii—"a bit of a dust storm"
Hiroshima—"a bad summer heat wave"
AND Wuhan—"just a bad flu season"

As far as Hupert knew, he was the only person at Weill Cornell
or Columbia who was assisting with Red Dawn projections, partly
relying on data from Lawler based on the amount of PPE that was
being used in Nebraska for non-COVID-quarantined patients. Hupert was aware that Nebraska was managing many of the repatriated
quarantined patients from the cruise ships. "PPE is PPE regardless
of the patient's true infection status," Hupert later recalled. At the
CDC, Lawler and Hupert had made similar assessments for Ebola
and the 2009 H1N1 (swine flu) pandemic, in which twelve thousand died in the United States, but Hupert understood that in this
case, he was a modeler operating without full knowledge of the data.
But how could any modeler get a proper assessment of the infection
numbers given the lack of testing in America and China's failure to
share data? Testing was essential to get a handle on COVID's spread,
and tests existed, but a combination of White House disregard and
CDC sloppiness doomed America's attempts to nip the pandemic in
the bud. Indeed, the CDC's rollout of test kits had been a debacle.
   Hupert tried not to overreact to the Red Dawn alerts, especially
as their frequency increased hour after hour. But many disaster preparedness experts and epidemiologists were galvanizing support, pro-
pelled by the massive accumulation of data in the scores of e-mails
flying back and forth.

By the second week in February, Hupert started getting e-mails from emergency physicians in Hong Kong and around the world who had been following his Red Dawn contributions. "We have seen pictures of what is going on at NewYork-Presbyterian. No one is wearing a mask. What is going on?" Concerned, Hupert copied elaborate diagrams of COVID safety procedures and taped them up in the doctors' lounge. "Weirdos like me were telling people to stock up on toilet paper and pasta," he said. "All through the month, I was hopping mad." Running numbers late at night, Hupert was stunned by the possible infection rate he estimated for the hospital staff. "I lost it," he said when his recommendations were spurned during a preparedness meeting in early March. Hupert presented slides of the shocking numbers he was seeing. "Two women who were running the emergency response were at the conference table. I said, 'You should not be at the same meeting.' People looked at me like I had two heads."

"Let's face it," Weill Cornell's director of critical care, David Berlin, later said, "we were stupid. Stupid not to be wearing masks in the beginning. There was so much we did not understand." Hupert told the group gathered at the table: "This thing is going to go off like a bomb." How many staff members could be infected? His estimate: possibly in the hundreds.

On February 9, Lawler texted, *Good work, Nathaniel!* to the Red Dawn chain, now grown to more than thirty members, among them Richard Hatchett, another of the country's premier epidemiologists. In the first week of February, Hupert had calculated new projections for the fall and then the stabilization of the mortality rate he was observing in Hubei province. Hupert communicated what he was seeing to his department chairs, Monika Safford and Art Evans, who shared his growing concern, but they were unable to convince the hospital to engage in a real discussion about the implications of their numbers. And there were some other numbers that came to the fore: On February 11, the World Health Organization named the new coronavirus "severe acute respiratory syndrome coronavirus 2," or SARS-CoV-2, and the disease it caused "coronavirus disease 2019," or COVID-19. Few in the world had heard the term *coronavirus* before. Within weeks, nearly everyone on the planet would be using it.

It was long understood by many in public health that the CDC was more or less in tatters, riddled with bureaucratic infighting and a lack of collaboration with other agencies. In the academic corridors of the CDC, real-time crisis management has always been a secondary consideration. The CDC investigations are wrapped in the *Morbidity and Mortality Weekly Report,* the agency's epidemiological digest that provides deep analyses of disease trends. Raw data and conjecture in a public health crisis is often risky, but at times it is the only guide to save lives, a paradox and impossible conflict for an institution that is funded to perform rigorous analyses that can take years.

The antediluvian CDC structures and its inability to quickly gather, process, and interpret data had created an information desert by February 2020, and it would implode publicly, many later commented, harming thousands of COVID-19 patients. Among its failures, the CDC could not generate reliable information about the number of actual COVID patients and how doctors were treating them. According to Scott Gottlieb, the former head of the FDA and now a Pfizer board member, the CDC estimates relied on death certificates, provided by the states, which, given the serious limits of Chinese cooperation, were often delayed by one or two months. Epidemiologists inside hospitals were forced to rely on data coming from China and now Italy, which was much more reliable. But it took no mathematical or medical expertise to see the catastrophe unfolding. France had announced Europe's first death on February 15, though Italy had raced ahead of it in terms of infections and fatalities. By February 24 cases in

Iran were beginning to explode, and that same week, Brazil recorded Latin America's first official death.

On February 29, the United States recorded its first death from COVID in a nursing home outside Seattle. Much later, investigators from the CDC would try to analyze earlier deaths in January 2020, the *New York Times* reported, but the results would be inconclusive.

Yet in the last week of February, almost no one presenting with COVID symptoms in the United States could be tested unless they could somehow prove that they had been exposed to someone from Wuhan. The combination was devastating. The lack of tests (and a good portion of the kits that were distributed would turn out to have flaws that made them unusable) and the decision to assume a woefully inadequate presumption of spread meant there would be almost no preemption.

A month later, an investigation conducted by ProPublica would uncover hundreds of e-mails from CDC staffers seeking answers. How could an agency that had eradicated smallpox globally and wiped out polio in the United States have fallen so far? But while the agency's increasingly obvious stumbles continued, NewYork-Presbyterian maintained that its hands were tied; it had to follow federal and state government policy about how to respond to COVID—something that was about to become even harder thanks to the White House and New York governor Andrew Cuomo's administration.

At Weill Cornell in February, the week that the modeler Jeffrey Shaman was going public with his apocalyptic modeling data from China, Nathaniel Hupert was desperately trying to alert his colleagues. He knew his time would be better spent trying to push out papers to ensure his funding and get global attention, but he had long believed in what he called "the morality of modeling," and as a doctor believed his first obligation was to patient care.

"What the hell is this guy talking about?" That had been Dr. Matt McCarthy's reaction to the first e-mail he received from Nathaniel Hupert. McCarthy, like Hupert, was one of the elite group of Weill Cornell hospitalists, doctors who provide care primarily to patients inside the hospital. McCarthy was known almost as much for his year spent as a lefty relief pitcher on an Anaheim Angels farm team as he was for his scholarship and clinical knowledge of deadly microbes and rare bacteria strains that became the basis of his bestselling book *Superbugs: The Race to Stop an Epidemic*, published in 2019.

McCarthy surely is the only southpaw in the history of Minor League Baseball who, after one season, wound up at Harvard Medical School. "You always looked stupid in a baseball hat," his sister told him when he was sent packing by the Anaheim Angels. The detailed journals he kept of his experience—the baseball babble, clubhouse segregation, and possible steroid use—became the basis of the bestselling 2009 *Odd Man Out*, which so angered several of his former teammates they accused him of making it up. By then, McCarthy had started his residency at Columbia and had already spent summers trapping Ebola-infected bats in Cameroon. Hearing of his plans to live under the trees and search for highly infectious bats, his father said, "Really, Matty? Why?" That experience he wrote about in *Slate*. In 2008, at Columbia, as a rookie resident, he kept another detailed journal that would become his *The Real Doctor Will See You Shortly: A Physician's First Year*. McCarthy often speaks of his passion to combine what he loves—deep research, taking care of patients, and writing.

At Yale, McCarthy was known for his ninety-two-mile-an-hour fastball, which led him to his last game in his senior year and his best performance, against Brown: a perfect shutout. Ten strikeouts, one walk, four hits, and all with a pro scout in the stands. He was drafted in the twenty-first round by the Anaheim Angels and in 2002, took off for Provo, Utah, where the Angels kept their rookie-level minor league team. He lived with a Mormon family and tried to pitch his way out of the bullpen. To entertain himself, he took notes. Lots of notes. Did the scout know that the square-jawed pitcher from Orlando was also a molecular biophysics and biochemistry major who spent his spare time working in the lab of the celebrated scientist Joan Steitz, a godmother of mRNA? Introduced to McCarthy by her son Jon, who also played for Yale, Steitz and her husband, Tom, a Nobel laureate, saw McCarthy's unusual focus immediately. The son of two professors of criminal justice, McCarthy had grown up in a world of academic research. "I would come into the lab and, however early, there would be Matt leaning forward on his bench staring into microscopes," Steitz said.

McCarthy had come to Weill Cornell to work with Tom Walsh, whose groundbreaking research career (detailed in *Superbugs*) changed the way doctors treat infections. A son of a reconnaissance sergeant who had fought on D-Day, Walsh flirted briefly with becoming a soldier himself but thought of his work with antibiotics as "a mission." It began in medical school when he cared for a patient with a rare condition: candida endocarditis, a fungal infection of the heart. It was a mystery to him and his mentor Bernadine Healy, a rising star in cardiology. Trying to learn how to treat such cases, Walsh went to work in her lab and found his calling. (Healy went on to become the first woman to head the National Institutes of Health.)

McCarthy was in place in 2012 at Tom Walsh's lab when the deadly outbreak of the mold *Exserohilum rostratum* infected batches of steroid injections to relieve back pain prepared at a Framingham, Massachusetts, compounding pharmacy. Thousands of patients across America had been injected with the contaminated shots; hundreds developed meningitis across twenty states. Sixty-four would die. "Only a handful of people even knew what this fungus was—and Tom happened to be one of them. And he was like, we have to jump

into this. We were in a world where the fungus had been an intellec-
tual backwater and what would come to be called Exeter Highland
became the biggest health issue of that moment. Tom knew we had
to focus on the diagnostics. We had to have a way to detect it. A
rapid PCR test. And then the treatment. And this is what I was
thinking of when COVID hit: We have to have a PCR to detect it."

In early February 2020, driving the thirty minutes from her house
in Great Neck, Long Island, Jaclyn Mucaria, head of NewYork-
Presbyterian's Queens hospital, was astonished by what was happening on Main Street. Despite the images from Wuhan with health
officials in hazmat suits, there were no known COVID cases in New
York. But "suddenly, everyone out shopping was in a mask, all of
the Asian Americans—blue surgical masks, bandannas, N95s. What
did they understand that we didn't? . . . They knew it was community
spread, even if they did not know the term."

At the same time, McCarthy had noticed an unusual number of
patients presenting with severe, pneumonia-like symptoms. "I was
seeing all kinds of patients who were testing negative for influenza
who could have had COVID," he recalled. Meanwhile, his in-box
was clotted with "hundreds of e-mails a day from people hawking
miracle cures for COVID, hawking new tests, all kinds of stuff, so I
was unable to read more than a sentence or two from any e-mail. I
saw an e-mail from Nathaniel and I read a sentence or two and just
moved on."

Hupert's second e-mail jolted McCarthy: "Treat every patient
as infectious." It was February 23. In northwest Italy, ten towns
were being locked down; schools were closed and sporting events
canceled. For days, McCarthy had been slammed with patients,
but seeing the Weill Cornell e-mail address, he stopped to read

Hupert's long methodical instructions laying out a strategy to cohort patients (that is, group together patients who shared certain risk factors). "I hadn't been thinking about the cohorting issue," McCarthy admitted. "I basically said to the person next to me in the office, 'Who is this guy?' The next thing I know I am meeting with Nathaniel and we started e-mailing all the time. I came to rely on him for an understanding of where things were going with this, because he was light-years ahead of everyone else in terms of understanding that the schools were going to close and commerce would come to a halt. He was talking about all of this before it was on anyone's radar. It became clear to me that the messages we were hearing on TV and in the media were increasingly divorced from the reality that we saw and [he] helped me and a lot of others come to appreciate [this] before New York even had its first case."

Hupert had another advantage when convincing McCarthy he was worth listening to. "Most of the people who do the modeling don't ever step into the room of a COVID patient. All they do is take data sheets and spreadsheets and draw conclusions from that," McCarthy said. "Nathaniel knew what it was like to be in a room with somebody on a ventilator. That was also what drew me to him.... I started reading these long e-mails from him and I said, 'If I am going to be in a foxhole with somebody, this is the guy.'... I wasn't sure who was actually listening to him at the hospital, but he turned out to be right about everything."

On 5 South in the ICU, Lindsay Lief was equally concerned. "All N95s have been removed from the supply room," she was informed in an e-mail from the hospital. All the ICUs kept a supply of N95s to protect those who took care of critically ill tuberculosis patients or patients who'd had bone marrow transplants. With its focus on lungs, 5 South's pulmonary needs were especially urgent. "I think they were worried that people were hoarding them or stealing them or something," Lief said. Normally, N95s would be in boxes in the carts next to the room where the gloves and gowns were kept as well as in a cleaning supply closet. No longer. "So if you had a patient that met the criteria," Lief said, "you had to call down to the supply room and they said, 'We will ship you a box.'"

Lief freaked out. "My nurse manager and I sent an e-mail to my senior vice president. I was like, 'This is unacceptable....A patient is dying and we don't even let a nurse in the room until I have this mask? This is what you are telling me? But I am not allowed to keep a mask in the unit? And we're going to call someone and wait?' They were like, 'Yeah.'I said, 'That's outrageous.'...I was forced into the situation where I was saying, 'Okay, so when the first COVID patient arrives, we are not going to bring them upstairs then, because who's going to go into the room and hook them up to the monitor?' And so, after literally a hundred e-mails, I got someone to say, 'You can keep five boxes in the MICU and they have to be locked.'" She knew such a limited supply wouldn't be enough for their day-to-day work in the unit and predicted that "when the first COVID patient arrived, we would have no N95s—none."

For years, the attendings in 5 South had relied on the wisdom and experience of Judith Cherry, a silver-haired Haitian American grandmother who had devoted her life to pulmonary critical-care nursing. Her colleagues affectionately referred to her by the nickname "Haldol," after a medication used to treat psychiatric disorders. Haldol can tame anxiety and nervousness, much like Judith Cherry did for her colleagues on 5 South every day. On the unit, Cherry, one of fourteen nurses and assistants, was known as the secret weapon who could upbraid a resident or fellow who was ordering medicines incorrectly. ("Are you sure that's what you want to do?") Such admonishing was always done with a smile—Cherry was never flustered or, it seemed, tired, despite commuting in from the last stop on the train in Rockaway at dawn. "Lindsay, I know where there are half-open boxes the hospital doesn't know about," she told Lief. "There are closets where they won't think to look." Cherry gathered them all, giving 5 South a secret stash of N95s—a two-week supply under normal circumstances.

In Lower Manhattan in late February, Nathaniel Hupert was also concerned about the masks. Leaving work at the end of the night, he saw someone from Patient Services standing by the elevator with two cartons of N95s. "What are you doing with those?" he asked. "And she said, 'I'm bringing them to one of the trustees. Is this super-bad?'" Hupert had just been asked to join the hospital's emergency response management committee and, stunned, he wrote to the head of it immediately. "It was so jarring. My first question to her was 'Do we have more?' And she said, 'Actually, none of my suppliers in Chinatown have any.'"

Hupert had grown increasingly alarmed about making it clear to Augustine Choi, the dean of Weill Cornell Medical School, that the hospital was about to be hit very, very hard. But getting on Choi's calendar seemed impossible; the world-famous pulmonologist was consulting with the governments of South Korea and China and had not slept in days.

Finally, a meeting was set for February 28. Hupert alerted his department chairs:

Draft Agenda for COVID-19 meeting with Dean Choi,
3 pm today

Immediate Recognition for Everyone:

- Handwashing and/or sanitizer. All the time. Everywhere. After touching anything on the outside or that has been shared by someone else (e.g. microphone)/Enforced on entry to the building by entry guard.
- No touching face without washing/sanitizing first.
- No handshakes or kissing—do the "Ebola elbow bump"
- Get at least 6 feet away from anyone who looks or acts sick—sneezing, etc.
- Cancel all face to face meetings, immediately and for the duration of the event

This is going to be historically bad, rivaling the medical consequences of 1918, but far exceeding it in terms of global financial impact. If we get through this, it will be the sort of thing that we will tell our grandchildren about. And no one seems to have a clue about what is coming (the administration isn't helping).

—Nathaniel

Presidents' Day weekend: Lindsay Lief had to schedule her time away from the pulmonary ICU months in advance, and this was a weekend of utter pleasure for Lief, her sister, Liz, their spouses, and their kids, who were all exactly the same age. After three days of perfect weather and a skiing lesson or two to work on her skills, Lief was feeling confident, and she took a tough slope. She was at the top of a mountain when she heard a pop.

Oh no, Lief thought. *I've caught an edge. This could be bad.* A knife of pain cut through her leg and she fell, her skis off to the side. Lief had been a dancer all through school and had a sense of a possible ligament tear. Collapsed in the snow, she saw that her husband, Jake, and her brother-in-law had skied ahead. She forced herself down the mountain. Lief thought, *There may be a chance if I ice it.* What she most feared was a torn ACL, the anterior cruciate ligament. If it's torn, it makes sitting feel like a spike has been driven through your kneecap and it weakens the affected leg. If she needed surgery, she would have to have it as soon as possible, she told Liz. *Maybe the first week of March.* From Taos, Lief texted to see if she could get an appointment. The specialists were at a conference that week, she was told. If she needed surgery, she would have to put it off, maybe until the second week of March.

Liz and Lindsay Lichtman grew up in Upper Dublin, a quiet suburb of Philadelphia. Liz and Lief were uncommonly close; they had been raised by their mother, Dina Lichtman, a psychologist and executive coach, after their parents' divorce. Lief's father, a dentist, remarried, but he too remained close to his daughters. Although it was rarely discussed, the subtext of history haunted the Lichtman family. Survivors of Auschwitz, Lief's maternal grandparents had met in a displaced-persons camp set up at Bergen-Belsen. Dina was born in the camp, and the family went to New York the following year. The family moved to Philadelphia, where they lived in public housing and struggled to rise to the middle class. As a child, Dina was often called on to translate for her parents. "I remember taking my father to the doctor one day and saying when we got home, 'I'm ten years old. I shouldn't have to do this.'" Her father had seen his first wife and child shot in front of him—he rarely talked about the past, but the tattoo of his concentration camp number on his arm was clearly visible in family photos. Lief was named after one of his sisters who had died in the camps. Lief's grandfather Roman often said, "The only thing that matters is freedom." And that is how Lief and Jake's first son got his name: Freedom Roman Lief.

From the time Lief was a child, Dina knew that her younger daughter had an unusual internal focus, rarely feeling the need to mention winning a school award. She seemed to require no outside affirmation—or perhaps, as is often the case with children in survivor families, she internalized her own dramas. "My mommy fixes heads and my daddy fixes teeth," Lief once said to her kindergarten teacher. Dina always encouraged her to become a doctor, and in her first year practicing, she helped take care of her dying ninety-two-year-old grandmother. Once, her grandmother, in and out of delirium, asked her, "Are you an American doctor?" And they both cried, understanding the vast journey that had been taken from Auschwitz to Weill Cornell.

It did not surprise Dina that her younger daughter, aware of so much needless death in her own family, grew up to save lives. At the University of Pennsylvania, at a bake sale to benefit South Africa, Lief met her future husband, Jake Lief, who had spent his high-school years in London and become passionate about South Africa and the possibility of breaking the cycle of poverty there. Jake and a South African teacher he had met in a shebeen in Port Elizabeth started the nonprofit Ubuntu Pathways in a storefront. He scraped together enough money to keep it going until his vision caught on. Today, Ubuntu Pathways is active on three continents and has educated five hundred thousand children; Jake often appears on lists of young visionary global leaders. It took Lief and Jake nine years to get married. "Jake kept asking," Dina recalled, "and Lindsay kept saying, 'Wait until I finish medical school. Wait until I finish residency.'" For a year, Lief taught in a medical school in Tanzania and often flew to South Africa to see Jake. "She was horrified by the lack of adequate care," Dina recalled. "In Tanzania, all you could do was give antibiotics, and people were just dying."

Lief and Jake's second son, Madiba, was named for Nelson Mandela. From the moment of their first date at Penn, Jake knew how deeply Lief felt about becoming a doctor. Whatever it took to get through the grinding training, she would do it—and a lot more.

4

The request from Laura Forese was not unusual: Could Yoko Furuya take her place monitoring an off-the-record American Hospital Association webinar for the heads of hospitals?

Substituting for the always-busy COO of NewYork-Presbyterian came with the department-chief territory—especially at the last minute. It was February 26 when Forese reached out to Furuya, NewYork-Presbyterian's chief of epidemiology and infectious disease. Furuya was among several all-star physicians within NewYork-Presbyterian whose undergraduate degree had not been in science. An English literature major at Harvard who had grown up in Pasadena, she had gone on to med school at Penn before eventually making her way to Columbia to do a fellowship in infectious diseases and get a master's in epidemiology from Columbia's Mailman School of Public Health. Unsurprisingly, when Forese got in touch, Furuya was intently monitoring what was now clearly a pandemic. Alongside David Calfee, deputy epidemiologist at Weill Cornell, she had been working on data models from Wuhan to Lombardy when Forese reached out.

Inside Weill Cornell, many were trying to activate a sense of urgency. Jay Varma, an epidemiologist and global emergency expert, was working as the CDC's senior adviser to the African Union when a college classmate called him from New York. "He was nervous,"

Varma said of the surgeon. "And he said to me, 'People here at Cornell and NYP, they are not getting the message.' He didn't understand why they weren't taking it more seriously."

This was not the first time Varma had been approached. Since January, he'd been fielding calls from friends from his Harvard undergraduate days and his residency in San Diego. Varma's passion had always been public health initiatives. A voluble media presence, he had pushed out 140 academic papers but had also helped run New York's response during the Ebola crisis. Among those who had reached out early was a friend who was the chief operating officer of one of the largest hospital systems in the country. "You are about to get destroyed," Varma told him.

"This was about an hour-long call where I told him all kinds of things they could do to prepare—just stuff off the top of my head," Varma recalled. Later the COO thanked him. "I cornered the market in PPE, and we never ran out. And no one in my multibillion-dollar corporation had advised me to do that."

Varma had long dealt with the problem of unpreparedness. "Hospitals do not understand public health," he explained. "They think public health is sick care. Public health is not the care of sick people." But hospitals didn't make money from healthy people. "They have an incentive to take care of really sick people," Varma said. He was also unsparing when it came to public health school academics. "They publish papers. They don't actually make decisions in emergencies."

All of this was, of course, somewhat self-serving, but Varma had a point: Academics were great when it came to research and large-scale projects dealing with nutrition, childcare, and environmental risks. But they were not trained or encouraged to focus on making hard real-time decisions that might result in short-term suffering. Varma, who had worked as the deputy commissioner for disease control for New York City before he went to Africa, lobbied the CDC from Addis Ababa for test kits from the third week of January, when it was clear how quickly the disease was spreading. On the telephone with his colleagues in Atlanta late on a Friday night, he presented them with a list of countries he wanted to supply test kits to. "We had prioritized the countries that got the most airline traffic," he explained. When the weekend passed and he hadn't heard anything, Varma called back. "I said, 'What's going on?' And they're like, 'There is a problem with our lab, but we're still trying to figure [it out].'" He heard nothing more, and, unwilling to wait for the CDC, he sent a deputy to Germany with instructions to get hold of some of the highly effective test kits there. This was yet another massive failure with regard to stemming the pandemic early on: Good tests were available outside the United States, but the CDC and the Trump administration refused to authorize their import and use, instead sticking with the crummy American kits. And still unwilling to defy the CDC's imperatives, Corwin and the rest of NewYork-Presbyterian's leadership were forced to keep their heads down.

By the third week in February there were airport temperature checks across Africa, including in Ethiopia, which surprised several ICU doctors from Weill Cornell who were there on a hiking trip. "Everybody on the continent was aware of what was going on," Varma said.

Varma had spent years advising the Chinese government after the SARS epidemic on rapid detection of the next pandemic and had focused much of that effort on Hubei Province, where Wuhan had modeled its local CDC after the American system. That experience made him aware of the large discrepancy in health-care systems— China's public health labs were modern, but the hospitals were so decrepit that gathering accurate data was often impossible. As soon as reports of the Wuhan outbreak hit the news, Varma told a colleague, "This is going to be a disaster." And yet, while he found plenty of people concerned, he was astonished at how few of them recognized the scope and severity of the situation. "I was arguing with people

all over: 'Why aren't we calling this a pandemic? Why do people believe this can be contained? If you just look at the volume of airline
traffic . . . this was going to be devastating.'"

At Columbia, Yoko Furuya was used to apocalyptic experts who often
attached themselves to what could be a seismic infectious-disease
event, but the AHA had pulled in the University of Nebraska's
renowned epidemiologist James Lawler, and his impeccable judgment more than hinted that this was going to be a much bigger deal
than previous doomsday pronouncements. She was watching from
her office when Lawler stopped his PowerPoint to allow the hospital
heads to take in the magnitude of what he projected was coming to
the United States. Furuya was rocked by what she saw.

Best Guess Epidemiology

R_0—2.5; Doubling time 7–10 days

Community attack rate—30 to 40%	US: 96 million
Cases requiring hospitalization—5%	US: 4.8 million
Cases requiring ICU care—1–2%	US: 1.9 million
Cases requiring ventilator support	US: 1 PV [personal ventilators]
CFR [case fatality rate]—0.5%	US: 480,000

PREPARE FOR DISEASE BURDEN ROUGHLY 10 x SEVERE FLU

Furuya looked at the first line: R_0—2.5. R_0 was a mathematical
term (pronounced "R naught") that predicted the rate of spread of
a disease. In this case, each infected person could spread COVID
to 2.5 others. (For several weeks, Furuya would have no idea that
Lawler had devised his projections with the help of Nathaniel
Hupert.) Lawler's number was in fact relatively conservative; at

Imperial College in London, Neil Ferguson, another respected modeler, was projecting an R_0 of 3 to 5. Still, if Lawler's projections were correct, American hospitals would be hit with a tsunami—possibly millions of patients.

Furuya took a screenshot of Lawler's slide and, later that night, wrote a lengthy e-mail to her emergency management colleagues and the NewYork-Presbyterian leadership:

As you can tell, things are rapidly evolving and there are rumors that CDC will shortly update their guidance.

My take is that the widespread transmission outside of China (more new cases outside of China in the past 24 hours than within China), the horse is out of the barn, so to speak, and maybe I'm overreaching, but personally I'm not sure a global pandemic can be avoided at this point.

The AHA webinar was very interesting and valuable; the tenor was basically that we should hope for the best and prepare for the worst.

I think the most sobering message was that the most predictive models they shared (which they call "middle of the road best guess epidemiology") suggest a potentially enormous impact on the US and significant strain on our healthcare system.

96 million cases in the US
4.8 million admissions
1.9 million ICU admissions
480,000 deaths

I think based on the uncertainty of the current situation, we should take these dire predictions with (perhaps large) grain of salt so I don't want to put faith or certainty in these predicted numbers because our understanding of the epidemic is evolving so rapidly that things could change substantially within days or weeks.

That being said, knowing this is at least a possibility is what spurred me to reach out to emergency management this afternoon so that we can immediately start working on our pandemic planning protocols, similar to what we did in 2009 with H1N1 flu.

The next morning, her colleagues tried to absorb what Furuya had written. What might it mean for New York? What might it mean for the United States? What might it mean for the world? And, of course, what might be the implication for the hospital?

In Bronxville, on February 27, the same day Furuya's e-mail landed, Michael Fosina was busy ignoring the headlines—well, one headline in particular.

That morning, as usual, Fosina had driven from his house in New Rochelle, parked in the hospital garage, and arrived at his desk, where a stack of the day's newspapers waited for him: the *Westchester Journal News*, the *New York Times*, the New York *Daily News*, the *Wall Street Journal*, *Crain's New York Business*, and, source of said headline, the *New York Post*: "Let's Drown Her Before We Burn Her!!! Johnny Rotten." That week, the Dow had lost 1,150 points in one day—the largest drop in history—but all the *Post* seemed to want to talk about was Johnny Depp.

Fosina, the president of NewYork-Presbyterian Lawrence, one of the last hospitals in the sprawl of acquisitions from the New York Hospital–Presbyterian Hospital merger, preferred print to reading online and often cut out articles for future use. He flipped through the *Post* quickly, then stopped on page ten to carefully read a small story in the right column: "Long Is. Eyes 83 Possible Victims." He was startled by the details: a quarantine order for eighty-three Nassau County residents—which included the towns of Great Neck and Huntington—who had traveled to China or knew someone who had.

Fosina thought, *Uh-oh.* Eighty-three possible COVID exposures in the suburbs? He took a pair of scissors from his desk drawer and carefully cut out the column, noting the date, then tossed the entire edition into a plastic storage bin he kept in his office.

For the next seventy days, he kept every edition of every *New York Post*. When the bin overflowed, he took it home and placed the contents in his den, then brought the empty bin back to his office. Fosina's family occasionally made fun of his urge to collect. He had a thank-you letter from former senator Jacob Javits to his father, once the Westchester postmaster general. He had front pages for Yankees World Series wins, both Kennedy assassinations, the day Neil Armstrong walked on the moon, and an array of other major events. "Someday," he told his sons when they teased him, "when we go back, even if it is now, we are going to say, 'What else was going on that day? This is history.'"

Later, he would wonder if the decision he made to begin a collection of the *New York Post* on February 27 was a premonition.

Finally, a meeting was arranged with Augustine Choi. It was February 28. Matt McCarthy and Nathaniel Hupert were included, as was Dhruv Khullar, another hospitalist who had become a frequent *New Yorker* contributor. When Hupert and McCarthy met for the first time, McCarthy, out of habit, extended his hand. The gesture was not reciprocated: "Nathaniel just shook his head and said, 'We're not doing that anymore. No more handshakes.'... I realized at that moment a new normal was about to happen to all of us."

When the men entered his office, Choi was studying one of the early globally shared lung X-rays from an autopsied COVID patient. He explained to McCarthy and Khullar all the implications of what they were seeing—the lungs now almost all white, with ground-glass opacities spread throughout. McCarthy took careful notes, understanding that this was something new and menacing.

Choi's extensive conversations with his colleagues in South Korea and China had done little to inform him about the new territory they had all ventured into, but he remained focused on the X-ray in front of him, as if studying it meticulously would reveal something they had somehow missed. When Hupert showed his models of his own projections of the thousands of patients he anticipated coming to the hospital, Choi said in passing, as if his mind were on the X-ray, "I think we will be all right."

On the same morning that Michael Fosina began to collect articles from New York's most popular tabloid, a trust and estates lawyer named Lawrence Garbuz awoke worried about his cough and scratchy throat. Garbuz, a fifty-one-year-old father of four, had built his Midtown law practice with his wife, Adina Lewis. She was an active presence on Facebook, posting long blog entries about their children, one of whom lived in London. Many of Garbuz's clients were members of his synagogue, Young Israel, a modern Orthodox congregation in the garden suburb of New Rochelle, where the houses often sold for close to a million dollars. Within ninety-six hours, he would have the most famous scratchy throat in America.

The Garbuz family kept kosher and sent their children to private Jewish schools. Young Israel attracted a vibrant crowd of intellectuals and professionals—writers, doctors, lawyers—who walked to synagogue on Saturday. Often after services, twenty or so would get together at one of the airy Tudor houses that dotted the streets in this upper-middle-class preserve. The last days of February had been especially busy for the family; they'd attended a bar mitzvah at the synagogue and a funeral. Garbuz stayed only briefly at the latter—he felt a cold coming on and did not want to expose anyone near him.

A few days later, his symptoms hadn't gone away, and he went to NewYork-Presbyterian Lawrence. There he was diagnosed with pneumonia and admitted. His family gathered around him, as did friends from Young Israel, all close together, none masked, because at that time nobody imagined that they needed to be.

And why would they? "Seriously people—STOP BUYING MASKS!" the surgeon general, Jerome Adams, tweeted that weekend. "They are NOT effective in preventing general public from catching #Coronavirus, but if health care providers can't get them to care for sick patients, it puts them and our communities at risk!" The level of willful misinformation caused thousands to become infected—and strained all common sense.

Members of the Trump administration were not alone in their wretched counsel. Dr. William Schaffner, a preventive-medicine professor at Vanderbilt University School of Medicine, told CNN that the rush to buy masks was "a psychological thing." He was both right and wrong—wrong in that it would turn out that masks were tremendously successful in reducing COVID but right in that fear ignited a frantic buying spree. On Saturday and Sunday, hundreds of shoppers wearing masks crowded into a Brooklyn Costco to buy cases of water and fill shopping carts with food and toilet paper. Before long, prisoners in upstate New York would be forced to make hand sanitizer. (Ironically, prisons would turn out to be among the most dangerous breeding grounds for infection.)

Adina's mother, a doctor, saw the X-ray of her son-in-law's lungs and was startled—both lungs were almost completely white, a sign of severe infection. One person, the *New York Times* would report, described his lungs "as full of cobwebs." There were no special precautions taken for his friends in the room—or for the hospital's staff. A nurse in the ICU told the *Times* she had said, "I think he has COVID." Adina's mother reached out to Mark Apfelbaum, a cardiologist at Columbia who sat in the same row at synagogue as Lawrence and Adina. "Could you come here and see Lawrence?" After Apfelbaum examined him, Garbuz wrote a note asking his fellow congregant if he was going to die.

At Columbia, Apfelbaum was widely acclaimed for his work on cardiovascular disease. While it didn't appear that Garbuz was suffering anything heart-related, something was definitely wrong, and Apfelbaum and Garbuz's own internist were concerned. "We made the decision to get him to Columbia as soon as possible," Apfelbaum said. The next day, Garbuz was put into a medically induced coma, placed on a ventilator, and rushed to an ICU at Columbia.

Without a test result, Garbuz was now a PUI, the standard hospital reference for a "person under investigation." He spent his first night at Columbia with his wife, Adina, their twenty-year-old son, and their fourteen-year-old daughter sitting anxiously in the waiting room. Within forty-eight hours, Adina and her children would test positive for COVID, as would the neighbor who had driven Garbuz to the hospital and members of another family who had sat near him at synagogue.

On March 2, there were seven messages waiting for Matt McCarthy when he got to his office. The first was from Ryan McCarthy (no relation), the secretary of the army. The army chief asked if McCarthy might come to the Pentagon to brief his leadership team on the coming threat. The second was from Jamie Dimon, the head of JPMorgan Chase. He too inquired if McCarthy was available to talk to his team. That was, to put it very, very mildly, not how Matt McCarthy usually started his day.

That morning, McCarthy had been one of several guests on CNBC's morning show *Squawk Box.* He was seated next to Scott

Gottlieb, the now former head of the FDA, who had honed his public appearances to the go-down-easy style of a talking head. Because of the success of *Superbugs,* producers often booked McCarthy when they needed an expert on bacterial and fungal infections.

As usual, McCarthy had been on the 4:58 a.m. train from his house in Irvington, arriving at the hospital around 6:00 a.m., which gave him an hour to make clinical rounds before he was due at the studio. Although McCarthy was usually upbeat, his shock at the near impossibility of getting a coughing and wheezing patient tested by the CDC had by now turned to fury. Unable to hold back, that morning, live on the air, he had declared that America's diagnostic efforts "are a national scandal. . . . They are testing ten thousand people a day in some countries and we can't get this off the ground."

Squawk Box host Joe Kernen tried to lighten the mood, but McCarthy's evenness and lack of pretentiousness made it clear to the viewers that this was a grave "just the facts" moment. "I'm here to tell you," he said, "right now at one of the busiest hospitals in the country, I don't have [the test kits] at my fingertips. I still have to call the department of health, I still have to make my case, plead to test people." As he spoke, a chyron ran across the bottom of the screen: CORONA CONCERN SPREAD THROUGH THE US. WILD SWINGS IN DOW FUTURES. 1,000 POINT RANGE SINCE LAST NIGHT. "We have seen one case in New York, I'll bet there are hundreds. I'll bet there are thousands in the United States and the longer we wait to get testing up and running, the worse this is going to be. . . . There's going to be thousands of U.S. cases by next week—and this is a testing issue."

Gottlieb tried to interject: "We have about a hundred public health labs that will have the capacity to do about a hundred tests a day, so ten thousand tests a day by the end of this week," he said, repeating the White House line. "This pandemic may not be so severe." But by then, Gottlieb had learned that the CDC testing kits were a catastrophe, relying on three testing reagents, one of which had been tainted in a lab; like a good soldier, he held the information back.

But there was no disputing the facts: The weekend before, New York City had reported its first COVID case. A health-care worker traveling from Iran feared she had been infected and remained quarantined with her husband. She was at last tested—"only the thirty-second test we've done in this state," McCarthy noted.

"The message today that we are hearing from this administration is that the risk is low and that things are probably going to be okay, you don't need to change your lifestyle," McCarthy said. "That's simply not true. There are thousands of cases here. We've already moved from containment to mitigation. We are trying to lessen the severity here. You are going to see widespread disruption to daily life. Do not believe the false reassurance." He added, "I live in Westchester, and when I'm walking around Westchester, I'm not really worried about coronavirus." He paused. "But when I get on the six train, when I am walking around Times Square, when I am in the emergency room every single day caring for patients, I'm very worried."

Soon enough—that very afternoon—McCarthy would revise his sense of the COVID spread and how much of it already lurked in Westchester a few towns away from his. But before then, there was another message. This one came from the communications office of NewYork-Presbyterian. At 1:09 p.m. the *New York Post* had posted its first major story on McCarthy's dire warning. The next morning, a summary of McCarthy's message—"Send More Test Kits, STAT!"— bannered two full pages inside the paper. The subhead was striking: "M'hattan Doc's Diagnosis of Fed Response: It's a 'Scandal.'"

It wasn't beyond reason that the hospital administration would want to control what its employees said; given that the hospital's malpractice cases had become international events and headlines every day, even an offhand comment about hospital shortcomings could have massive legal impact. There was an elite community of writing doctors at the hospital, among them Richard Friedman, Helen Ouyang, Siddhartha Mukherjee, and Dhruv Khullar. Their celebrity was a PR coup, though at times it was nerve-racking for the administration and legal team.

There was also history to be reckoned with.

What happened to the eighteen-year-old Bennington student Libby Zion on the night of March 4, 1984, is now considered a case study of the dangers inherent in unsupervised and overworked residents and interns. Zion, home visiting her parents, had a low-grade fever and an earache after a tooth extraction. Libby's father, legal affairs correspondent and author Sidney Zion, and her mother, Elsa, were at a Park Avenue dinner party when their son called to report that Libby was spiking high temperatures and was agitated. The parents came home, saw how sick she was, and brought her to the emergency room of New York Hospital. Libby told the nurses and the second-year resident that she was on erythromycin and an antidepressant, and, after consulting with the Zion family internist, the resident admitted Libby to the hospital. At this point, an intern, who was also responsible for many other patients on different floors of the hospital, was charged with overseeing Libby's care.

Nine hours later, after she had been given several painkillers and an antipsychotic to calm her muscle spasms and flailing, Libby was tied to the bed; her temperature rose to 107 degrees. She coded and, at approximately 7:30 a.m., died of a cardiac arrest.

The case set off a media frenzy. Tabloids documented each new wrinkle in the charges and countercharges that ensued. Sidney Zion asserted that New York Hospital interns had killed his daughter, while the hospital claimed that Zion was on cocaine and didn't tell the doctors. For years, New York Hospital pushed back, attacking reporters and columnists who wanted to investigate the story and continuing to suggest that Zion had been on cocaine.

Ultimately, the hospital paid a minimal fine—thirteen thousand dollars—and admitted responsibility. But real change took root only when the Libby Zion Law passed; it mandated that residents and interns in New York State work no more than eighty hours a week. That standard has now been adopted by every hospital in America, ushering in a new era of hospitalists (in-house staff physicians).

After the yearslong public relations debacle, the hospital implemented new measures to control information and safeguard its reputation. There is now a clause in the residents' contracts stating that all media interviews must be cleared through the administration. Those who want to address the public—in an interview, an article, or an online post—have to get approval first. NewYork-Presbyterian was especially sensitive to HIPAA patient issues. In 2016, the *New York Times* reported, the hospital had to pay a $2.2 million fine because the ABC reality TV series *NY Med*, featuring Mehmet Oz, filmed a dying patient whose face had been blurred. His family had not given consent for him to be filmed or for the footage to be broadcast. They learned about it only when the patient's widow happened upon the episode while watching TV.

In McCarthy's case, however, it was promptly made clear to him that the hospital's corporate side wasn't pleased. A hospital-wide e-mail went out immediately: *All requests for interviews must be funneled through corporate comms: We speak in one voice.* McCarthy had been careful on *Squawk Box* not to identify himself as a NewYork-Presbyterian doctor—he was "an infectious disease specialist and author of *Superbugs*"—figuring that might allow for a loophole. Apparently, it did not. He was called into the office of the hospital's SVP and COO, Kate Heilpern, chastised for his "alarmist tone," and stripped of his title of medical director of the Greenberg Pavilion's fourteenth floor. Heilpern implied that if he broke ranks again, he might be fired from NewYork-Presbyterian.

This was not easy for Heilpern.

She had infinite respect for McCarthy's intellect and ability as a doctor, but she was an administrator on the cusp of managing a crisis of epic proportions amid the wholly new reality that the federal government, as she later said, "was not really open for business in terms of helping on so many levels." And the decision had not been hers; she was carrying out the wishes of those in the corporate suites. Heilpern's was the tapioca hospital language—"hurdles"; "the need for discussion on how to proceed"—that made sense in many situations, but with a pathogen circulating, the rules counseling comity and restraint perhaps needed review. For Heilpern, the chaotic situation recalled her experiences controlling disaster communication in Atlanta at Grady Memorial Hospital during various emergencies: a pedestrian walkway collapsing at the Atlanta Botanical Garden; a bus carrying members of a baseball team crashing; requiring "physicians, medical students, and residents—everybody in the hospital" to speak with one voice. The dissonance of using that same playbook to address the public in the face of this possibly fatal mysterious new disease would divide the hospital.

Anthony Hollenberg, chairman of the Weill Cornell department of medicine, was often called upon to navigate the at times highly contentious split-screen reality. "Private institutions can manage their messages," Hollenberg said. "Academic institutions cannot. That was the fundamental conflict." Hollenberg firmly believed that doctors should be able to speak out about their concerns without fear of reprisal. Further, he believed that McCarthy, one of the hospital's best infectious-disease doctors, was right. In a pandemic, there was no question that the public had a compelling right to know. Hollenberg's focus was on patient care, not corporate public relations. "We had far more important things to worry about than if something came out in a tweet or an article about inequity or new standards of care. Who really cares? We're here taking care of thousands of patients. . . .

"The department of medicine's role was really to marshal our resources to manage the health of our patients and the wellness of our faculty in training. So aim one, do whatever we could to take care of New York. Aim two, do whatever we could do to take care of our residents. Aim three, do whatever I could do to take care of our faculty." As head of the department of medicine and an employee of Weill Cornell, he was, he said, the "middle manager." He reported to both NewYork-Presbyterian CEO Steve Corwin and to the medical school dean, Augustine Choi. "I felt it was very, very, very important to support our faculty," Hollenberg said. In repeated discussions, he emphasized how concerning the issue was to the world-class doctors who believed they had a moral imperative to alert the public. "The differences would never be resolved," Hollenberg added. "But that didn't stop us working incredibly well together to get the job done. . . . We moved on."

The assumption in the hospital was that this was coming as a direct order from Laura Forese. Soon after, NPR asked the hospital if McCarthy could go on; the hospital said no. (When asked about this incident later, Forese said she had "no memory" of it.)

At 6:30 in the morning on March 3, Dr. Andrew Amaranto, the head of the Lawrence emergency department, was on his way to Bronxville listening in on the Tuesday chiefs call with Corwin and Forese. Usually these calls were relatively predictable—budget updates, personnel concerns, the purchase of new devices, and so forth. This was not one of those calls.

Amaranto had not been at the hospital when Garbuz was admitted, but he had reviewed that day's cases. "We are a small team. We were thinking, 'This guy has pneumonia. Let's treat him for pneumonia.'" Now, driving across the George Washington Bridge from his home in New Jersey, Amaranto learned Garbuz had tested positive for COVID. "I thought, *If this guy has it, I knew we were a tinder box. I was thinking, Anything is possible.*"

Forese had been bracing herself for the first COVID case to hit NewYork-Presbyterian. That same morning, she called for a car to pick her up at Columbia with Yoko Furuya to assess the situation at Lawrence. As they drove, Forese was strangely calm. "I thought, *Okay, the pandemic is here. We are prepared. Bring it on.*" On the quick trip to Bronxville, Furuya and Forese talked about the remarks they would give to be streamed across the NewYork-Presbyterian system, which employed thirty thousand people. How to control the message? That was always uppermost in the corporate suites.

Forese was known around the hospital for her discipline and her mind that worked like an engineer's, as her father had been. From time to time, Forese ran into the parents of children she had successfully operated on, and those moments made her wonder if she had been right to go into hospital administration. She had been an academic superstar—a Phi Beta Kappa who graduated summa cum laude from Princeton and rose to become COO of NewYork-Presbyterian and vice chair of the department of orthopedics. A stylish blonde, she was, per usual, impeccably turned out, as if she had been to the salon that very morning. In her first briefing of what would be a daily event, Forese, joined by Fosina, sat at the Lawrence conference table, a cool, corporate smile fixed in place. It was unconscionable, she said, that a patient's name had been released. But Forese avoided mentioning the obvious: that the mayor was responsible. Forese made it clear that such an action was "against hospital policy." Forese then spoke generally of all the unknown aspects of the days ahead. On her left was Michael Fosina, looking appropriately somber, a captive to a situation that would quickly spiral out of control. On her right was Furuya, whom she asked for an assessment of the situation.

Forese had been trained in the cool corporate hospital-speak that began and ended with the objective of never imparting fear, and her calm in the briefing was exemplary. "Our emergency rooms are in good shape," she declared. "There will be no issue with the PPE." And then, incredibly, at the end of the briefing, Forese (who would later say she was working off the guidelines of the CDC) advised the NewYork-Presbyterian staff that "masks would not be necessary" unless staffers were in direct contact with an infected patient. It was advice and regulation that countermanded every bit of common sense understood by public health officials since the black plague.

Relieving McCarthy of his title was mostly a warning shot fired from the corporate suites to keep him in line, because technically McCarthy was employed by Weill Cornell, not NewYork-Presbyterian, where he had admitting privileges. When word reached Art Evans, the iconic Weill Cornell chairman of the hospitalists, that McCarthy was being muzzled, he responded immediately: "You do not give Matt McCarthy his titles. We do. And you are not taking them away."

Evans, a native Texan and son of a radiologist who was part of the Baylor hospital leadership, was not cowed by the power politics as played in corporate medicine. Fifteen years earlier, the tall, lanky Houstonian had been recruited to Weill Cornell from Cook County Hospital—the setting for the series *ER*—where he'd been chief medical officer. At the time, Weill Cornell was one of the last hospitals in America not to have adopted the hospitalist structure. Evans subsequently grew the division from eight to eighty-five physicians, who care for more than 250 patients daily and teach more than 200 students and residents annually. For decades, private internists were the commanders of the medical care of their personal patients, and the residents were charged with carrying out their instructions. "The practice," Evans said, "often led to poorer outcomes, as the residents had no training as attendings making decisions." And that wasn't all of it;

Weill Cornell's swarm of internists were threatening to mutiny should changes be made, and the resident program was put on probation. Evans arrived like a sheriff to cut through the resistance of the internists, what a rival at Columbia called "the Upper East Side navy-blazer-and-bow-tie crowd." It was not an understatement to say that his deft negotiating and aura of command had saved the residency program.

Evans was, in his quiet way, more than just offended by what he saw as the disrespect shown to one of Weill Cornell's most accomplished young doctors; he was infuriated that McCarthy had been threatened. "Doctors who have something to say should be able to speak the truth without being censored," he said. Later that week, he told people at a faculty meeting, "I am here to tell you that if Matt McCarthy is fired, then I will resign."

Further, in a meeting in his office, Evans informed McCarthy, "I have complete faith in you. This is going to be a once-in-a-century pandemic. And I want you to assume leadership and see these COVID patients. It is your generation that will get us through all of this." On March 8, Evans followed up with an e-mail to Weill Cornell leadership:

Hospitalist-PA team dedicated to COVID-suspicious patients

Can we please rearrange patients tonight so that all COVID-suspicious patients (i.e., COVID still on differential regardless of whether meets DOH testing criteria) on to the PA5 (Matt McCarthy).

During the week, all patients admitted to Hospitalist-PA service that are suspicious for COVID (based on hospitalist assessment; regardless of DOH testing) will go to PA5 (McCarthy)

This grace note of nonengagement defused much of the anger rocketing at McCarthy, but if NewYork-Presbyterian was going to gag one of its most respected voices at a time when the public was desperately in need of responsible information about the lack of testing, what did that bode for dealing with the reality of a city in a pandemic?

The censorship of McCarthy—the first of many NewYork-Presbyterian doctor-researchers who would be gagged by the corporate side, in the process depriving the public of crucial information about the possible spread of the pandemic—was, many believed, a classic case of corporate liability concerns trumping the urgency of warning millions of a once-in-a-century health-care cataclysm that would within days paralyze the city and threaten the health of thousands. It would as well confirm the long-standing tension in the hospital between Weill Cornell's medical school and its distinguished staff and their corporate masters on the hospital side at NewYork-Presbyterian. The difference could be understood most easily in the contrasting priorities of a nine-billion-dollar business (the hospital) and the academic freedom conferred by a first-rank medical school on its doctor-scientists. In the best of times, there was a constant thrum of conflicting agendas over funding, over patient care, over messaging—and now NewYork-Presbyterian was scrambling to try to impose disaster communications guidelines. The comms team would explain its decisions with the same rationale that later came from the Trump White House: We did not want to create panic.

But panic was coming. On March 2, the day that McCarthy appeared on *Squawk Box,* the *New York Post*'s headline was "It's Here: Manhattan Woman Has Coronavirus." The next day, Mayor Bill de Blasio jumped in with additional information, tweeting, "We can officially confirm some more information on the second coronavirus case connected to New York City. The individual sought care on February 27 at Lawrence Hospital in Westchester. He works at Lewis and Garbuz, P.C., a law firm in Manhattan."

Almost immediately, there were two additional tweets from the mayor. The first explained that the "patient has two children with a connection to New York City, a daughter who attends SAR Academy in the Bronx, and a son who attends Yeshiva University in Manhattan. They're currently in isolation at home." The second stated that personnel from the Department of Health and Mental Hygiene "are on the ground at the law firm, SAR Academy and Yeshiva University. Disease detectives are following up with anyone who had close contact with the patient or his kids to get them tested for coronavirus."

Garbuz, still comatose, had been outed.

For years, Julia Iyasere, Anna Podolanczuk, and Lizzy Oelsner had texted several times a day about small matters and large. On their first day as residents in 2008, the trio and Matt McCarthy had immediately bonded. Columbia was one of the few residency programs in the country that put you with three other people with whom you then spend eighty hours a week for the next three years. Call nights, worries about a misdiagnosis, scrub-ins on surgeries, decisions about patients—it was all done together. Unsurprisingly, the relationships forged at Columbia usually lasted a lifetime. Although they weren't always forged. "You are told, 'This is going to be the most difficult period of your life'—and all you can think is *I hope these people like me. I hope they are hardworking. I hope they are reliable.* . . . It's like an arranged marriage—where everyone gets married," observed McCarthy in *The Real Doctor Will See You Shortly.* On the residents' first day, McCarthy recognized the tall woman with the great mane of curly hair immediately and knew he had encountered her in the halls of the chemistry and physics labs when they were undergrads, but they had not seen each other since. She dazzled McCarthy with the easy way she interacted with her patients and the other doctors and her quiet aura of projecting that no one was going to push her around.

Within a week he told Iyasere, "You are going to be running this hospital someday."

In his book, McCarthy changed the names, but it wasn't hard to figure out who was the sleek sophisticate with the etched cheekbones and polished style (Manhattan-raised Oelsner) and who was the quiet, research-driven science nerd (Podolanczuk).

Podolanczuk was the daughter of two Polish research doctors, a teacher and an engineer, who had tried for years to enter the green-card lottery that was offered by the State Department; an uncle in the United States entered her mother's name, and she won. Podolanczuk, twelve years old at the time, spoke only a few sentences of English. The family moved close to relatives at the New Jersey shore; Podolanczuk's mother worked as a nanny and her father as a handyman, and while it took years for Podolanczuk to feel comfortable speaking English, she had no problem with math and science and earned a full scholarship to Brown.

For her part, Oelsner had worked as a management consultant before she went to medical school. She had her first child during her medical residency training and had to take a leave due to the 2009 influenza epidemic.

The pod lived one another's terrors—McCarthy pricked himself with a needle while drawing blood on an AIDS patient and had to go on massive medications; he was frantic with worry that he had it and could give it to his fiancée, Heather Morris. In one of his first days as a resident, he misdiagnosed a professor who had crumpled with a heart attack, and he'd thought his medical career was over. But his friends lifted him up, helped him recover, and he had done the same for them at other times.

The hospital, with its gleaming interiors, was anchored in the Dominican community in Washington Heights, which meant exposure to a panorama of medical disparities rarely discussed by any of their attendings. Each resident had to spend time seeing the Medicaid indigent at AIM (Associates in Internal Medicine), the primary care clinic. Everything about it was in stark contrast to the medical wonders of Milstein Hospital on Fort Washington Avenue. The paint was peeling; the patients seen on the clock in twenty-minute increments. The staff were more or less physicians in training with one attending, servicing Washington Heights and Inwood. The interns called the elevator entrance "the Tuberculator" because of the homeless who had taken up residence inside.

On his first day at AIM, walking through the muck of the summer heat, McCarthy was struck by the neighborhood as an immigrant's tale. In the beginning of the twentieth century, it was all Irish; in the 1930s, the fleeing European Jews—including Henry Kissinger—arrived and thought of the German-speaking neighborhood as Valhalla; and after the war, Holocaust survivors filtered in. Growing up in the neighborhood, Mark Apfelbaum had attended yeshiva with the children of survivors who had found refuge, as his family had, around 180th Street. Stickball, Nedick's, the RKO Coliseum, the wonders of the new world like the Morris House, the Polo Grounds to watch the Giants, not far from 555 Edgecombe Avenue, where Duke Ellington was a frequent visitor and Paul Robeson lived. It would morph in the 1960s and 1970s into a drug-dealer haven where shooting galleries and stabbings defined the streets, but that did not dissuade the devotees, like the late Jim Dwyer of the *New York Times*, a bard of the neighborhood, from celebrating its progress as it renewed itself. Through all of this, the many buildings of the Columbia campus hovered as a cornerstone, but also, even twenty years ago, only faintly serving the needs of the community despite the astonishing medical breakthroughs in heart transplant and biomedical research that were going on within.

Iyasere and Podolanczuk had been struck by how quickly the focus pivoted from hospital protocols to the realities of their new neighborhood. McCarthy's training group was told by the head of the department, "You will be doing a great service for this community." Great service was definitely in order—noted McCarthy, "One in five were obese. Half did no physical activity. Residents were nearly one-third more likely to be without a regular doctor than those in New York City overall, and one in ten went to the emergency room when they were sick, or simply needed health advice." His first clinic patient had eighteen different medical problems noted in an alphabet soup of acronyms, from HTN (hypertension) to BPH (benign prostatic hyperplasia), and was unaware his kidneys were failing.

Years later, the quartet was still close, particularly the three women. At 11:00 o'clock on the night of March 2, 2020, Podolanczuk, who was home on maternity leave with her newborn, texted Iyasere: *Did you see Matt? He was shut down. Have you been watching Schitt's Creek? What are your plans?* With the message was a link to Matt's CNBC clip on YouTube. Podolanczuk posted the link on Twitter too, tweeting: "Here is some info from the experts."

Lizzy Oelsner, another member of the pod, texted back the next day: *I thought he was terrific.* Iyasere did not answer—she was at Milstein, helping to transport a suspected COVID patient.

Julia Iyasere, the daughter of two academics—one a Nigerian Shakespeare scholar and the other a Ukrainian American English professor who taught at California State University, Bakersfield—had grown up cosseted in a world of internationalists who cooked dishes from Lagos and made Russian pastries. (Her father would go home to Lagos and return with bags of spices and food, and Iyasere would later speak of her Nigerian heritage as rooted in the sights and smells of his deliveries.)

Iyasere's introduction to Columbia was when her sister was a resident. She would come and visit her in one of the apartment dorms on Haven Avenue where Steve Corwin once lived. The day before she started her residency, Iyasere experienced a sharp wave of panic and called her sister, now at Mass General, crying hysterically. "You'll be great," her sister told her. "Stop crying. No one feels bad for you. Don't let fear keep you from doing something you love. Show up every day, on time, with a smile on your face, excited to learn. They'll tell you where to go and what to do until you're ready to do it yourself."

Almost immediately she saw the racial differences in the populations they served and the care they got. Iyasere had never thought of herself in racial terms. Once, as a child in Bakersfield, she was shocked when a woman asked her mother, "Is this your daughter?" On another occasion, after scoring highly on a test for a gifted school, she was asked to come in and undergo formal IQ testing. Much later, her mother told her that the testers thought she had cheated. As the daughter of a father who had grown up in another country, Iyasere had far fewer overt sensitivities about racial slights; what drove her was an overwhelming passion to try to right the century of health disparities that had savagely affected the medical care of Black Americans. Still, there were only two other women of color in her residency class, and they were often mistaken for one another.

At the beginning of the pandemic, "I was trying to figure out: What are the protocols?" For example, what was the best way to transport feverish patients with suspected COVID? "There was a real sense of worry," Iyasere recalled.

Iyasere stayed late at the hospital on the night a suspected COVID patient arrived, developing the new protocols, and not a moment too soon—their next patient arrived on Tuesday, two days after Lawrence Garbuz was admitted. Per Iyasere's rules, she and three others, including the chief physician assistant and a hospitalist, put on PPE gowns, double-masked, and went to the ED, where they had security clear the area and a path. "We had three security guards ahead of us," she remembered. Security made sure no one accidentally got in the way. "I remember vividly talking to the nurses, putting them in a room with a double door, dropping off the patient. Then I took all of my PPE off right away and thought to myself, *Okay, when I get home, do I wear these clothes in my house? I am not sure.*"

In the blur of the first days, as more patients were admitted, the fear intensified. "We had to be super-careful—and I knew we had to get the patient out of the ED quickly. It was very late at night, and when I was done, I sat down with the chief PA in-hospitalist. 'What are you still doing here?' And I said, 'I don't really know what else to do.' There was so much impotence. There was so much to understand about the disease. This is a sense of fear we had never had before. Now it was, 'Check my mask three or four times.' I had to make sure that I didn't feel anything, no air coming in." In the first week, she was in a room with a patient who was on noninvasive, positive-pressure ventilation. He unexpectedly pulled off the mask and coughed. "I felt the droplets hit my eye, under the eye shield. I left the room and pulled off my eye protection and mask. I just lost it." She began to sob. "I thought, *You are not a good doctor.*"

On March 3, *New York Times* reporter Sarah Maslin Nir was in the paper's newsroom following the Super Tuesday voting—Joe Biden fighting for his political life in South Carolina—when Garbuz was outed by the mayor. Despite the election, she was fixated on the previous day's story of the woman who had traveled to Iran and then was diagnosed with COVID on her return to the city. "I thought, *She travels, okay.* Then when I heard about Larry Garbuz, I thought to myself, *Wait, Larry Garbuz didn't go anywhere.*" Garbuz worked in Manhattan and lived in one of New York City's nicest bedroom communities. "If he is sick," Nir concluded, "so are many others . . . community spread has happened." Her reporter's gut told her she needed to get to New Rochelle—right away.

"It was about five p.m. My editor Cliff Levy said, 'Wait, I have these nitrile surgical gloves . . .' and he handed me a pair of blue surgical gloves from his stash. I turned on my heel and took the gloves and took a picture outside the *Times*." She posted the photo with the caption "Guess what assignment SMN is off to later? #purellbathlater." (One person commented: "A purellitzer prize winner for sure," a reference to Nir's stunning exposé of the treatment of Korean manicurists in the city's salons, a finalist for the 2016 Pulitzer in local reporting.) Nir arrived in New Rochelle and parked the *Times* pool car near Eden Wok, a kosher Chinese restaurant. Its workers were anxiously peering out, looking for customers. At Maestro's, a local Italian restaurant, one customer told her, "I recognize that the gentleman now in the hospital was someone I have seen walking up and down the street." Then Nir made her way to Young Israel, a short drive from the center of New Rochelle. The doors were locked—the building was closed. While she stood outside, one member of the congregation arrived and was perplexed that evening prayers were canceled.

Nine people close to Garbuz were now infected—and a thousand people were asked to self-quarantine. Unsurprisingly, the *New York Post* ran a half-page photo of Garbuz and Adina.

For the next few days, Nir parked herself at Eden Wok, whose owner was preparing meals for the one hundred quarantined families as a gift. Nir was back in New Rochelle within the week when the governor declared a one-mile "containment zone" that included the schools of the younger Garbuz children, the synagogue, and the surrounding houses. *Containment zone* was something of a misnomer—traffic was unrestricted, although large gatherings were banned—but it was without a doubt unnerving. Nir watched the National Guard roll in, all of them wearing hazmat suits, and thought it looked like a scene from a horror movie; she followed them to a Jewish community center, where they took children's building blocks and LEGO bricks and doused them with Clorox and the prisoner-produced sanitizer.

"They were well-meaning but bonkers tasks," she said. "Wash every kindergarten block in bleach solution." Given the confusion about how the virus was transmitted, fear of LEGO bricks was somewhat understandable, but the intensity of the effort was shocking for some onlookers. After the community center, the National Guard set up the first site of what would soon become a national horror—soldiers in hazmat suits with drivers in miles of cars having their noses swabbed at the windows. Still, at the triage center, Nir noticed a buffet lunch set up for the volunteers. "None of this made sense. . . . I thought, *Oh, fuck. Everyone here is going to get sick. They are going out in the contagion zone and then coming back here to eat.* This was before anyone talked about airborne anything."

That week, a group of teachers staging a protest in New Rochelle swarmed Nir, screaming that they wanted their school closed—it was just out of the containment zone, but, said one of the protesters, "The kids from that synagogue go to our school. The brother goes. What is the point of the geographic zone? It makes no sense." When Nir called to check some facts with them a few days later, several had gotten COVID.

On the day testing began, Nir phoned her seventy-four-year-old mother, the psychologist Bonnie Maslin, who was getting ready to move to a new apartment. "I said, 'Mom, this thing is here. It's not coming here. It is here. And you have to get the hell out of Dodge.'" Nir's mother explained that she had to move her stuff to her new apartment. Nir was emphatic. "I said, 'Mom, I am in Wuhan, in Westchester.'"

Their discussion ended unsatisfactorily for Nir, but her mother called back and agreed. "She left for Long Island," Nir said, "and did not come back for a year."

When Nir returned to the city and had a lunch on her stoop on Perry Street with her friend Mary, she was careful to sit six feet away. "My friend brought snacks and seltzer and wiped everything down with Clorox wipes. I thought, *That's interesting. When did Clorox start making unscented wipes?*" She remembered a throwaway line from a story in January about a woman who had mentioned that when she got COVID, she had lost her sense of smell. When Nir got home, she started trying to smell everything—kitty litter, pepper—and frantically Googled *sense of smell and COVID*. She came up with nothing, so she started Googling in different languages, targeting Italy and France, places that had been struggling with COVID. She found two small studies, from Iran and Belgium. She immediately reached out to Roni Rabin, the paper's health reporter. "'Roni,' I said, 'I'm telling you. I can't smell a thing. I've never experienced anything like this. Here are these two studies. I promise you that this is a symptom of COVID. I'm going to get tested. I promise you I am going to have COVID when I come back. You have to report on this. It's not out there yet.'" Nir was correct on both counts—she had COVID, and loss of smell was a symptom. Although there was much anecdotal evidence from around the world about the loss of smell, Rabin's piece broke on the same day the WHO began to investigate the link. It would take Nir over a month to recover, and for weeks after, she suffered from vertigo. She was convinced she got COVID from one of the screaming teachers who'd surrounded her in New Rochelle.

It would take four days for Iyasere to watch McCarthy's *Squawk Box* appearance, and in that brief time, Columbia admitted seven patients, most of whom were from New Rochelle. But the spread had, ominously for the medical staff, gone further. Crishila Livacarri, Garbuz's nurse, contracted COVID almost immediately, as did her husband and teenage son. In a lawsuit against the hospital, Livacarri, who grappled with months of long-haul symptoms, charged the hospital with "gross negligence" for failing to quarantine Garbuz immediately "although he showed every sign of COVID-19." That was only the beginning, though. Despite those signs of COVID, Garbuz's doctor had to desperately argue with New York State's department of health that a test was in order even though his patient didn't meet the state's criteria—he had not been in China. And the nurses treating Garbuz were not given N95 masks or PPE.

At Lawrence Hospital, five staff members would lose their lives. If they had been wearing masks, would their deaths have been prevented? Whenever this question was raised, NewYork-Presbyterian's answer was some version of "We could not get ahead of the state and the CDC." It also became standard for the hospital to say, "We do not know whether they were infected here or in the community—there was so much spread." Unsurprisingly, the lack of PPE, the inadequacy of testing, and packing infected patients into spaces meant for far fewer people (if they were meant for people at all) resulted in a number of COVID infections among the entire NewYork-Presbyterian staff.

The morning of McCarthy's CNBC appearance, Frisby was one of the first to arrive at Lawrence. All that weekend, Xenia Frisby had been trying to get Garbuz tested and was repeatedly told the same thing as Garbuz's doctor: per the state's criteria, Garbuz was not eligible. Frisby didn't have a problem with that—after all, Garbuz had never been in Wuhan or even in China, and he did not seem the type to roam Chinatown in search of the perfect dumpling.

One of Frisby's first, elemental lessons in medical school was known as "horses and zebras." The logic was straightforward and efficient: If you hear hoofbeats, the odds are they come from horses, not zebras. In other words, when diagnosing a patient, match the symptoms with the most common ailment. A lawyer from New Rochelle has a cough and a fever—those are the hoofbeats, garden-variety pneumonia the horse.

But driving to Bronxville that Monday, she received a call from an infectious-disease doctor, a conversation she would later describe as "that call you never want to have."

As every emergency medicine physician knows, any conversation that starts with "Hey, remember that patient you saw a couple of days ago?" is not going to end well. "Hey," this infectious-disease doctor said, "remember that patient you saw a couple of days ago? He tested positive for COVID."

The same morning, Laurie Ann Walsh, the chief nursing officer, was in her office on the far side of the hospital. "The director of the oncology unit comes over and says, 'Can I come in?' And she said, 'My daughter just notified me that Lawrence has a first patient.' And I was like, '*What?*'" Walsh found Fosina in a conference room with a few people she didn't recognize. Walking in, she asked the hospital chief what was going on. With Fosina were two doctors from the state's department of health, based in New Rochelle. One, Eleanor Adams, had attended medical school with Matt McCarthy and had been a bridesmaid at his wedding alongside one of his ushers, a Yale baseball teammate named Ron DeSantis. Neither DOH doctor wore a mask.

In February and the first days of March, McCarthy had been deluged with texts and questions from his college classmates worried about their families, but McCarthy didn't hear from DeSantis at any point during the pandemic, which struck several who knew of their friendship as bizarre. DeSantis, now governor of Florida, would soon propel himself to the top of the Republican party in part by his refusal to shut down the state and to go to war with schools and businesses that wanted to impose a mask mandate.

At Columbia Medical Center, on March 2, Garbuz had been put in a medically induced coma and placed on a ventilator—a godsend, he would later tell friends. Almost the first words he heard from his wife, Adina, when he was extubated were "Don't look at social media."

There were very good reasons for this. Before being hospitalized, Garbuz had attended a funeral and a b'nai mitzvah and unwittingly exposed more than a hundred families to the virus; ninety people would become infected. The stigma was immediate. It mattered not that Garbuz had been unaware that what felt like a small cold was actually COVID and that the department of health was insisting you could catch the virus only if you'd been in China or in close contact with someone who had. The tabloids pointed the finger at the comatose Garbuz, accusing him of reckless endangerment of the most dire sort. In the *New Yorker*, writer D. T. Max noted that a New Rochelle laundry refused to wash the family's clothes, and for more than a week, the mail wasn't delivered to the Garbuz house; finally, Adina Lewis complained to the mayor of New Rochelle.

During all of this, Lewis, an active Facebook user, put out several long posts imploring New Yorkers "running on the hamster wheel of life" to "take a moment and take care of yourself." On Purim, a spring holiday, she would write that she was trying to see this cluster of virus as a blessing and that her husband's "illness was able to make us all aware of the problem." Lewis's first post elicited scores of good wishes but also condemnation from those who were enraged: "Larry is no hero in my book! Nice try, lady!" wrote one reader. Another responded, "I did have a family member pass due to COVID-19. I will NOT hail your husband as a hero!" Lewis's second post elicited an even more scathing reaction. A resident of Rye wrote, "He did not go to one party he went to three. He continued to travel on metro north. He was coughing. His hands were filled with germs. Anyone he touched got sick . . . It was thoughtless and reckless."

Shaming and demonization are often attached to people who expose others to disease—especially those diseases without cures. In 1907, the New York City cook Mary Mallon was the first asymptomatic carrier of the typhoid bacteria in the city, and she inadvertently infected seven of the eight wealthy families she worked for, earning her the nickname "Typhoid Mary." Mallon was put into quarantine, but unable to understand why she was being blamed when she had no sign of the disease, she escaped, changed her name, and infected a new family, becoming the scourge of the city, Max noted, lambasted in cartoons showing her cooking skulls.

The need to enforce the wearing of masks during the 1918 flu pandemic prompted the *San Francisco Chronicle* to publish the names of those who did not comply and refer to each of them as a "dangerous slacker." But in the first weeks of March 2020, the people getting shamed in New York City were those who did wear masks, because it was a sign that they didn't trust the CDC and the hospitals that were saying that face coverings were an overreaction. Such castigation was a grotesque and ultimately costly reaction against anyone who questioned the CDC's irresponsible magical thinking and faulty analysis.

At Columbia Medical Center, the sign outside Lawrence Garbuz's door stopped Gregg Rosner in his tracks: DROPLET PRECAUTIONS. "It was the first time I had been scared in medicine," he said. Rosner, a cardiac intensivist, was revered in the Young Israel community for the meticulous care he had taken of a member of the temple who had been struck with a rare bacterial infection. After Garbuz was taken to Columbia, Rosner's cell phone began to vibrate. "Thirteen different people asked me to check on him," Rosner said. It was always like that when someone in that community was ill.

Over a decade earlier, Rosner, then a resident at Harvard's Brigham and Women's Hospital, found himself treating pregnant women on ventilators at the height of the swine flu pandemic. But from the moment he arrived as a cardiology fellow at Columbia, he knew he'd reached an elevation far above anything he'd experienced. The hospital was a clearinghouse of impossible cases looking for solutions, and all the fellows were plunged in from the first moment. "I was handed the cell phone numbers of all the cardiac surgical attendings," he said. "The heart surgeons wanted to interact with us. They would summon us to the OR and gave us unprecedented access to what they were doing and what they were thinking. The atmosphere here was like nothing I had imagined—the surgeons were just pushing the envelope with every discipline, doing the cases that no one else would do!"

As the situation in Italy worsened, anxiety spread through the hospital. "I had a cancer outpatient who had a cough and needed some follow-up scans," Rosner recalled. "We put a mask on him and sent him to the oncology department and got a frantic call. 'What are you doing? You can't do this! The patient has a cough.'" While some of NewYork-Presbyterian's leaders were projecting calm, it was clear, before the hospital had admitted a single COVID patient, that the troops were not unruffled. In February, Rosner had heard about the tabletop exercises using Fleischut's team's modeling numbers being staged in Laureen Hill's office overlooking the Hudson River, a hushed aerie of hospital power at the end of a corridor lined with portraits of Columbia's leaders from the turn of the century.

Hill had trained as an anesthesiologist; she became the department chair at Emory, then ran the hospital at Washington University in St. Louis. Now COO of Columbia University Irving Medical Center, she had an uncanny ability to shape her history into we-got-this inspirational moments, such as the time she helped rescue a group of Vietnamese who had been in a van crash outside Hanoi by manually ventilating them with Ambu bags with their families at a rural clinic. Her history also included an MBA degree, a sign that Hill had corporate aspirations. "Laureen hides her steel with velvet," a colleague said of her, a skill that was on display from the first moment of the testing fiasco.

The task was far from clear. How many COVID-positive people might be out there? A few hundred? A few thousand? Half the city? The CDC was still completely fumbling the rollout and no one in New York could get the state to override the agency's demands. But the dirty little secret was that while the CDC's failure was beyond obvious, it also provided, many believe, an excuse and a cop-out. As the pandemic kicked into gear, there would be a lot of "we would if we could" and nowhere enough "we did it because we had to."

Of course, that wouldn't be how people told the story afterward. Former New York City health commissioner Oxiris Barbot later told the BBC that she was trying to warn de Blasio that "this is going to be truly horrible. We could see tens of thousands of people could die if we don't act quickly," but insisted she was shut down by a panic that gripped the mayor's team, who told her, "Oh my God, you can't say that to the public because we're gonna lose their trust." The mayor's office strongly denied her charge, telling the *New York Post*, "All we wanted was a clear prognosis on when to shut down the city and how far we had to go. She was unable to produce either." Barbot cried during the interview with the BBC.

There would be plenty of blame to go around, but it was obvious that Barbot—perhaps made the scapegoat by de Blasio—got it wrong. The same error was replicated by the state. In retrospect, the recklessness of some of her recommendations is startling. A month earlier, on February 1, one of the major Chinese and Chinese American communities in the city, in Flushing, Queens, had canceled its annual Lunar New Year celebration. Clearly they had heard enough from China to make them very concerned. Barbot saw things differently. That same day, she tweeted, "As we gear up to celebrate the #LunarNewYear in NYC, I want to assure New Yorkers that there is no reason for anyone to change their holiday plans, avoid the subway, or certain parts of the city because of the #coronavirus." A week later, she appeared on *Inside City Hall*. "We are telling New Yorkers: Go about your lives, take the subway, go out, enjoy life, but practice everyday precautions. . . . If it were likely to be transmitted casually, we would be seeing a lot more cases." Two days later, she tweeted, "I want to remind everyone to enjoy the parade and not change any plans due to misinformation spreading about the

#coronavirus." It was some of the worst advice that could possibly have been given. The day after that, the city government tried to buy two hundred thousand N95 masks but were told that the regular vendors had already run out.

And it kept going. On March 2—the day that Matt McCarthy was on CNBC warning about the testing chaos at Weill Cornell—Barbot, contradicting her counterparts in Seattle and San Francisco, offered a delicate assesment of the situation. "We know that there's currently no indication that it's easy to transmit by casual contact," she said on the morning that Lawrence Garbuz was diagnosed, completely contradicting her claim. "We want New Yorkers to go about their daily lives, ride the subway, take the bus, go see your neighbors."

Two years later, the *New York Times'* Joseph Goldstein and Sharon Otterman would reexamine the misguided policies and misunderstanding of the menace that affected the city's early slow response and failure to take action.

In Queens, at the city's Department of Health and Mental Hygiene, Barbot and the city's premier epidemiologist, Dr. Demetre Daskalakis, studied a large screen that tallied the number of emergency room visits, which began rising in the first week of March.

They understood, they later said, that the low number of tests—fewer than one hundred New Yorkers had been tested—meant there was no way to assess the crisis. The mayor saw this number and thought, he later said publicly, it meant "there is clearly a higher bar for transmission." It was March 9. San Francisco would institute a complete lockdown one week later, saving, many experts estimated, thousands of lives. In New York, emergency rooms all over the city were crowded with coughing patients. Barbot would insist she warned the mayor that the city was facing a disaster to rival the 1918 pandemic, but as late as March 10, she urged that Broadway shows remain open if there was hand sanitizer provided, according to a memo obtained by the *New York Times*.

Barbot's public statements were reinforced by the mayor, who attempted to reassure New Yorkers that the city hospitals had "twelve hundred extra beds" and were on hold for a mask order of three hundred thousand. It would take another three days for the mayor to stop saying the virus could not be spread by casual contact. On March 6, de Blasio issued his first emergency order for protective gear, masks, and hand sanitizer, but inside City Hall, the *New York Times* would later report, there were shouting matches as de Blasio's emergency team tried to talk sense into the mayor, who continued his daily two-hour workouts at the YMCA in Park Slope.

This overconfidence—arrogance, even—was echoed in Albany. "We think we have the best health-care system on the planet right here in New York," Governor Andrew Cuomo declared. "So, when you are saying what happened in other countries versus what happened here, we don't even think it is going to be as bad as it was in other countries." With regard to the countries in Europe now dealing with a virus that had broken free, he was right that in New York, it was not "going to be as bad." It was going to be much worse.

As associate chief quality officer of NewYork-Presbyterian Lawrence, Frisby ensured the hospital's standards of quality, and she was a fierce investigator of patient outcomes. "In hospitals," she reflected, "human error occurs. The question is why? Was there fatigue? Was it a complete slip? There's a whole science and methodology behind it where we characterize based on the type of error. Was it bias? Was it ingrained?" One of her first assignments at Lawrence had been determining the cause for a misadministration of radiation by two different techs, both very experienced. Frisby could not understand why this mistake was repeated. She watched the techs work and created a "spaghetti diagram," drawing a line each time they moved. "As they moved, I said, 'Okay, so they go in front of their computer monitor. Now they go to the center. Now they walked back to the monitor.' I just basically drew their path on a piece of paper that maps the route of the person." Frisby discovered that the technicians had to check on at least twenty different items and walk twenty-five times from one spot to another just to conduct a single CT scan. "It was obvious how easily errors could be made. Also, these guys were dripping sweat in a room that was freezing, they were running around so much. It was clear they needed more support and a more efficient workplace. I said, 'Let's move the printer closer. Let's put the garbage basket in a place where you can be closer so you don't have to continuously walk across the room. They were injecting dyes and constantly having to reposition the patient—sometimes as many as forty-five times. This was in the emergency room where a trauma patient could be bruised from head to toe and we were scanning to look for brain bleeds and fractures." The improvement was immediate.

Frisby had learned about coronaviruses in a college microbiology class and drilled down on them in virology. "All of the aspects were there—that they were the reason for a common cold. We learned about their replication and their cycles—all that kind of stuff. But that in their mild form, they were not a threat to life." Unfortunately, they didn't always come in the mild variety. The SARS epidemic a decade earlier had been caused by a much more deadly and virulent coronavirus. Then MERS—coming from the Middle East—erupted. When SARS and MERS mutated again, Frisby noted, "They became less deadly. But with COVID, it's an entirely different ball game."

Frisby and Fosina followed a careful script when dealing with staff who had been exposed to COVID. "I would always check in. I would say, 'Are you okay? How are you doing? Are you having any symptoms?' And some would say yes, and some would say no. And then I would say, 'We have a survey. I have to ask you these questions: What kind of PPE were you wearing? Were you wearing a mask? Were you wearing eye shields? What kind of interaction did you have? Was the patient wearing a mask?" This was to every member of our staff. I would ask them, 'How long do you think you were with the patient?'... They would answer the questions and right there I would formulate what risk category they are in." If infection was likely, Frisby would counsel them, explain how they needed to protect their families. She told many that they had to quarantine right away.

The anger that came at Frisby and Fosina was immediate. "I was getting calls saying, 'This is bullshit,'" Fosina said. "And then a lot of external calls trying to make sure that the hospital was isolated from the world."

"I had one doctor who started yelling at me, 'I have to be with patients in my office,'" Frisby recalled. "And I said, 'This is not me, this is the state mandating it.'"

Matt McCarthy's suggestion that New York City was unprepared was perceived as a comms nightmare for the hospital administration, who worried about losing their number one in the city rating, and for the trustees, who were, like everyone in New York that week, trying to stockpile N95s. As Forese drove to Bronxville, Corwin spoke to his closest advisers, among them the former chairman of the hospital Frank Bennack Jr., who'd run the Hearst Corporation for decades, and the chairman of the board, Jerry Speyer, the understated global real estate power responsible for saving Rockefeller Center. For Corwin, the amiable Bennack, who had risen from a radio announcer to newspaper publisher in San Antonio to running the multibillion-dollar Hearst empire, was "pure gold ... his judgment and integrity were impeccable. I always consulted with Frank and [former Morgan Stanley chairman] John Mack and Jerry Speyer." Both Speyer and Bennack said the same thing: "You and Laura are going to have to split up. We can't afford to have the leadership go down."

For all the upset at the hospital, the city and the state and the
CDC and the federal government had waffled and stonewalled and
failed to declare an emergency. But Corwin couldn't argue with his
advisers' logic. He already felt his health was in danger. Inside the
hospital, he said, "The doctors were not wearing masks in their meetings with each other. There was a willful suspension of disbelief. My
original gestalt was that you could not believe this was happening,
and then . . . this is going to be a disaster. We were following what
was happening in Italy." Corwin understood the lack of masking
as a product of doctor training: "It is unusual to wear masks in a
hospital setting—usually, you just wear them in a surgical setting."
And of course, it wasn't just the doctors; almost no one at any of the
NewYork-Presbyterian hospitals was wearing a mask.

One of the first tasks Arthur Evans assigned McCarthy once he
became head of the hospital's COVID specialists was, along with
his team of six other hospitalists, to sift through the barrage of
global findings and come up with treatment plans. "I felt electrified,"
McCarthy later said.

McCarthy felt that he had been preparing for this since his time
in Cameroon. In the first days, he ran into a very senior doctor who
told McCarthy he was extremely worried about what was happening.
McCarthy replied, "This is our Super Bowl. This is the thing we have
been training for." It was, as McCarthy said, "really how I felt at the
time. Like, 'Holy shit.'" At one point, Evans called a group meeting
on Zoom. There were eight hospitalists on the call. "He said that he
believed in us," McCarthy recalled. "And that this was our time to
step up. And that what we were doing was serving as role models
for people, not only in the hospital, but really around the country—
because it hadn't gotten around the country yet."

At that moment, there were just three PUIs in the hospital, but
it was obvious there were going to be many more. How many?
McCarthy woke up every day at 3:00 or 4:00 a.m. and read the latest

data the moment he was on his train. He made a note in his journal that Evans ended almost every conversation with "How can I be of help?" and decided he would start to do that as well.

McCarthy's partner as NewYork-Presbyterian's first COVID hospitalist was the physician assistant Rudy Tassy. Tassy was known at the hospital for his quiet confidence. He was a man of few words, not because he was shy but because he could ably diagnose a patient or situation without the need to chat his way through it. ("Lab value," as McCarthy described it.) He knew exactly how the hospital worked, not just bureaucratically but psychologically, which turned out to be an invaluable asset as the pandemic went on. He knew when action was needed, and he knew when the action needed was to defer. McCarthy found him reassuring. "He was thinking three steps ahead," he said, trying to figure out not only the case in front of him but what would happen in a month.

And that reassurance, that ability to see what was coming, was invigorating. McCarthy had been home, up at 3:00 a.m., reading an issue of the *New England Journal of Medicine* and thinking about the partnership when, corny as it later sounded, a song by Queen popped into his head. Some of the lyrics to "Don't Stop Me Now" were a bit raw, but the chorus suddenly spoke to McCarthy: *I'm having a ball / Don't stop me now / If you wanna have a good time / Just call.* Queen's lead singer, the late Freddie Mercury, had famously used the song to power himself through his bad days, and McCarthy instantly connected. He needed to hear that, no matter what was coming, he could not—and would not—be stopped, and here, however cheesy, was that battle cry.

But it was a contest that could not be won simply by outscoring an opponent; so many people thought of medicine as pills and numbers, but McCarthy, like Lief and an army of rebels who believed the Osler model was corrosive, felt emotion was central to good medicine. "I am bringing a little joy to them," he thought then. "We are going to be setting the tone." Maybe it was the hour that added so much weight to Mercury's proclamation, but it seemed auspicious.

That setting the tone came up on his first morning as a hospitalist; he and Tassy met in his office and put on their shields, then posed for a selfie. He heard himself saying the exact same thing that his baseball coach had always said before games: "Well, are we going to do this?" Tassy said, "Let's do it," and got a fist-pound. "We are going to be setting the tone for the hospital—people are going to be looking toward us. We have to show them we are not scared," McCarthy recalled. "And I said, 'We have to show everyone that we are focused. And that we are enjoying ourselves.'"

He would later reconsider the term *enjoying ourselves* as they grappled with the overwhelmingly serious issues. Tassy and McCarthy were trying to come up with a psychological strategy about how to handle the patients, what they should say, and how long it was safe to be in the room with them. There was the acute human side—how did you tell patients that there was almost no medication that would help them? He had practiced his opening lines: "We are going to do everything we can but we are not sure we have anything that really works." There was no pleasure in that. At night, Tassy would take the subway back to the Haitian American community in Flatbush where he had been reared. His family was in quarantine, at his insistence. He tried to convince everyone he had gone to school with to take precautions, but he wasn't sure how much anyone was listening. For that matter, he became deeply concerned about the temporary rooms that had been put up at Weill Cornell; they had no glass windows to the hallways, just to the outside. Tassy began to hear about patients who were having severe mental distress, far more life-threatening than anxiety. He resolved that he would try to make all of his patients laugh within moments of meeting them. As the only African American physician assistant in the hospitalist service, Tassy believed he had become adept at knowing how to navigate all the complexities of his singular status. The physician assistants were in fact a melting pot of ethnicities, but the striking fact remained: Tassy, one of the first to be hired under the new hospitalist system fifteen years earlier, was the only Black person among them. That reality had always troubled him and many others at the hospital.

Still, it had been his dream to be in medicine. Like McCarthy, Tassy thought beyond the individual patient. He and many of the residents were often swamped with paperwork and sleep-deprived, which could make them forget why they were doing what they did. But the pandemic was the biggest reminder possible: *This is why we are here.*

Their first patient was a talker. "Rudy and I were in the room and he talked and talked. And the thing that I thought about was: *Is it risky to stay in this room for more than twenty minutes or thirty minutes?* Listening to the patient is one of the most powerful things I can do. . . . But in this case it was different, right? And I started thinking about the clock ticking after about fifteen or twenty minutes." With every word the patient uttered, droplets and mist were sent into the air toward those who were listening. McCarthy and his colleagues were each wearing a double mask and a face shield, but when their patient wasn't talking he was coughing continuously and was very short of breath. "I thought, *I need to excuse myself, just for safety purposes,* because we don't know exactly what the risk profile was for transmission," McCarthy said. McCarthy was concerned that they would have to intubate the patient.

"We are going to get you through this," he told the patient. But how? He had resolved to be completely honest about what they were facing.

"We don't have the resources yet to really help you," he said, somewhat contradicting himself, but the *yet*—that was what he was banking on, that something would come up soon. So he would repeat the line again and again: *We are going to get you through this.*

But he wasn't sure it sounded believable, and as things got worse, he had to accept that it wasn't. He was exchanging endless e-mails about the emerging data on what they should be doing. Should they really be using hydroxychloroquine? What should they be doing about cohorting patients? But nobody knew.

There was also the question of discharge. What did it really mean to "get through" COVID? Nobody was totally sure if COVID might come back or if the recovered patient was still infectious, but the hospital needed the beds. "Is this person really going home to their partner," McCarthy wondered, "to their family? What are we going to do to protect others?"

At Columbia, Dr. Heather Morris, a kidney specialist, was trying to handle the same situation. She had met McCarthy when they were both residents, and they married soon after. At night it was impossible to watch anything on TV—sports, Netflix, anything. McCarthy could not stop looking for answers.

Almost immediately, McCarthy's children, both under five, noticed the change in their parents' behavior: "They started asking, 'Why are you and Mom always talking about coronavirus? Why are you always on your phone?' And it was hard to explain that I was trying to, after a day of seeing patients, keep up with all the new information coming out. Clearly, something was different. I was leaving at three or four in the morning. And they were like, 'Where is Dad in the morning? Why is he on the phone?' and 'When will this be over?' We tried to keep things light, to shield them from it as much as possible, but it's hard when your kids can't play with other kids. We just kept saying, 'We are trying to keep people safe,' and 'There is a virus,' and 'You can still learn, even if you aren't in school.'"

This is going to be really bad, he thought. "There wasn't much we could do other than put our heads down and try to save people's lives until everyone recognized what we were seeing."

5

At Columbia, in the second week of March, on the liver-transplant floor, it was more or less business as usual, despite the presence of Lawrence Garbuz in the hospital. It was still business as usual in the city too, the last days of normalcy in an uncanny twilight. The restaurants and bars were still open, bands were still playing, hundreds of coffee shops were still in operation for those who wanted a latte or just a public restroom, the subways were still running. Dozens of members of British theater royalty were on their way to New York for the jammed final previews of *Girl from the North Country*. At the Whitney downtown, lines formed for *Vida Americana*, the blockbuster Mexican muralists show. But whether you trusted New York's tabloids or their more sober competitors, fear was settling in.

From Madrid, Xenia Frisby's daughter Ariadne reported that there were drones flying over her neighborhood near the Puerta del Sol, one of the busiest in the city, less than a mile from the Prado. Ariadne was still teaching, but she told her parents she wasn't feeling well. She had a bad cough and was walloped by fatigue. "What do you think I should do?" she asked. Frisby told her to stay home if she spiked a fever, but she began to worry. She called Kang: "Ariadne may have COVID." Then Ariadne called again. The American embassy in Madrid was insisting that all U.S. citizens leave the country before it shut down. From a Spanish friend, she was able to get a PCR test.

She tested negative and caught the first flight she could that landed anywhere near New York. Upon arrival she quarantined with friends in Queens and then tried to figure out what to do next.

In Brooklyn, on the morning of March 4, Susie Bibi missed Marcus's disco aerobics and the Donna Summer soundtrack that always powered her through the day.

Bibi lived in the wealthy community of Syrian Jews on Brooklyn's Ocean Parkway, in a stretch of redbrick houses and Tudor mansions not far from Coney Island. A mother of five and grandmother of twelve, she looked two decades younger than her age. She prided herself on her impeccable house and exquisite clothes, cooking elaborate meals that she served the family in the dining room of burled woods and silver vases with massive orchids in oranges and purples cut just so and chairs covered in olive-green velvet. Her voice sang, the vibrato of Brooklyn piped through the upper sinuses then expelled in a whoosh of words.

The SYs, as they called themselves (a shortened form of *Syrians*), had originally come from Aleppo and Damascus and made their way to Brooklyn, where in the 1950s they sent their children to public schools to educate them to do business outside the closed world of their community, but they also insisted they follow the Edict, the 1935 ruling by Syrian rabbis that they must marry within the community to ensure that the Syrian Jews would remain united.

Bibi often texted her friend Heidi to meet at the 9:00 a.m. aerobics class at the Sephardic Community Center on her corner. A self-described gym rat, Bibi worked out daily and obsessively to keep her weight at 107 pounds. She stayed for the second class and then exercised with weights in the gym until around eleven, then came home to shower and steam and go about her day. Bibi's rabbi teased her that she was like Joan Rivers because of her comic timing and not taking herself too seriously. "Fran Drescher from *The Nanny* . . . Mrs. Maisel . . . everyone has called me that too," she said. "I didn't even know the rabbi knew who Joan Rivers was!"

Over the past few days, she'd had a cough on and off, but now it had turned worse; she'd been diagnosed with bronchitis, and the hacking had kept her up much of the night. The gym was off. She texted Heidi: *I need to rest and have tea and soup—it is helping me.*

Heidi, on the way to Florida, texted from the airport: *There is no one here. It is eerie. We are getting out of the city. Everyone says that the pandemic is coming.*

Most New Yorkers weren't flying or driving anywhere. Instead, they were staying put. The appeals to continue life as usual were being made precisely because New Yorkers were adjusting.

At the moment, Bibi was not thinking too hard about Heidi's departure but about her cough and the wedding. Her son, Jack, twenty-four, was planning to propose, and in the Sephardic tradition, the boy's family gets the ring and showers the bride-to-be with gifts. For Bibi and her husband, Reuben (or, as she called him, Ruby), the pressure was on. "I kept saying, 'Ruby, let's hurry and get to the diamond district and get a stone for the girl's ring.'"

Reuben was more aware of what it took to make a nice wedding ring, being in the jewelry business. He was also more aware of COVID than most, since he had been in Hong Kong in December. "I travel to Hong Kong, to Asia, at least five times a year," he explained. "So I was following what was going on in Asia very, very closely." The Chinese government was increasingly concerned about political unrest in the former colony, and it seemed to some that it was only a matter of time before Beijing unleashed a violent crackdown. But, Reuben said, while COVID "didn't really reach Hong Kong yet . . . they were somewhat prepared because they wear masks going back to regular SARS. So a lot of people wear masks there."

On December 14, 2019, concerned "for us as Americans between the protesting and the COVID so close," Ruby's hotel manager told him, "If I was you, I would leave Sunday morning." So he did. The news about mysterious cases of pneumonia in China didn't come out for a couple of weeks after the hotel manager encouraged Reuben to depart. She had heard something from Wuhan.

Only days before Bibi's skipped workout, she and Reuben had been at a jewelry show at the Javits Center, Manhattan's sprawling convention center, and she realized it wasn't as bustling as it usually was, which was fine with Bibi because she was feeling so dragged down by her bronchitis. Still, she could hear her grandmother's endless bromides: You never know what tomorrow will bring. "You know what," Susie told Reuben, "let's just go and get all the gifts now."

In Flushing, Queens, Booth Memorial was a landmark built in 1892—there is still an avenue named for it—a Salvation Army hospital that had an adjunct wing for unwed mothers, as they were called in the 1950s. After decades, Booth was taken over by NewYork-Presbyterian, which renovated it completely.

Much had changed on Main Street in Flushing over the years. Always a central artery for the fiercely ambitious working class, it was now the shopping district for the thousands of Asian Americans who have moved to the area. But the most dramatic transformations of the past century had one thing—or, rather, one person—in common: New York power broker Robert Moses, who treated Queens and Brooklyn as experimental fiefdoms. His fixation on building playgrounds and parks could obscure the means by which he seized the space and the larger scope of his grandiosity. His vision of cloverleaf highways, bridges, and tunnels left little room for the area's neighborhoods, farms, and waterways. Moses loved parkways and cars. He gashed and paved his way through the five boroughs, but he seemed to have a particular fixation on the swamps of Queens, the thousands of acres of garbage dumps that had, Robert Moses once joked, "rats big enough they could wear saddles" and so many furry creatures that trappers sold their pelts to the furriers on Seventh Avenue.

As hospital drama, the tale of the two Sharma brothers of Queens could have been concocted by a screenwriter. They were a year apart, their mother a doctor whose office was a quick bike ride from their house in Elmhurst. "Do you know how amazing your mother is?" the Sharmas often heard as they made their way through the neighborhood.

Their home was a few miles from Booth Memorial Hospital. Firstborn Rahul informed his younger brother, Manish, that he was going to be an ER doctor and added, "That is what you will do too."

Manish became the head of the Queens emergency department, Rahul the chief of emergency at Weill Cornell. And so the brothers Sharma rose to the very top of the NewYork-Presbyterian leadership.

NewYork-Presbyterian Queens was just a few miles from the dumps that Moses had transformed into the site of the 1939 and 1964 World's Fairs. Nearby were the houses of Kew Gardens that in the 1950s had welcomed shtetl Jews who were barely literate in English on their way to Levittown and the Trumps of Jamaica Estates. The area was also the stomping grounds of some of New York's gaudiest con men, like former Queens borough president Donald Manes (who would wind up committing suicide to avoid jail).

In the first days of March, Jaclyn Mucaria, head of NewYork-Presbyterian's Queens hospital, had started allotting rooms for COVID patients and bringing in HEPA filters, but by March 5, two days after Lawrence Garbuz was diagnosed, "We knew the number of rooms was not enough," the ED nursing director Suzanne Pugh said. "We went from two rooms to five rooms to thirty-five rooms. And over two or three weeks, I said to Manish, 'I don't know how we are going to do this.'" Some of the first attacks of anti-Asian violence were here too. As Trump screamed about the "China virus," shopkeepers were beaten up; women by the E and F train stops feared for their lives.

A very small proportion of the patients in the far-flung NewYork-Presbyterian system had been to China before getting sick. But in this part of Queens, with its massive Chinese American population, that was not the case. In the first week of March, Pugh found herself confronting an onslaught. Every hour, someone would come into the ED saying, "I have traveled to Asia. I have symptoms of COVID-19." The number of patients who descended on the small community hospital soon overwhelmed the lobby of the ED.

That weekend, Pugh was upstate visiting her father when she got a call from Laura Forese, informing her of the first COVID case that had hit Lawrence Hospital in Bronxville as Pugh's emergency department filled up with coughing patients. "She wanted a call with all of the ED chairmen—there were maybe eighteen or twenty of us on the call. She told us what was happening at Lawrence and said, 'I want you all to know what is going on. ERs are our front line and I need you to hold it together.'" After the call, Pugh phoned her assistant director. "I said, 'I am coming in. You have a kid. One of us has to be there.'"

On the Upper East Side, during rounds on March 6, Kristen Marks, one of Weill Cornell's infectious-disease specialists, turned to the noted epidemiologist Roy Gulick. "Hey, we should think about how we are going to treat this disease." It seemed like such an obvious statement—it *was* an obvious statement—but they were only days into COVID coming into their building, and with a very modest sample size, systemizing a course of care seemed quite a leap. It was that way everywhere—in no country where COVID had landed was there consensus about what to do. At this point there was no treatment.

"That's a great idea," Gulick replied. "Let's get four or five people together to say what we know about this disease and what therapies we may want to pursue." And after rounds, they sat down and compared notes. What had people been seeing? Which therapies should they try to get hold of? They were in uncharted territory—here were some of the greatest research infectious-disease doctors in the world, and they had nothing to offer except a ventilator in the ICU. So little was known about the virus and its transmission that they brainstormed in a small conference room with no masks on and no decent options.

The atmosphere was fraught. What data was new? What were they seeing in China? What were they were doing in Italy? The pair knew so much that they had no need to show anyone how much they knew.

They settled on two treatments, one of which was hydroxychloroquine. This was before the president of the United States began to tout it, and by the time he did, it had become pretty clear the drug was nearly worthless in the fight. But right then, they had a single study—imperfectly done, they all knew—that showed some activity in a test tube against the SARS-CoV-2 virus, a study so small that under normal circumstances, they might not have even have printed it out for review, but what choice did they have but to try it? The second drug added, in a similarly desperate move, was Zithromax, a commonly used antibiotic.

The data was coming in from Italy and China. The coronavirus, although sometimes causing only mild symptoms, could race through the system and cause organ failure. A patient could decompensate within hours. And if a patient's immune system, desperately working to kill the virus, overreacted and produced too many cytokines (small proteins that regulate the immune response), that hyperinflammation—known as a "cytokine storm"—could be fatal.

One other decision was made. Gulick had spent months planning his sixtieth birthday party and had friends flying in from all over the world.

Gulick had invited more than a hundred people to a celebratory dinner set for March 16, but it was clear to him that the party could not go forward—not that many people in his apartment, not now—and he canceled. "I don't want to be a super-spreader event," he acknowledged. Instead, he invited eight friends to sing songs around the piano. Two would become infected.

On 5 South, all Lindsay Lief knew of Nathaniel Hupert came from e-mails that went to her and the five other medical directors of the ICUs at Weill Cornell. The first, dated March 7, 2020, was unnerving. All around Weill Cornell, the hospitalists were trying to take action, increasingly worried that the administration was slow-walking an emergency situation. Hupert submitted a model that astonished Lief: He was predicting over two thousand COVID patients at all ten hospitals of NewYork-Presbyterian by the end of March. At the time, there were only fifteen COVID patients at Weill Cornell.

Lief stared at his name in her in-box. "I wondered, *Who is Nathaniel Hupert?*" They had never met, but she vaguely knew he was connected to the medical school's Center for Global Health.

Lief studied Hupert's models. No one at the hospital had mentioned anything that came close to Hupert's number. Two thousand COVID patients? Where would they put them?

"I thought, *My God . . . this can't be.* It was my first sign of reality." She noticed that he was predicting that the numbers at the hospital would peak by April 9. She thought to herself, *A month of hell. If I can only hold on for a month.* He was less successful in getting hospital epidemiologists to pay attention.

Hupert kept digging deeper, examining every bit of data he could get from his modeling team of Peter Jackson and John—"Jack"—Muckstadt, the former dean of the engineering school at Cornell, a scientific adviser for the CDC, and Cornell's director of pandemic and disaster response. He advised the air force and Amazon among scores of other institutions about improving their efficiency systems, and had worked with Hupert through his time at the CDC. Using numbers that he had gleaned from China and Italy, he told Art Evans that the hospital was going to have to find four times the number of doctors and health-care workers. Evans said, "I hope to God not! We can do three times, but four? There isn't a way in hell that the hospital won't collapse." He drilled down on what was coming at the hospital: "WC (1,800 employees) + NYP (20,000). If 30% attack rate and 50% asymptomatic rate and 0.5–2% symptomatic case fatality ratio, then 16–65 deaths (among staff) over next 3–6 months." (There would be 34—exactly in the range Hupert had predicted.)

But all the modelers, including Hupert, made a massive mistake—they predicted COVID, as Hupert later said, "as one huge wave up front, not taking into account (maybe not believing) that it would be so effectively attenuated by measures and yet keep coming back." Later, Hupert revised the numbers with better information, but his estimate of how many patients would be admitted to New York-Presbyterian—between two thousand and three thousand—was prescient.

At Columbia Medical Center, there was, frankly, nothing that was going to stop Veronica Roye from taking her long-delayed vacation to New Orleans for a bachelorette party with friends from Columbia's nursing school. On the liver-transplant floor, the surgeons were jammed with cases. Tomoaki Kato was known for his quiet outreach and extraordinary surgeries for anyone who could not afford it, and now a teenage boy needed a liver transplant. The equation was pretty straightforward for Kato: "If the surgery goes well," he said, the teenager "can go on for years." If not—well, it was too dangerous to wait. Kato knew that he had a very short window to save the teen. He told his scheduler to look for a date sometime in March.

The first week of March, across town at Weill Cornell, Brad Hayward, one of 5 South's critical-care attendings, was on call, and in addition to trying to keep the unit running smoothly, he was trying to keep his mother calm. Hayward's father was a steelworker from rural Pennsylvania, a man who had seen his son's sensitivity and unusual gifts early and began buying him chemistry sets. He encouraged him to go to college on any scholarship he could get and move away from the small town he had always known. Hayward struggled to pay his medical-school loans, but he never regretted that early inspiration, and he loved being part of the 5 South family.

Now, however, he wondered if his parents were having second thoughts about the direction they'd encouraged him to go in. In February, Hayward had kept thinking about the pattern of SARS and MERS, the rush of cases and then the falling-off. But, okay— what to do with that knowledge? "What is our plan?" his mother asked him, the plural possessive revealing their close bond. Hayward punted—"I haven't seen any cases yet," he told her—but the truth was that he didn't have a plan. Or the plan was to wait until they had a patient in front of them and go from there.

That didn't take long. The first call had come in from the ED—a patient with shortness of breath and a fever. At 2:00 a.m., Hayward rushed down and called the desk on 5 South. "I don't want to send alarms but the surge is here."

The nurse's assistant on the 5 South desk called the supply room. Hayward let them know they had a COVID patient and needed

N95s. "And the people on the other line said, 'What are you talking about?'"

For days, Lief had been sending e-mails about the lack of N95s. Luckily, Judith Cherry had alerted the team to her stash of half-empty boxes. "Judith Cherry saved lives because of her actions," Lief said. "After that, we got them to agree that the MICU could always have six boxes, on our own, and we would not have to ever call Central Supply to get them again." There was something else that Cherry gave them, and it might have been just as important, if not directly so. "I think she kept the spirits up," said one of the 5 South pulmonologists. Having people like Cherry and the other nurses who "were passionate about their jobs, passionate about us getting through this, keeping everyone's morale up, really made it much, much easier. Just the positive reinforcement for what we were doing through Judith was really valuable." (As it turned out, a later test showed the patient was negative, after which he had been sent home.)

Kirana Gudi had been on duty on 5 South with Lief. Gudi, the vice chair of education at the hospital, had been chief resident during Lief's training and they had been close ever since. She, Lief, and Hayward were in the small office monitoring a young man with a fever who had just flown in from Rome. At his mother's insistence, he had stayed at a hotel at first but then decided that what he had was a bad cold and not COVID-19, so he stopped quarantining, possibly infecting dozens of others. He would become 5 South's first case.

He was admitted to the hospital with shortness of breath. His mother stood outside the glass doors that looked into his room in the ICU, talking to her son on a cell phone. "She would yell at him, 'Sit up and take a deep breath,'" Hayward said. "This was as he was starting to desaturate. She did not want him on a ventilator." Visitors were still coming in and out of the ICU. "Each time we would try to go over and see how he was doing, she would tell us, 'You are going to make him nervous.' Then she would call him on the cell phone and say, 'Take a deep breath. Put the mask on.' All of the things you say so that we wouldn't run in there."

It was, of course, impossible to get him tested. "All of the forms had to be processed in triplicate and every specimen had to be hand-delivered to the DOH, who would only pick up at the hospital twice a day," recalled Hayward. "And there were no weekend pickups at all. So that weekend, Lindsay and I were at the hospital and we were looking at each other saying, 'How are we going to deal with this if we don't even know who has it and who doesn't have it?'"

Particularly frustrating was that Columbia actually had the means to test. Testing for COVID was a simple matter of combining two reagents. In the labs, scientists pulled the recipe off the web and tested each other, off protocol. And endless hours were spent trying to negotiate with the governor's moribund department of health to activate Columbia's massive Roche machine, which could run five thousand tests a day. The Roche 6800 at Columbia was one of a few in the city. It was the size of a small room and was in a lab where the head scientist, Kevin Roth, worked fourteen-hour days trying to stockpile enough reagents. It was known throughout the building that research scientists were coming in to get tested despite the lack of approval, but patients were out of luck.

The hospital's policy was to bring anyone who needed six liters per minute of supplemental oxygen to the ICU, to prevent the spread of infection. The patient's mother had studied the disease and was close to a doctor who advised her to keep him on a mask that covers the mouth and nose and delivers highly concentrated pure oxygen. At Weill Cornell, the micro lab was scrambling to assemble reagents to start their own tests as soon as the state signed off. Not long after he was finally tested, the young man came back positive; he was put on a ventilator, then quickly taken off it.

And then, Gudi recalled, all of a sudden the hospital seemed to fill with PUIs—all treated by the general-medicine ("gen-med") teams with a small amount of oxygen until they deteriorated and had to be admitted to an ICU. She watched as the hospital scrambled to accommodate the patients' needs—the gen-med teams that would become COVID teams; the decision to keep the patients to one floor of the hospital that quickly became three floors, the operating rooms that were turned into ICUs. All of it happened within ten days as the city continued to stay open, the subways and theaters still packed. "It felt like there wasn't a plan anywhere," Gudi said. "We were putting it together as it was unfolding. We were learning how to don and doff. I hate even hearing those words because it brought us back to the Ebola crisis when we were fellows practicing endlessly and realized during those drills that we were contaminating each other. . . . Those drills would go on and on and we would say, 'God knows what will become of us. If Ebola comes here, we are all dead.'"

In Queens, the first official case was diagnosed on March 8. Chief medical officer Amir Jaffer had been working nonstop with Manish Sharma and Suzanne Pugh, trying to reconfigure the hospital to accommodate the scores of patients who were crowding the emergency department. The city—and, for that matter, Main Street—had yet to slow down, although Flushing seemed quieter as more Asian Americans chose to stay home.

Jaffer had grown up in Karachi and then London, where his father was the John Deere representative for Pakistan, and now lived in Manhattan. On Thursday, March 12, Jaffer got into his car to make the drive home to his apartment on the Upper East Side. "It was late at night and I was beginning to have chills. I thought to myself, *Oh my God, I am not doing good. All of these chills—this might be COVID.* I went home and suffered all that night. I had sweats. I had a fever."

The next morning, he reached out to Sharma and told him that he was not feeling well. He then headed to Queens, met with his boss to request time off, and took a test.

"I got back my results the next morning," he remembered, "and I had already started quarantining myself. My daughter is in a separate bedroom, but my wife and I share the other. I think I had already infected her.'"

Jaffer did okay over the weekend, but on Monday, he started to have shortness of breath. "I called Manish, who told me to get right back to our emergency room. I have so much confidence in our team that I wanted to be in Queens, not at Cornell. My daughter drove me. Manish looked at my levels and oxygen and thought they were low." Sharma told Jaffer they were going to keep him at the hospital. But Jaffer wanted to leave.

"I was using hydroxychloroquine—it was the early days. And also azithromycin. That was on a drip. And I was on oxygen. My doctor was the chief resident I had trained. I'd had him as an intern. He said, 'Dr. Jaffer, I have seen a lot of people now who look as sick as you and I do not recommend you leaving the hospital.' And I said, 'I really want to go. I need to go home.' And he said, 'Amir, as your doctor, you are going against my recommendation.' And I left."

Concerned, Laura Forese went to Queens to see for herself what was going on. She did her daily broadcast with Jaffer, who talked about what happened to him in the hospital. "We have your back," she told Sharma. "I promise."

That night, Jaffer's heart started racing, and his daughter and wife took him to the emergency department at Weill Cornell and said, "You are not leaving." Jaffer was put on oxygen and admitted.

Weill Cornell pediatric nurse Karen Bacon could hardly grasp what the doctors at Metropolitan hospital in East Harlem were trying to tell her: *We need to intubate you.* She remembered agreeing to it at the time, even though she wasn't fully grasping the gravity of the situation. It didn't occur to her to ask, "Why don't you try a BiPAP first?" BiPAP was similar to a ventilator, but it was noninvasive and could be used at home for sleep apnea and other moderate pulmonary difficulties. But she just didn't have the energy to speak up. She could hardly breathe.

It was March 8. The next day, Italy announced it was locking down the north of the country, including Milan. The news sent a tremor of panic through many in New York City. Italy was the first western country to impose such authoritarian sanctions. "We are facing an emergency," the Italian prime minister said. "This is the moment of self-responsibility." But flights would continue from Italy to New York for five more days. The president announced that the chance of anyone in America getting COVID was "extremely low." For weeks, Bacon had been dealing with bronchitis, a hacking cough that made her leave the room when she was with her patients. She had dreamed of taking care of children since her school days in Jamaica, Queens. She loved calling herself "a Queens girl." Her husband, Quinn, was a security officer whom she'd met through someone in her church. They'd married just before Thanksgiving, her wedding gown a confection of organza that she'd bought in Manhattan at Kleinfeld's, the bridal shopping shrine.

Bacon's parents, a New York Department of Education paraprofessional who assisted teachers in Queens classrooms and a heavy-equipment engineer and proud union member, pushed Bacon hard to get into nursing school and to complete her BA, which you needed to become a registered nurse. She got her degrees online and combed the openings at NewYork-Presbyterian from the moment she could apply. "It was number one in the city," she said, "and that is where I was determined to be." Two positions popped up. One was at NewYork-Presbyterian Queens, a short drive from her house. The other was at Weill Cornell, a longer commute. She hesitated, imagining how easy it would be to get to Queens, but her father said, "Karen, you have worked hard. You deserve to be at Cornell."

Now, all of thirty-two years old, she had made it to Cornell, where she felt immediately at home. The race issues that had so troubled Veronica Roye a few years earlier did not bother Bacon. "I just know that if I am in a room, the patient will address the white doctor or the nurse and I am invisible—and that's just something I deal with." But when it was her turn to shine, the illumination could be dazzling. A teenager watching Marvel movies during chemotherapy? Bacon knew all the Marvel movies and could make small talk about superheroes. A six-year-old with a sarcoma fighting for his life? She could spin jokes with every variation of her last name—eggs and bacon, bringing home the bacon, bacon bits—until the silliness made them both forget, at least for a moment, the fear. Like Lindsay Lief, she never for a moment questioned her choice of profession.

And then it was February 2020. Bacon noticed that there were lots of nurses out sick; everyone seemed to have a cold and a hacking cough they couldn't get rid of. Bacon's started late that month and, determined to tough it out, she took every cold medication she could think of and hydrated herself. She hated missing a day of work, and she didn't want to miss her mother's birthday, which was on March 6, it was a big deal to Bacon, as she had an uncommon closeness with her parents, whom she unabashedly revered.

The cough worsened. Italy shut down completely. Bacon wondered: *Could this be COVID? How can I get a test?* In the first days of March, she had to call in sick to work. She was coughing nonstop, at one point so much so that she went to the emergency department in a local hospital near Cobble Hill in Brooklyn, close to her parents' apartment. She was told, "It's bronchitis." No one suggested she should be checked for COVID.

More cough medicine and a nebulizer to help her breathe. On her mother's birthday, Bacon was so overcome with coughing and breathing difficulties, she told her, "I have to go rest. I cannot breathe." Her mother worried that it was COVID. "There is no doubt in my mind," she said of her daughter's illness. Bacon went to another emergency department, this time near where she had grown up in Jamaica, Queens. The hospitals were public—Bacon did not want to drive into the city to try to get into Cornell. She was sent home again with an albuterol inhaler—a classic treatment for severe bronchitis. In the middle of the night, she could not breathe—and it wasn't just that. Bacon texted her boss, *I'm spiking fevers having chills and body aches and just freezing cold*. Her dad said, "You are going to the hospital—now." Bacon resisted. He said, *"Now."*

As Matt McCarthy had made clear on *Squawk Box,* there were no COVID tests available at Weill Cornell without getting into a massive fight with the DOH about a possible Wuhan exposure. Bacon was referred to Metropolitan hospital, a public hospital in East Harlem on the Yorkville border that was the setting for a Frederick Wiseman documentary and George C. Scott's 1971 film *The Hospital*. It was the only place that would agree to set aside a COVID test for her. "Sure, we have a swab for you," she was told when she said she was a nurse. "Come right away, and we will hold it."

On arrival, Bacon was put into a room, and she understood, almost immediately, this was a mistake. "It became clear to me very quickly that I wasn't going to get the right kind of care. They assumed because I was a nurse, I could operate my own oxygen. They came to the door and expected me to get up and carry it and start it—I was so out of breath that I could not move. I couldn't even get to the bathroom on my own power. I had air hunger; I was gasping." Her oxygen dropped to the low nineties, and not only was she unable to lug around an oxygen tank, she could not eat. Quinn dropped off some soup but was not allowed into the room. "Please, can you call your attending?" Bacon asked the respiratory therapist. "This oxygen is doing nothing. I need the high-flow."

Bacon knew she needed an advocate. Where was her family? Could she pull up an online picture of the small version of a BiPAP machine, the one that looked like a toaster but could deliver so much more oxygen? It seemed so obvious—what did she have to say to them so they would try it?

But it seemed the staff had gotten tired of hearing her opinions about what should be done. Bacon texted her boss that they'd removed the call bell from its socket, making it impossible to get immediate assistance.

The response was rapid and suitably angry: *Are you fucking kidding me?* She pleaded with Bacon to advocate for herself. *Karen, this can turn serious very quickly.*

A few hours later, Bacon wrote again: *They gonna move me to a different icu. Bcuz I need extra respiratory support.* Now, long after Bacon had asked for it, the doctors raised the idea of using a BiPAP, but by this point she needed more than that. Asked by her boss how she felt, Bacon texted back, *Sleepy. Really sleepy.*

Her boss insisted she call patient services and ask for help immediately. *I try they don't listen,* Bacon responded, her oxygen level getting lower. Her boss asked if Bacon wanted to be transferred to Cornell. She did.

Bacon kept texting her friends and her family: *I don't like the care I am getting here.* As she struggled for air, she was finally moved to the ICU and put on high-flow oxygen.

It's about time, her boss wrote.

Bacon's next message: *They may have to intubate me.*

What??? What's happening? her boss replied. Not getting a response, she added, *I love you so much! Please text me if there's anything I can do . . . I'm here for you and am praying for you.*

But Bacon was trapped behind the wall of illness; the words stuck, and she could not breathe. The doctors just kept saying, "We need to intubate you." And she found herself too weak to argue. All she could think was *Lean on the people you love. They will help you.* She gathered enough strength and texted the nurses she worked with in the pediatric unit: *I am at Metropolitan Hospital. They want to intubate me. I do not like the care I am getting. Help me. Love you, love you guys so much.*

"I thought I was going to be semi-sedated so I would still be able to react. I had no idea that I was going to not see my husband or family for almost two months. No idea."

Months later, Karen Bacon would learn that her friends wasted no time enlisting Rae-Jean Hemway, Weill Cornell's director of pediatric nursing, to lobby the hospital to admit her. Hayward was on call when he got a text: *One of our nurses is intubated at Metropolitan Hospital.* He was deeply concerned. "If one of our nurses got it, will we all get it?" Immediately, he called the Weill Cornell Transfer Center to start the process of getting Bacon to Cornell.

Moving a patient is never easy, and a sedated patient on a ventilator all the more precarious. The hospitals were less than two miles apart, both on the East River, a ten-minute ambulance ride.

Later, Lindsay Lief said that Bacon "was our very first health-care worker . . . We were determined to bring every single infected health-care worker to Five South to try to save them." Kirana Gudi, her former supervisor and the vice chair of medicine, kept meticulous notes: "March 10th: We admitted the first health care worker to the ICU today—the test is actually positive. . . . Everyone starts to worry that we will get it too." Lief began to fear for her sons, still attending public school every day. She talked to her husband, Jake. *What are we going to do? What if I expose them?*

In Lower Manhattan, at dawn on March 9, Hupert walked out of the hospital on William Street and snapped a photo that he would keep on his phone for the next several months: the red dawn of New York City with a Rothko-esque sunrise of blazing oranges and golds cut with the black silhouettes of office towers and the pedestrian entrance of the Brooklyn Bridge, soon to be completely deserted. Throughout the day, as he now did every day, he would be trading e-mails with fellow modelers as well as James Lawler and John Hick, one of the key authors of the *Crisis Standards of Care* from the National Academy of Medicine. In one e-mail to Hick, Hupert mentioned the lack of PPE and told him that when walking around Lower Manhattan, he'd started wearing a painter's canvas smock and a welding mask he had bought at Ace Hardware in New Jersey. If the hospital wasn't going to help out, he'd help himself.

That morning, although the mayor still was not ordering a lockdown, Lizzy Oelsner was worried and moving fast. Her daughters' school had left a message that it was shutting down "for the next weeks"—no specific reopening date planned. Putting aside the research-grant application for the National Institutes of Health that she had been preparing, Oelsner spent the morning packing for a few weeks in Vermont. She was writing a COVID-related research grant that was due on March 31. Her team was scrambling to submit the application in time. She was also texting back and forth constantly with her pod. As Oelsner drove her children north over the Triborough Bridge, she saw the city in her rearview mirror and thought to herself, *My God, what will happen to us all? This is a complete catastrophe.* She wasn't sure they would ever be back in the city again.

Gudi had been on call three straight days and often worked long into the night. "I thought, *I am going to take the morning off today.* It was my best friend's birthday. I wrote in my notes, 'I thought I was going to take the morning off today and actually do laundry and tend to my children. But by 7:40 a.m. I had answered five phone calls and several e-mails so I just decided I would go in.'"

Gudi had planned to use the time to teach the residents what

COVID treatment was going to look like, but as soon as she walked into the hospital, she learned that an emergency meeting had been set up in the trustees' boardroom in the Whitney wing. She walked down the narrow hallway lined with portraits of leaders of the hospital, including King George III, who had granted a royal charter to the hospital in 1771. "Lindsay and I were both in the meeting. Everyone was talking at once, saying, 'What do we do? What do we do?' Lindsay and I both started to cry because of what we had already seen in the ICU." The questions came without answers: Where were the ICUs going to be? How were they going to move the patients? Not every room on 5 South was a negative-pressure room, so how were they going to accommodate all the patients? Nathaniel Hupert was at the same meeting, with his first models predicting 2,500 to 3,000 patients. He turned to the heads of the emergency department and said, "How can you even be in this room together and not wearing masks?"

For many years at Weill Cornell, residents and training fellows first encountered the pulmonologist Kapil Rajwani during his virtuoso performances in the patient-simulation suite constructed in former squash courts at the top of one of the hospital buildings. Rajwani's nickname on 5 South was "the Ninja," for his almost mystical way of intuiting when "something bad could be happening in the ICU," Brad Hayward said. "You don't even have to call him and, suddenly, you turn around, and he's there." He demonstrated that same prowess in the simulation laboratories, which used high-tech mannequins to teach residents how to intubate patients and insert central lines with cutting-edge equipment. Gathered around the high-tech patient's bed, leaning in to hear Rajwani's instructions, residents saw Rajwani's visionary diagnostic ability and quiet ferocity when a patient was in trouble.

In the first weeks of March, as one critically ill patient after another needed intubation, Hayward was often short-tempered with anesthesiologists who wasted what he thought was crucial time searching for extra-long nitrile gloves to cover their forearms or special neck wraps to protect every bit of skin. The quietly thoughtful Rajwani did not discourage the younger Hayward from going after any anesthesiologist who delayed intubating patients. Sometimes fifteen or twenty minutes passed as they prepared to intubate. "I am going in myself," Hayward would say at this point. "We are not going to lose this patient. We don't have those extra-long gloves and you do not need them."

Rajwani and his wife, the critical-care specialist Lourdes Sanso, lived in Astoria when the pandemic began. Sanso was in charge of the residency program at NewYork-Presbyterian Queens. "Whenever we wanted to understand what was happening," recalled Fernando Martinez, chief of Weill Cornell's pulmonary and critical-care medicine, "we would just ask Kapil, 'What is Lourdes saying about the situation?'"

Rajwani took the subway to work. At first, he was one of the few people on the train wearing a mask. "I'd get looks from people," he remembered. "'Why are you wearing a mask? Are you crazy?' . . . Then each week that passed, I saw the crowds on the train thin out, essentially no one on the train except a handful of folks, so just watching that was eerie.

"When we first were seeing folks," Rajwani said, "the plan was—or at least the information we had—was that steroids essentially could worsen things based on some literature from past viral diseases, through the lens of the prior SARS pandemic and the MERS outbreak." None of those studies had been substantial, but they had been accepted as common knowledge. But the closer the 5 South team looked, the more they wondered. "As we were dealing with it," Rajwani said, "we were seeing that the nature of the viral infection was a little bit different than what we were used to. There was a lot of inflammation in the lungs, but also systemically, in terms of fevers and inflammatory markers that we were seeing—and the fact that we just had nothing else—folks were just continuing to get worse."

"No one had seen anything like this before in respiratory illnesses," Rajwani said. "And there was a suggestion in the previous data that using steroids for SARS or influenza could be harmful. But this was different—it was inflammation. And steroids are the best way to deal with that."

Rajwani had discovered there was some experimentation with steroids going on in parts of the world, but there was no data—just a flicker of anecdotal results. In London, the first days of a clinical trial had been established to check the safety of the steroid protocol. Fernando Martinez, Rajwani, Lief, and Columbia's ICU chief Dan Brodie reached out to colleagues from Mass General and in Italy. But there were many who thought that steroids could be harmful, especially the infectious-disease experts. "It was a situation where we were discussing it constantly, debating all of the pros and cons. But the patients had been in the ICU with us for eight days," Martinez said. "And they were dying. They would have died—and we knew that."

Added Rajwani, "We decided that people that had been sick for greater than a week would be reasonable folks to consider trying the steroids on. Those are the folks that were . . . if they were not getting better by then, they were going to end up in our ICU." Especially hard was seeing family members who'd been infected, "both next to each other, husbands and wives, or you see a husband and you're talking to him about how he needs to get intubated and telling his wife and saying potential goodbye, and seeing that . . . we had some together, and then one was getting better and one was getting worse. The wife was getting better and she was actually going to be discharged and she didn't want to leave. She was like, 'No. How am I going to leave my husband here?' knowing that she can't come back and visit him." If they did take a chance on steroids, 5 South would be the first critical-care unit in New York to do so. The ultimate plan was to use steroids throughout the hospital.

"There were reports from Wuhan that they had used steroids, or mixed reports," Rajwani said, "but there wasn't anything concrete. It just felt like the way the disease was progressing that you needed to do something to tamp down the inflammatory process. We looked into the literature, saw some of the dosages people had used in either viral instances or other ARDS [acute respiratory distress syndrome] pictures, and came up with a protocol that we thought would be reasonable to try." But Martinez also noted that there had been studies showing that steroid therapy in SARS-CoV-1 made things worse. It prolonged viral shedding. "That was the reason for the hesitation this time around," Rajwani explained.

There was some discussion about whether some sort of clinical trial was necessary before going forward, but, Rajwani said, "Given how fast things were moving and just the speed at which we can get a clinical trial approved and organized, it was going to be probably much longer than I think we wanted." Yes, using steroids was an experiment, but people were dying. "It was more of a 'We don't have anything else and we need to start doing something,'" he said.

The cooperation between Cornell and Columbia should have been seamless—they were, after all, part of the same system. The two schools often had to compete for grants and funding. As a result, sometimes information didn't spread as quickly uptown or downtown as an outsider might expect—especially in a pandemic. But in the spring of 2020, there were daily calls between the medical school leaders on exactly what they were seeing, as well as plans for collaborating on academic papers.

Everyone was calling anyone they could for whatever new glimmer of treatment possibility was out there. Things "were happening in other parts of the world that we weren't aware of," Rajwani explained. "Really, not until we dealt with our version. We were start-ing to get some information from Europe and we had some better sense of what we were dealing with, but the initial reports that had come out of China, they had their own versions of gag orders, et cetera. It really made it hard."

He did have a close partner beyond the hospital borders. Ibra-him Hassan, one of his co-fellows from Cornell (and the best man at his wedding), was in Qatar, where the ICUs were also filling up. The two of them "would exchange notes frequently in terms of what they were seeing and what we were seeing in the ICUs and how the disease was progressing. He was my go-to person in terms of things that they were doing.

"I think the sharing of information, just as clean as possible and regular, made things move along faster. People were able to say, 'This didn't work. Don't waste your time on this. We've tried X, Y, and Z,' or 'We've tried this and it didn't work.' When you're working in the dark, you're feeling like you're trying to figure out something for the first time. It motivates everything."

Given the risks, Rajwani and his colleagues decided to be conser-vative with the dosage. The steroid they tried was called methylpred-nisolone, and the dosing was weight-based. (Eventually they would determine a standard dose.) Later, when it became clear that steroids helped many patients, a randomized trial was conducted, and the data corresponded to what the 5 South team had seen.

But while steroids helped, the effect was far from instantaneous, and there was still a spectacular backlog of sick patients trying to get in. "Whenever you could, if you had a few open beds, you would try to negotiate a transfer here or there," he said. "Lindsay did the bulk of it during the daytime . . . but we all had our opportunity to take those calls. The heartbreaking ones were when you said, 'Sorry, I don't have any beds for you tonight.'"

The thirty-eight-year-old Hayward had been given the onerous task of determining which patients were put on ventilators and which were not. As the first attending to be summoned to the ED— and with his extra training in palliative care—he understood the complexity of counseling families. "Can you save this person? Or, if you can't, can you alleviate suffering in some way?" Anytime there's a critical-care consult or somebody becomes critically ill, these questions come up, so to have one person able to address them all is like a two-for-one deal. Kelly Griffin, who ran 5 South at nights, and Hayward made the most harrowing decisions again and again from the earliest days. "I was on the schedule and the next week I was back in the ICU and I said, 'I feel like we are used to seeing what the trajectory of patients looks like.'" Hayward and Griffin spoke often and were close. "The system kept changing. It didn't make sense for us to keep trying to teach someone else," Hayward said. Triage decisions were highly delicate and intuitive, based on deep clinical knowledge. In the first week of March, with only ten COVID patients admitted, the idea of battlefield conditions seemed remote, although Martinez and Brodie had been told by Italian doctors about the carnage they were facing and warned of how unpredictable the disease was. "I told Lindsay and Brad and Kapil and all of the team, 'This is going to be really bad in New York. We have to do everything to prepare,'" Fernando Martinez said.

Park Slope is an elegant Brooklyn neighborhood of brownstones and cafés and bookstores that borders Prospect Park, codesigned by Frederick Law Olmsted, a Staten Island farmer who toured England in the 1850s and returned to New York to create first the nearly 850-acre Central Park and then Brooklyn's more than 500-acre oasis of fields and ponds. New York-Presbyterian Brooklyn Methodist is a historic community hospital a few blocks from the park, and in early March, the respiratory therapist Felix Khusid was in its ICU when he noticed something peculiar during a routine procedure.

"What the hell is this? Is this Dracula blood?" he asked one of the doctors who was in the ICU. The blood, which usually spurted through a needle, came out in gluey clots. "Have you ever seen anything like this?" he asked the intensivist.

"This blood—it wasn't just dark," Khusid recalled. "It was, like, literally so hypercoagulated that it was almost like mercury from the thermometer that you shatter. Usually, if you try to get rid of air bubbles in the syringe just to make sure you have pure blood, some of the normal blood from the syringe would splatter. Not this one."

The fact that Khusid was the one to notice this was not a surprise; he was as expert as any physician on blood and coagulation and how the airways and lungs could benefit from every kind of oxygen device. He could talk your head off about ventilators that flutter, not roar; ventilators that didn't overwhelm the lungs with their blasts of air; and ventilators that were garbage. His knowledge was encyclopedic: He could reel off serial numbers and manufacturers as effortlessly as a Yankees fan spewing World Series stats. Khusid had an autodidact's passion for the history of ventilator machines and the decades of advances in administering oxygen since the 1940s, when respiratory therapists were called "oxygen jockeys" and used rubber tubes and masks or oxygen tents.

It was impossible not to pay attention to Khusid. First, there was his accent, with the strong sound of his childhood spent in Ukraine. Khusid's backstory somehow flowed into every encounter, his speech peppered with exhortations to Hashem (a Hebrew reference to God); he often mentioned the experiences of his parents, Jewish doctors in Odessa who had come to New York speaking almost no English. And while his family—thanks to an international pressure campaign—had been able to flee the virulent anti-Semitism of the Soviet government, like so many refuseniks, they had to give up their

careers to emigrate, leaving behind practices in radiology and gastroenterology.

Since January, Khusid, insatiable in his desire to understand the
new disease, had been on multiple calls with the hospital respiratory
therapists (RTs) to discuss the equipment needed. Nothing about
this was casual for him. Khusid had been determined to be a doctor
when he landed at Kennedy Airport in 1981 at the age of sixteen.
The Khusids were met by representatives of HIAS, the renowned
Hebrew Immigrant Aid Society, who gave them a cash stipend of
one hundred dollars and directed them to a hotel at Seventy-Ninth
and Broadway that housed the homeless; they'd stay there until an
apartment could be found for them. At his first American grocery
store, Khusid's father filled a grocery basket with what he thought
was inexpensive tinned meat. "Why are you buying so much cat
food?" a Russian-speaker asked him. To support themselves, his parents cleaned offices and hotel rooms.

Khusid was stunned at the size of the Checker cabs and at what
New Yorkers put out in their trash at night—TVs and radios and
books and uneaten pastries and bread still in its wrapping. One
night he spotted a newish radio and lunged for it—and so did a
homeless man nearby. A fight ensued; the homeless man got the
cord, Khusid the radio. Back in the room, he found some wires
and put it together and now he had a way to listen to music and
the news.

A few months later, an apartment was found for the Khusids in
Starrett City, Brooklyn. Khusid had to enroll at South Shore High
School, then one of the largest high schools in the country, although
he still spoke almost no English. He was placed in a class for the
intellectually challenged. "This is what level you tested," he was
told. Almost immediately, Khusid went to the blackboard and filled
it with complex equations of integrals and derivatives—assuming
that math was a universal language. "You can do that?" the stunned

teacher asked, and promptly found the proper place for the young man who had already had years of physics, chemistry, and calculus. It was a good welcome to America, and it was followed by another piece of good fortune a few years later. He had whittled down his dream of medical school (it was not affordable) and was training to be a respiratory therapist when, in his final semester at Long Island University, the welfare payments he relied on for support inexplicably stopped. How to turn this around? Khusid wrote heartfelt pleas to three powerful politicians, including Governor Mario Cuomo ("I thought of him as a bleeding-heart liberal for guys like me"), Mayor Ed Koch, a champion of the Russian Jewish community, and ultraconservative senator Al D'Amato, the lone Republican. Cuomo and Koch dismissed Khusid, but D'Amato responded immediately, sending him a letter that "arrived in a fancy red box with a gold seal that said 'U.S. Senate' and a ring binder with instructions to deliver a scathing letter to the local welfare office." D'Amato told Khusid to get back to him if the office did not reinstate his payments. Thirty-four years later, Khusid wrote to D'Amato to thank him. "I will never forget the impact you had on me and my family," Khusid wrote. "Thanks to you, I finished my studies and quickly found work as a respiratory therapist." He went on to tell D'Amato he was now the administrative director of respiratory therapy at NewYork-Presbyterian Brooklyn Methodist and had two children, one a urologic surgeon at Mount Sinai Hospital and another who had just started medical school at Weill Cornell.

In his first years as a respiratory therapist, because he spoke Russian and understood Yiddish, he was dispatched to the Brooklyn home of the grand rebbe of the Lubavitchers. The rebbe was a small man who came to rely on Khusid to assist with his breathing, and Khusid's name and reputation rocketed through their neighborhood in Brooklyn.

Long before Methodist Hospital (as it was originally known) was acquired by NewYork-Presbyterian, Khusid's reputation was such that Columbia ventilator experts put him on an acquisitions committee to weigh in on their choices. Known at the hospital as "the mad scientist," Khusid had a basement office that was jammed with every ventilator that had ever been used since the nineteenth century, a Miss Havisham museum parlor of equipment that featured Victorian copper tubes and a working model of the Babybird machine, named after its inventor, Forrest Bird, an aviation entrepreneur and doctor who helped develop the first mass-produced ventilators. One of Khusid's earliest acquisitions was a green-plastic-covered Bird Mark 7 model that had replaced the iron lung. The ventilator, which still had its blue sticker reading PROPERTY OF BROOKLYN RESPIRATORY HOME CARE, was a gift from one of his former professors. Not long after Brooklyn Methodist merged with NewYork-Presbyterian in 2016, Khusid was told that his dozens of machines had to be moved. He refused. "If they go, I go," he said. "This is history." Soon after, he received a visit from the head of HR, who spent an hour looking at Khusid's parlor of curiosities and then quickly rescinded the order.

Khusid had done his clinical rotations at Kings County Hospital Center, the largest public hospital in Brooklyn, at the peak of the AIDS crisis. Khusid had felt helpless seeing so many young people dying and not knowing what to do to save them—a feeling that would overcome him again in March 2020.

Lawrence Hospital in Bronxville, with its first wave of patients from New Rochelle, was the first hospital in the NewYork-Presbyterian system to be roiled by the staffing and infection issues that would within days overwhelm Queens and Brooklyn. The hospital, many believed, was the Alaska of the system, far afield from the Cornell and Columbia heavyweights. But it was also the proverbial canary in the coal mine, as cardiologist Mark Apfelbaum would later say, where the first signs of community spread were seen.

In the first days of COVID's Lawrence Hospital debut, Apfelbaum had turned to Jessica Forman, the physician assistant he relied on most. Forman had worked with Apfelbaum at Columbia at the outpatient center, helping to monitor cardiac patients with stents and artificial valves. Her specialty was atrial fibrillation, an arrhythmia that increases a patient's risk for stroke. To help prevent strokes, patients with atrial fibrillation are traditionally treated with blood thinners. The problem with blood thinners, however, is that they increase the risk of bleeding, either spontaneously or after a trauma. There was a new device that decreased those risks in patients with A-fib. "The Watchman device plugs off the left atrial appendage, where more than ninety percent of stroke-causing clots originate," Forman explained. "After you implant it, patients are able to come off blood thinners." The Watchman device had been available in Europe for years before the U.S. FDA approved it in March 2015, and it took nearly another year for a national coverage decision to be made, effectively limiting this lifesaving treatment to patients who could pay up to $125,000 for it out of pocket—a fact that infuriated her at the time.

Forman said she went into medicine to help people understand and battle the inequities of the U.S. medical system. The daughter of a doctor who had run medical schools in the Midwest, Forman, forty-seven when the pandemic began, was raising her thirteen-year-old daughter, Talia, on her own. She came from tough stock. Her grandmother had hidden in the forests of Belarus during World War II and made her way into Russia and the Ural Mountains. Like Lindsay Lief's mother, Forman's mother was born in a camp for displaced persons in Germany. The only possessions her grandmother had then were pictures of the family she had left behind—and she believed that those pictures, often carried by refugees, were what gave her grandmother and mother the will to keep going. Still, she remained in perpetual wonderment: What had given these women their resolve? How did they keep going forward when everyone around them was suffering and doom was almost certain?

"Do you think you could help us out in Bronxville?" Apfelbaum asked Forman. The idea was to pull her to Bronxville to help out in the new jerry-rigged ICU. It was the second week of March. Forman drove up and arrived at the hospital to see TV vans waiting near the parking lot. "When I pushed through the wooden doors of a new ICU they had put together, I saw that every single patient was on a ventilator. There were four people in the same room." Although Forman worked full-time at Columbia, she had assisted at Lawrence in the past, though never in an ICU setting. "I was immediately swept in by how much people were helping each other, and learning all of these procedures."

One person she knew at Lawrence was the interventional cardiologist Anthony Pucillo, a Renaissance man who had trained with Corwin and Apfelbaum at Columbia. A few years earlier, Pucillo had recruited Forman into a book club—W. Somerset Maugham, Thomas Hardy, and the like. He had a passion for jazz and American standards and—most of all—Frank Sinatra. The cardiologist often regaled Forman with stories about his training days in the 1970s, when he would come in to do a cardiology consult in shorts and a crop top; back then, the residents smoked cigarettes at the nurses' station.

Pucillo was doing everything he could to keep Lawrence staffed and also debating possible treatments. He found himself arguing with the Columbia team about the possibility of starting the COVID patients at Lawrence on blood thinners. While treating that first rush of COVID patients, Pucillo had noticed that many of them were clotting but also bleeding. "At the time, we were not sure of the exact mechanism," Forman said. "Or what was causing it—or where it was, in the brain, or the lungs or the hearts." They found that some COVID patients had elevated levels of cardiac troponins, indicators of damage to the heart muscle. The result was, in Forman's words, "a two-headed monster." Somehow you had to figure out how to do two contradictory things at once: thin and coagulate.

Forman thought about the doctors in the nineteenth century who were constantly experimenting, and she saw all of her own training in a different, urgent light. New ideas were needed, and they were needed right now. "It was terrifying but also exhilarating as the doctors became mavericks trying out ideas on their patients they hoped would work," she recalled. "Everyone was looking for guidance. Everyone was very transparent." As Rajwani had done when he was considering using steroids, Forman reached out to a colleague, in this case a friend in a hospital in Boca Raton. They spoke nightly, and when Forman heard about possible new protocols, she brought them to the Lawrence ICU director, who usually said, "Let's try this new protocol because, what the hell, it's not like anything else is working." As it turned out, Forman said, "All of the patients we didn't try new protocols with died." That didn't mean everything they tried worked—if only—but there were glimmers of hope. (Forman tried the combination of steroids, zinc, and vitamin C and saw immediate results with one patient.)

Forman decided that she could not keep Talia at home, not with the possibility that she could infect her. Early on, Forman had told her daughter, "Talia, I think you are not going back to school this year. . . . I don't see that anyone will be going back to school." Now it had to go further; Talia wasn't going to school, and she wasn't even going to stay in the place she thought of as home. Talia's father lived in Wurtsboro, a village of about a thousand people in Sullivan County, New York, an hour and a half north of the city. "Basically in the middle of nowhere," Forman said. But safer for Talia, at least for now.

———

On the first floor of the Columbia Medical Center, the COO, Laureen Hill, was hunkered down, making plans, haunted by a more primitive sort of danger. In February 2018, a twenty-seven-year-old had driven his car into the emergency entrance of a Middletown, Connecticut, hospital, then set himself on fire, all of it on Facebook Live. That the man seemed to be mentally ill (he claimed to be Jesus Christ and was attacking the hospital because it was one of Donald Trump's "headquarters") was irrelevant. She had just started at Columbia, and as soon as the news broke, Steve Corwin immediately called. "We need to act quickly," he said. And act Hill did, changing all the codes and entrances at every vulnerable entry point. She had concrete blocks installed in the driveways, added new security measures, and coordinated with NYPD plainclothes detectives so they would be ready should something arise. It wasn't just Middletown that was on her mind; in 2017, an immigrant from Uzbekistan had driven his pickup truck down a crowded bike path along the Hudson River, injuring eleven and killing eight. He stopped his rampage when he rammed into a school bus near Stuyvesant High School, got out of the truck, and ran down the street yelling "Allahu akbar!" as he waved a pellet gun and a paintball gun. It was the deadliest domestic terrorist attack since 9/11. Hill had seen what was going on in Europe in countries where COVID was raging—people were scared but also angry at the doctors who were telling them they had to lock themselves down but weren't offering a cure for what ailed them. What if the pandemic incited the same sense of rage in New York City? What if the enormous Columbia hospital complex was overrun by panicked crowds or there was a violent incident if the system could not admit all the patients, as happened in Italy?

She understood that hospitals were open to the public and were porous—almost anyone could come in. She thought of the Middletown hospital incident as foreshadowing—what would happen if New York had a true catastrophe in a pandemic and Columbia was overrun? The guards at Columbia were part of a special police detail and they had weapons; the driveways were blocked with concrete barriers, and security checks for everyone entering were now mandatory. The 2018 episode haunted Steve Corwin as well. The board debated: Should the hospital security teams be armed? They decided they'd arm security only at Columbia, because of its location in the high-crime area of Washington Heights—a policy that would be rescinded by the summer of 2020.

Hill worried about how to protect the hospital. She left her office late one night and rushed for the subway at 168th Street, and there she saw, standing on the corner, a guy selling N95s clearly stolen from the Columbia supply room. She'd thought that every mask she could control had been locked down. *How did he get those?* she wondered. *What am I going to do?*

Rosanne Raso was a true New Yorker, born in Park Slope, where her father had a pork store—Raso Sausage—on President Street and another in Bay Ridge. People in Raso's close-knit Italian family were never shy about expressing their opinions, a quality she shared and that helped her serve her nurses well as their chief advocate. She thought deeply about every aspect of her nurses' lives and was fiercely protective of their morale (a word she used frequently), battling whoever tried to implement a policy she thought would harm them. And because she was not only Weill Cornell's director of nursing but a fellow in the American Academy of Nursing and the editor in chief of the magazine *Nursing Management,* read by more than fifty thousand people all over the country, she had an outsize influence on how nurses were treated.

In the early days of the pandemic, Raso found herself facing perhaps the most overwhelming of all the problems the hospital was dealing with—how to provide trained nurses to take care of the most infectious patients. She would have to protect her staff, who were understandably worried about their own health. Word had circulated through the hospitals about all the nurses who were suddenly desperately ill—Karen Bacon in the ICU; Crishila Livacarri in Queens. She was obsessed with what was going on in the ER. "So, you have a ninety-eight-year-old who belongs in a nursing home, gasping for breath, and it was like, 'Really? Do we use a vent on her? And she's going to be paralyzed in the ICU for months? It just doesn't make any sense.'" She heard about patients who struggled to breathe but refused to be put on a ventilator and then died. The doctors and the nurses just had to watch them struggle to breathe—and they were horrified. "The families could not even be in the room with them when they died," she said. And she was especially worried about all the ethical issues that might even put her nurses' lives in danger.

Lacking guidance from above, Raso found herself counseling her nurses about their impossible choices. "What do you mean, he struggled to breathe? What we normally do for end-of-life patients that are on comfort care is give them a lot of morphine so that they are comfortable. . . . Do we do any end-of-life stuff that we normally do so that there was no suffering?" And how would anyone dealing with a COVID patient know if this was an end-of-life situation? There were larger ethical and legal implications of giving high doses of morphine—a nurse or a doctor could be accused of murder.

"We did not know what to do. . . . We were told not to let people wear masks in the beginning. That was terrible. But we were following the CDC," Raso said.

The first days of the pandemic siege, the nurses raged about the lack of scrubs, the lack of PPE, "but then the enterprise went over the top taking care of the nurses—providing meals, hotel rooms, getting scrubs, and the morale lifted," Raso said. They talked to their friends in other hospitals and realized those hospitals were so much worse.

Worse, but their own staffing issue was horrendous. "I walked into one of the patient rooms," Raso recalled, "and the strongest nurse we have was sobbing. She was so overwhelmed with grief. Her patient load had doubled and she had a helper nurse who did not know how to be an ICU nurse." She was not alone; everyone was dealing with double loads, and, as was the case for everyone treating COVID patients, it all took so much time. "If the bell would go off and a patient was in need," Raso explained, "the clerk goes to the console, who goes to the aide, who says, 'So-and-so is calling.' And then you have to put on PPE, which is very time-consuming. And you have to undress when you come out of the rooms. So the nurse is doing rooms and by the time they get in and get out and undress and re-dress to go to the room, it could be ten or fifteen minutes at least and that probably feels like a hundred years." The 114 ICU beds were all taken, but most of them had large glass windows where the nurses marked the blood gas numbers and kept track of medications. "Student nurses were not allowed in," Raso said. "It was too dangerous for them— and no extra help until the worst of it was over." In a meeting with Kate Heilpern and one of the corporate nursing directors, Raso wrote the number of nurses that she needed on a whiteboard. The corporate nursing director told her, "Take a Google Doc with the hundreds of nurses and just slot them in where they are needed." Raso flared: "Are you kidding me?" The director was suggesting that staff members, no matter their expertise, could just be yanked from one department and stuck in another. "Later that day I was over in the Koch building across the street from the hospital, where we had opened up a pop-up ICU in the middle of an ambulatory surgical unit, which was another craziness," she said. "And I saw [COO] Kate Heilpern. She asked me, 'Rosanne, how are you doing?' It was my worst moment. I said, 'Kate, if I could quit right now, I would. I am being undercut and undermined every day about staffing. I still have morale in the building and people are trying to destroy it. I know what I am doing.'"

Heilpern was shocked. "You are not quitting," she said.

The word always used for Noah Ginsberg, the head of Columbia's lab services, was *unflappable*—he was the master negotiator who had spent days in his Ford Explorer driving from FedEx warehouse to FedEx warehouse to meet the shipments of reagents the hospital was trying to stockpile for the coming days. Now Ginsberg found himself in the middle of a traffic jam in Times Square on the way up to the Bronx to FedEx because deliveries were so unreliable. (Ginsberg was sending cars and planes back and forth to Albany to pick up test kits because he could not trust FedEx.)

The traffic jam was the result of a city still going full tilt—the crowds were out in the surprisingly good early March weather. As Ginsberg waited for a light, he noticed the Disney characters that populated Times Square were all wearing masks with their costumes. *Holy shit,* he thought. He took his cell phone out, snapped a photo, and sent the picture to Senior Vice President Laureen Hill. *What are they getting that de Blasio and Cuomo are not?*

March 11, 2020, was a freakishly warm day in the city. Kerry Kennedy Meltzer, an internal medicine resident at Weill Cornell, and five other residents volunteered to do a COVID-19 information briefing at a Park Avenue South women's shelter. Slim as a wand and speaking in a low voice, Meltzer carried herself with restraint. Later, she would think of this night with intense embarrassment and berate herself for how deluded they had been to follow the guidelines that were coming from the CDC and the city and, for that matter, what was being told to patients at Weill Cornell. "We were advising a group of mostly Hispanic and Black women. We told them, 'Do not worry about this. Just wash your hands. Do not worry about wearing a mask. Think of this as something like the flu.'"

The day before, New York State had finally shut down New Rochelle, but the city remained wide open. A week earlier, Meltzer had been in Florida visiting her grandmother and uncle. "I was telling my uncle what a lot of people smarter than me were still saying, that it wasn't necessary to wear a mask! I would see people wearing masks on the streets and I would get annoyed—it was like they were taking masks away from the health-care workers. I was saying to my friends, 'This is so ridiculous that they were wearing masks.'"

Being mistaken on medical issues was a matter of the greatest sensitivity to her. Meltzer, a daughter of Maryland's former lieutenant governor Kathleen Kennedy Townsend and a granddaughter of Robert F. Kennedy, had grown up in a family obsessed with public service. The elderly grandmother she worried about was Ethel Kennedy. For years, Meltzer had tried to ignore the hectoring e-mails and obsessions of her uncle Robert F. Kennedy Jr. She tried to explain his fanaticism as coming from a good heart and a belief that corporations that manufactured chemicals had poisoned the environment with toxic waste. While that was demonstrably true—a fact that Robert Kennedy Jr. had exposed with Monsanto—his original campaign had been transformed into a far-flung everyone-is-evil global effort that included as its targets pharmaceutical companies and, in particular, vaccines.

As much as she loved her mother's brother, Meltzer had grown fed up with his endless campaigns against vaccinations and could not even imagine the harm he had caused to the many children whose parents followed his advice not to vaccinate their kids against measles and mumps. "I don't know why you don't block him," she told her older sister, the public health expert Maeve Kennedy McKean, a lawyer and human rights activist who ran the Georgetown University Global Health Initiative and had advised the State Department on AIDS during the Obama administration. But she couldn't block him—his corrosive messages seeped through social media, and he repeated them in his media appearances, and there was no way to completely muzzle his ludicrous, and dangerous, opinions. But if Meltzer couldn't stop him from talking, maybe she could find a way to talk back.

The same day that Meltzer and the Weill Cornell residents spoke at the women's shelter, at City Hall, Corey Johnson, the thirty-seven-year-old speaker of the New York City Council, sent a direct message on Twitter to CDC epidemiologist Jay Varma.

Varma and Johnson had met each other when they collaborated on an AIDS initiative for the city, but since Varma's move to Ethiopia, they had not stayed in touch.

"Jay, this is Corey Johnson. Do you remember me? I have a question for you about the new epidemic," Johnson wrote.

It was a few minutes before 9:00 p.m. in Addis Ababa. "We were leaving a birthday party at a hotel," Varma said, "and I called him, and he said, basically, 'I'm really worried. The governor and the mayor, nobody can seem to make a decision or take this epidemic seriously.' And I said, 'This is going to be a mess.'" Varma told Johnson that New York City should have already imposed restrictions on people's movement, should be closing the schools, should be doing all sorts of things to get ready.

The next days were a blur of calls and texts as countries around the world scrambled to close their borders. At the time, Varma was alone in Ethiopia. His older kids were already in the United States at college and boarding school, and by orders of the CDC, his wife and youngest had just evacuated in the effort to get nonessential Americans out of the country as COVID began to spread across the continent. He and his wife hadn't thought about returning to New York for at least a year, and they'd sublet their house in Park Slope as a result. His work in Ethiopia was deeply fulfilling, and the whole reason his wife and daughter weren't there now seemed precisely the reason he needed to stay there.

Still, he felt a patriotic and personal obligation to help New York. Plus, his wife and daughter were there, staying in a hotel. So, at night and in the early morning, he began writing out a hasty emergency plan for the city, sending Johnson advice about what should be done.

There were also numerous phone calls when Varma could get away from work, and in one conversation, Johnson asked him, "Could you speak to the mayor's deputy, Emma Wolfe?"

Wolfe was not only New York's deputy mayor but also de Blasio's chief of staff. She and Varma had met when he was at the city's health department but they were essentially strangers. Varma had told Johnson earlier, "Shut the city down. *Now.* And you must implement full-scale testing and tracing."

Wolfe asked if Varma would be willing to come back to New York and help them out. Varma insisted on speaking directly to the mayor. "I am not leaving Africa unless I have a direct leadership role," he said.

De Blasio and Varma had met when Varma and the department of health were dealing with the Ebola and Legionnaires' outbreaks. Now, on the phone, the mayor told him, "Well, we're committed to having you come back and you being my main adviser to help strategize for all this and our senior spokesperson for these things."

Varma had a clear understanding of the mayor's complexities. "He's very committed to certain things," he said. "He takes a lot of time to make decisions. Then when he finally makes them, because he's not a really day-to-day manager, he expects things to just happen." Varma, given reassurances by de Blasio, asked his wife what he should do. She said, "Of course get back here."

At Weill Cornell, Kirana Gudi, vice chair of medicine, was in lockdown in her office, her days a blur of questions that were impossible to answer. How many ICU beds? And with this many ICU beds, how many floor beds? How do we staff both of these at the same time? In one meeting, Tom McGrath, the head of business affairs for the department of medicine, took Nathaniel Hupert's calculations and said, "It is going to be three hundred twenty-something ICU beds and double that for the floor beds." Gudi walked through the numbers. "Okay, if we take this ICU, this ICU, the ones that we have, that is this many beds. Then we will need many, many more. Where can we put them? I don't know. . . . And then it was, 'Let's make a schedule. Here's where we can get this many residents from the department of medicine—we will take them out of outpatient, we'll take them out of lymphoma, we will take them off of cardio.'" Not admitting certain cases had distorted everything—the hospital had had no heart attack patients for three months. "I don't know what happened to all of those people," Gudi said.

"Cardiology fellows started taking care of those patients, and we took the residents out of that, and then we took residents from other departments. And we knew that if we got to two hundred and ninety-eight patients, I ran out of house staff. There was nobody else I could pull from anywhere. And early on, Art Evans and the chair of medicine, Tony Hollenberg, and I felt this was internal medicine's disease. Like we knew, 'This is what we know how to do, right?' So we were going to put ourselves out there before we started involving obstetricians, except for a few, and there were the lovely ENT residents who we sent to the pediatric ICU." Eventually, doctors and nurses from across the hospital would be called to treat COVID patients.

At Columbia, trained in disaster medicine, the COO, Laureen Hill, would later say, without a hint of embarrassment, that destiny had presented her with a crucible that would be the test of her lifetime. On March 11, almost a week before the hospital stopped all surgeries and the city shut down, she texted Stephen Rush, medical director of a unit of the PJs, the air force's elite pararescue force. The PJs were combat medics and rescue specialists who had been trained for unconventional (and conventional) rescue operations; they could enter enemy territory via water, land, or air, deploying in pretty much any way imaginable to reach, treat, and evacuate wounded American soldiers. The PJs were the only such group in the American military. (Such were their abilities that in 2018, they had been brought in by the government of Thailand to help rescue members of a soccer team trapped in an underwater cave.)

Help us, Hill messaged Rush.

They had met a decade earlier on a bike trip in Italy. As they pedaled through the Amalfi hills, Rush had explained how in his forties, feeling stuck in his career as a radiation oncologist in suburban Long Island, he decided he needed a greater challenge. When he saw that a job had opened up as a flight surgeon in the U.S. Air Force National Guard on Long Island, he had grabbed it and eventually risen to become a medical director, sharpening the training around the country. Among the groups he helped were the PJs.

After the bike trip, Hill and Rush had stayed in touch. At one point, "Doc Rush" (officially Colonel Rush), trying out a new training program for the PJs under his command, asked Hill if she could help him write some acute-care protocols. Over the next decade, he would reach out to Hill occasionally to review one of his articles or record a session on airway management. She also reviewed equipment the air force wanted to bid on.

"When I moved to New York, I wrote to him and said, 'Guess who is coming to New York?' And he said, 'What, where, how?' And I said, 'Senior vice president, Columbia Medical Center, COO,' and all I got back was 'Holy shit.'" When Hill arrived, she learned that Rush's daughter was a social worker at Columbia and his son was a radiology resident there.

Hill wasn't sure how Rush and the PJs could be brought in to help out if the hospital was overrun with cases or what the procedure would be to pull in recently retired medics. After all, the training that PJs received for rescues meant that many of them had ventilator and ICU expertise. They had a proven genius in getting people and equipment in and out of almost unreachable places under near-hopeless conditions. Hill decided she would keep Rush in the loop, just in case.

Within three weeks, two hundred retired PJs would be helping with patients and building two field hospitals, at Columbia and NewYork-Presbyterian Allen.

In Queens, ED nursing director Suzanne Pugh knew her concern about capacity at the hospital was justified, but she wondered if it was shared at the executive level. "I don't think the corporate office trusted us at first. By the third week of March, our numbers had risen exponentially, and the acuity was outrageous. We were putting people on ventilators at a rate that was hard to believe. It was so startling that Dr. Forese herself called and said, 'This is crazy. You can't possibly be seeing this number of patients. This cannot be true.' She wanted to know, 'Are you admitting appropriately?'"

Pugh tried to control her temper. "I was like, 'Oh, right. You are sitting where you are, and I am at the hospital looking at the patients.' It was frustrating," she said. While the explosion of cases in Queens was predictable, given the borough's Chinese American population, the rate of infection was stunning. "We started seeing eighty to a hundred patients a day," Pugh said. "And had no place to put them." It made sense, but the curve was so steep, it was literally mind-boggling. "Laura had a hard time understanding. Columbia and Cornell had about fifteen or twenty [COVID patients] in their ERs, and Queens had a hundred. She couldn't understand. 'How could Queens have a hundred patients?'"

Forese quickly assigned a clinical person to analyze the Queens charts, and that person told her, "No, this is very real." If she needed more confirmation, it came from outside her system: Elmhurst Hospital, one block from NewYork-Presbyterian. "When they left us," Manish Sharma, chief of the emergency department at NewYork-Presbyterian Queens, said, "they would go home and later wind up in Elmhurst." Unsurprisingly, Elmhurst became far and away the city's most overwhelmed hospital, and details of its sky-rocketing patient load began to hit the papers. "There was one week-end when they totally closed," said Manish. "They had no beds, no equipment, no ventilators." It was a wake-up call. "Before that," Man-ish said, "we had three or four calls where they were saying, 'Oh my God, are you sure?' And we were saying, 'Oh my God, yes.'" Within two days of Pugh's call with Forese, the hospital was provided with a large tent to try to handle the overflow. In a weekend, they converted a downstairs storage area into thirteen rooms for COVID patients.

At Weill Cornell, Bradley Hayward would think of the first weeks of March as a blur, a time-lapse dissolve of streets becoming de-serted and stores shuttering as he walked toward the hospital from his apartment on the Upper West Side, his passage through Central Park almost disorienting. The pond was still there, the bridges were holding up, the fences were still up, the views of the surrounding buildings the same, but with each crossing, it felt more like a facade.

And then there were the signs that appeared in windows: N95 MASKS IN STOCK. LIMITED SUPPLY. WASH YOUR HANDS LIKE YOU JUST SHOOK THE HAND OF THE PRESIDENT!! LIVE MUSIC @930/HAPPY HOUR 4–830—that one on a blackboard at Brandy's, a piano bar on East Eighty-Fourth Street off Second Avenue, residue from the last days of the city without abandon.

On March 12, there were ninety-five people who had tested positive in all of New York. Matt McCarthy texted a close friend that when China had twenty-two cases, they had already built two hospitals. Yet the White House, seemingly concerned only with the possibility that a pandemic could tank the market, believed—in line with their overall antipathy to science—that the disease could be contained if another cruise ship, the *Grand Princess,* was kept from docking. ("I don't need to have the numbers double because of one ship that wasn't our fault," the president announced when he refused to let the passengers disembark.)

One week earlier, speaking at a Fox News town hall in Scranton, Pennsylvania, the hometown of Democratic hopeful Joe Biden, Trump had been asked if he thought the COVID pandemic would have an effect on the economy. "It's all going to work out," he said. "Everyone has to stay calm." That same week, Rush Limbaugh told his fifteen million listeners that COVID-19 was like the common cold and that "all of this panic is just not warranted."

As anyone who has studied infectious diseases knows, the fastest way for a disease to get out of control is for a large number of uninfected people to gather with a few infected people (or maybe even just one infected person). New York's St. Patrick's Day parade has long been one of the city's most attended celebrations. The weekend before, Ellen Corwin had turned to her husband and said, "What is the cardinal going to do about the St. Patrick's Day parade? You must call him. Now." In fact, it was Laura Forese who would make the call.

In her mind was the catastrophe that had overcome Philadelphia in September 1918. As the Spanish flu ravaged the country, Philadelphia's leadership had taken the position that hysteria about the pandemic was unwarranted, and they went ahead with the city's Liberty Loans Parade. Thousands flocked downtown to support the fundraiser for the doughboys overseas. Within days, scores of Philadelphians were collapsing on the street, unable to breathe as their lungs filled with fluid. Thousands became infected. The morgue, which had room for thirty-six bodies, had hundreds of corpses to process. Of all the cities in America, Philadelphia had the highest death rate from the Spanish flu—more than twelve thousand dead—in part due to its failure to cancel the parade.

All this history loomed in Steve Corwin's mind too. Like George W.

Bush, he and Ellen were both familiar with what was detailed in John Barry's *The Great Influenza*, and they understood what happened when you ignored history. But not the mayor of New York, who not only refused to cancel the parade but insisted it take place—this despite the fact that Boston, Chicago, Philadelphia, Pittsburgh, and even Ireland had canceled their own parades. In the end, it was Cuomo who made the call, and the chair of the parade's board, Sean Lane, made the announcement that the event would be postponed indefinitely, the first time New York's Irish had not been celebrated in 258 years.

At Weill Cornell, from 5 South, Hayward was repeatedly summoned to the emergency department to evaluate patients who had come in with COVID symptoms. Those evaluations were not always strictly medical. Hayward had done a fellowship in hospice and palliative care, so he was experienced in counseling the dying—and their families. On 5 South he was the expert on moral and ethical issues about end-of-life matters. Over the next year, that expertise would be employed more times than he had ever imagined possible.

There was no question of his deep commitment to his patients, which helped him empathize with their situations—but that emotional connection sometimes made his work even more heartbreaking. Early on, he would be called to the ED to consult on several of his own patients, some of whom he had grown fond of during the course of their relationship. Now Hayward had to decide whether to intubate them or not. When Hayward got to the patients' rooms, they were sometimes on six liters of oxygen—the maximum the 5 South team felt comfortable with after studying the protocols coming from Europe. "At that point, early in the pandemic, we had made the decision to intubate early because we thought it might be beneficial—there was no other way to treat acute disease. But these patients were saying, 'I don't want to be intubated. I don't want to be intubated.'

And they were often also kind of delirious." Hayward would call their children, who would consent to intubation. The team then intubated the patients and moved them to one of the pop-up ICUs.

Hayward continued to follow these cases closely, as did the patients' families, who, as they thought more about the brutality of intubation, often regretted allowing it. "The families would withdraw [their permission for] the ventilators," Hayward recalled. "Their thought was that their loved ones would not want to live this way." The patients would be taken off the ventilators, and, as expected, they died.

Hayward was haunted by the outcomes. The staff was in constant communication with doctors in Italy and former colleagues in Seattle who said that if patients did not improve on six liters of oxygen, they should be intubated. But every disease had its peculiarities, and at the time there were no real protocols—at NewYork-Presbyterian or anywhere else in the world—for treating COVID patients. No one had had the opportunity to do research, to assemble reports; there was no handbook that said, *In this situation, you should do this*. Hayward wondered if they'd made a terrible mistake, that perhaps the patients' fears of intubation were justified.

"As a group, that was what we thought was medically sound," Hayward said. "And now we see that some people may not have needed to be intubated. And it makes me wonder: If we hadn't had that policy, would he still be alive now?" There was no way to know.

"We were acting as a cohesive group. We would say to each other, 'What is the limited data we have? We have been calling pulmonologists all over the city.' It was like, 'Have you guys seen this?' People were having weird rashes, for example. And we would say, 'Are your patients having rashes? Are all of your patients clotting their dialysis machines?' It was scary." It was, admittedly, an interesting time to be a doctor, he said, "because we were all discovering things at the same time. We had so many different phone calls talking to people around the country." Nobody had any certainty though. "We were seeing what we thought was the right next step—and then changing. We kept changing our protocols as we learned more."

Everything about the disease was new: The white clouds of infection on the X-rays. The mucus that felt like chewing gum. The fact that patients' oxygen levels were so low but at first they did not seem sick. "You would expect that with oxygen levels this low, they would be much sicker. And they were saying they felt fine. It was a disconnect. We were wondering, *Am I crazy? Why are they requiring so much oxygen and they are saying they are not feeling sick?* It was very difficult. Patients would call in to our pulmonary practice and say, 'I have fevers and chills but I feel fine.' We would say, 'You have to check your oxygen levels because if they are low, you will have to go to a hospital.' But then we would say, 'But you shouldn't go to the hospital because it's risky to go to a hospital.' Our usual way of evaluating patients was turned around." Everyone in the country was following New York's lead, since it had become the epicenter of the virus, but even the best of the best at NewYork-Presbyterian were at sea. From Los Angeles, the mystery writer Charles Finch sent Matt McCarthy, among his closest friends from Yale, a message on Slack. *What's the first date on the calendar that we'll wake up and not think about corona for an entire day? May 12th?*

That's when it'll be peak corona, dude, McCarthy replied.

What? This is not the peak?

Charlie, it hasn't started yet, McCarthy wrote back.

Nathaniel Hupert was unable to sleep, he was so terrified by what his modeling numbers were showing. When not checking his calculations again and again, he dealt with patients at his office in Lower Manhattan. Like his colleagues, he remained stymied by the scarcity of equipment and common sense. Frantic to get one patient from Chinatown tested, he explained to someone in the city's department of health, "The guy is from Chinatown! No, he hasn't been to Wuhan but he lives in the Asian community where there is every opportunity for exposure." No dice.

In a swirl of frustration, he sent his first models to the Greater New York Hospital Association, the all-powerful lobbying group run by Ken Raske, a player of such connections that he helped direct how the state regulated all of New York's hospitals, from the rules about Medicare reimbursements to the hospital unions' compensation. Raske had left Michigan and come to New York when the city's hospitals—including Columbia—were more or less bankrupt, trying to navigate the new world of corporate medicine. He had arrived in debt and built up an empire of influence, including supply companies that sold hospital PPE and equipment. He was now paid over ten million dollars a year and presided over an impressive suite of offices near the Hudson River with a boardroom that could seat one hundred. It was there, in the first days of March, that Raske and his staff hunkered down in the deep green leather chairs that circled a U-shaped table—twenty chairs to a side—to monitor the news from Italy and China on the big screens that nearly covered three walls of the room. During his time in the job, Raske, a husky redhead who lived close to Young Israel in New Rochelle, had negotiated with two governors with the last name Cuomo—Mario and then his son Andrew, with whom he remained close.

Still, Raske had no control over the hiring of management-consultant behemoth McKinsey and Company to advise New York State at a cost of ten million dollars, approved in the state capital of Albany with little debate. McKinsey would quintuple its own earnings in 2020, bringing in over a hundred million dollars in revenue advising cities and states. McKinsey was running an aggressive campaign to rake in state and national business, ProPublica would later report, including having one of the company's partners in the Washington office badger a former colleague now working in a leadership role in the Department of Veterans Affairs. On March 19, McKinsey partner Scott Blackburn wrote an unusual e-mail to Deb Kramer, the undersecretary of the Department of Veterans Affairs, stating that they had to hire McKinsey in the next twenty-four hours. She responded immediately. "There is no time to spare," the Veterans Affairs contracting document stated, adding that "every day wasted by a lack of situational awareness down to the community level, and the inability to model scenarios . . . increases the risks to the citizens of this nation." Kramer approved the twelve-million-dollar price tag.

Hupert had been hearing about McKinsey's New York City projections—forty thousand ventilators and over a hundred thousand patients to hit the hospitals—and was increasingly baffled by their magnitude. He understood the catastrophe that could happen if the state relied on wildly inflated numbers—a belief in the severe shortage of beds and equipment could result in patients, still infected with COVID, to be placed in facilities without adequate safety protocols, endangering thousands of lives. At first, many would commend the governor for wanting to be prepared, insisting that hospitals double the number of beds and the city commit tens of millions of dollars for field hospitals. All of this was admirable and might prove necessary if the McKinsey and Columbia and NYU numbers turned out to be correct. What was so disturbing for the city and state leadership, as well as for the hospitals and modeling teams, was the awareness that the urgency could be short-lived and set off a cascade of unanticipated consequences that could also threaten lives. Hupert was commuting back and forth between his home in Princeton and the hospital in Lower Manhattan, getting into standoffs with the hospital's epidemiologist Harjot Singh because of the welder's shield and the painter's garb he now wore. "You can't wear that around the hospital," Singh told him. "You could infect everyone with that." Hupert ignored her. His overwhelming desire was to get someone in leadership to pay attention to his models.

For the first ten days of March, he was in frequent touch with Celia Quinn at the city's department of health, whom he had known when she was part of the CDC's elite virus detectives, the epidemic intelligence service officers, tracking Ebola in the field. He was also in touch with Raske's deputy, who had been trying to get Raske to focus on Hupert's projections: ten thousand patients, more or less, in the city hospitals.

On March 12, the day after Cuomo declared a state of emergency, Hupert finally received a message from Raske to call him. "Nathaniel, the governor and Michael Dowling [head of Northwell Health] and I have been reviewing your numbers. We would like you to come to work for us immediately as our full-time modeler."

"Okay," Hupert said. "But you need to reach out to NewYork-Presbyterian and have me relieved of my clinical duties."

And still, the mayor and the governor would not shut down the city. Raske, desperately concerned by the projections McKinsey and other modelers had come up with, wanted a backup. He was convinced that McKinsey's numbers were "patently absurd," he later said. The reality would be horrible enough—within six weeks ten thousand patients would surge into the New York City hospitals. "We were five percent away from breaking the backbone of the New York health-care system. And we would not have had any place to put these sick people—and we would have ended up stacking them up in hallways," Raske remembered. Frantic at what the hospitals were about to face, Raske's staff reached out to Amtrak to resurrect the World War II hospital trains. "We knew what bad shape the patients were in and we knew we could not fly them out on C-5 supersonic military transport flights but we thought we could use trains and ship them to Boston, Philadelphia, San Antonio—wherever there was space in a hospital," Raske said. Within a week, he had organized a daily 10:00 a.m. briefing call with the chairmen of the five New York City nonprofit academic hospitals—Montefiore, NewYork-Presbyterian, Mount Sinai, NYU Langone, and North-well Health, which includes Lenox Hill Hospital.

In Midtown at the corporate office, the chief information officer of NewYork-Presbyterian, Daniel Barchi, was in constant communi-cation with Steve Corwin and Jerry Speyer. On March 13, he began to e-mail a leadership circle of hospital chairmen around the country whom he knew well. "We were the absolute first major city to have to deal with this," Barchi said. "And I wanted them to have a sense in real time of what was coming." His e-mails were stark—and deeply troubling.

3/13

Friends:
It is getting very real very quickly.
  My quick advice is

• Bolster your organization's ability to support work from home (including equipment and timekeeping)
• ensure you have significant teleconference/webex capability
• make new future appointments default to telemedicine visits when possible both for safety and to minimize appointment cancellation (many patients electing to cancel in-patient visits)

- ensure your EMR teams are ready to make rapid changes to add decision logic for screening or for special test ordering (who can order/how do you manage/support)
- We set up an information line … with information and added it as an option to the phone tree of all our practices, EDs and hospitalists to decant significant call volume. If you listen to the end of the message, you can choose an option to talk to a PA. It is also a front door to our online urgent care telemedicine visits.

Barchi had no idea that his quick corporate memos—written as notes to his friends—would become a template for how medicine would be practiced for years to come.

The second week in March, the city and the country were react-ing to an onslaught of breaking news: The president had banned all travel from Europe. Tom Hanks and his wife, the actress Rita Wilson, announced they had contracted COVID at a film shoot in Australia. The news of their illness made headlines around the world and brought into sharp relief how real—in case anyone still had doubts—this public health crisis truly was. On and on it went as the world turned upside down—the NBA suspended basketball. And somehow in the frenzy, the film producer Harvey Weinstein was found guilty after years of alleged sexual assaults, and was sen-tenced to twenty-three years in prison in a Manhattan courtroom where few wore masks. That Friday, Forese told Steve Corwin, "We are going to need to shut down all elective surgery." All that week-end, chief of surgery Craig Smith and the other division leaders dis-cussed at length how this would work, which surgeries would be triaged, which would go forward. The new policy was put in place immediately, and on March 16, NewYork-Presbyterian announced it would be the second major academic hospital center (following Mass General) to temporarily stop all elective surgeries. The news shook the city and the country—at no time in America had a public health crisis caused this level of hospital disruption.

The decision to stop performing elective surgeries was not just about keeping the noninfected from entering the hospital and getting COVID—it was about real estate. No operations meant no need for operating rooms.

"Steve, are you busy tomorrow? I hate to bother you."

At Columbia, critical-care anesthesiologist Oliver Panzer sounded apologetic when he reached anesthesiologist Steven Miller late on the evening of March 13. Panzer had just come from an emergency meeting in Hill's office with Dan Brodie and Dave Wang. At the meeting they laid out yellow tape on the floor and on large charts to see which operating rooms could be turned into ICUs. "We are going to the ORs tomorrow and could use some help," Panzer said. With Panzer and Wang had been the head of construction, Edo Volaric.

"The atmosphere was somewhere between intensity and anxiety," Miller recalled. "How do we make it safe? Where do we put the beds? Where do we put the hoses? We stole them from all over the hospital . . . we knew it was going to be bad and we were preparing for worst-case scenario."

Columbia had thirty-two operating rooms throughout its substantial facilities. The engineering teams had three days to turn all but eight of them into ICUs and then add thirteen more ICUs from other spaces. "We started laying out all of the floors—we thought we might be able to stretch to put eight people in a room," Miller said. "Where do we need more pipes for oxygen? What would we do for internet connections? Where are the jacks going? There were so many logistics." The next step was to bring in the engineers. "How do you retrofit twenty-three operating rooms? Where could thirty-six ICUs go? How would we have ventilators to cover?" It was easy to map all of this out and forget a huge detail—such as how they would get the patients in and out of the rooms.

The anesthesiology chief Ansgar Brambrink had tasked Oliver Panzer and David Wang with the immense mission of converting all the ORs to ICUs in just ninety-six hours. "As the pandemic hit, we were creating the largest ICU in the city. The ventilators weren't running short yet, but we knew they were going to run short," said Miller. "Were there going to be machines we could repurpose to ventilate the patients? The anesthesia machine is basically an older-model ventilator and also delivers anesthetics. And the anesthesia department in any hospital is the number one department for ventilating patients." At Columbia, there were approximately 110 surgeries a day, and an anesthesiologist was at every surgery. How to repurpose those machines? Miller was known in the department for his passion for mechanical tinkering, an engineer without portfolio who was often asked to help out with balky anesthesia machines. His amateur skill set was now called upon to make the machines mobile and set them up so they actually worked in their new purpose.

The original plan was to do the fourth floor first, the cardiac floor. There were more electrical outlets, for starters, and more anesthesia machines than on other floors in the hospital. Critical care had evolved to be one patient per room to reduce noise and help staff focus. "Repurposing these rooms took medicine back to the 1930s and 1940s, where critical care was a ward—a giant room with a curtain." The ORs were outfitted with built-in gas outlets that allowed them to be refitted rapidly. The decision was made not to use inhaled anesthetics as sedation with intubations—a patient could have a rare bad reaction, and a patient having a bad reaction in a room with six patients and a total of forty patients on the floor with overwhelmed doctors and nurses running between that floor and another one that also had rooms of six patients and a total of forty patients . . . what might have been rare but controllable was just too risky.

Converting the ORs had doubled the hospital's ICU capacity, which was essential if they wanted to have even a hope of keeping up. But, of course, more room for the very sick meant more risk of infection for those working in the hospital. Hill, a critical-care anes-thesiologist by training, pressed the doctors: "'Just tell me, what do I need to do to keep the staff safe?' We came up with the idea of using the massive industrial-strength HEPA filters."

For all of this to work, you needed air systems that allowed you to regulate pressure inside and outside of rooms. This was, to put it mildly, problematic. Explained Miller, "When you open the door, it sucks the air in . . . the only way the system can be regulated is with a positive-pressure system." However, "if you turn off that system, the room [is] sweltering within minutes and there would be no airflow."

They decided they would turn the positive-pressure system on very low, and, by punching holes through the doors and walls and then installing two industrial fans per operating room along with giant industrial filters, they would create, as Miller described it, "a massive negative system" in each of the ORs.

"It was like a forty-eight-hour process. It was unbelievable. I did not oversee the conversion of the operating rooms to the OR-ICUs—or the ORICUs, they called them. But it was an in-credible feat." Stripping down and refurbishing the rooms was a revelation—that it could be done so quickly, but also they would notice what the rooms lacked. "We worked in ICUs for years, and we never thought about where the electrical outlet for something was," he said. As it turned out, among the many complications the NewYork-Presbyterian doctors and nurses dealt with during the surge was just how many rooms lacked extra outlets. When you put four people into a space meant for one, you needed four times as many outlets—but they weren't there, so what could you do?

By March 14, Lindsay and Jake Lief had made the agonizing decision that it was far too risky for Freedom and Madiba to stay in the city. Lief was especially worried for Madiba, who was only six. Jake's parents had a house in Maine, but that was many hours from New York City. That kind of distance was agony for the family to contemplate. Lief reached out to Liz, whose husband, Daniel Squadron, had been a state senator. What was really going on in New York? If anyone would know, it was Daniel. The Squadrons had a house a few hours away from the city, near Hudson, New York. Now if only Jake and Lief could find an affordable cottage to rent close to Liz.

On March 14 at 3:30 p.m., Lindsay texted Liz:

Lindsay: *Why aren't schools closed*

Liz: *I thought cause what you said. Hospitals and other essential services would shut down?*

Lindsay: *Yes I guess You upstate? Jake is about to rent something.*

Liz: *Yes. Where?*

Lindsay: *Do you think you are coming back?*

Liz: *I don't know*

Lindsay: *Elizaville*

Liz: *I feel so weird about everything*

Lindsay: *Looks like 20 minutes from you. Me too*

Liz: *I would feel better if they were up here*

Lindsay: *They refuse to go to Maine because it's too far from me and I feel guilty. And I keep breaking down into tears 100 times a day*

Liz: *Do you want to talk?*

Five days later, Lindsay texted Liz:

Lindsay: *Morning. How are you? Meant to text yesterday. How's Daniel and what's going on with Anne?*

Liz: *I'm ok! How are you????*
I love you. Thinking about you all the time.

Lindsay: *Thanks. Love you too.*
How were boys?

Liz: *Boys are good. Looking forward to seeing you in a few days.*

Lindsay: *good. (Me too)*
Jake said they're struggling.

Liz: *It's so hard. Poor little sweeties. Their cousins will help. Don't forget they are "mag a nets"*

Lindsay: *I mean, I actually think I forgot until they FaceTimed me the other day!*

Liz: *Did they say it? Remember we were nervous when they were babies that they wouldn't be besties like the big ones*

Lindsay: *Yes. Madiba was squishing his face to the camera and they were talking about [it]. Yes. funny.*

Liz: *Cuuute*

Lindsay: *Yes Love You. I'm going to bed.*

From her West Village co-op, the medical director of the Allen emergency department, Lorna Breen, had no intention of changing her yearly ski vacation with her sister Jennifer and her brother-in-law, Corey Feist. In the first week of March, Breen was on her way to Big Sky, Montana. Breen's alpha glamour was part of her nature, as was her meticulous planning. Breen—the medical director of the emergency department at NewYork-Presbyterian Allen, the campus at the northernmost tip of Manhattan with one of the most at-risk populations in the city—often scheduled events months in advance and would send her calendar to those she was close to. The trip was over spring break, a chance for Breen to share her passion for skiing and snowboarding with her niece and nephew. But by that time, the hospital was veering toward a crisis. There were still those who thought that maybe, somehow, New York would not become Italy or Wuhan—the last moments of magical thinking before the city shut down.

Already, the first pop-up ICUs had been built in Bronxville, and Lawrence Garbuz was on a ventilator. One hundred twenty-five of Breen's colleagues at Lawrence Hospital were already quarantined. Laureen Hill had already established her command center and was preparing Columbia for what was coming. Lindsay Lief had seen Nathaniel Hupert's modeling and was preparing the ICUs at Weill Cornell for a thousand patients. Italy was going into complete lockdown, and Italian physicians were texting their Columbia colleagues about the crisis as Breen, the confident, adventure-loving ED doctor who drove a sports car and always wore Jimmy Choos, flew to Montana. She had a wide-open smile and radiated confidence, but she was deeply concerned about burnout in her workplace.

All that week, Breen mostly stayed off the detailed emergency-planning Zoom meetings conducted by NYP emergency department director Angela Mills and her medical directors. As Mills was implementing a new structure and assigning a crisis-management person for each ED to interpret all the shifting protocol policies for the staff, Breen tried to dial down. When Breen returned to New York, the ED that had been completely under her control was organized in a crisis structure that she had not helped plan.

The fact that Breen went on her planned vacation did not surprise Mills. "These doctors are under such stress, they need the break. It's important." Breen was known for her sangfroid—as well as a certain hauteur, which alienated some of the nurses. She carried herself with the confidence of the daughter of a trauma surgeon. Breen was the third of four children; she and her younger sister, Jennifer, had shared a bedroom. Their mother, a former psychiatric nurse, occasionally dressed them in identical clothes. But when Breen was in high school, her parents divorced. Breen went to the Wyoming Seminary in Pennsylvania for boarding school and became determined to follow her father's career path, as her older brother had (he became a radiologist). She was a straight-A student—"the smartest one in the family," her sister told *Vanity Fair* writer Maureen O'Connor. Breen went to Cornell as an undergraduate, got her medical degree at the Medical College of Virginia, and did a combined residency in emergency medicine and internal medicine at Long Island Jewish Medical Center.

Breen appeared to share her father's easy aura of "We've got this covered." She seemed always in motion—she played the cello in an orchestra, ran marathons, belonged to a Bible study group, and liked to salsa dance and throw rooftop parties, O'Connor noted. But for all the activity, she was fiercely protective of her private life; it was as if a moat kept her from intimate connection.

Angela Mills was Breen's boss and mentor; she admired Breen's rigor for patient care. They had known each other for only three years, since Mills moved to Columbia from her job as the ED director at the Hospital of the University of Pennsylvania. Mills was highly sensitive to race disparities in health care and was drawn to Columbia because its ED served the diverse communities of Washington Heights and Inwood and parts of the Bronx. With Breen, she helped bring stroke care to the Allen and a telehealth program for neurologists.

Breen had a special closeness with her sister, her brother-in-law Corey Feist, and their children. A decade earlier, their six-year-old son had contracted the flu during the H1N1 pandemic and was in an ICU at UVA's University Hospital, where Corey was the head of the medical group. That was Breen's first intimate encounter with a pandemic. In Montana, however much she wanted to disconnect from the new pandemic, in between black-diamond runs with her twelve-year-old niece, Breen kept a keen eye on the news and took calls from colleagues. Every so often, according to *Vanity Fair*'s O'Connor, she told her sister and brother-in-law, "This is really bad. This country isn't ready. We don't have the supplies. We don't have the protocols."

Craig Smith, the chief of surgery, had a special status at Columbia—and, for that matter, in the world of cardiac surgery. Of all the heart centers in the United States, Columbia is among the most elite. For decades, it has performed thousands of heart and lung transplants, a fact that was largely the result of the work of Smith, who has also led Columbia HeartSource for the last several decades, an organization that creates cardiovascular centers of expertise at hospitals around the nation. He had trained over 350 cardiothoracic surgeons and published hundreds of academic papers, and his lab churned out many experiments with lasers and high-tech tiny robotic devices for surgeries, including those that allowed Smith to perform coronary-artery bypass operations without making significant incisions.

His patients referred to him as "the Marlboro Man" for his taciturn demeanor and discipline. He was also known as "the Robot" for his daily 5:55 a.m. arrival for his 6:00 a.m. rounds, where his patients would wait for the few sentences that would signal if they were on their way home. It was no wonder that Smith was called upon to perform Bill Clinton's quadruple bypass in 2004 (which he subsequently discussed on Larry King's TV show).

Smith was born in Cleveland; two of his grandparents were doctors who taught him the value of discipline. His family moved frequently, but Smith excelled at athletics, playing three positions in football—usually quarterback. He was a Phi Beta Kappa at Williams. During a summer job working in a steel mill, he got caught in a giant piece of industrial equipment and broke his pelvis in multiple places.

Before he decided on medical school, he spent fourteen months as a telephone lineman, and he eventually chose perhaps the most physically grueling of all surgical specialties—cardiothoracic surgery.

Smith had often performed two or three open-heart procedures a day, but when the pandemic began, that was put on hold indefinitely. While the loss of revenue to the hospital resulting from the ORs being converted to ICUs was unimaginable, that was not what concerned Smith. How to capture this moment for his department? On March 15, at home in his Bronxville study, he opened his laptop and began to type.

He wasn't the only one of his peers to write themselves beyond the bounds of established policy; throughout the NewYork-Presbyterian system, department chairs were attempting to adequately inform their medical staff about what was actually going on in the hospital. Hospitalist Art Evans's nightly roundup would post at 1:00 a.m. with the summation of the facts—the cases, the ICU beds, the number of NewYork-Presbyterian staff who were infected or hospitalized. His fact sheets were a bracing tonic and were strictly against the comms policy of the corporate side, but the need for them underscored just how much the silos of the NewYork-Presbyterian system— Corporate versus Medicine—impeded the staff's ability to organize and manage the care of those admitted. Though the memos were first issued for the hospitalists, Evans began getting requests from critical care to add them to the update list. "It was imperative that the doctors know exactly what was going on," he said.

Smith decided to write a daily letter to the Columbia surgery department detailing what he was seeing. The first one expressed concern but offered comfort too: "Our OR schedule-adjusting process feels like the eye of the storm if we look at what's swirling around us in the ER and the medical ICUs," he wrote, commending the "around-the-clock" efforts and the stamina of the department in paring down all "non-essential parts of their missions," the clinical, research, and the educational outreach. Smith pointed out "an alarming shortage of resources (primarily PPE) that are equally essential in the OR and in the front lines of the COVID-19 battle." His tone was somber; the hospital was somewhere in the nether zone, preparing for the worst but hoping the comet would miss Washington Heights. "Let me emphasize that we're not overwhelmed yet! It's a beautiful sunny day," he wrote. "We have our families and friends. No matter how many of us get infected, the vast majority will do well."

A few days later, the clouds were gathering. The "hard data has become alarming," he said. "I wish I could use a more comforting word." Smith reeled out the numbers—about three hundred NewYork-Presbyterian cases confirmed, two hundred awaiting results. "This approaches a 50 percent increase in one day. . . . Projections presented at noon today estimate that the NYP system will reach peak COVID-19 volume within 22–32 days, at which point the NYP system will need 700–934 ICU beds. The lower estimate exceeds our ICU capacity."

That day, Smith had learned of the dire shortage of the "already extremely scarce" N95 masks. "NYP normally uses 4,000 non-N95 masks per day," Smith reported. "Currently NYP is consuming 40,000 such masks a day, which is estimated to reach 70,000 per day. . . . With great effort Dr. Corwin has successfully pried 150,000 masks out of the reserve." He closed his letter with the first flourish of semi-poetry: "The next month or two is a horror to imagine if we are underestimating the threat. So what can we do? Load the sled, check the traces, feed Balto, and mush on. Our cargo must reach Nome. Remember that our families, friends, and neighbors are scared, idle, out of work and feel impotent. Anyone working in health care still enjoys the rapture of action. It's a privilege! We mush on."

Almost as soon as he posted this to the department of surgery, there was a tsunami of forwards. Smith's Balto reference became a viral phenomenon. Who was Balto? What happened in Nome? (Smith was referring to a 1925 dogsled mission to deliver diphtheria antitoxin to remote Nome, Alaska. Balto was the name of one of the lead dogs. The statue of the heroic Balto, erected in 1925 near Central Park's East Drive at Sixty-Seventh Street, has for years been a popular meeting spot at the zoo.)

Smith was not expecting any attention outside of his Columbia bubble, and, he later told people close to him, certainly the last thing he expected was an icy call from Laura Forese chastising him for "giving out confidential information." Adding to the subtext of Smith's brisk reaction to Forese was the fact that he had trained her husband, the thoracic surgeon Robert Downey, and he was now in the complicated position of having to field calls from Forese, whom he had known since she was in medical school. He was seventy-one, and his global reputation was formidable; he did not defer to corporate masters. (Forese, who described Smith as "a friend" and "an eminence in the medical school," said she had no recollection of the incident.) Around the hospital, it was known that Forese could be opaque when dealing with situations she was trying to control. Empathy, even feigned empathy, was not her strong suit.

Smith could be equally bristly, taking special delight in delivering rebukes with a droll theatrical panache. To use the word *surgery* in his presence was to invite a swift usage lesson, delivered in staccato: "A fast correction," he said to an author he was meeting for the first time, "we do *operations*. . . . I hope you understand the difference. I like precision . . . surgery is the art and science of surgery. Operations and procedures are the things we do. Have you ever met a chemistry professor who is going off to do chemistries? And does a radiologist go off to do radiologies? We do operations and procedures, but we practice surgery."

Forese's call did not go down well; Smith ignored her.

At Columbia, one possible downside of surgeon Tomoaki Kato's commitment to taking on cases that nobody else would was that his patient load was often heavy. There were things he could and did leave to others; his staff would do the follow-up with patients after an initial post-op visit, for example. But some things could only be done by a surgeon, and Kato just didn't have it in him to turn away someone in need.

Such was the case in March 2020. Like hospitals across America, New York-Presbyterian was postponing, canceling, or not scheduling elective procedures; they needed the beds, they needed the supplies, and they needed the staff to handle the exploding pandemic. But organ transplants are almost never elective—you get the organ and you live, you don't and you generally won't. And it isn't easy to get a donor organ in the first place, which is why, when the right organ is suddenly available, a plane might have to be chartered to land at the edge of a hurricane and pick it up. So even when the city was in lockdown, Kato did operations if they could save a life.

There are stories of athletes who, without looking at the scoreboard, seem to know exactly how many seconds remain and execute the perfect pass or shot just before time runs out. So too a great surgeon. "The most important time is the time you take the organ out," Kato said, "because once you take the organ out, the clock is ticking and the patient could die, so that is the time that you have the most level of tension." When planning an elaborate case, Kato would, in his own words, go into "a tunnel." The distractions of the outside world sloughed away, and his focus was entirely on what he needed to do and how he would do it—how he would solve the problem that was soon to be in front of him. The irrelevant was put aside. The irrational (and Kato rarely exhibited anything that might be considered such) was shelved. Clarity was key.

But clarity was context too. Even though the virus was already raging through the New York metropolitan area, in some ways, everyone at the hospital was in what Kato described as a "detached state." They knew things were bad—very bad—but like most, they didn't know the extent of infection. Many thought a sort of "ordinary safe" was enough. "You knew that you had a potentially very infectious agent," said Corwin, "you knew that people had to mask up, you knew that you didn't necessarily have everything that you'd want to have, everybody buttoned up. At the time, there was conflicting guidelines about what the appropriate protective garb was." They would learn soon enough how dire the situation was.

7

On the morning of March 11, New York City and the rest of the world awakened to the announcement that the WHO had finally declared the coronavirus was, in fact, a pandemic. For weeks, the WHO had used "a public health emergency of international concern." That morning, Andrew Cuomo sent the National Guard to New Rochelle to enforce a containment zone, a perimeter that encircled the areas around Young Israel. By afternoon the subway platform at Times Square had become an eerie ghost town. It was March 11, and across America, there had been only twenty deaths—thirteen of which had taken place in Washington State at the Life Care Center of Kirkland, the assisted living facility in the Seattle suburbs. That day, the center announced that sixty-five of its employees could not get tested despite showing symptoms.

In New York City, as attendance plunged at Broadway theaters, the producer Scott Rudin announced he was slashing the ticket prices for hit shows *To Kill a Mockingbird* and *The Lehman Trilogy* from around two hundred dollars to fifty. But the *New York Post*'s front page showed an enraged Joe Biden, on the campaign trail, shouting at an autoworker at a Michigan rally. "Don't try me pal, you want to go outside?" A banner at the bottom read: "New York Town on Covid-19 Lockdown." That morning in New York, Daniel Goldman, a legal analyst, had a sense that what he'd thought was the flu might actually be COVID-19. Goldman, then forty-five, a graduate of Yale University and Stanford Law School, had put in a grueling year as one of the special prosecutors in the impeachment case against Donald Trump. Awakening in the city that morning, Goldman saw the headlines: "Trump Declares National Emergency"; "Up to $50B in Aid, Testing Expands." Panic had set in on the Upper East Side. Regulars at the Fairway Market on East Eighty-Sixth were used to waiting on long lines for the cashiers, but the lines now were massive, snaking through the aisles of the store, making shopping itself difficult. Up and down the East Eighties on Park Avenue, doormen were loading suitcases into SUVs as thousands left for their country houses.

Back on December 9, 2019, Goldman, dealing with a peril of a different sort, had commanded national attention in front of the House impeachment committee. Central to the proceeding was Trump's attempt to blackmail newly elected Ukrainian president Volodymyr Zelenskyy into investigating his political rivals in exchange for $391 million in foreign aid. In his concluding remarks, Goldman declared, "President Trump's actions and words show that there is every reason to believe that he will continue to solicit foreign interference in our elections. This undermines the very foundation of our democracy."

Goldman had been in London the week before, not allowing himself to consider the possibility that COVID-19 had overtaken Europe to such an extent that he would be vulnerable. Three days later, back home, he'd started to exhibit the symptoms of COVID, but because the CDC and the White House had forbidden the use of test kits approved by the World Health Organization, Goldman could not get a test anywhere. Cuomo's testing restrictions didn't help either. The lines to get tests at urgent-care clinics wound around the block, but Goldman did not meet the criteria New York State was still insisting on. Had he traveled to China? Had he been in contact with anyone who had been in Wuhan? He reached out to a longtime friend, Matt McCarthy, whom he had first met when McCarthy was still at Yale. He had been following McCarthy's frustration with the testing debacle, but both were concerned he might have COVID.

Arriving at Weill Cornell, Goldman saw that what McCarthy had described was correct. The doctors were overwhelmed trying to get patients tested. He was placed in a hallway on a bed near other possible COVID patients, although everyone was in masks. Later, he would call out the "incredibly unsanitary conditions"—and this was early in the siege. It was March 11, and the city was still rocking.

A telegenic prosecutor who winds up in a bed in an ED hallway for six hours is every hospital CEO's media nightmare. How long did it take for the masked and feverish Goldman, lying on the bed as unmasked patients and doctors walked past him, to alert the doctors to his presence? And after that, how long before the ED team, besieged by so many others like Goldman, understood that his level of notoriety made his presence "a situation" that required the counsel of the chairman of the emergency department, Rahul Sharma?

However well known Goldman was, Sharma knew there were onerous state and CD protocols that on March 11 were still being challenged. However misguided those rules later turned out to be, Sharma could not deviate from what the state and the CDC had allowed. And by those rules, Goldman was not sick enough to qualify under New York guidelines. All of which Sharma conveyed to Steve Corwin, who agreed completely. For Corwin, this was yet another example of the crisis fast descending on the hospital and the city. And for Goldman and for so many others who could not get tested, it was a lesson that COVID would teach the privileged: There were few levers they could press to bend the rules.

For all of Andrew Cuomo's later grandstanding about his leadership, his failure in the first weeks of March to expand testing meant that there were thousands like Daniel Goldman all over the city who were trying to do the right thing but getting blocked by a paralyzed

DOH. And, to maximize inefficiency, the state was still insisting that tests had to be done through the Wadsworth state laboratory all the way up in Albany rather than at a New York City testing facility or in the hospitals themselves.

"There is nothing we can do for you here," Goldman was told at Weill Cornell. "Go home and quarantine." But he was also told that it was fine for his family to continue to go around in the city. Incredibly, that was still the protocol in New York State and in the city; de Blasio had not shut down the schools or taken the sort of truly aggressive action that would have signaled to residents that adjusting their routines would be a very good idea.

The next morning, having been tipped off, Goldman awakened at five and drove to Greenwich, Connecticut, where he was able to get a test in a roadside site set up by the state. The test came back positive. In a fury, he reached out to *Morning Joe*, where he'd developed contacts during the impeachment saga, and the next morning he was on the air describing the chaos at NewYork-Presbyterian. "It's not the doctors' fault," Goldman said. "They don't have the tests. The doctors were incredibly frustrated." It was the same point that Matt McCarthy had tried to make ten days earlier before he was shut down by the suits at the hospital.

Not long after Daniel Goldman appeared on *Morning Joe*, Steve Corwin was sent a link to the video. He watched as Goldman used the word *unsanitary* to describe the emergency department at NewYork-Presbyterian's jewel-in-the-crown hospital and heard about the six hours Goldman had waited to be seen. By any measure, it was a public relations disaster. Goldman, in a crisp red-and-white checked shirt, sounded like he barely had a cold, but his complaints didn't seem like an overreaction; the *Morning Joe* hosts were clearly concerned, and the fact that even a high-profile patient like Goldman had been treated so poorly would lead those of lesser celebrity to assume that if they went to a NewYork-Presbyterian hospital, they would not be treated any better. It was not the way Corwin wanted to start his day—now he had a comms issue too.

In case Corwin needed reminding, the Sunday *New York Post* was still in his apartment: "Heaven Help Us!" the headline blared next to an image of blue-surgical-gloved hands in a prayer position with a rosary wrapped around them. Smaller headlines read "COVID-19 Forces Catholic Church to Cancel Mass"; "Teachers to Stage Sick-out as NYC Schools Stay Open"; "Two NYers Die, State Cases Explode to 613." From Ethiopia, Jay Varma texted furiously: *Why aren't the schools closed yet?* That day, an emergency meeting was set up in the NewYork-Presbyterian executive offices on Lexington Avenue. Incredibly, there were many on the leadership team, including Peter Fleischut, the hospital's chief transformation officer, still not wearing masks. The NewYork-Presbyterian modeler Matthew Oberhardt, in close consultation with Nathaniel Hupert, gave a presentation of what the hospital might expect—thousands of cases. "At one point, he asked for some Advil. There was no drama, but it was clear the strain he was under—we all were," said Fleischut. After that, for Fleischut, "It felt like every day was the same day." The next week, when he went for his morning run, there was no traffic at all. "The city was a total ghost town."

The day after Goldman's *Morning Joe* appearance, Corwin went on the show to try to undo the bad PR. Cuomo was the lead-in from his press conference the day before, his voice somber as he said, "At this point New York State will not be able to flatten the curve enough to meet the capacity of the health-care system." Then Mika Brzezinski, in full crisis-anchor mode, said: "New York governor Andrew Cuomo still fears his state's best efforts might not be enough as concerns mount over the demand for respirators, ventilators, and other equipment needed." She cut to Corwin, appearing remotely in a somber navy suit and green tie. "I believe," she said, "somebody that we know walked into one of your hospitals and was sitting in a hallway and he ultimately was diagnosed with the coronavirus. . . . How are health-care workers in your ERs and in the hallways of your hospitals being separated to be protected?"

"We worked it out in our emergency department. I saw your segment yesterday with the patient who became COVID-positive," Corwin replied. "Part of the issue is the availability—or lack of availability—of testing. So we wish him well."

"Steve is always walking the line between being a doctor and an administrator," Ellen Corwin later said. "He wasn't going to change the rules for anyone." But Brzezinski did not appear particularly sympathetic.

In response to a question from coanchor Willie Geist, Corwin laid out some of the questions being asked by New York-Presbyterian and all the hospitals. "Do you have enough ICU beds? Do you have enough health-care workers? Do you have enough ventilators, et cetera? So we're a four-thousand-bed system, thirty-five hundred medical-surgical beds. About ten to fifteen percent of those beds are ICU beds. Maybe a little bit more. We have five hundred ventilators. We have an additional capacity for two hundred and fifty ventilators." The implication was clear: That might not be enough.

Corwin insisted people needed to socially isolate. "There's no treatment for this at this point, no vaccine." Yes, the hospital staff could keep people alive for a stretch, maybe even send them home safely, but they were improvising, juggling, hoping researchers would figure this thing out and say, *This is what you need to do*. Social distancing was an essential first step, and it was free and available.

Of all his worries, one of the most intense was the amount of PPE the hospital had if New York became Italy. Corwin had already told his board members to work their contacts and see if anyone could help them with Alibaba and the Chinese media-and-gaming giant Tencent; the companies' massive footprints might mean they had access to PPE, and maybe the hospital system could get a million masks from China. Rob Glaser and Anand Joshi, NewYork-Presbyterian's supply director, ran a team of hundreds to procure supplies for the hospital, and from the first days, Glaser worried about counterfeit N95 masks being churned out in China. Given the frantic and competitive efforts simply to get PPE, there was no time to investigate the specific factories they were coming from or determine if they complied with OSHA standards. Before masks could be used, the hospital staff would have to laboriously test them, and they discovered a huge percentage of them were bogus. The first testing site was set up in the warehouse of Weill Cornell, where staff checked the masks for seal and smell—if you could taste sucrose through the mask, it had to be discarded. "At what point do you realize: 'Holy shit, this stuff is no good'?" Corwin said. The masks they got from Tencent were good, Corwin concluded, but the masks from Alibaba were not. (In an early interview, Corwin mentioned the fakes that were coming from China, which enraged Chinese authorities, who interpreted his remarks as anti-Asian, and anti-Chinese in particular, and delayed deliveries. A back-channel discussion with the American president of Alibaba quickly smoothed things over, but it was a reminder of China's heightened defensiveness, likely exacerbated by the habit of some, including Trump, of referring to COVID as the "Chinese virus.")

"It wasn't like the world, given the geopolitics of the Trump White House, was trying to help us," Corwin reflected. "Were they going to send supplies to us or to Europe? Once you combined the geopolitical stalemate with the actual crisis of manufacturing, it wasn't like they were opening their arms and saying, 'Yes, we are going to help you.'"

"You can't even begin to describe the weight that is on my shoulders because you know there is nothing you can do about it. We had never seen death like this. And there was no way to prevent it." It seemed like everyone coming in ended up on a ventilator, Corwin said, "and even if you were on a ventilator, your chances of recovery were not great." *What are we going to do,* he wondered, *if we run out of ventilators?* Without a ventilator, there was no way to intubate someone who needed to be intubated. So what would you do—send the patient home to die?

As the city closed on March 16, scores of New York-Presbyterian staff no longer felt safe on the subway. Joe Ienuso, New York-Presbyterian's head of facilities. and Steve Corwin made the decision to find a hotel room for every staff member who requested one. "We had a hundred-and-twenty-room hotel near Weill Cornell, but we could not find rooms for every staff member." Three thousand rooms were ultimately taken in hotels throughout Manhattan, Brooklyn, and Queens. In the third week of March, Ienuso, who lived on First Avenue near the United Nations, parked his car and tried to find something to eat after a grueling day at the hospital. "Everything was closed. My entire neighborhood was dark—all the bars, stores . . . no people. . . . It was surreal. When I was in the hospital, the pace and being surrounded by people was very normal. . . . We were walking the halls, we were problem-solving. It was preservation—there were so many issues, mechanical, architectural . . ." And one that concerned him but that he did not mention: psychological.

The complexity of managing eleven hospital campuses and hundreds of acres of real estate was the mandate of Ienuso. It required a team of more than two thousand employees. His skills had been honed when he oversaw the 240 buildings of Columbia University and by the years he had clocked in at Northwell, learning hospital management.

Ienuso had worked with former mayor Michael Bloomberg on leadership committees because of his deep understanding that New York is a city of neighborhoods. From the earliest weeks, Ienuso's team was brought in to the immense struggle of how to manage the facilities and do what was required. "We were in constant conversation with Laureen Hill and the epidemiologists to try to understand the air-quality needs, how we would have to amend all our facilities. Said Hill, 'At one moment, a patient could be well, and thirty minutes later, they would need to be intubated.' The leadership of NYP were in constant communication—Steve, Laura, Laureen, Kate, Jaclyn Mucaria in Queens. It was virtual and physical, and part of the worry was that we all had to stay well. Steve said, 'I don't expect any of us are,'" recalled Ienuso.

But sometimes what seemed like a solution to Joe Ienuso quickly became its own nightmare. That was the case with the design of the temporary rooms—wooden walls with a door—that, following Cuomo's orders, were quickly assembled in a rush to accommodate all the COVID patients. These were not, Ienuso felt strongly, the sort of hospital rooms he or anyone among his staff of two thousand would ever have deemed close to acceptable. Rosanne Raso, director of nursing, understood the crisis conditions that had led them to be built in such haste—there was no other solution to double the hospital occupancy—but the rooms already felt claustrophobic to patients who would be isolated from their families and from most human contact; a quarantined COVID patient would see no human face unless a nurse or a respiratory therapist came in (and even then, that face would be masked).

A few of the cells (that's what the rooms felt like) had a window to the East River, but the incoming light was really just a difference without distinction. What if a desperately ill patient with no good options had a breakdown? Or tried to harm him- or herself? Raso crafted scenario after scenario in her head, knowing her nursing staff could not possibly accommodate all the demands. They couldn't even monitor what was going on in the rooms without taking twenty minutes to correctly don and doff full PPE, of which there was not enough.

The potential of damaging the psychological well-being of the staff was overwhelming, and Raso knew she had to start talking about this and try to implement a plan. "We decided that when we would tell patients that they had COVID, we had to evaluate their mental status at the time. Because the patients were alone. There was no visitation. You are behind a closed door." Patients who had been in those rooms spoke of how the feeling of isolation had been overwhelming, the mounting panic increasing their shortness of breath, each hour making them feel they had been forgotten and might never be retrieved—ever. Raso took in all the stories and later commented, "Imagine that you are the patient."

Lindsay Lief also had concerns about the temporary rooms without windows; the ICUs all had glass windows and doors that allowed doctors and nurses to monitor patients from a hall. In the temporary rooms, she said, "You couldn't hear or see the alarms going off with the filtration system." If it was bad enough for a patient to feel abandoned when nothing was happening, imagine how petrifying—and dangerous—it would feel when those alarms were ringing.

8

At last Nathaniel Hupert had penetrated the power circle in Albany. On March 17, on a chilly night in Princeton, he stood in his garden trying to get better reception on his cell during a conference call with the governor and the most powerful hospital leaders in New York, including Steve Corwin, whose worry was evident. The atmosphere was one of extreme urgency and agitation as New York's health leaders tried to understand their options and cope with a crisis of unimaginable proportions.

On the call were the governor, Corwin, Northwell's Michael Dowling, the Hospital for Special Surgery's Lou Shapiro, and Ken Raske, president of the Greater New York Hospital Association, the organization that actually made hospital policy. All of them knew that if the McKinsey and Columbia projections were accurate—if 120,000 to 140,000 patients were going to overwhelm the hospitals at the same time—then, as Corwin would later say, "We could just pack it up and go home because there was no way any hospital could survive."

At that moment in his garden, Hupert fully believed that the horrifying numbers were correct—he had yet to understand they were relying on inaccurate data assumptions—and as he listened to the speakers, he took meticulous notes.

March 17, 2020

Michael Dowling
Ken Raske
Governor Cuomo
Steven Corwin

Governor Cuomo
Projection is a projection
Moderate—45 d 110,000 requiring hospitalization
37,000 ICU
Possible calamity on the size of Italy
Pulling out all the stops
Army Corps FEMA
  1. Flatten the curve
  2. Build new beds
  3. Increasing your capacity
When the bear is chasing you, you run like hell
We have to prove that we have the best health-care system
None of us can live with not doing well

Michael Dowling
Who the hell knows if the numbers the government said are
true, but we have to go with something.

Steven Corwin
Start from inside out:
  1. Preserve most critical care capability first, requires PPE
  2. Med students, retirees won't be able to handle those patients
If we have to take a revenue hit, we are going to take a revenue
hit, I could give a rat's ass.

Ken Raske

Exponential use of state stockpile N95 (now into "expired
  reserve zone")

PPE

Every COVID patient requires 5–7x normal PPE

China now shipping PPE

Expanding production in USA

$0.35 becomes $5–8 per mask

Hand sanitizer in global shortage

COVID test kits

Lou Shapiro

Given up 90% of capacity and revenue

The notes Hupert took reflect the hour-by-hour metric as fear and the realization of the state's lack of preparation took over New York. For the hospital heads, the economic questions were overwhelming. How, wondered Lou Shapiro, the chairman of the Hospital for Special Surgery, would his institution survive if 90 percent of the patients and revenue were gone? How did you maintain five to seven times the normal amount of PPE? Dowling, who had punched his ticket in Albany as an adviser to Andrew Cuomo's father and was now running the largest hospital group in the state, understood that the numbers might not be accurate, but the assumption that they were, many would later suggest, affected every future choice, including Cuomo's disastrous decision to return patients with COVID to the nursing homes—and later attempt to cover that up.

On that call, Corwin later remembered thinking, *If these numbers are correct, we can't get through this.* But he thought as well, *If they are directionally correct, and we are going to do everything we can to maximize what we have, then we'll see. And we can take it so far before we get to the breaking point. But we're NewYork-Presbyterian—we're going to be the last man standing and we are going to do everything we can to prevent us from getting to the breaking point.*

"I had my own modeling numbers," he said. "There was disagreement around some of the modeling numbers. . . . I had to pull out all the stops. Once you pulled out all the stops, there was no governor on that, right? I mean, you just know that it's only the question of whether it is going to be terrible or horrible and what the difference is going to be. It did not influence my decisions one way or another."

Nothing about those numbers seemed possible, Ken Raske later said. Yet, watching the rapid acceleration of cases in that period, how could you justify not preparing for the worst, even while you were hoping for the best?

One year earlier, at thirty-three, Mike Schmidt had been anointed the state tax commissioner, the youngest in New York history. He had four thousand employees, and unlike the Internal Revenue Service, he was determined to keep the office open, despite the panic of the staff. Now Cuomo had added to his portfolio an entire new responsibility: head of the New York State task force in charge of the pandemic. Schmidt moved from his apartment in Brooklyn to Albany for the next two months. There was pushback inside the governor's inner circle on the modeling projection put forward by both McKinsey and, for a time, Columbia. How could this number be valid? By late March, Schmidt assembled modeling teams from all over the world to accumulate data for projections for what seemed to be a failure to share data across agencies, most notably New York State and New York City agencies.

In the first days, his team was overwhelmed with incoming concerns from employees. The level of fear was palpable. "There was an incident where someone spilled a burrito in a common area of our buildings, right? Someone else thought it was vomit. The perception was that was vomit in a common area, and literally, we had all-out panic. I told my chief operations officer, 'You have to figure this out right now.'. . . And he was like, 'It's a burrito.'. . . It just hit us all so fast. . . . I had a very strong conviction that, as tax department employees, the state was depending on us for revenue, and citizens were depending on us for refunds, and that as a result our business had to keep running. The basic infrastructure of society had to continue."

The tax department ran the largest call center in the state, and tens of thousands of New Yorkers made all kinds of inquiries about their tax issues and other issues as well. "I got a call or an e-mail or something in early March," Schmidt said. "It was like, 'Hey, there's this coronavirus thing . . . the governor is doing an event . . . we want to announce a call center where we just answer questions about it.' And as soon as I got this call, I thought, *My God, this is going to be a bear.* It was our first sense of how big this was going to be."

In Albany, all decisions are made by "the Chamber," as the governor's office calls itself, and the tight cohort of aides who cosseted Cuomo. It included his chief of staff, Melissa DeRosa, who commanded each day's press briefings, and Robert Mujica, the state budget director, whom Schmidt worked closely with. Schmidt said, "It was all hands on deck . . . with all of us doing everything." His first task was to set up a COVID call center, which wound up getting two million calls and used the National Guard to field them, and he brought in staff from twenty-eight agencies.

Schmidt started splitting his time between the tax department's main offices and the call center site just outside of Albany, but by mid-March, Mujica contacted him with another temporary assignment: "The governor wants you to work on the pandemic modeling." Schmidt had no previous experience in public health, but he was unusually skilled at the analysis of state and federal revenue.

For the next two months, Schmidt added the modeling expertise to what was already an overloaded portfolio. How would the sales tax be extended? How could the state budget be passed? What was the implication for the state of the CARES Act—the $2.2 trillion aid package that Trump would sign into law on March 27, 2020? "It was all happening at once," he said. "And it was absolutely insane."

At the same time, Cuomo pulled in Jim Malatras, then the president of Empire State College and later the chancellor of the State University of New York system. Trained as a social scientist, Malatras was known for his statistical analyses and had been running his own pandemic projections for the state's universities when he joined the group gathered in the war room in the Capitol. Brought in after McKinsey's first projections, Malatras found Cuomo's staff very aggressive; they were demanding instant answers. They "would not listen to anything for five minutes," he said. "Cuomo, who I have worked with a long time, overblew a lot of stuff himself."

When Malatras arrived, he noticed that the McKinsey team had already embedded on the second floor of the Capitol. They seemed to be always present, in the halls, at frequent meetings. "As I started to dig into the numbers," Malatras recalled, "it was already the end of March. The whole issue was around the 40,000 ventilators and the 140,000 beds McKinsey projected the state needed. Crazy numbers. Once you started digging into it, it seemed overblown. But that was their most severe case—they had other projections that were less severe. But they stuck to the severe model. Maybe it was out of fear. They didn't want to be wrong if they underestimated."

Malatras and Schmidt assembled a group of modelers who had a more realistic picture. Ironically, Malatras would later say, the modelers that the White House task force gathered were "the most accurate," but no one would listen to them because they had come from the president's advisers. Another reason was that the modelers had been pulled together by four-star admiral Brett Giroir, a Harvard magna with a long career in public health who had been anointed Trump's COVID-19 testing czar. In the larger medical research community, Giroir had been criticized for his "track record of letting ideology drive decisions at the expense of women and children," Washington senator Patty Murray said when he was nominated to be the acting head of the FDA. At the U.S. Department of Health and Human Services (HHS), he had attempted to stop the NIH's one-hundred-million-dollar research grant allowing the agency to use fetal tissue to explore vaccines and treatments for the Zika virus and treatments for Alzheimer's and Parkinson's.

But on the White House Coronavirus Task Force, Giroir had "assembled the best of the federal government . . . the emergency defense agencies . . . Treasury. . . . They had people coming from everywhere." Malatras said Giroir had suggested to him that he hire top modelers from the University of Washington's Institute for Health Metrics and Evaluation (IHME), whom Malatras and Schmidt came to rely on. "[Mike and I] scoured the earth. . . . We used a lot of different people during that process to really dig into what this was actually going to look like because the original stuff everybody talked about was just doomsday projections," Malatras said. "I had no idea McKinsey was there when I got there already. . . . They must have already been on a contract with the state or something. BCG [Boston Consulting Group] was involved too. . . . McKinsey was working with Columbia, NYU, and others."

Schmidt said, "I would get calls from people saying, 'Schmidt, why are these numbers so different?' And I would say, 'Which one of the assumptions do you want to talk through?' Because each of these models were so different on so many things."

From his attic in Princeton, Hupert fielded several calls from Cuomo as well as Schmidt as he pored over the data sets. At one point, he became convinced that the city was coming close to herd immunity. Was that it, or were the numbers dropping because, as Schmidt and Cuomo came to believe, the pause would work? "All of the models said it was five-days-plus for incubation, then ten days for the hospital. And then two weeks for the numbers to show. . . . It really is easy to forget the amount of uncertainty at the time. . . . It was just terrifying. People were dying. And it felt like the wave was about to crash. And we had scenarios we could look at, like, 'What's happening in China?' You couldn't understand if the information was correct. China's got more control of their people. It was the fog of war. Everything was so uncertain and the stakes were so high," Schmidt recalled.

Schmidt was often frustrated as he waited for Hupert's projections, which sometimes arrived late. But in his attic in Princeton, Hupert was seeing entirely new data that showed the Cuomo team's models, many would later say, were catastrophically mistaken. He was the first person to suggest that ventilators be moved to the hardest-hit areas and among the first to understand that the projections of patients expected in Brooklyn and Queens were being used, possibly incorrectly, to model what was going to happen in all of New York City.

March 28, 2020

Mike,

Sorry upstate not done yet. Will be tomorrow.

Watching today's address; three points I can glean from the data and models now:

1. There will be three peaks most likely: NYC, then Westchester and Nassau/Suffolk, then upstate. Not sure if that is

important to tell people, but important for Governor to be
prepared for. May be up to two weeks apart.
2. This is good news because we can move vents and other
things to follow the peaks.
3. This means that we may not need as much space or space.
For example, I think there are few scenarios in which we
need 140,000 beds . . . simultaneously.

More tomorrow,

Nathaniel

The following day, Hupert e-mailed David Shmoys, the head of
information engineering at Cornell, and cc'd Schmidt and Malatras. The e-mail was a single-spaced detailed rocket essentially
saying *Hold on, the state is operating on terrible numbers.* He sent
his latest model from his group—the Cornell COVID Caseload
Calculator—and amped up his previously neutral academic language.

> Finally, I am wrestling with acute concern about whether we
> should be relying on NY City hospitalization data from last
> week to parametrize our predictions for the whole city. . . .
> Basically, it has become apparent from the last 48 hours anal-
> ysis of where cases are coming from. . . . The problem for the
> modelers is that the rates of hospitalizations from these areas/
> households is not necessarily reflective of the city as a whole,
> so if you match a curve to that really steep rise in cases, you risk
> completely overshooting the estimate for the City. . . . Combined
> with that is the dual problem of not knowing, in any way, the
> true extent of infection in the city, the rate of symptomatic
> infections, or the rate of hospitalization for systematic infec-
> tions, and you see that we are largely in the dark. Nevertheless,
> the NYU and Columbia groups have put their chips down on

very frightening scenarios that the City is rushing to send to a press conference.

Hupert never received an answer to this e-mail, but he did get an e-mail from Schmidt canceling a scheduled conference call. "That was the last communication I ever had from the New York State task force," he said.

Without letting Hupert know, Malatras had taken his advice and started moving ventilators from upstate. The tabloid headlines blasted how dire the New York City lack of ventilators was. De Blasio had raised the level of anxiety in the city with his press briefings.

"In the chaos of those days, I don't think we reached out to Nathaniel to tell him how important his work was," Malatras said. "The biggest fight I had with New York City was that they were just wrong [on their ventilator projections]."

By early April, it was clear that the McKinsey team was trying to reassess their early data projections as well. "It was a two-week period of absolute intensity," Malatras said. "We were really having people drill down into their daily analyses.

"Mike and I were spending all of our time on it. We brought in people from Drexel and from the University of Washington. . . . The McKinsey people, to be fair, said, 'Get us more data showing something different.' They were backtracking. . . . They went down to about seventy thousand at one point after a Mount Sinai study showed that the virus was in New York much earlier than had been thought. . . . But we ended up in New York with eighteen thousand." (McKinsey and members of its modeling team did not answer multiple requests for comment.)

Malatras was most concerned about the state and the hospital's frenzied push to acquire ventilators. "McKinsey had projected we needed 40,000. We scrounged around and ended up with about

18,000. And New York wound up needing only 6,000." The focus in Albany, Malatras said, was the fear that the hospital system could collapse. "It was all going at one hundred miles an hour," he said. "The governor was at the epicenter of this unknown thing. It was all happening in two weeks. The governor was concerned—that is why we brought in all the modeling groups. We couldn't go to him and say, 'Oh, by the way, it's twenty-five thousand.' And then later say, 'Oh, we fucked that up. It's actually ninety thousand.' He would have lost all public confidence. Buying more equipment than you need is forgivable. Not having equipment is not forgivable."

The *New York Post* ran a story on March 27 reporting a de Blasio press conference—a conference that Hupert refused to attend. "After next Sunday—April 5 is when I get very, very worried about everything we're going to need. The people power we are going to need, the equipment, the supplies, obviously the ventilators," the mayor was quoted as saying. On that same day, de Blasio attempted a mea culpa about his failure to shut the city down for weeks, a catastrophe that may have been responsible for thousands of needless deaths.

In Albany, Malatras came to understand that Hupert and the modelers at the University of Washington could be right. He tried to alert Cuomo to the new findings: "We think it is looking like we are going to be in the twenty thousand to thirty thousand range, not one hundred and forty thousand."

Malatras later explained what he had tried to get across. "We may be overplaying this. Getting a governor to pivot like this takes a lot of work, because they hedge in the academic space. It is, 'This is what it is' one moment and then, two days later, 'No, actually, it is this.' But in the public space, if people freaked out, [a governor] just can't say, 'Never mind.' . . . You were trying to figure this all out in a model which is essentially garbage in, garbage out."

Cuomo was now in an untenable position. "He had been on a call with the other modelers for weeks who had projected one hundred and forty thousand or one hundred and ten thousand. . . . They were all in the same ballpark. . . . And it was like, 'You crazy people, you have been making me say this for weeks and now you are coming back to me and saying it's totally off,' but [the state] had taken actions too," Malatras said.

On April 6, Cuomo insisted that Malatras stand in front of the PowerPoint slides and try to walk back the higher numbers that Malatras still struggled to understand. At the daily briefing, the soft-spoken Malatras danced his way around the larger reality of the previous McKinsey assumptions. "As the governor said, we have been looking at projections and modeling from the beginning to determine the size and scope of the severity. We were working with many organizations and using the projections from Imperial College, Cornell, and McKinsey. And some of the original projections, um . . . that we first saw at the beginning of this were at least 110,000 and said that the peak would come at the end of April." The *New York Times* Albany bureau chief, Jesse McKinley, tweeted: "@GovCuomo's aide Jim Malatras says the projections are now showing that the state unlikely to need 110,000 beds for #Coronavirus. New projections show much lower demand, near 20,000-30,000 range if the new chart is believed."

Two years later, Malatras was still trying to understand how off base much of the modeling had been.

"I pushed McKinsey pretty hard. Now they would say the data— and I'm not blaming them—but Columbia, McKinsey, and the NYU folks were way the hell off," Malatras said.

"I would go back to the University of Washington models, which said twenty-six thousand beds," Malatras said, close to the number that Hupert had projected. Malatras took this to Cuomo. "I think there was a little of this 'Oh, shit, you guys better be right, because now I am saying what you want me to say and it's not what we have been saying. We've been saying the sky is falling. The sky isn't falling.' I think what public health was saying was, 'Well, we've learned more information.' That was my interpretation."

But Cuomo stayed with the 140,000 projection, even in the book he published later that fall. "All of the models said we would need 110,000 and 140,000 hospital beds on any given day at our apex. We went from 53,000 beds to a total of close to 90,000. They said we needed to do everything we could do to 'bend the curve,'" he wrote in *American Crisis: Leadership Lessons from the COVID-19 Pandemic*. "That's what people had been telling him. That is what he was planning for. So very much his die was cast with that number in mind, so everything around the whole governmental response was 40,000 ventilators or 140,000 beds or whatever it was. And that was the worst-case scenario that everyone was planning for. It was hard for guys like him to break out of that," Malatras said. The total number was almost exactly as Hupert and Cornell had predicted—25,000.

How did everyone get it so wrong? "They were looking at Wuhan and you were operating in a void of reliable data," Hupert said.

By early April, Schmidt and Hupert realized that they needed to rely on data projections, not mathematical models that were consistently unreliable. "I came to a place where I was like, 'This is not a complicated modeling exercise.' This was more like, 'Okay, how many beds do you have? How many ventilators do you have? How many got used up last week?' . . . We are in the world of extrapolation based on numbers. . . . I felt we just needed to take this down to earth a little bit. If there is a model we can't explain in plain English, then it's not worth sharing with people, right?" Schmidt said.

All that month, the issue of masks rocketed through the NYP system and through every hospital in America. (What had been obvious to the crowds of Asian Americans in Queens had clearly been less obvious to the CDC leadership.) There had been the hope that the president would invoke the Defense Production Act, forcing private industry to manufacture ventilators, swabs, and N95s, and that the federal government and FEMA would further come to the aid of the nation's governors. But Trump's staff made it clear that the blue states would have to grovel for federal aid, since their voters and leaders did not support him. On a conference call, Trump told the governors, "We're backing you a hundred percent. Also, though . . . respirators, ventilators, all the equipment—try getting it yourselves." Washington governor Jay Inslee told Trump, "That would be equivalent to Franklin Delano Roosevelt on December 8, 1941, saying, 'Good luck, Connecticut, you go build the battleships.'" But Trump was not going to lend a hand. "We're just the backup," he responded, noted author Lawrence Wright in *The Plague Year*.

But it wasn't just that Trump wasn't helping—he was actively undermining efforts to fight the pandemic. At a Weill Cornell staff meeting, many in the room talked about how their mental health had been affected by the White House's propaganda—"Nothing's wrong, it's just like the flu"; "The only reason this is on is that the Democrats want Trump to lose"—and its bizarre medical "recommendations." Trump and his allies would promote cures and treatments that had no basis in medical science, with disastrous results. McCarthy told a friend about a patient who died in the ICU after ingesting an aquarium cleaner called chloroquine, convinced it was the same as the hydroxychloroquine the president had been pushing as a remedy—which also didn't work anyway.

Matt McCarthy texted writer Charles Finch that he was so slammed at the hospital, he was now leaving for work at 3:00 or 4:00 a.m. The 6:00 a.m. updates on the COVID patients were often revised by 8:00 a.m., the flux of those dying and those taking their places so volatile as to change dramatically even in those two hours.

McCarthy sent a picture from an empty train car and said he had not seen anyone except a conductor in what seemed like ages. But he told Finch that there had been "a flurry" of good news—some definitive studies saying that masks were beneficial. "A medical win," he said. It was hard to read McCarthy's text and not think, *Are you kidding me?* And yet there were millions of Americans who not only didn't believe those studies but would never believe them, thanks to a plague of White House–encouraged disinformation and hostility. Trump's success had been built partly on demonizing the "educated elites," and scientists and doctors fit right into that category. Trump demanded his supporters trust in him, period.

On March 31, the *New York Times*' Matt Richtel broke the story of the El Paso anesthesiologist Henry Nikicicz, who in March had finished an emergency intubation of a man in his seventies and then put his N95 mask back on when he saw a group of people walking down the hall in his direction. In the next days, Nikicicz was suspended when he refused to adhere to El Paso Medical Center's policy of no masks in the hallways. His boss texted him in all caps: *UR WEARING IT DOWN A PUBLIC HALL. THERES NO MORE WUHAN VIRUS IN THE HALLS AT THE HOSPITAL THAN WALMART. MAYBE LESS.*

The idea that virus levels at Walmart might be so stratospheric that the hospital was less dangerous was deemed a harmful fiction, as was the fact that people were coming into the hospital because they were infected with COVID.

In Bronxville, the underestimation of COVID's threat put hospital staff in danger and encouraged a sometimes fatal obliviousness among those visiting the hospital. Xenia Frisby, associate quality-control director of NewYork-Presbyterian Lawrence, grappled with a patient in the ED who had COVID symptoms but refused to stay in the hospital and wait for his test results. "He said, 'You can't keep me against my will.' And he left the hospital. He turned out to be positive and came back in terrible distress a few days later. We could not save him." She was haunted by the number of her staff and their families who risked infection because of his actions.

Trump reveled in his power over the states more directly, especially those in the Northeast. Massachusetts's Republican governor Charlie Baker was infuriated when a shipment of three million masks he had purchased from China was seized at the Port of New York; the supplier had been offered a bonus if they were sold to FEMA instead. "I've got a feeling that if somebody has a chance to sell to you or to me, I am going to lose every one of those," Baker complained to the president. "Price is always a component. Maybe that's why you lost to the feds, okay? That's probably why," Trump condescendingly replied, trying to remind everyone that nobody knew how to make a better deal than he did, morals be damned.

It would be up to the governors of the Northeast states—Baker, Connecticut's Ned Lamont, Andrew Cuomo, Rhode Island's Gina Raimondo, and New Jersey's Phil Murphy—to act together. "If I close down bars and Andrew keeps them open," Raimondo explained, "that doesn't solve any problems. . . . Everybody's going to go down there to drink, and bring back the infection." (Raimondo wasn't always in for the kumbaya of her larger neighbors. When New York exceeded 114,000 cases at the end of March, she deployed the National Guard to checkpoints up and down I-95 with orders to stop all cars with out-of-state plates. She also issued an edict that anyone from New York had to quarantine for fourteen days before entering her state.)

Left empty-handed by the White House, the governor of Massachusetts called Robert Kraft, the owner of the New England Patriots as well as a friend of the president, who dispatched his jet to China repeatedly to aid not only Massachusetts but also New York—and

NewYork-Presbyterian. Critical care pulmonologist and vice chair of medicine Fernando Martinez texted NewYork-Presbyterian board member Stephanie Coleman, whose husband, Chase, ran one of the largest hedge funds in the city. That week, the *New York Post*'s front page showed Mount Sinai nurses wearing garbage bags as PPE, an image that Ken Raske later claimed was staged by the nurses, who were enraged at the hospitals' lack of N95s, but it punctuated the fact that there was a shortage, and people were going to die because of it. "I was stepping way out of NewYork-Presbyterian boundaries," Martinez admitted. "The medical-school chairs are siloed from approaching the board. But I had gotten to know Stephanie and I didn't hesitate. I didn't care if they fired me." Coleman responded immediately and sent her plane on two different occasions to get masks and ventilators for the hospital system.

Stay in the present, Jeanne Rizzuto was told. *The calm-down app will help you.*

At home in Riverdale, a quiet residential enclave in the Bronx, Rizzuto, a literacy and math coach for kindergarten and first grade, was set to give birth to her second child in late March or early April. Rizzuto's husband, Albert Tirado, a fireman in the Bronx, started worrying about COVID in early March after he sought medical treatment at a local hospital before protocols had been put in place. He had hurt his wrist in a fire, but could he catch something from someone? At that point, they weren't testing people, Rizzuto recalled, but the next week the case in New Rochelle popped up, which made her nervous. Rizzuto was following all the news closely from Italy and Wuhan and was in close touch with her sister, Gabi, a pathologist in San Francisco. Stock up on formula, Gabi told her. Stock up on diapers. As San Francisco, ahead of New York, saw its first cases, Gabi's instructions became more urgent. "I began to think, maybe I should be more concerned because she was concerned," Rizzuto reflected. "Then my mom started texting me. Maybe I should be more concerned here? Because she was concerned?" she said.

In the first days of March, Rizzuto was avidly watching the news. "I began to get really nervous when the first patient in New Rochelle was transferred to Columbia-Presbyterian. But I thought to myself, *Okay, they brought him to Columbia because that is the best hospital, and that's why I am giving birth there too.* I said to Albert, 'We shouldn't go to the shopping center in Riverdale. It's not a good idea.' Albert said, 'I agree.' My parents were supposed to watch my two-year-old, Alfonso—that's when I started getting really nervous. I told them, 'Don't come down.' Gabi texted me, 'I think it's a bad idea for you to see Mom and Dad. You need to protect them.' I had already decided that."

Rizzuto was under extraordinary pressure. Like her fellow New York City public-school teachers, she'd been working on-site up until that point. Then, on Sunday, March 15, Mayor Bill de Blasio announced the suspension of school until after spring break. The teachers, meanwhile, were required to go into the empty buildings for professional training to help them transition to remote instruction. Rizzuto decided to take sick days, hoping to avoid people and accidental exposure while still pregnant.

Another week passed. Rizzuto had already started to dilate; she doubted that she could make it to forty weeks. On Friday, March 20, she went to bed early and slept through a call from her ob-gyn, Dr. Jaclyn Coletta-Lucas. Rizzuto awakened to a message. "Was I having any contractions? She called me and said Columbia-Presbyterian was putting in a policy that there were going to be no support partners let in the birthing room."

There were only two hospitals in New York that had instituted the drastic rule: NewYork-Presbyterian and Mount Sinai. The announcement set off a fierce barrage of criticism aimed at the hospitals;

online petitions circulated against this policy, and two hundred thousand people had signed one of them within a day. In Albany, Cuomo was agitated—this level of anger from women was dangerous for him. Cuomo sent Ken Raske to get Corwin to back down.

Raske asked Corwin, "Do you really want to go against the governor?" On March 28, Melissa DeRosa, the governor's top aide, tweeted, "Women will not be forced to be alone when they are giving birth. Not in New York. Not now, not ever." Laura Forese took a call from the state health commissioner, Howard Zucker, about rescinding the policy. But executives Laureen Hill and Forese were concerned—there was not even enough PPE for their own staffs.

At first, Rizzuto was sanguine. "I was trying to look at this from a public health perspective. If I could protect the doctors, then the doctors could deliver more babies. . . . I was trying to think rationally about it. . . . I wasn't going to be by myself—one of my friends said, 'You are going to be with your baby.'" That was the plan.

Rizzuto continued trying to stay calm as she awaited the birth of her second child. "I felt so terrible for the women who were having a baby for the first time. This was my second and I knew what to do. . . . I kept saying these positive mantras over and over. I asked everyone I knew to help me and send me positive affirmations. I asked people for songs. I was planning to bring my computer to the hospital."

March 24 was a Tuesday. That day in New York City, the headlines detailed the horror of what was happening in Queens at Elmhurst Hospital. One resident told a reporter that she performed chest compressions on three dying patients at once. In the middle of the night, Rizzuto woke up with terrible contractions. A week earlier, the city had announced a complete lockdown. Only essential businesses could stay open. New Yorkers had to shelter in place and would be allowed out only for exercise and food and drugstore runs. That announcement sent a seismic shock through the city; on cable news, the stories were all pandemic, all the time. Almost immediately, the New York City teachers union went after the school chancellor, Richard Carranza, accusing the board of education of a massive cover-up about the level of infection to keep the teachers working before the lockdown. "It was getting dire in the city. . . . I avoided the news. I called Dr. Coletta-Lucas. She had delivered my first child. She said, 'Come in right away.' Albert drove me to the hospital and kissed me goodbye. He was trying to smile, but I was in an absolute state. He handed me my car seat and the nursing pillow and then drove away.

"The transporter met me and was so nice, but I wasn't in the mood to engage. He said, 'Is this your first baby?' And I said, 'No.' And he said, 'Oh, you have got this!'"

Rizzuto had never seen so many people in masks. "The security guards, and the women at the desks . . . I looked around and I was very scared that everyone was in a mask—and they gave me a mask right away. The woman at the front desk was wiping everything down. Then they took me to a little room and wiped everything in there down. They asked me about symptoms. I said, 'Everything is normal.'"

Rizzuto was taken to room 8 at Sloane, the women's hospital of Columbia, the exact room where Alfonso was born. She was then given a COVID test. "Keep your mask on until you get the results," Rizzuto was told. "They decided to start Pitocin to give me more contractions. I was feeling okay and the nurse stayed with me. I was e-mailing with some of the teachers at our school. I was thinking: *I can do this.* The epidural was magic. It worked immediately! And having the nurse in the room was really helpful. Dr. Coletta-Lucas came in and said, 'You can do this! You are strong.'"

Rizzuto tried not to react to the strange sense of doom in the hospital, the kabuki theater coming from the nurses in the labor room that everything was normal when everything was conducted by FaceTime—even giving birth. "Albert was on the phone with me and he was crying. He said, 'You are strong.' I was pushing and pushing. I FaceTimed my parents. And then Nicolas appeared and they laid him on my chest. It was perfect."

Rizzuto breastfed the baby and about an hour later, she prepared to go to the recovery room. Then Coletta-Lucas appeared in the hall wearing full PPE. "Jeanne," she said, "your COVID test came back positive."

Rizzuto was stunned. "I said, 'What?'" Coletta-Lucas tried to reassure her. "She said to me, 'You are going to be okay.' I remember thinking, *What is going to happen next? Will Nicolas be okay? Am I going to be okay?* All of these things. *I have to call Albert. I have to tell my sister.* I pictured myself in the ICU getting intubated. I was thinking, *Will I even get to know my baby?* We were debating names, and I was holding him, thinking, *Is he breathing normally?*"

The nurse came in and said they needed to get Nicolas to the NICU since his oxygen levels were in the eighties. Rizzuto was told she could not accompany him, as she was COVID-positive.

It was Columbia's first case of asymptomatic COVID in a mother in labor. Almost immediately, the head of the department, Mary D'Alton, the chair of ob-gyn and a world authority on fetal health, was alerted. "Please let me see him," Rizzuto said. "But they wouldn't let me in the NICU [newborn intensive care unit], not with COVID. That [first] night was terrible. I could not sleep. Every time the nurse came in, I said, 'I am so sorry you have to be in the room with me.' I felt like I had the plague." Rizzuto called Albert and their upstairs neighbor; both assured her she would be fine, but what did they know? The doctors and scientists didn't know how to treat COVID—they weren't even sure why and how some people caught it. The next day, Rizzuto went home, but Nicolas remained in the NICU.

Coletta-Lucas called and told Rizzuto that Nicolas had tested negative. "You are going to be okay," she said. "And so is Nicolas. When he comes home, you can breastfeed, but every time you touch him, you have to wash your hands before—and wear a mask."

Rizzuto wondered about Alfonso and Albert. It was impossible to get them tested, so Coletta-Lucas suggested they be kept apart from Rizzuto and Nicolas. She and Albert explained to Alfonso that he could not come into the room. Even he and his father would have to be careful about how close they were to each other. "We said, 'Mommy and Daddy wear masks now.'"

Rizzuto reached out to a therapist repeatedly. "She had me focus on remaining in the present," Rizzuto recalled, "but I felt so much shame that I had COVID. I could not even talk about it. I felt I had done something to bring it on."

Rizzuto watched the Cuomo briefings daily. "He talked about how the hospitals were so overwhelmed." Nicolas remained in the NICU—he was put on oxygen and his white blood count was high. "I was allowed to call the doctors all day long, but I was so traumatized I could not process what was happening." If Nicolas recovered, when would she be able to see him? Who would pick him up from the hospital? First, the hospital told her that her husband could pick up the baby but then said he couldn't because he had not been tested. They recruited a family friend to bring the baby home, but at the last minute, Albert was allowed to go: "The nurses brought Nicolas down from the NICU and tossed him to Albert in the lobby of Columbia-Presbyterian," Rizzuto said. Subsequently, everyone in the apartment "wore our masks and washed our hands and we did not leave the apartment. Cousins brought food." Rizzuto's asymptomatic case made medical history while she was still in the hospital. When she was finally released, the apartment COVID procedures continued. "Weeks went by and finally, we could take our first family picture without any of us in masks."

At Weill Cornell, by March 20, Lindsay Lief was under enormous strain and attempting to ignore the desperate throbbing in her leg.

She tried to camouflage what she was feeling in her texts to her sister, Liz.

The hospital was overwhelmed with patients. Lindsay texted Liz:

Lindsay: *What can I do for Jake today. He's struggling and says the boys are a mess and I can't think of anything to do*

Liz: *We are doing lots of small things and then long walks outside. Like 30 mins Minecraft. And then a snack break*

Lindsay: *Anything special you can think of I can get for Jake for his bday*

Liz: *And then an hour long scavenger hunt to find a heart shaped rock or something*

Lindsay: *I feel overwhelming guilt on top of everything else.*

Hayward and Lief had the 5 South teams working six days on and two days off. Some of these days were sixteen hours long, starting at dawn. Shortly after midnight every day, the head of the hospitalists, Arthur Evans, posted an update of hospital deaths and staff COVID infections. Many physicians, like Matt McCarthy, waited for Evans's e-mail before they went to bed. Evans had advised the Weill Cornell attendings to stay in frequent touch with one another. He feared for their states of mind. Now at the end of the day, the ICU doctors met by the elevator bank. At first, the group was kept small due to COVID safety protocols. But as word spread through the hospital, dozens appeared, far too many for comfort. The compelling urgency to discuss and understand what they were seeing kept the fifteen-minute elevator-bank meetings in place.

Hayward had just ended a long relationship with his partner, Anthony. Now Anthony had COVID. Hayward was in constant touch with him, but his days off in his empty apartment became unbearable. The staff of 5 South was his family; 5 South was where he needed to be. "No more off days for me," Hayward told Lief. "I am not going home to sit in that empty apartment. I will just stare at the walls and get more depressed. I need to be at the hospital taking care of patients." For the next few weeks, Hayward worked almost continuously.

At Columbia, the signs appeared in the third week of March. They looked like they had been printed in haste—and they had been. Up and down the halls and near all the pop-up ICUs, the flyers appeared.

NEW!!! SURGERY SWAT TEAM!!

WHO: Two senior surgical residents; surgical attendings as available

WHAT: Surgical Workforce Access Team—available to help with any procedures (CVC, A-line, Chest tube, NGT/OGT, foley, etc.) to help expedite

COVID and non-COVID patient care

WHEN: 24 hours a day

WHERE: FIND US OR WE WILL FIND YOU. WE BE-
LIEVE HEALTHCARE IS A 24 HOUR TEAM SPORT!

NO STRINGS ATTACHED

It was no surprise to anyone who knew her that surgeon Beth
Hochman taped up some of the signs herself. She would often
enter a room at a gallop, as if she were running a warm-up lap
before her next trauma surgery. Tall and lanky with wide-set eyes
and a focused gaze, she often wore an L.L. Bean fleece and was
prone to making jokes. Hers was a natural elegance, a bright com-
posure that could feel out of place in a world of surgical mandarins
with no lack of ego. Her aura of self-possession was lightly held,
but her concern over the fate of those suffering from COVID
was not.

While Hochman may not have had the ego of an alpha surgeon, she definitely had the work-until-you-drop grit. Her group
handled all the ED and inpatient emergency surgeries. "There
is a lot of bread-and-butter stuff," she said. "Appendix, gall-
bladder, hernia kind of stuff." She also rotated in and out of the
ICU.

Very little fazed Hochman, a Harvard magna who had already
interned at the WHO in Geneva and at the State Department before finishing her degree at Columbia. After her general-surgery
residency, she did fellowships in trauma and surgical critical care at
Penn. Hochman had worked in seven different countries, including
Kenya and India. When the pandemic rolled in, she had just returned
from Namibia and Ethiopia, where resources were so scarce that
sometimes two patients had to share the same bed. Such deficiencies

had taught Hochman a lot about the urgent need for both supplies and humility.

Adopted by two real estate developers who moved from Baltimore to Boca Raton, Hochman had always been mysteriously drawn to medicine, and in college she majored in biochemistry. She'd always known she was adopted, but when she was in college, she received a message from her birth mother, a neurosurgeon married to a pediatric surgeon, her birth father. Hochman was astonished. When she met her birth parents, she discovered that her uncles were also surgeons, some of them in the Boston area. "I was adopted privately when I was in the womb and my parents were in medical school and could not deal with a baby," she said. "When I first heard from them, I let them know I was fine—and was at a good school in the Northeast." Her birth parents, who were at Vanderbilt, arranged for her to intern with her doctor uncles in Boston, which became the real beginning of her surgical career.

Hochman may have appeared perpetually calm, but like everyone at the hospital during these months, her anxiety had ramped up tremendously. When she learned that basically all of surgery was going to be shut down, she said, "I was not alone feeling tremendously stressed and overwhelmed by it. Like, 'Okay, now, okay, we suddenly have to completely change everything we do, and we have to be able to do it by tomorrow.'" As the associate director of the surgery residency program, she set the schedules for the residents. She immediately called Steven Lee-Kong, who ran the program, and said, "'Steve, I feel like I am drowning.' But he was basically the only person I said that to. . . . I didn't want to reveal that."

Hochman had been on spring break in the first weeks of March, feverishly reading everything she could about COVID to prepare briefing books for the department. Once back, she was pulled into every kind of planning meeting with Laureen Hill, ICU head Daniel Brodie, Julia Iyasere, and Lauren Wasson, the head of the residents' program. Hochman was put on disaster-preparedness planning.

For weeks, Brodie had been in touch with colleagues in China and Italy and had been trying to prepare the hospital: "He was telling us, 'Actually, by the way, this is a true disaster, and they're overrun and we're about to experience it. And we should be getting ourselves prepared.'" Hochman took it in and thought, *Oh, wait . . . this thing is real, and it's coming to us, and it's going to be awful. And you know what? We've got to make sure everybody knows.*

Hochman was struck by Hill's calm and targeted focus: *Beth, here's the problem—can you do this thing? Dan, what do you think?* Of great concern to Hochman was the timing of the Epic rollout. It would be a great tool to keep track of patients, but it was going to slow things down at a moment when they had to work faster than ever.

By the third week of March, Hochman was focused on how best to use the surgical staff with all the operations now put on pause. All that week, Hochman was locked in strategy sessions with the ED and surgery leadership—what to do with the COVID patients crowding into the Columbia ER so they could make room for more COVID patients? There was no manpower to off-load the pressure on the ICUs. "Central lines, intubations—these are not short procedures; they can often take an hour." She asked, "If our surgeons aren't doing anything, how can we help you? We are good technicians, we're good procedurally. How can we take a burden off of you? Instead of the standard procedure of waiting for a resident or an attending to call them to the ED, why don't we have triage just dump them in our hands immediately? And we can take that burden off your hands."

Hochman, a former chief resident, reached out to one of the surgery program's current chief residents, Sophia Tam, who was at the Allen. They talked about the many problems in recent days that were due to ICU manpower shortages or the inexperience of staff who had been shifted to new duties. As they discussed the situation, they came up with an idea: the creation of a 24/7 strike force of surgical residents—a surgical SWAT team for the overwhelmed ER. Loaded with backpacks of equipment, they would roam through the pop-up ICUs and rooms. Hochman immediately texted a group of fellows, including Peter Liou, about the plan. Liou responded immediately with two fire emojis.

The ER plan quickly expanded to the entire hospital. Hochman and Tam set up a dedicated Epic portal for the surgical SWAT team—you could sign up if you were available—as well as a SWAT pager and a contact team in Epic, an unexpected boon to the introduction of the new electronic medical records system that had generated so many complaints. "Anyone could text us or page us or reach us through Epic if they needed something," Tam said.

As word spread, attendings volunteered to work with residents, racing from patient to patient throughout Columbia and the Allen; in the next month alone, they did bedside procedures for almost four hundred patients, fanning through the ICUs and the ER.

In late March at Weill Cornell, a group of nurses was tapping on the glass of Karen Bacon's room. She was a patient in the peds unit where she worked, now converted into an ICU for COVID patients. Not that Bacon knew. She was caught somewhere else in the hospital: *They were trying to kill her, someone chasing her through the halls of the hospital . . . and then her aunt was in a room, trying to awaken her . . . and then a low voice saying, "Karen, look over here."* Two weeks had gone by, and Karen Bacon—in and now maybe out of an ICU hallucination—had no idea how she had gotten from Metropolitan to Cornell, but there, staring through the glass, were all the nurses from 6 North, waving and crying, and by her side, Annette and Kourtnie, friends from her unit, were sobbing.

She saw posters and signs taped on a wall: WE LOVE YOU, KAREN. GET WELL, YOU ARE OUR FAMILY. Was this too a hallucination?

Bacon could not speak because of the tube down her throat. As she faded back into delirium, she tried to shout to them: *Please do not let the man kill me. Please.* She was crying and, she realized, no one could hear.

In late March, first-year medical resident Kerry Kennedy Meltzer started her rotation in the emergency department at Weill Cornell. She was sent to the area that had been cordoned off for COVID patients.

For days she had been telling her friends and family that she was scared for them but not for herself; she was only twenty-eight, and "so few young people were getting COVID," she would later write in the *Atlantic*. That all changed when she saw her first patient. She would later write of this night and her inability to test a young adult patient who presented with a dry cough and a high fever. Like the other doctors and nurses, she wanted to test them to see if this might be COVID, but given the rules and their current capacity, that was impossible. The chest X-ray came back clear, and their oxygen levels were high enough that she wasn't concerned. "Assume you have COVID-19," Meltzer instructed the patient. "You need to quarantine at home."

But one young patient followed another. They were having diffi-culty breathing, running fevers, and in some cases they had been with friends who had COVID. Still, their oxygen levels and chest X-rays did not warrant them staying in the hospital. But late at night, pa-tients in more desperate condition appeared. What Meltzer saw on their X-rays shocked her—the lungs were white clouds. "A chest X-ray is usually black—these patients' X-rays showed white on both sides [of the chest]." These patients had been quarantining and running fevers. They were so weak, they could not walk across the room. Even after a few feet, they were out of breath. "They were so out of breath, they were tripoding," she told me, demonstrating the hunched posture with hands on the knees that helps to draw in air. These patients were so sick that they were admitted to the hospital. The next day, when she returned to the hospital, they were on ventilators. Meltzer cited a study that had just come from the CDC—40 percent of those getting COVID-19 were ages twenty to forty-four. One doctor in the ICU told Meltzer he had never seen so many people in the ED. She texted her sister Maeve: *This is the hardest thing I have ever done.*

Meltzer had always wanted to write, especially about her experiences as a training doctor. When she came in from the emergency department, she told her husband, "I want to write about the young people coming to the ER." She sent a draft to the comms office, as stipulated in her contract with the hospital. "They absolutely did not want me to publish it," Meltzer told me. "I had written I was scared by what I was seeing. I was twenty-eight, around the same age as some of my patients. They said, 'We don't think you should say that.' They didn't think my future patients should know that about me. And they had a lot of HIPAA concerns—so I could not identify the sex of my patients. This was all coming from corporate PR. But I felt strongly that we needed to tell people about what we were seeing."

Meltzer began her residency in the summer of 2019, spending weeks with Lindsay Lief and Brad Hayward in 5 South. She was a newlywed; her husband, Max, was a book editor. Once a week, the interns would have breakfast with Lief and Hayward and talk about the difficult cases of the previous week and about all the deaths and the nuances of coping with this level of illness. That summer, her twenty-two-year-old cousin, Saoirse Kennedy Hill—the daughter of Courtney Kennedy Hill—died of a drug overdose. Saoirse had battled depression since she was at prep school but was set to graduate that summer from Boston College. Hill, like Meltzer, was the grand-daughter of Ethel and Robert F. Kennedy, whose children included Robert F. Kennedy Jr., Kathleen Kennedy Townsend, and Courtney Kennedy Hill.

When Meltzer heard about Saoirse, she immediately flew up to the Kennedy compound at Hyannis to once again grieve and try to console her family. Shortly after, she returned to her rotation on 5 South, a twentysomething patient coded, and she was called on to do chest compressions. She was surprised that the other residents were aware of what had happened in her family—Meltzer's style was not to discuss intimate tragedy, however public. "Can I take this for you, Kerry?" a friend offered. "This could be really hard." He realized what it might trigger; she did too.

That summer, Saoirse was often in Meltzer's thoughts, and she would later try not to think her cousin's tragedy was somehow a pre-cursor of the crushing grief of all who would lose their loved ones in the many months ahead.

At Columbia, Chief Resident Cleavon Gilman would later say, he may have been the most unlikely doctor in all of NewYork-Presbyterian. He had grown up poor in northern New Jersey, never knew his father, and his stepfather died of an overdose. He was frequently harassed by the police, once at gunpoint. Difficulties from a terrible stutter prompted him to drop out of high school. He eventually returned, but after he graduated, his prospects re-mained dismal. "I could have been a bouncer at a strip club or a drug dealer," he told a reporter. "Those were the only opportuni-ties." If he hadn't gotten out of there, he believed, he would have ended up in jail or dead.

Thanks to an extremely unlikely coincidence, he escaped. Sitting on the curb waiting for the police to let him go after they'd falsely accused him of carrying someone else's license plates, Gilman glanced up and saw a billboard: JOIN THE NAVY AND SEE THE WORLD. He did.

Gilman's high score on the military vocation test gave him career options, and he chose the medical path. Once he finished boot camp, he went to the Naval Hospital Corps School in Great Lakes, and was trained to provide medical care. His initial assignment was to Walter Reed National Military Medical Center outside Washington, DC. One day he was taking care of a patient when he looked up at a TV showing the Twin Towers. He stopped, transfixed. He had been to New York many times. But al-Qaeda's attacks hit close to home in a literal sense too—Walter Reed was not far from where American Airlines Flight 77 smashed into the Pentagon. Before the morning was over, Gilman knew that the United States was going to fight back and that his time at Walter Reed was about to end.

He was sent to Camp Lejeune to train with the Marine Corps as a hospital corpsman. In 2004, he was deployed to Iraq. He and a surgical company built a hospital; an especially challenging task, as they were frequently under attack while doing so. "The first few days out there we were mortared and a few of our own people were casualties." The first attack came in the early evening. "I was taking a shower. . . . I was like, 'What is that?'" The mortars were very close; he could feel the encampment shake. "People were saying, 'Get out of the shower, get your flak jacket, get your pistol—we're under attack.'" He was told, "'They need a corpsman at the clinic, at the hospital,'" and faster than he ever had, he dried off and dressed. "We ran across from the barracks over to the clinic and there were just multiple casualties, people who had severed legs, spinal-cord injuries."

During his time in Iraq, Gilman would again and again and again race to help save soldiers suffering from the most grievous damage. "When you're in it, you're just in it. You clearly don't have any time to think about anything else but what you're there to do.

It's the quiet times that I think are the hardest . . . you think about these things."

After six months in Iraq, Gilman headed back to the United States with a plan: He was going to become a doctor. Some of the inspiration had come from the African American doctors he'd worked with in the military, role models for a kid from northern New Jersey who hadn't known someone Black could be a doctor. But inspiration alone wasn't going to get him an MD.

"I was like, 'How do I go here?'" He was advised that he wouldn't get into the batter's box without a college degree, but even that seemed out of reach. At best, there was community college, so after five years in the navy, that's where he went. His relentless work ethic led to great grades, which in turn led to the University of California, Berkeley. Excellence there took him to medical school at UCSF, where he again excelled. The next step was finding a residency program. A visit to NewYork-Presbyterian made it an easy choice. "I just knew that Columbia was the place for me, I had a feeling." He walked into the pediatric ED and said, "I belong here." He called his fiancée and told her, "Babe, this is the place." Hundreds applied for the emergency residency program in 2016; a dozen were admitted, and Cleavon Gilman was one of them.

Part of the reason Gilman had immediately loved Columbia Medical Center was its location. He was from the East Coast, and it was nice to be back (though he had to get used to the cold again after so many years away). But more important, he loved the patient population. "I loved something about it being in New York, where you don't feel your color. . . . I just melted into the street talking to the patient population: Look at this big Black guy, but just like everybody else." It was the music, the culture, the fact that he could joke with his patients, laugh with them, feel truly at home with them. "I walked into there and I just see people who look like me, the patients and the Dominican population out there, the Puerto Ricans, and the

Blacks as well too. This is why I got into medicine, right? So I can come back and serve my community." And it wasn't just the patients: "It's the security guards, it's the people answering the phones, it's the people in the cafeteria, it's kind of vibing with everybody. That also happened in the pediatric ED too, the little kids as well of color who I see out there. And they're smiling . . . these people from our backgrounds to see people of color who have become a physician."

On March 24, Gilman saw that there were thirty patients waiting for admission, "and they were just super-super sick. We had to intubate, we had to jump around rooms to rooms to intubate, and the janitors could not keep up with cleaning the rooms. That's how quickly we were turning over the rooms, to intubate patients and to stabilize them." It was like being on the edge of a hurricane, "stretchers in the hallway, back to back, back to back. People with masks on, with oxygen on, very frail." Everywhere was the sound of coughing. "There was just an onslaught of sick patients that came in hypoxic, and they looked as if they had just hopped off the treadmill. . . . I just remember them being at all ages, twenty-year-olds, thirty-year-olds, fifty-year-olds, they were super-super sick. They just had this look of helplessness in their eyes; they could not believe they were breathing that bad or were that sick.

"A notification occurs when you have an unstable patient who arrives into the emergency department. And with these patients, it would be how quickly they were breathing and how hypoxic they were, eighty percent oxygen." Notification after notification—they never seemed to stop. Residents, Gilman recalled, "would have on these backpacks with intubation meds in them, kind of like being in Iraq with our medicine. And there were three of them and whenever we had an intubation, we would call them up; they would intubate the patient and then the surgeons afterwards would come in and [put] a central line in the patient because they needed a lot of medications, they needed access." Sometimes there wasn't even time for the doctors and nurses to learn one another's names.

But although it was chaos, it was not without order. "From a military standpoint," Gilman said, "how Columbia handled this pandemic is remarkable. How they created these intubation teams of anesthesiologists who would help us out in the emergency room."

One of the things that frustrated him was how people could fall back to thinking of those who'd died of COVID as a generic "them" or simply a number. The belittling—and sometimes demonizing—of the poor and those with preexisting conditions especially upset him. "People don't realize that the first patients sick during the pandemic were wealthy patients who were able to travel to Europe," he pointed out, "not people in the projects. These were people who had access to money and were able to travel to Europe and overseas."

March 26, 2020

Dear Colleagues,

I can begin today with a sunny ray of optimism regarding our PPE supply. It was just announced by NYP that a surgical mask should be worn in all hospital and clinical areas by anyone working in proximity to other people. The mask is not necessary when alone in an office, or in other non-clinical settings. Even more noteworthy, each "direct care giver" will receive one N95 mask, although use of the N95 is still officially restricted to aerosol-generating procedures. N95s should be covered with a face shield or a surgical mask to prolong their functional lifespans. Resterilization should be available very soon. Importantly, "direct care" giving is not the exclusive province of nurses or physicians. For example, housekeepers working in clinical areas are providing direct care; housekeepers in office areas are usually not. Setting aside Talmudic details of each use-case, this is an important step towards broader use of all masks, and is a signal that supplies are expected to increase soon.

Testing policies also show tentative signs of relaxation. Testing is still not approved for asymptomatic or mildly symptomatic patients, but for mildly symptomatic patients testing might be approved when the result would "make a difference." That can mean minimizing risk of spread to vulnerable persons (elderly, immunocompromised). It can mean clarifying risks surrounding planned procedures (radiation, chemotherapy, perhaps surgery). The new NYP policy in obstetrics to test all women admitted to labor & delivery falls in the latter category. As with PPE, setting aside the minutia, this is a positive sign. Widespread testing will be an unalloyed good.

Stepping out of the sunshine and back into the cave, I must report that the number of patients on ventilators at CUIMC more than doubled in the past 3 days, a pace that exceeds the overall increase in new cases. We have not exhausted our existing supply of ventilators, but if we keep doubling every three days, we might. This development has placed sudden pressure on ICU capacity. ORs have already been converted to ICUs, and an entire 36-bed floor (7GN) is now fully renovated for conversion to ICU space. Consequently, a call went out yesterday for MD volunteers to staff ICUs. Within a few hours 20 surgeons had volunteered. Once again, the selflessness demonstrated by everyone in the Surgery family inspires me.

On the front page of the *New York Times* yesterday is a story that deeply distresses me. Across the U.S. pharmacists are pushing back against physicians who are prescribing large amounts of hydroxychloroquine and azithromycin for themselves and their families—with refills. Doesn't that make you proud? One of the few positive things we can say about this pandemic is that it gives us a precious opportunity to carry out proper double-blind, randomized controlled trials of therapeutics. . . . Because the numbers are so large, and growing so rapidly, such a trial could be carried out very fast. Enrolling large numbers quickly also allows us to rely on meaningful hard end-points, which avoids bundling a bunch of soft endpoints into a composite, solely for the purpose of dredging statistical power out of smaller (and cheaper) trials. The hysteria surrounding [hydroxychloroquine and azithromycin] is almost entirely anecdotal, propped up by a handful of tiny, unconvincing trials. Ask yourself this: if 98% of patients survive, and many have relatively minor illness that resolves in a week or two, what value is an anecdote in which patient X starts taking [hydroxychloroquine and azithromycin] after a few days (when he's feeling really lousy), then (lo and behold) he improves? Sacre bleu! And now the MDs featured in the *New York Times* are fanning the flames, nudging us along from ignorance to superstition. Almost 100 years ago (1928) Bertrand Russell said "What is wanted is not the will to believe, but the will to find out, which is the exact opposite." Our profession's response to this crisis has been extraordinarily uplifting and reinforcing—I hope we do the right thing here.

Craig R. Smith, MD
Chair, Department of Surgery
Surgeon-in-Chief, NYP/CUIMC

At Weill Cornell, the news that the New York police were in the hospital traveled quickly through the floors. Rosanne Raso and the hospitalists and others knew what it was about, as did hundreds of thousands of others when a story appeared in the online edition of the *New York Post* on March 27 with the headline "Man with Cancer Commits Suicide at NYC Hospital After Getting Coronavirus."

The *Post* had only been able to pull in notes from the police blotter, which the paper had somehow gotten hold of via a tip from sources inside the force. The patient was sixty-six and was admitted to the hospital with pneumonia as well as throat cancer. He was put in isolation in one of the hastily built wooden rooms without a window or a way to see to the floor, and he hung himself.

Outside the hospital, the calamity of what was happening to the city pushed aside what could have been another Libby Zion case—the appearance of clear neglect or lack of awareness of what was happening to patients inside the Amazing Place. The front page of the *Post* featured the new reality: "Hell on Front Lines . . . NYC Hospitals Overwhelmed with Virus Patients, Equipment Shortages." The head of facilities, Joe Ienuso, was told he had twenty-four hours to change the isolation rooms for COVID patients who had been lucky enough to secure a bed.

For weeks now, Jessica Forman, the physician assistant helping to run a pop-up ICU in Bronxville, had been working twelve-hour days, sometimes without a break. Forman was far from the only one exasperated. On the other side of the hospital, Xenia Frisby found herself absorbing the angst from the nurses who felt unprotected by NewYork-Presbyterian's policies. "I had to call a meeting and just repeat the CDC guidelines about the masks," Frisby said. "And there was a period when so many nurses were already out on quarantine or already sick. We told them, 'We are very low on N95s. And unless you are treating COVID, we can only give surgical masks.' And they came at me hard. 'What are your qualifications for making these decisions?'" The whole hospital had only 250 masks. Why couldn't it get more? "A lot of the PAs were upset—and in the ER staff," Frisby said. "Many of them became COVID-positive."

"The guidelines were constantly being changed on us," cardiologist Anthony Pucillo said, "sometimes three times during the day."

Frisby lamented, "We, as a leadership team, lost a lot of credibility with the staff."

Forman had thrown herself into the role of being an ICU PA without portfolio. She would walk into a patient's room and reconnect hoses that had somehow come loose. "I had to learn how to suction lungs—and quickly. And how to troubleshoot." Sometimes patients had to be put on their stomachs to help them breathe, which required elaborate choreography with tubing and other attachments.

Almost immediately, she and cardiologist Mark Apfelbaum had noticed the virus produced mucus so heavy and adhesive, it was like rubber cement. "I saw the coagulated mucus early," Apfelbaum recalled. "It was thicker and grayer and firmer than anything I had ever seen before. I remember thinking we were a little bit helpless."

Through it all, Forman was surrounded by nurses from the cath lab who had volunteered to help. "There was real danger. I had never [seen] people step up this way. There was so much camaraderie. And there were no rules of engagement." There was also no treatment regime that worked. "It came down to a tremendous amount of distress. I would be on the phone with the families of the patients over and over again during the day. They would ask me: 'How are you treating them? Are you using Zithromax?' It was whatever they heard on the news that day. They would say: 'Why can't you use remdesivir? Is this because he is Black?' It was so hard." Forman would FaceTime or go on WhatsApp with families three times a day, staying for extra shifts just so she could personally update them.

Heartsick about the lack of human contact for the patients on ventilators and the cold detachment of having to look at them through masks, Forman made a photograph of herself for her badge so patients would know who they were looking at. And she appealed to hospital administrators to bend the rules and allow wives to look through the glass into the room where their husbands were being treated. By the second week of March, no family members could come into the ICU; there could be no exceptions. That's when she was trying to help a young couple. The husband was not doing well, and the wife wanted desperately to be with him. "She screamed. And tried to run into the room. The nurses had to hold her back. It was the most horrible primal sound—the grief. We did not know what to do. It was creating moral distress for everyone on the team. Part of the job was telling people that aggressive measures were futile. Family members couldn't accept that because they couldn't see what we were seeing, but when we tried bringing family members back so they could see for themselves, it didn't solve the problem either. They couldn't understand why we wouldn't do things we knew weren't going to help, such as giving CPR, which would aerosolize the virus. It felt to some extent like we were torturing these bodies by prolonging the inevitable. Meanwhile, there were more people waiting to come into the ICU."

Driving home late at night, Forman would call her parents in Las Vegas to discuss the harrowing physical conditions—caring for so many patients who were so desperately ill was taking a terrible toll. She also spoke of the horror of being with her patients while their families FaceTimed with them. She had become close to a Dominican woman who would speak to her hospitalized mother for hours during the day, praying and telling her, "Mommy, you are a lion. Mommy, I am praying for you." Forman would upload pictures of the mother and send them to the daughter. In turn, "She sent me pictures of her mother when she was healthy—such a beautiful woman." And, because sometimes there were happy endings, the patient made it through.

"We were so worried about her," Forman's father, Mitchell, recalled. "The strain on her—it was as if she was in combat."

As spring drew closer, fear took over the city. On March 23, the city had recorded one hundred COVID deaths. Seven days later, there would be one thousand. The parks were now mostly deserted. And there were still days to go before there would be any sign of the pandemic's peak. "The first symptom," Columbia transplant surgeon Tomoaki Kato recalled, "was a backache." He decided to stay home but didn't suspect anything major was amiss. After all, who doesn't get a backache every now and then? If your job involves using your body, as surgery does, a backache is a good reason to take the day off.

Then the fever came—and went, and then came again, here and there, up and down, but never planting its flag at a particular temperature. Kato checked his oxygen levels, which hovered around 93 percent, a symptom of COVID.

On Tuesday, March 24, he was taking a shower and "that was when the pain came." Initially, Kato had been reluctant to go to the hospital, since at the time NewYork-Presbyterian and other area hospitals were telling people to stay home unless they had risk factors for severe disease, such as immunosuppression or long-standing lung issues. After drying off, he checked his oxygen level; it was only 90 percent—which made sense, since he was struggling to breathe. He had headed to the hospital a thousand times as a physician. He now headed to it as a patient.

Those who saw him when he arrived were horrified. He was given supplementary oxygen; the doctors tried to deal with his elevated heart rate, and they took an X-ray of his lungs. The image was extremely disturbing: these were the lungs of someone who was suffering from acute COVID.

At Columbia Medical Center, it was inconceivable to the cardiologist Gregg Rosner that Tom Kato would ever be his patient. Rosner knew Kato; from time to time, Rosner was called on to do a preoperative evaluation for one of Kato's patients to assess whether his or her heart was strong enough to withstand surgery. The week of March 24, Rosner was on service doing his yearly three and a half months as the chief of the cardiac intensive care unit. "It was shell shock," he said. "The patients were coming in faster than we could take them. I was not exactly unused to treating critically ill patients. But this? I did not know up from down, left from right."

What Rosner did know was not comforting. The news from Italy was filled with accounts of health-care workers dying, and nobody seemed to know what sort of protection was needed. Whatever it might be, it was clear that NewYork-Presbyterian would not have enough of it. "I said to my staff, 'I will see this through with you guys, whatever that means.' I didn't know what it meant, but I thought it sounded good." Rosner, along with a single colleague, proceeded to run a COVID ICU on a grueling schedule of twelve days on, two days off, for four months straight. "All that first week, the patients were coming in and there were things about this illness that no one had seen before," he recalled. "We were learning as we went."

What did they see? "We saw kidney failure that required dialysis, then the rapid destruction of lungs," Rosner said. "When we first started, none of this was known. We did not know if the medicines we were giving were the right thing. Give steroids, don't give steroids. Give antivirals, don't give antivirals. Dialyze, don't dialyze. High-flow! Intubate! Every one of those decisions which now seems so clear, but no one in the U.S. knew." He would go to bed at 11:00 at night after reviewing all the patients in the ICU and wake up at 4:30 in the morning to find half the patients dead and replaced with different ones. "And it was over and over again," he said.

Many of Rosner's conversations were focused on just getting his staff to come to work. "The black Jell-O blood. That was new too. There were people clotting everywhere. You would put in a dialysis catheter, and by the time you had finished, the catheters had clotted.

People were scared—and understandably." Everyone was a patient
of some sort, immediate or potential. Rosner was bombarded with
questions from his staff: How are we going to survive this? How are
we not going to get sick? What do we do if we get sick? Can I go
home? Do I have to come to work? "In the hospital, people were still
not wearing PPE. After the New Rochelle patient was in our MICU,
I still wasn't wearing a mask, and my wife was like, 'Are you crazy?'"
And when Rosner donned a small surgical mask, patients would ask
him, "Why aren't you in a moon suit?" But the hospital and the CDC
hadn't said you needed to be, so . . .

Then Rosner got a call. "I was told that there was a VIP in
McKeen—that is one of our fancy floors—and that this VIP might
need to come to an ICU and they would prefer he be treated in the
cardiac ICU because he wasn't as well known there as he was in some
of the others." Rosner didn't reflect on the strangeness of that remark
or wonder why he wasn't given a name. "I said, 'Whatever. We have
a bed. We will make a bed.' And then we got a call that it was Tom
Kato, and I said, 'Oh, that is terrible.'"

Rosner hastily went to see Kato where he was, and he did not look
good. He was visibly distressed and pale. He was being seen by hospitalists and a team of pulmonologists, and Rosner interrupted to announce
that Kato needed to come to the ICU. There was a back-and-forth
about whether to relocate him, but eventually everyone agreed that he
needed to be moved. As well, those closest to Kato knew that they had
to find, as quickly as possible, two of his surgical fellows: Dusty Carpenter, who was racing through the hospital collecting mucus samples
for a T-cell COVID NIH project, and most of all, Peter Liou.

The transplant fellow Peter Liou and his boss, Tom Kato, shared
many traits, not least of which was musical training—and the understanding of chance. In 2007, Liou, trained as a classical pianist

in Cleveland, was on campus at Columbia, upset that he had missed a rolling deadline for medical school because of an appearance at a music festival in France. He noticed a flyer for the Columbia Polish Society's annual Chopin competition. Liou thought, *Why not enter?* The contest was the next night—Liou played Chopin's *Andante Spianato,* which he had performed in France, and won.

The next day, Columbia University president Lee Bollinger reached out to a professor who had been present. "I'm looking for someone to play at the annual trustees dinner." When Liou got the call, he almost turned them down, expecting only to play background music. But then he was told, "We are paying you one hundred dollars for ten minutes." The offer was too good to refuse.

At the event, Bollinger introduced Liou as a Columbia undergraduate majoring in biochemistry and music who hoped to go to Columbia's medical school. It was hard not to be astonished by his accomplishment—in ninth grade, Liou had debuted at Carnegie Hall with the Cleveland Orchestra Youth Orchestra. He played both violin and piano and performed several times in New York after that. "I knew I wanted to come to college here," he said. "There was so much opportunity for a musician." Among those listening to him at the dinner were the dean of the medical school, Lee Goldman, and Clyde Wu, a Columbia medical school alumnus, who was not only a trustee but also a classical music aficionado.

Cue the lights: Liou was accepted to the medical school (with a scholarship, no less) and, hoping to become a pediatric surgeon, he later matched at Columbia for his residency. Liou planned to take a year off before his final year of residency to work in the office of a Park Avenue hernia specialist. The job fell through when the surgeon was involved in a legal scandal. Suddenly, Liou had to figure out exactly how he wanted to spend that year. Kato's astonishing procedures and genius were legendary in the department, but he operated in his own orbit, surrounded by carefully chosen fellows.

Fortuitously, Liou heard that Kato's longtime physician assistant was leaving, and asked Kato if he would be able to take him on for a year, adding, "I will do anything you need—research, anything." Kato told him, "I would like to, but I have no funding for another fellow." In this case, "funding" mostly meant a budget to cover the additional malpractice insurance that came with adding a fellow, and Liou figured that if he could somehow get another fellowship elsewhere at the hospital, he could use that insurance coverage and be available to Kato for free. Doing two fellowships seemed insane—one alone could be overwhelming, but doubling that? But Liou knew what it would mean to learn from Kato, and he found a way.

Liou spent two years as Kato's fellow and was enthralled by the dramatic possibilities of organ transplantation. Liou was especially drawn to Kato's most extreme surgeries, the ex vivo procedures performed only for the most difficult tumors and cancers. "They wrap around critical blood vessels that you really cannot cut out without cutting the organ," Liou explained. "So what we do is take all that out and take the organs out, so they can be replaced in the body. While they are on ice, you can take the tumors out and you can sew the organs that are now tumor-free back in the body." Kato was so bold and optimistic that it sometimes seemed to Liou that when others looked at a patient's CT scan and threw up their hands, Kato was energized. Liou, too, often disagreed with Kato about the chances for survival of a patient Kato was trying to save. "More often than not, I will go into a surgery thinking, *There is no way this is going to work . . . we are going to harm the patient and not help them.* And then two or three weeks later, the patient will walk out of the hospital and is doing amazing." Liou remembered a patient who was so weak from a virulent tumor involving her kidneys, stomach, and intestine that he gave her no chance to survive. "It's a risk, but let's try," Kato said. She too left the hospital and, defying all predictions, lived a few more years, returning to the hospital to thank the doctors and nurses who saved her.

In February 2020, Liou took a vacation in Southeast Asia. When he came back, he wore PPE through the hospital at a time when no one was wearing it, explaining that what he learned in Asia really concerned him. "When people would see me, they would say, 'Oh my gosh, are you sick? What's going on? You were just in Asia.' So people stayed away from me just because I wore a mask." Liou and Kato did a surgery together on March 7—a hernia operation. "We were talking about [how] crazy COVID was in China and how it was coming here." Liou was stunned when he received a text: *Kato has COVID.* Then Liou got a call from the medical ICU. Kato was deteriorating.

In the ICU, Rosner assessed Kato and realized he had to be intubated. "And there is a pulmonologist and there is a hospitalist—and there is hesitancy," Rosner remembered. "They did not want to intubate him. We know when patients are intubated that they do not do well." Indeed, Rosner and the others knew that when you intubated someone, mortality increased to 80 percent or 90 percent, depending on other issues.

It was Rosner's ICU and he was charged with making difficult decisions. "[Kato] was panting fifty times a minute by the time he got to us," said Rosner—something had to be done, and it had to be done immediately. "Good friends of mine who I trust with my relatives said, 'I think we can wait. I think we can wait.' And I said, 'Guys, he needs to be intubated.' And I look at him—I will never forget it—and I say, 'Tom, we need to intubate you.' And he looks at me and he goes, 'Oh.' And I said, 'How are you breathing?' And he said, 'I am not breathing well, but I don't want to be intubated.' And I said, 'I think it is for the best.' And he said, 'This is scary. Will I live?'

"I looked at him," said Rosner, "and I said, 'Tom, I know this is scary. You are going to get the best care in the world. We'll do everything we can.' He called his wife and then we got the anesthesia team. One of the last people he e-mailed was an anesthesiologist who was his close friend, who he asked to do the intubation. He was in tears walking out of the room. Again, we knew the data. And the chance of coming off that ventilator was not great. So we intubated him, then the decision was made later that night to move him out of the CCU to one of the neuro ICUs, where we had been doing ECMO for this disease." (ECMO stands for "extracorporeal membrane oxygenation," a process in which a machine acts as both heart and lungs for the patient. Later, doctors would deploy ECMO in many different units, but early on it was in just two of the neuro ICUs.)

"We take care of so many sick patients, but when it's someone that you regard as an amazing person and your mentor [who] is that sick, that's when it really hits home," Liou reflected. "I tried to make sure the best people were doing the ECMO. That was Josh Sonnet, the head of thoracic surgery. I came to the hospital, and it was very emotional. The transplant surgeon Adam Griesemer was also there. That night, Dan Brodie called me to reassure me, 'We will move the world's resources for this man because we know how many people he has saved and will continue to save.'"

"It was the low point for me in the entire three months," said Rosner. "That he could die. The tragedy of this. You can't replace anyone. All human deaths are tragic. All life is sacred. But Kato has a skill set so unmatched—if you lose someone like that, mankind is worse."

There would be many, many cases of COVID at NewYork-Presbyterian during the first year of the virus's invasion of New York, but it's unlikely that any patients were much worse off than Kato. Within hours after he was put on a ventilator, he lost consciousness. From there, things got worse: bacterial infections, sepsis, kidney failure, and then his lungs deteriorated to the point that even a ventilator couldn't help.

The news about Kato's condition stunned the staff and devastated Corwin. It was one thing to talk about the undercount of nursing-home deaths or the many who had died already, but, he said, "I felt, on a personal level, I love the guy. I meet with him regularly on a variety of things. He's brought tremendous credit to the institution. And now I've got somebody who is a friend, who looks like he's going to die, and that was horrible. And I remember Laureen Hill basically saying, 'Steve, we're going to do everything, I don't know if he's going to make it.'"

Rosner tried to alleviate some of the horror of his days by listening to audiobooks—*The Boys in the Boat, Unbroken*. He woke up every morning at 4:30 in his home in Armonk, an hour from the city, his three kids—ages four, eight, and ten—still asleep. "Twelve days on, two days off. I leave for work and change in the parking lot. I walk in. Gown up. It was like you were going to war. You leave the hospital. Undress. Pack the clothes. You are in your underwear in the parking lot. It was really just the health-care staff who was there. I would come and unpack my clothes and try to be normal with my family, but in my mind I am seeing people die and families screaming on FaceTime in the background. And they can't be there when their loved ones are dying. And it was: Repeat. Repeat. Repeat." It would go on for months.

And throughout, there was Tom Kato, intubated, comatose, the ECMO machine drawing out blood, oxygenating it, then returning it to his body, doing the work of his heart and lungs. Rosner checked on Kato several times a day. His surgical fellows Dusty Carpenter and Peter Liou were by his bedside. "And every time there was a complication, it was like a gut punch," Rosner said.

Kato, many believed, was never coming back.

In the third week of March, at home on the Upper West Side, the pulmonologist Anna Podolanczuk had taken enough of her maternity leave. She loved her newborn and four-year-old, but right now she knew where she was needed—at the Allen, which was under siege. The Allen, atop Manhattan, on the edge of the Hudson River, a short bridge away from the Bronx, shared land with the Columbia University soccer field. The small community hospital—focused on the local, largely minority population—had a new heart unit but sent most of its more complicated cases fifty blocks south to Columbia.

When Podolanczuk walked into the small emergency room at the Allen, she saw crowds of patients on stretchers in the hall and almost no nurses. Where were the nurses or, for that matter, the doctors? In particular, where was Lorna Breen, the forceful high-fashion perfectionist, the medical director of the emergency department at the Allen who was known for her love of the excitement of the department? Breen had been a mentor to Cleavon Gilman. She had also worked closely with Angela Mills, chair of the Columbia emergency department. Breen, Podolanczuk was told, had recently had COVID. Podolanczuk was surprised—Breen could work longer hours than almost anyone. If someone so strong and diligent about COVID protocols could get infected, Podolanczuk wondered, what did it mean for the rest of them?

The hallway stretchers were not even the half of it. The farther she went into the hospital, the more it felt like she was in a scene painted by Hieronymus Bosch. "The ICU was filled with COVID, the ED was filled with COVID," she said. Acute respiratory distress syndrome (ARDS) and viral pneumonia were everywhere. She noticed that a lot of those caring for these patients had been redeployed from other departments and were not ED doctors or pulmonologists. Patients had oxygen levels of 70 percent, "and we are telling them, 'We have to intubate you. . . . Let me call your family. We don't know if you are going to make it out.'" Outside, one ambulance after another was unloading gurney after gurney of elderly patients. The ICU had twelve beds, and they were able to squeeze a few more in, but that was that. "It looked perfect on paper," Podolanczuk said. "Everyone we couldn't take we were going to decant downtown—meaning to Columbia—but, of course, the patients coming into the Allen were old and they weren't stable enough for transport." In the end, she said, "We had no place to put anybody."

Perhaps most disconcerting, there seemed to be no one to take care of all the sick patients. "I was angry at the nursing bosses. I said, 'We can take care of these patients, we have the doctors.' And the nurses kept saying, 'No. We need at least one nurse for two patients! And we will not accept one other patient.' And I would say, 'You have to.'" But they wouldn't or it would take too much time to argue or if they did, it would be nurses without ICU experience. "There were multiple drips, and if you don't know how to titrate these drips, if you make one little error, it's life or death." Podolanczuk understood the substitute nurses' concerns—they hadn't been adequately trained for this. But she and the other doctors were forced to do all of it themselves, which took them away from other tasks.

Podolanczuk, who was continuing to breastfeed, sometimes wore portable pumps underneath her doctor's coat, not even thinking about risk as she intubated one patient after another. The sheer scale of misery at the Allen overwhelmed her. "In the beginning, it was, 'This is what I am trained for and I am ready,'" she said. "Then I went to the Allen, and I started crying, and I could not do it." She could medically take care of them, but without adequate nursing support, "It was just too many. I could not do it. I was there from the end of March and into the first week of April, when it was at the highest level and there was *no* plan. There were thirty people in the hospital that needed ventilators, and we had thirty-one ventilators. I was literally making decisions like, 'Do I send this patient who just got extubated out when I worry that they might die tomorrow? Or do I make a bed for the patient who is twenty-five and needs to be intubated or will they die in the ER?' It was an impossible situation."

Late at night, an emotionally scorched and exhausted Podolanczuk would return home, strip, shower, store her pumped milk, nurse her four-month-old, and try to process what she'd gone through. Fortunately, her husband was able to feed the baby during the day, and she treasured the fact that she could be with her kids, knowing that some of her colleagues had sent their children and partners far away so they'd be safe. Hiring their babysitter "saved our lives," but it also brought home to Podolanczuk the cost to the hospitals of staff not having childcare or support; if that wasn't there, how could you possibly expect people to continue to come in to work, especially since work was a hot zone? She had started sleeping with the baby because "there was no way I could get up with her all night." One night, in a state of total exhaustion, she tweeted a selfie blurt from her bed, then collapsed. When she awakened, her phone had blown up—thirty thousand had watched her and were now following her tweets.

Anna Podolanczuk and Julia Iyasere and Lizzy Oelsner were texting one another all day long: *Yesterday there were 20 patients in the ER and now there are 25. And we have no beds.* Remembered Iyasere, "I got calls all day, 'I need more. I need help. We have no one here.'"

As might have been predicted, given the nonstop intubations and lack of fresh air, Podolanczuk tested positive about a week later. Her fever spiked to 104. "Anna was texting us her oxygen saturation level," Iyasere recalled. "And I would text her, 'How are you doing?'"

"I felt the most awful I have ever felt," Podolanczuk remembered. "I had two comforters on top of me and I was shivering. It wasn't pneumonia—that was my expertise. I took Tylenol, and it worked. And then my four-month-old got COVID. And we would just lie on the floor, staring at each other." Whether she could return to the hospital was only one question. COVID was so new that there was no way of predicting what its long-term effects might be. Podolanczuk might not just be done as a doctor in the current war—she might be done as a doctor, period.

Now back in New York City, Lizzy Oelsner finished her grant proposal the third week of March, whereupon she was told by her supervisor, "I need you to report to Columbia tomorrow. Now would be better." Oelsner took the bike she'd ordered for Vermont and sped up the West Side Highway bike path. "There was no one outside," she recalled. "No one." She arrived in the ED and was handed PPE. She had heard about the atmosphere but was still shocked by what she saw. "There was a uniformity of doom. . . . Imagine that you stepped into a room and there are literally two hundred people coughing. They are surrounded by people trying to do their best, but literally, one of them was wearing a scuba mask." ("NYP put out the word that we should not be talking about that," she said, referring to the lack of PPE.)

"You could read about it," she said, "but to walk into it?" Oelsner was getting texts from friends asking how long they had to wait after wiping their FreshDirect deliveries with Clorox wipes, and she was here, where the issue of what to do with a FreshDirect order was from a different universe. "There is personal fear and there is public fear. These were individuals who were really sick. There are people who are being dropped out of cars and they are blue and their cars are driving away. . . . You have the drama coming at you. You walk out, you walk back, two more people are intubated. You are told more people are being intubated, and you know there is virus everywhere. Zero walls, zero negative pressure.

"Friends were texting me about shopping in stores without 'a negative-pressure environment.' A negative-pressure environment? Are you kidding me? People were still living in that world—and

we were in a place where there was no negative-pressure environment . . . and no PPE. People were showing up and they were doing
their best and their best was not good enough. And you knew the
disease was so bad, many were going to die no matter how good you
are. And that is always the case in the ICU. . . . You are in a high-
class place with the best science, and the rate of death was thirty
percent to forty percent."

   And yet, while there was admiration for them, Oelsner and many
of the doctors and nurses and support staff who broke their backs
and broke their hearts felt there was a lack of sympathy for what they
did. "Some people would say, 'This is what you signed up for,'" she
recalled. "And we said, 'Oh no—this is *not* what we signed up for.'
And we said, 'There are plenty of doctors who did not work and left
town and did not do a thing.'"

In the third week of March, as he walked up First Avenue from his
apartment on Seventeenth Street on his way to Weill Cornell, the
cardiologist Hadi Halazun was struck by the eerie silence. The clamor
of trucks and deliveries that often stalled traffic near the downtown
hospitals and the United Nations at Forty-Second Street had slowed.
There was hardly a taxi on the streets. Halazun had decided to stay
off public transportation and try to enjoy the spring weather before
he plunged into the maelstrom of the pop-up cardiac ICU he had
been asked to oversee. One week after it opened, Halazun's ICU was
overrun with patients. The roar of the HEPA filters and the constant
beeping of the machines were unnerving. Like his colleagues, Halazun had never seen so many desperately ill patients all at once. The
cardiology department had scheduled a nightly Zoom call to discuss
how to keep the CCUs—the cardiac care units—fully staffed. At
home, before one Zoom meeting, Halazun poured himself a stiff
whiskey, then another, but he was not prepared for the degree of re-

sistance he heard from several colleagues on the call. "There was a real sense among some that they did not want ICU duty," Halazun said. The skills required for cardiac intensivists took years of training to develop, that was one issue, but another was simply fear. At the end of that call, Halazun, now a few whiskeys into the night, sat at his desk and began to type.

On March 26, Halazun e-mailed the entire cardiac division at Weill Cornell:

Dear All,
I don't usually write this division list, but I feel it is important to share a few brief thoughts from what can only be termed as the front lines.

First, make no mistake. This is a war. There are no rules; they are made up as we go. They change daily. People will die. You may get hurt. But loved ones at home are cheering for you. The world is relying on you. The camaraderie and support is incredible. Your brothers and sisters on the front lines have your back in unimaginable ways. You are serving humanity.

Forget that you are a cardiologist. You are "just" a doctor now. You are a COVID doctor. Your expertise will come in handy once in a while, but you will have to learn things that you never thought you would need to, and trust me, you will learn it fast. You'll think you are doing a shitty job at first, but everyone appreciates your stepping up to the plate. Algorithms change daily and you will feel dumb and inadequate, but then your favorite ICU doc will come and tell you, "I don't know what the fuck I am doing either, I'm making it up as I go." It is then you realize that we are all in this together.

Put your ego aside. Do fellow work. Do resident work. Do

intern work. You are not a vent or ARDS guru. Accept it, get over it, learn and move on. Contribute any way you can. Recognize that the TRUE frontline providers are the nurses and respiratory therapists who are at the greatest risk of getting hurt. Support them in every way that you can.

Be Proud. We are truly beyond privileged to be asked to serve our society in ways others can't. Sitting on the sidelines of this pandemic must be frustrating to those who cannot help. We are truly in a unique position in time and place to be the "heroes" that our children will one day look up to. Don't shy away from it. Don't fear it. Jump in.

There is a saying I live by, which is, if you are standing close to the water on the beach, you'll be hit by a wave. You can let the wave knock you down, or you can surf it. Either way you'll get wet. I say to you all, put on that surgical mask, and let's surf the fuck out of this wave; we're getting wet anyway.

> But stay safe,
>
> Hadi

He sent the letter to the forty-plus cardiologists who had been on the Zoom call. The letter was instantly forwarded, then widely tweeted, and then it went viral. Almost immediately, Halazun received a sharp e-mail rebuke from the communications office of New York–Presbyterian, demanding that he immediately remove the letter from the site where he'd posted it, even though it had already been forwarded to thousands of people. Halazun received dozens of media requests; several outlets asked him to film the conditions inside the ICU. "We were forbidden to do that," Halazun said. "Even though we were in the first stages of the pandemic and could have prevented a tremendous amount of disinformation being spread by people doubting the severity of COVID-19 had we been allowed to get the word out." Angry at what seemed not only opaque but in fact dangerously misguided corporate policy, Halazun discussed it with his division chief. "The letter is already out there," his chief said. "Why get them angrier? I would take it down." Halazun did. After the severity of the threat against Matt McCarthy by the corporate side, the Cornell doctors were justifiably infuriated and wary of being bullied; they were focused on managing the masses of patients who now crowded every floor. But Halazun's letter found an audience. *People* took a screenshot and ran with it. Halazun rewrote it and published a weakened version on the op-ed pages of the *New York Times*. "We are America's doctors, and we have been redeployed. Yesterday we were your pediatricians. Your cardiologists. Your surgeons. Today, we are all Covid-19 doctors. Your appointments are canceled, and our offices are closed. We've been called to the front lines. . . . We have lost some doctors already. They were our colleagues. They were our friends." The *Times* published Halazun's op-ed on March 6, the day before the peak of the New York City surge. Ten days earlier, the president, in an interview on Fox News, had said, "I would love to see the country opened up and rarin' to go by Easter," exacerbating the spread of magical thinking and bolstering some people's belief that COVID-19 was a hoax. That week, there were thirty thousand confirmed cases in New York State. The Senate passed a two-trillion-dollar COVID relief bill to aid America's unemployed and shore up businesses struggling to survive.

Halazun had already made the decision to leave Weill Cornell and go into private practice, but two years after the pandemic began, he was still haunted by NewYork-Presbyterian's corporate communications fiats, which kept information from the public in the crucial early stages of the New York surge.

Back in Queens, chief medical officer Amir Jaffer, struck down early with COVID, had improved and been released. "I was home after four days, and I was determined to go back. And my boss said, 'You need to work from home.'" He closely monitored the flood of patients who were now in every hall and room imaginable.

"By the third week of March, there was one day when we saw a hundred and forty patients," ED nursing director Suzanne Pugh recalled. "We had to see them outside in the tent—the inpatient team could not keep up."

On March 26, 208 patients were admitted. "We put them in classrooms, we put them in lounge chairs, doubling up," Pugh said. "We had them in the halls. I took pictures. One hundred fifty-eight of them were out of the ED. Every hallway was filled with someone in an oxygen tent. . . . You talk about a war zone? I tell people, as bad as you think it was, it was worse." They ran out of stretchers; they put patients in a boardroom. "We ran out of sedatives. Fentanyl drips. The tube is in your throat saving your life. What do you do if you awaken? You have to rip it out." The doctors were scared to go home.

It was like being onshore as the tsunami arrived. "We had a room downstairs that had been built for a surge," Pugh explained. "The idea was that each room could take two stretchers. We didn't have room for stretchers—then we ran out of stretchers. We basically took every lounge chair from every room in the building. I was able to put two lounge chairs and two oxygen outlets in every room. I was able to get fifty-five patients in there. . . . We used the classrooms and we used the patient waiting areas for lab tests." When elective procedures were canceled, they were able to convert the endoscopy unit into another space for COVID patients. A post-op recovery room was converted into a space that could hold twenty-four patients, and within two hours, every bed was full. The influx was so massive and the frantic efforts to take care of patients so intense that Jaffer, now back, didn't know that his own brother and cousins were in the hospital in Pakistan.

The shunning of the Asian American population set in immediately. And for that matter, anyone connected to a New York City hospital was suddenly persona non grata. Pugh's attempts to rent a house for the Fourth of July weekend failed when the owner Googled her and saw that she worked at NewYork-Presbyterian in Queens, an area with a lot of Asian Americans; he told her the house was no longer available. Even her uncle, afraid of what she might bring, refused to let her visit his lake house. "No one who owned a Laundromat would allow any of our staff to bring their scrubs in. I went to my dry cleaner with my lab coat and the cleaner, who I have gone to for years, said, 'No, not today.' And I said, 'What? Can I bring them tomorrow?' And he said, 'No.'" And it wasn't just the Asian population. "Early on, one woman who had gone to Italy with her entire family group came back. I saw her and I said, 'Just wait. Your entire group will be in the hospital within a week.' Twenty-five of them were admitted."

Elmhurst had closed by declaring "an internal disaster," which was, ED chief Manish Sharma realized, the only way a hospital could legally close. "I called someone who works there," he explained, "and I said, 'Is this true?' And he said, 'We had no N95s yesterday—none.' That night I left at two in the morning and I drove by and I said, 'I have to see this.' It was dark. Everyone was in full hazmat suits outside. There were security people by the ambulance entrances to keep people out. If you walked in, the doors were locked. They had ambulances there, but the ambulances were only there to take you someplace else."

Manish Sharma asked NewYork-Presbyterian for the same consideration. "We were completely overwhelmed. We had taken two hundred patients in and had no place to put them. We were like, 'If you walk in, there is no place, we can't even put you down on the floor.'

"We were in an emergency huddle in the boardroom. Everyone was there. Jaclyn Mucaria, the head of the hospital. Pierre Saldinger, the chief of surgery. We were all saying, 'What can we do? We have nothing even left for the next patient.' And I said, 'Why don't we ask what Elmhurst has asked for? An internal disaster.' NYP said, 'Okay, ask the DOH. Go ahead.' And we went to the DOH and they said, 'No!' Because we were part of a network. They saw what closing Elmhurst had done. And it wouldn't have helped anyway because we knew that some patients were going home. At least we thought. The admissions went from five to seven days to fourteen to twenty days. Our ICUs generally run about forty-two people . . . now there was at least a hundred. And another ninety-six patients waiting for beds. They were on ventilators and they were coding. Fifteen in the ED in one day. Eleven in the ICU on another. . . .

"It was very hard on our staff. We had to tell them, 'It is not the intubation that is killing them. It is that at this level of intubation there is a seventy-five percent chance you are not going to make it. For people to see this with forty-, fifty-, and sixty-year-olds? This is not normal. We were used to seeing seventy- and eighty- and ninety-year-olds."

The sounds in the ED were horrifying. The panting. The beeping. "We didn't have enough gowns for the patients," Pugh recalled. "People just took their shirts off. They had fevers. They were coughing. They were gasping for air. They were sitting in chairs with oxygen next to them. We had techs running around and getting the oxygen. Every square inch of the ER had someone in it."

March 30, 2020

Dear Colleagues,
I would love to say otherwise, but new-case rates compel NYP and the entire tri-state area to increase ICU capacity dramatically, as fast as possible. For the NYP system alone this means

increasing from a baseline of ~400 ICU beds to ~1100—almost a tripling in capacity. These beds will be coming on line daily, in the largest possible aliquots, over the next few weeks. All NYP construction resources are being directed at this with military focus and intensity. Simultaneously, "field hospital" facilities are springing up here and across the region (Javits Center, USNS Comfort, possibly Riverview Terrace, and more). Field hospitals are familiar elements of forward areas in armed conflicts and in natural disasters. Yes, it is getting that serious.

Triage is a fundamental operating principle in field hospitals. Triage determines who should be treated first, how they should be treated (surgery, fluid resuscitation, etc.), and who should be kept comfortable. Broadly construed, we will all be operating more and more on field hospital principles as we move through the next few weeks. In the "how they should be treated" part of the spectrum, NYP is moving quickly to implement a form of triage that offers the promise of relieving pressure on inpatient beds. Some carefully-selected COVID patients will be sent home with oxygen, an oxygen saturation monitor, and strict telehealth followup at 12–24 hour intervals. Does this entail incompletely understood risk? It certainly does, but triage is an essential part of the resource/utility-balancing situation in which we find ourselves.

Redeployment haunts my days. To the redeployed I've emphasized that we're not leaving you alone, that we will keep reinforcements flowing out. Think about the impact of redeployment on the ranks left behind, who are steadily reduced to those inappropriate for duty. They may be older, or medically compromised—or they may be your ensconced leaders, barricaded in the war room. The entire group of re-mainders, I assure you, suffers from a thirst combined of guilt and FOMO [fear of missing out] that will never be slaked. In contrast, those redeployed are thrown into rapidly evolving organizational structures made fluid by the fog of COVID. On that side of the wire, new leaders must emerge, and fast. It is a time for battlefield promotions. Whether you're a frustrated leader-in-waiting, or a reluctant leader who needs to be catalyzed by events, this is your time. Dandelion seeds go nowhere without wind. Our next generation of leaders will emerge in these few weeks.

Craig R. Smith, MD

Chair, Department of Surgery

Surgeon-in-Chief, NYP/CUIMC

By the time the medical director of the Allen emergency department, Lorna Breen, returned from her trip in mid-March, Columbia was in full-on crisis mode. That weekend, Laureen Hill had an emergency session in her office, laying out the ICUs that would take over the ORs. Weill Cornell had instituted the hospitalist-PA COVID teams. "Things were ramping up so quickly," Mills said. "Especially at the Allen. It's a very small footprint. Normally we put patients in the hallways so that they're getting their care. But with COVID and all of the coughing, we couldn't do that because it was so infectious.

"When Lorna got to the Allen, I imagine she was shell-shocked. All of the protocols had changed. We changed how the leadership would be with the administrator for the day who would figure out, 'How many beds are there? Do we need to transfer this person to Milstein?'"

The idea was to free up the doctors—the Allen was under siege. Breen, known for her obsessive research and preparations, would go to uncommon lengths planning for everything she did. Even applying for an MBA program was an exhaustive process, as Breen analyzed and reanalyzed each program. Coming back from her ski trip, she found the Allen ED—with all the new COVID protocols—was no longer completely under her control. "Morale was very low," Mills recalled. "People were worried they were going to get sick." As chaos overtook the New York hospitals, the Allen ran out of stretchers and the ED did not have enough oxygen tanks to accommodate the demand. "She was thrown into the middle of it without being part of the buildup of the crescendo," Mills said. "She was a planner and a researcher and a preparer. . . . There seemed to be an overwhelming sense of doom . . . it was like a runaway train." The medical director acts, in part, as an assist to the other doctors; with no real treatment for COVID, that role was also confounding. "My sense of it was it might have been too overwhelming for her, that she just couldn't catch up or figure it out."

On a department video call days later, Mills noticed that Breen was in bed. "I thought, *What is this?*, then I realized that Lorna had COVID too." Breen had a slight fever and a headache and a lot of fatigue, but her oxygen level was holding steady. "I said, 'Lorna, you do not need to be on this call! Get some rest.'"

At Weill Cornell, Lindsay Lief's close confidante Kelly Griffin ran 5 South four nights a week. An expert on global health before finding her way to medical school, Griffin had been a champion equestrian, and that hard-core focus was both a boon and a bane—a boon because she now had to focus as she'd never focused before, but a bane in that she couldn't figure out a way to step back for a moment to clear her head. Every night, she drove in from New Jersey, leaving her teenage sons at home; before she knew it, they'd be off to college, and she'd think about the time she had missed, but what else could she do? Greater absences called.

Griffin and Lief started a text chain and daily meetings with the other ICU directors. When PPE ran short, Griffin's mother made chintz turbans for all the women, which Griffin called "our schmattas." One morning, nursing manager Anthony Sabatino arrived to see Griffin sobbing in her office.

"By the third week of March, we had so many intubations, we had to set up a special place for the patients to be brought," Fernando Martinez recalled. "It became an assembly line of intubation . . . battlefield conditions. We had anesthesia teams that sat in this room all day long." Meanwhile, Hayward, Griffin, and the other attendings were taking turns consulting, one desperately ill patient wheeled in after another. "On one day," Martinez recalled, "Brad had twenty consultations in a row. We were intubating everyone—that is what the Europeans were doing in March and we did not know how else to treat them. . . . Brad would wheel one person in and insert the ventilator and he was constantly being paged: 'This person is really bad. He is failing. When can you get someone in to intubate him?' And Brad would have to say, 'There are five people ahead of you.' He was under siege."

Hayward was assisted by one pulmonary fellow and two residents. The residents would get the first pages from the hospitalists: "Patient X is decompensating!" Elyse LaFond, a second-year pulmonary fellow, was particularly astute at evaluating a patient's condition. Called to the ED, she would sometimes override the attending doctors who did not have the advanced pulmonary critical-care training, even though they were technically her seniors. Recalled Martinez, "One time they had intubated someone and we thought that they hadn't intubated them correctly, that it wasn't in the trachea but that it was actually in the esophagus. And she said, 'You need to show me that it is in the correct place' to the attending. That takes a lot of courage. . . . She was very skilled at saying things in a way that did not make people upset."

The art of triage meant probing and evaluating patients who were sick, then understanding how sick they really were. What kind of monitoring might they need in the hospital that's above the regular level of monitoring? Did they need to go to an ICU, and which ICU did they need to go into? Could they be stabilized? "Everyone was sick," Lief recalled. "On oxygen masks." They'd call her or whoever was in charge of beds that day and announce they had "another one to be intubated." She had time for one sentence: Age, medical problems, how sick they were at the moment, and how sick they were expected to be immediately after intubation. The patients were often breathing extremely fast, their oxygen saturation low despite the oxygen masks. Lief would put on all the PPE and "talk to the patient, see how hard they are working, what their numbers are, make sure they are agreeable to intubation, talk to their team about their trajectory—rapidly worse versus stably bad."

Often there were multiple people on different units, and it would be up to Lief to find each a bed, if there were any. Hayward would call the airway team, which at the time consisted of an anesthesiologist along with a nurse anesthetist. Respiratory therapy would find a ventilator. "Sometimes there was a delay because although they existed, we didn't always know where each one was. The anesthesia team would come. They would spend what seemed like forever meticulously putting on PPE—in excess of what we normally wear covering hair, neck, et cetera." PPE, PPE . . . it was never enough just to be a doctor or nurse on 5 South, you had to be a treasure hunter too.

Same thing if you were the boss. "You have to call the head of Halyard [hospital supply] and get them to help us," Joshi, the supply director, had told Corwin.

Corwin immediately placed the call to Halyard's president. NewYork-Presbyterian was one of Halyard's largest clients, and Corwin hoped that would count for something. "I am up against the wall. You have to help me out. You have to get me PPE," Corwin said. But everyone wanted it.

In the third week of March, NewYork-Presbyterian's chief of finance, Mike Breslin, got a surprising phone call from the hospital's JPMorgan Chase representative, who had recently heard from the FBI. Breslin had just made a wire transfer of nine million dollars to DTM, a New York start-up reportedly in communication with Shanghai Dasheng, a manufacturer of hospital supplies; it had been recommended as a legitimate source for N95s, the masks that filter out 95 percent of airborne particles. The nine million dollars was a partial payment for the three million N95 masks that the hospital needed over the next few weeks. Breslin was startled to hear that the FBI had stopped the wire transfer—the banker told him that "somebody in the government was flagging the nine million because it was going to a bicycle company in Shanghai." *Uh-oh*, Breslin thought, *what is this?*

Millions of counterfeit masks had already flooded into the United States. Hospitals across the country had been plunged into chaos, all competing with one another to acquire masks and PPE. NewYork-Presbyterian had been assured through trusted contacts that Shanghai Dasheng was a legitimate operation.

Corwin had grown increasingly frantic about being able to supply the ninety thousand masks a day that NewYork-Presbyterian needed. "We were asking everybody with any connection to get the masks. We were casting a wide net, and that means you are not going to go through your usual channels," Corwin said. Mount Sinai Hospital was also sending millions of dollars to Shanghai Dasheng.

The FBI warning about the bike company came as a shock to all, but the American liaisons who vouched for the company assured Breslin and supply chief Anand Joshi that the business had many holdings, including the bicycle shops.

On the morning of April 6, Joshi received an e-mail:

Some good news. I just got the latest on shipping. We have two flights a day booked daily. Which means we estimate arrival to you and Sinai starting Sat 4/11.... Based on this we are now actually looking for final payments to secure all the bookings and move forward.

Cautiously optimistic that the hospital might soon receive three million masks, Joshi put through the second wire, for a total of eighteen million dollars. Although the hospital system was approving hundreds of millions of dollars on purchase orders to cover its sudden enormous expenses, eighteen million was still a lot of money.

But there had been a worrying sign from a banker at Blackstone who was helping the hospital secure masks: "Hi, Anand. Just wanted to make sure you saw the below. I think the Dangshen [*sic*] n95s I was looking at are on this counterfeit list."

The next day, Joshi e-mailed the heads of DTM Healthcare, which was serving as the intermediary between New York-Presbyterian and Shanghai Dasheng. He expressed concern and got a response that was fairly anodyne in its reassurances. Joshi remained worried.

Those worries were well founded; it turned out that DTM had been caught up in an attempt to sell American hospitals millions of masks they were incapable of delivering. There was an attempt by the hospital to press their case with the Manhattan district attorney, but chasing down $18 million that may or may not be in Shanghai was not the way the DA's office wanted to use their resources, hospital executives later said. The profiteering and counterfeit market set off by the lack of federal leadership allowed scores of buccaneers to rake in billions of dollars. The president failed to sign an executive order demanding that American companies manufacture the hospital supplies that were now made primarily in China. Hospitals were forced to compete in the shadiest markets for shoddy merchandise that could kill thousands. (DTM did not respond to repeated requests for comment.)

In March, Mike Breslin had been given a mandate by Corwin and board chairman Jerry Speyer. "We were not going to run out of supplies for our employees. We have to take care of our employees and they have to take care of our patients. . . . Whatever it took, whatever we needed, we're not going to run out of supplies," Breslin said.

Anand Joshi tried to retrieve the eighteen million dollars that had gone to Shanghai, but it was not to be.

In May, the Associated Press broke the story of the counterfeit masks sold under the name of Shanghai Dasheng.

Ultimately, the hospital was able to get millions of masks from its Atlanta-based supplier, which coordinated flight after flight from Shanghai's Pudong airport despite the lockdowns, a feat that Joshi is still not sure how it accomplished.

It went without saying that when it came to some supplies, not everything was shared equally. After an especially harrowing siege of one intubation after another, Hayward and LaFond and the residents took a break and went to 14 South, which had two-thousand-dollar-a-night suites for the rich and offered views of the East River and private chefs. "We went up to a lounge to evaluate a group of patients we had just seen," he said. "No one was there—the pandemic had closed down all of the normal procedures and this had been reserved for visitors and there were no visitors. The lounge had a pantry and a freezer stocked with gelato. I said, 'You know what, let's just take a break and eat some of this expensive gelato.' It had been such a crazy day. And then the corporate patient manager appeared and said, 'You guys aren't allowed to eat this.' He yelled at us and told us, 'You guys have to leave unless you are seeing patients.' I sent Elyse and the residents to the elevators and said, 'Do you realize what we are going through and what we are doing? There is no one on this floor to eat this gelato. And is it really the institutional priority making sure that fellows and residents who are sacrificing their lives don't get to eat the gelato that is reserved for rich people and VIPs? If you are going to restrict us from eating this, then we are going to stop coming up here to help you with your patients.' Obviously I didn't mean that, but I was so angry and frustrated." None of it made sense to Hayward. "This was an area where the patients aren't allowed—and there were no visitors allowed in the hospital. So all of the food was going to go away.... I said, 'We are going to come up here and look out the window whenever we want to. And that's the way it is going to be. And if you have a problem you can escalate it up to your management. I don't care.'"

In the land without private chefs and views, Lief and Hayward constantly looked for beds to move the patients to as soon as the decision was made to intubate, allowing the ED to keep the intake going. (Columbia's procedure was different—those intubated would often remain in the ED.) After the tube was placed, the MICU team—Hayward and Griffin and whoever was relieving them—would transport the patient to the bed. Eventually, the engineering department appeared and cut windows in all the doors to the new rooms—a huge relief.

Walking the halls of 4 Central and 4 North, Hayward and his team would often hear the nurses say, "'Oh no, here they come,' because they knew we were there affirming the intubation decisions. I felt like I was the Grim Reaper. It wasn't a good feeling to be associated with that.... We were like a harbinger of doom."

Very late at night, Hayward would leave the hospital too worn out to walk home. With the city shut down, the fleets of yellow taxis seemed to have vaporized. An Uber could take twenty minutes to arrive. But at York Avenue, Hayward spotted a yellow cab, a gift.

Opening the door, still wearing his scrubs and N95, he heard Rush Limbaugh on a tangent. All he could make out was *crazy Nancy Pelosi.* "Do you mind turning that off?" Hayward asked. He had walked out of the hospital to see the morgue truck in the driveway and was reeling from the number of patients he had placed on ventilators. Who among them would be next to the morgue in a black body bag? Hayward looked out at empty streets. There was still a line that snaked down Broadway at Trader Joe's, many of those waiting for entrance unmasked.

Hayward asked the driver to let him out there, but when he approached the line, people moved away from him; it was as if he carried the pathogen in his backpack. He had brought blue surgical masks home with him for his neighbors, but he stopped to offer some to those in line. "You really should wear them," he said. And then he left some at his neighbors' doors. As a doctor, he had always felt immune from diseases, but not any longer. The next night, leaving the hospital, the same taxi driver was waiting. And the next. For three days, the same driver appeared at the same time. "I have to make money," the driver told Hayward, who paid him in cash at his request.

"Is it really as bad as they say in there?" he asked Hayward.

"It is," Hayward replied. "It is scary in there."

I could have told Brad's taxi driver that. If only he had asked me.

Night after night, Marjorie Walcott watched the bleary group she called "my doctors, my sweethearts" as they stumbled home or tried to nap in their cubicles on 5 South. She was there on the night that Hayward, frantic that five people in the ED all needed ventilators and there was only one available, remembered he had the cell phone number of Weill Cornell's COO, Kate Heilpern, who had tried to take Matt McCarthy's title away just a few weeks before. "Kate," he told her, "forgive me for calling you on your cell. But there are no ventilators and five people who need them." "Brad, I will get on it immediately. You were right to call me." Hayward would always think of this night as a moment when someone showed real leadership.

For the twelve years Walcott had worked on 5 South cleaning rooms, she had never felt more protective of all of her team than she did that spring. Arriving at work every day for the night shift, she promised them bottles of Barbados rum when she finally got to visit her island again, inviting them to come stay at the small block house she was trying to build, brick by brick, with the money she saved from her seven-hundred-dollar-a-week salary.

Walcott was sixty-one. Each afternoon, a close friend picked her up at her apartment in Crown Heights to drive her to the hospital. "I never missed a day," she said. "And often I did double shifts when the other cleaners got sick." Walcott was used to the hum of 5 South, but watching Hayward and Lief and Kelly Griffin under siege became, she recalled, "an out-of-body experience." And then there was Walcott's nightly ordeal of cleaning the rooms with so much infection and death. She had come to believe her ritual protected her: "Before I go in, I would sign the cross and I would always say a little prayer, 'Father Lord, please protect me. I'm going to clean this room so that another sick person can come in here and maybe recover.' . . . Because they were dying so fast over there on-site. So, I would always be afraid. All the time I would be afraid. And I would go in and I would clean that room. And one day, the clerk said to me, 'Marjorie, you know something?' She said, 'You are not going to die from COVID. You know what is going to kill you? The mask.' Yeah. Because shoot me. When I went in to clean those rooms, it took over an hour and I put two N95s on. And I was struggling to breathe. But

I would wear them." Walcott was never worried about PPE. "My doctors told me, 'Take whatever you need from our rooms.' I had all the keys for their offices. I had my own closet and kept my PPE there." She quickly developed a system for cleaning up the massive amount of human waste and infected supplies in each patient's room. "I kept the garbage cart right at the door. Because I had so much to take out of those rooms. And when the patient leaves, I have control where everything goes. At first, the doctors did not know what they were dealing with. They were all just trying. And then they started learning a little more, a little more. Sometimes I would get ten bags of garbage out of one room. Sometimes twenty. Most of it were supplies—sometimes not even opened. We had to tie the linen and put it in a special place that was separate from the others. My two floors? They were all COVID."

As a young woman in Barbados, Walcott had worked in a small nursing home and had a special love for the old, finding an almost mystical power in making sure their needs were addressed. The daughter of a former sugarcane cutter who had traveled to the Everglades from Barbados to labor in conditions so brutal it was not uncommon for the workers, brought to the States with restrictive visas, to lose fingers or collapse in the heat as they struggled to make their quotas. Walcott's father ran away to New York and found work in a morgue—work as onerous as the sugarcane fields. He fled again and wound up at Weill Cornell. As a child, Walcott recalled her father coming home to Barbados "dressed in a suit like he lived in a big ranch in New York." Weill Cornell seemed to her like a place of infinite possibility. When she came to New York in her thirties, Walcott discovered she had multiple brothers and sisters from her father's many partners. "My family was very, very poor and finally, I just said, 'You know what? I'm going to give it a trust to see if I can better myself.'" Before she resettled in New York, she spent years in

Florida and found work in an assisted living home, then reunited with a brother only to discover he had AIDS. He died not long after. While Walcott was in New York for a visit, a girlfriend told her, "Why don't you get yourself straightened up so you could move here and get a job. . . . We will help you." Soon after, she reconnected with her father and stayed with him in Harlem for months as she attended school to get her home attendant health care license.

In her own apartment at last, Walcott welcomed close friends from Barbados to share her two rooms. When they arrived, they had brought a gift—Barbados rum for a friend working at Weill Cornell. When the friend arrived, he told Walcott, "Why don't you let me carry your résumé to my manager?" Walcott gave it to a cousin to quickly type for her and within weeks, she had been hired to clean 5 South. Twelve years earlier, Lief had been almost new to the ICU; Hayward started seven years later. From time to time, Walcott thinks of them as her own children.

Then the pandemic hit. Through March and April, Walcott had lunch every day with another cleaner, Edthea Buckley, a friend originally from Jamaica. "She was more frightened than I was. And then because she cleaned, she got COVID. And she was out for almost two months. My doctors and my nurses got burned out. We all got burned out. It was overwhelming. You see, they didn't know what they were dealing with. You understand?

"So many of them were dying. One day I cleaned the same room, the first room in the evening and the last room at night, twice. That is how fast they were dying. And then they bring a person who was already dead and put them in the same room. It was gruesome. So many nights I said hello to the dead people." Often when Walcott saw a nurse, they would warn her, but not always. "I have said good night to so many dead people. And I would have my bleach and bleach everything in the room. But it was overwhelming. I would come home at night and I would see all those bodies being pulled outside the door. When I fell asleep, I thought I was at work still. I wasn't at work. I was in my bed. But that's when it played in my mind. Okay, it was just a dream."

"Marjorie, why don't you become a clerk?" David Berlin, the unit head, asked her when she wound up with cellulitis and throbbing veins because of all the hours on her feet.

"Absolutely not," she said. "Dr. Berlin, what I love is cleaning rooms."

9

In Bronxville, Jessica Forman was not only an uncommonly good PA, she was also uncommonly qualified for the larger moment. She held a master's degree in bioethics from Columbia, so she reached out to Kenneth Prager, the chair of the hospital's medical ethics committee.

Prager was a throwback who had ably adapted to the new world of medicine, the sort of person who kept track of every emergency Zoom meeting with his own handwritten notes, filed in manila folders. His window office was ornamented with a plaque documenting his work with refuseniks, a 1955 Brooklyn Dodgers team poster, and assorted religious texts. At seventy-seven, he still saw pulmonology patients. Surprisingly, he was also the brother of Dennis Prager, the conservative talk-show host and writer who, as the pandemic took over New York, was on the air decrying the lockdowns—"the greatest mistake in the history of humanity." If that didn't make dinner conversation interesting enough, Kenneth Prager's son, Joshua Prager, was a well-known writer who was deep into the reporting of a surgically detailed new history of *Roe v. Wade* that was set to be released the following year.

The Prager brothers had been raised in Brooklyn and attended yeshiva. Kenneth Prager was modern Orthodox and, early in his ethics career, found the insights of Jewish medical ethics to be extremely helpful both in his clinical practice and in his classroom.

The elements of medical ethics can be traced to the Talmud, the compendium of Jewish law. In *Superbugs,* Matt McCarthy, who attended Prager's lectures at Columbia, discussed the example of the ambitious young World War I medic Gerhard Domagk, who survived the slaughter of the First Battle of Ypres. Returning to Germany, Domagk completed medical school. He was determined to work in a laboratory and eventually joined IG Farben, which had the largest chemical plant in the world. Domagk was particularly obsessed, McCarthy noted, with finding molecules to treat gangrene, diarrhea, and pneumonia, which led to his experiments with streptococcus, the bacteria responsible for, among other maladies, the sort of battlefield wound infections Domagk had witnessed as a soldier. Eventually someone in his lab had the outside-the-box idea to try on the lab mice a dye that IG Farben used to make wool take color more easily. The results were astonishing—sulfanilamide protected the mice from bacterial infection. More experimentation followed until IG Farben was able to file a patent for the first effective antibiotic—thirty-six days after that, Adolf Hitler became chancellor of Germany. Within several years, Farben became infamous as the company that concocted the chemical gas used to poison Jews in the concentration camps.

The Nuremberg Trials would reveal the horrors of antibiotic, sterilization, and transplantation experiments that went on in the camps at the hands of medical providers in Nazi uniforms stripped of their insignia. (In his book, McCarthy pointed out that when it came to the Nazi movement as a whole, "The professional group with the largest percentage of Nazi Party members was medicine.") Called in for expert testimony at the trials, a founder of the U.S. Naval Medical Research Institute said, "There was no politician under the sun that could force me to perform a medical experiment which I thought was morally unjustified." He would come to understand that in his own country, this was far from the truth.

In 1972, one year before Prager returned to Columbia from his time as chief resident at University of Chicago Medicine, news broke about the appalling research that had been done in Alabama on poor Black men, many of them sharecroppers. Begun in 1932, the "Tuskegee Study of Untreated Syphilis in the Negro Male" was supposed to last six months—it lasted forty years. Hundreds of men were left untreated so researchers could study the effects of the disease. (Government researchers, aware of the risks, never obtained any form of consent.) The experiments continued even after penicillin became the standard treatment for syphilis in 1947; the many hundreds of men used as guinea pigs were never told there was actually a drug that could cure them. Scores of participants died young or infected their wives, who then transmitted the disease to their unborn children. A sweeping reform of patients' rights resulted from the viciousness, but the reverberation of medical sadism from the U.S. government deeply affected the management of the pandemic of 2020—and fed into the paranoia and terror that surrounded every aspect of the public health response, from mask mandates to the distribution of vaccines.

In 1975, twenty-one-year-old Karen Ann Quinlan was not allowed to be taken off a ventilator after five months in a vegetative state despite her parents' request. Quinlan had mixed Valium and alcohol while on a crash diet and had accidentally overdosed. She was taken to a local New Jersey hospital in a coma. Quinlan's parents were devout Catholics, but after months of vigil, could no longer bear to see their daughter on a ventilator and asked for her to be taken off. The doctors treating Quinlan refused, telling the parents that they could be charged with homicide if they complied. Her parents filed a lawsuit, which was ultimately decided in their favor in 1976 by the New Jersey State Supreme Court. But when Quinlan was taken off the ventilator, she began to breathe on her own. She lived another nine years, on just a feeding tube, in a nursing home.

The Quinlan case triggered a debate about whether patients should be kept alive by artificial means. Prager says it informed end-of-life ethical policies at Columbia and his work helping doctors and nurses navigate such wrenching circumstances. But COVID and the massive use of ventilators and shortages in equipment had confounded the ethicists and the committees that were given the impossible decisions.

Forman reached out to Prager, who was putting in long nights with the doctors in the ICU, and he told her, "We aren't going to have a written policy. We have some scripts about how to talk to family members."

In other words, they were on their own.

Forman, head of quality control Xenia Frisby, and cardiologist Anthony Pucillo had formed a secret palliative-care team to struggle with all the ethical issues about the shortage of ventilators. If they were down to their last ventilator, who would get it? And how would they proceed? What would their potential liability be with the state?

"So many people don't talk about end-of-life decisions," Forman reflected. "It was clear there was a shortage of ventilators. We were told to use our best clinical judgment, and that really varies from patient to patient. It was just the fact that you could not make centered decisions versus public health considerations. It was hard to ask clinicians to function in both capacities: as a public health steward and a clinician taking care of one patient. That caused a lot of existential distress for the doctors."

There was also the challenge of how families could advocate for their loved ones when prevented from entering the hospital. Would they be able to make decisions without seeing the patient? Screens might give the illusion of intimacy, but just as Corwin could never truly understand what was happening in 5 South via iPad, a relative could not truly discern the condition of a loved one on FaceTime.

How to speak to patients was one of many urgencies Prager was trying to grapple with in March and, in fact, something he had been dealing with for decades. In the late 1970s, as a young pulmonology attending in the Columbia ICU, Prager had begun to question himself about whether continued aggressive treatment of hopelessly ill patients was appropriate. "What were we doing to these people? There were patients on ventilators, some of whom were going to die, no matter what. The notion that we might be doing more harm than good was a new feeling, a revelation. I never felt that way before because during my years of training when there were no ICUs we did everything for every patient. Technology was very limited and critically ill patients either got better or died rather quickly." In the years before he'd started thinking about this, technology—or lack thereof—had made these sorts of existential debates irrelevant. Columbia had no ventilators at all; it didn't even have dialysis.

Prager began to read the work of Rabbi Immanuel Jacobovits, who, starting in the late 1950s, had pioneered the discipline of Jewish medical ethics. Among Jacobovits's big questions were some of Prager's: How do you approach a situation when people are dying? By continuing aggressive treatment, are you doing more harm than good? Is it ever ethical to withhold a treatment?

"There are a few Jewish sources which said that if someone is imminently dying, and there is an impediment to the peaceful passing, you have to remove the impediment," Prager said. "Some of these ancient sources involve primitive notions of medical care. For example, there is a rabbi who wrote in the 1500s that if a man is a *goses*"— a person who is moribund, who is actively dying—"and there is a woodchopper outside the house and the noise of the woodchopper is preventing the soul from departing the body, you have to remove the woodchopper in order to allow a peaceful death and the departure of the spirit—of the person's soul." Prager likens this to pulling the plug. "Isn't this analogous to somebody on a ventilator who's trying to die? And yet, this is a very contentious area, because many rabbis feel that the notion of a *goses* no longer applies today. We have so much powerful technology—and so they feel that nobody is ever truly moribund. . . . That then leads to the question of whether there is an ethical distinction between withholding or withdrawing life support, which is viewed in contemporary medical ethics as the same. I disagree. I feel there is both an ethical and emotional difference between writing a Do Not Resuscitate order and removing a patient from a ventilator."

The more he thought about such conundrums, the clearer it was to Prager that NewYork-Presbyterian was going to have to come up with a triage policy, no matter what the state decided. COVID had stretched the doctors to the breaking point, he said. "And our resources were strained unimaginably."

To help devise a formula, Prager reached out to Joseph Fins. Prager was twenty years older than Fins, but they had worked together during the H1N1 flu epidemic when the hospitals were concerned about the shortage of ventilators. In 2008, a New York State task force, chaired by bioethicist Tia Powell, came up with a long and detailed statement of criteria for triaging ventilators in case of a severe influenza pandemic. "It was a policy for deciding—based on both ethical and medical criteria—who shall live and who shall die," Prager recalled. "Who gets prioritized when you have a limited number of ventilators or ICU beds?" There were ongoing and heated discussions about withholding and withdrawing ventilators: "Even though the medical ethics literature equates withholding and withdrawing, I and others do not think they are ethically equivalent," he explained. "Doctors are forced to consider the practical effects of these decisions. It is one thing when you decide that it is medically inappropriate to put a patient on a ventilator, and it is quite

another to conclude that it is medically indicated to remove a patient from a ventilator with the likelihood that he or she will die
soon afterwards." From an emotional point of view, Prager pointed
out, it would be "infinitely more gut-wrenching to take somebody off
a ventilator, leading to their immediate death, than to say, 'We recommend against having you put on a ventilator.' It's a big difference."

Prager and Fins were part of a group of clinicians, hospital lawyers, and administrators who met frequently by phone to deal with
the multiple medical, ethical, and policy issues that the hospital and
its staff frequently confronted. Among those in the group were Dan
Brodie; Katherine Fischkoff; the chief medical officer of Queens, the
chair of medicine, Joseph Cooke; and, from the Allen, Gerald Neu-
berg. While the issues at hand were decidedly moral, there was a critical legal element as well. Said Prager, "The issue was, 'Is the state going
to give us legal protection if we have a triage policy?' Will we be legally
protected if we say to families, 'We're not putting your father on the
ventilator because he doesn't fit the criteria for survival'? And possibly
even taking people off?" And what about the families of the doctors
who would make those decisions—what would you say to them if
those doctors were convicted of murder and sent to jail? Near the end
of March, Hayward sent an e-mail to Fins, interrogating him on this
point: "I can appreciate that the enterprise wants to protect itself, but
until then, who is protecting me? More important, who is protecting
the patients? And their families?"

Prager's group drew up plans for a triage policy that included the
creation of a committee of ethicists and ICU doctors who would
make the life-and-death decisions—who gets put on the ventilator
and who does not. They even drew up a rotating schedule for the
committee. "There were all kinds of details that had to be worked
out. Will the committee be anonymous? To do otherwise might
expose the group to unwanted pressures and legal liability. Who is
going to tell the family that we're not going to put their loved one on a

ventilator? An administrator, high up in the organization? A doctor in the trenches? Is it going to be someone from this subcommittee?" Eventually, it all ended up being for naught. "We would never put it into effect because the state would not come through and say, 'You are going to have legal protection.'"

In daily conversations with Fins and Rick Evans, the head of all patient care for the NewYork-Presbyterian system, the bioethics chairs at the medical schools understood why so much frustration was coming from the hospital ICUs. Prager was aware of the PTSD and of what the doctors would quickly call moral injury, but he wondered if all the bioethics training the younger doctors had had was, in fact, only a semi-useful crutch that in the end they should have understood wasn't going to save them from a reality that was out of their control.

But why, those making the impossible decisions kept asking, did you even have a medical ethics committee if it wasn't telling you what you should do? "This was the real McCoy," Prager proclaimed. "This is the stuff you read about, but we had to rise to the occasion. We're presented with this; we're in once-in-a-century circumstances—a wartime kind of thing. What am I going to say, 'This is too much for me. Hey, I'm going to bed'? The ethics input was crucial." There was no lack of discussion among the ethics committee members. "Normally, we meet once a month," Prager noted. "We had six emergency COVID-related meetings. Among the issues we discussed were the ethics of triage policy, futile CPR with its attendant risks to MD and nurses, and medical futility in general, the role of palliative care, dialysis shortages, and inadequate PPE and on and on."

It was normal that those who had to make the terrible decisions would have preferred to follow someone else's orders, perhaps even at some cost to their own autonomy as caregivers. Prager would get calls in the middle of the night updating him on ventilator shortages and asking him what to do. "One of the jobs I had—and that Fins had—was to hold the hands of people and say, 'You are doing the best you can. There is no easy answer over here. Don't think you are acting unethically. You're having to make triage decisions et cetera on the fly. Use your best clinical and ethical judgment: That's the best thing that can happen at this point.'"

Both Ken Prager and Joe Fins, the chairmen of their departments at their respective medical schools and experts in the field, were forbidden to speak to the media about the complexities of triage. In March, as the tension and anger around the lack of ventilators roiled the doctors, Prager and Fins were told in no uncertain terms that they would not be allowed to speak to the press. Fins was forbidden to talk to *New York Times* reporter Sheri Fink, whom he had known for years. Fink, author of the acclaimed *Five Days at Memorial*, was also a doctor and an expert on all the complex issues that surround medical ethics. Fins later said he was approached by every media outlet from the *Washington Post* to the *Los Angeles Times*, but was forced to stay silent as residents and Columbia's emergency room doctor Craig Spencer, who had contracted Ebola in 2014, were allowed to comment on a subject he had written more than five hundred academic papers about.

Prager recalled: "Joe [Fins] was quite upset about it.... They didn't see the wisdom of it [talking to the press]. We weren't going for banner headlines. I was disappointed but not surprised. Disappointed because I felt that I could share with the public a unique perspective about the stressors hospital workers were subjected to as they tried to rise to the occasion. . . . Not surprised because the hospital is ultra-conservative, so afraid [about negative PR] and concerned about its image and didn't trust us to be discreet and speak appropriately about these things. It would have been a real plus for the hospital to have someone who could speak to the time, effort, and thought that was given to doing the right thing. I wish the hospital had a little more confidence in us." Somehow, what was never communicated to

Prager or Fins or the medical team at 5 South was that Corwin, who had been the ICU chief of Columbia for years, had a strong sense of what the doctors were going through. He had resolved, he later said, not to operate just by the algorithms but also to strongly support any decision the individual doctors felt compelled to make. How that would play out legally was another matter, but however close they came to running out of ventilators, in the end, they had enough.

Rick Evans, who had once trained to be a priest and then spent a decade administering to the homeless, was haunted by his first experience as a hospital administrator in Hoboken. He watched the 9/11 attack on the Twin Towers from his office window, then rushed to the waterfront and tried to assemble all of the equipment to receive patients. "We cut off the rail lines at the PATH station, fearing another attack. We had three hundred and forty-two wounded descend on our small hospital. If you were injured, you were transported by ambulance. By the afternoon, we had tents erected for treatment. Clinicians and car stations. If you weren't injured, we hosed all of the ash off of you. I was up all night and the next night, trying to counsel all of the families who had lost loved ones." It was hard to imagine anything more intense and upsetting. "But in March and April of this year? Oh my God—as bad as 9/11 was, I never felt that day what I felt here. So many terrified doctors and nurses and patients—I was in the hospital all day and all night. The morgue truck was right out front. I knew how scared everyone was. Our staff felt like they were not going to be able to come home and see their families. It was hard not to despair."

And then there was the overriding question: Who would get the ventilators in such desperately short supply? "We kept calling the ethicists," Hayward said. "The palliative-care doctors. 'We don't want to make these f— decisions.' This is not how we trained."

"I think those first couple of weeks we were putting folks on a ventilator very quickly," Kapil Rajwani, a pulmonologist on 5 South, reflected. "It made sense for the purposes of clinical safety because we didn't know what we were dealing with and we didn't want a crisis situation. It made sense in terms of why that was the decision at that moment with the information we had. Later on, when we got to the point where now we had so many intubated people and needed so many ICU beds so quickly, and we had the situation where there's a ventilator shortage, we realized that probably wasn't the best move."

That was later, though. For now, the ethicists seemed stuck in philosophical loops, discussing the issue as if in a graduate seminar and not in the midst of an emergency. Right now, this minute, 5 South had to make the call that one person should be given a chance to live and another should not—and Hayward and the rest of his team were left without guidance.

"They were not talking to me. They were not doing their job. They were just kicking the can down the road. It was enraging."

Fins understood the immense strain Hayward and Lief were under. On March 24, Lief e-mailed Fins: "We are desperate. We are down to our last 20 or so ventilators, which at this rate, could mean we are out tomorrow. We are intubating elderly people. Can we move forward with the governor? We don't have time."

The next day Fins answered: "Lindsay, I am trying. Been in touch w NYPH senior leadership and am talking to ACP [American College of Physicians] leadership tonight so that they can lobby Cuomo. I wish I could wave a magic wand. Proud of your leadership. All best, Joe."

Working late into the night, forbidden by his department to round in the ICUs, Fins sat in his office drafting and redrafting triage policies that would never go into effect. "I had written eleven or twelve versions of a triage policy, actually. But that was just to be ready. And if the hospital leadership had said, 'Okay, we are going to do this,' it would have taken a week to get it together and there would have been a delay. . . . It would have been a failure if we had not provided Steve and Laura with options. . . . My concern was that the doctors had to contend with a brand-new disease which nobody understood at the time. And it put an unfair burden on people like Lindsay and on Steve [Corwin], as an administrator, and on me, because the state abdicated. And they did not institute crisis standards of care. . . . And my view was, as flawed as they may have been—the limitations of the SOFA [sequential organ failure assessment] scores—it probably was the right decision to make. I don't think Cuomo wanted to acknowledge that there were shortages."

In the last week of March, he picked up the phone to hear Lief crying. "And this is a person who is fearless. This is an ICU doctor. It takes a lot to faze an ICU doctor. . . . But the untenability of the situation . . . Here were people who were so incredibly skilled at what they do, and their professors and their teachers . . . all of us were reduced to medical students in the face of a disease we did not understand."

Later Fins would write for the New York State Bar Association: "Although the official line from the state was that there were enough ventilators to go around, the reality was that the systems buckled. . . . The state did not do what they were supposed to do—which was to give us guidance. . . . The doctors were very concerned about liability." Everyone in medicine understood the reason: After Hurricane Katrina, an opportunistic prosecutor went after a doctor in New Orleans who had been forced to make triage decisions as she attempted to care for patients in a hospital with no power and inadequate supplies. Fins wanted to make sure the doctors would not suffer the same consequences. In March, he was also studying data from Spain that showed that almost 18 percent of health-care workers were contracting COVID. "They were three weeks ahead of us. So, if during a resuscitation some of our people got sick, they would be taken out of the fight and they wouldn't be able to take care of the next one hundred patients."

There were no easy decisions. Elderly patients arrived, some suffering from dementia and nursing-home neglect so profound that their muscles had been allowed to atrophy, and their limbs could not be moved. Hayward said, "We can't intubate these people. They should be allowed to die. They will just take up ventilators." He called the ethicist and said, "We should not resuscitate these patients." The ethicist responded that if a family wanted their family member to be given CPR if their heart failed, the doctors had to do it, adding, "You have to do everything the families want." Hayward couldn't believe it. "We said, 'It is actually impossible to do CPR on these patients. Do you want me to injure them in order to do CPR? Is that an ethical thing to do?'" Performing CPR on patients in such a fragile condition would actually result in serious bodily harm. "And I said, 'You should come in, and you should do it. This is not ethical.'" It was a legal issue too—not only regarding accusations of malpractice by patients' families or by someone else who claimed the time spent on futile attempts to save some patients resulted in the deaths of others but also in potential criminal charges should their decision be seen as intentionally killing patients.

"The emergency room doctor would be so upset about it," Hayward recalled. He told his colleague, "This is why we have a hospital ethics department, this is why we have administrators—so we don't have to take these personal decisions as our own." And the patient load was only increasing.

Again and again, they would tell Hayward and his colleagues that "they were waiting for New York State to issue crisis-care guidelines—or to sign off on them. And we would say, 'We all know that is not going to happen. We all know that the government is not going to say it is okay to let people die. Then there will be a Sarah Palin death-panel controversy.' And they kept saying, 'We are waiting for the state.' And we kept saying again and again, 'But you and I know that the state will never say that. We are asking you as an organization to help us!' And they would not. I am still very bitter about it. . . . The amount of moral damage they did to a lot of people while they get paid millions of dollars is disgusting."

The third week of March, an anesthesiologist reached out to Prager on a Sunday night. "Ken, I have been asked by the hospital to embark on an experimental protocol of seeing whether we can have two people on one ventilator. I am having ethical qualms about this—two people on one ventilator. It hasn't been done before." Corwin had written to hospital vice president Laureen Hill and COO Kate Heilpern, citing the emergency directive the FDA had issued sanctioning "modifications to FDA-cleared ventilators and anesthesia where the modification will not create an undue risk in light of the public health emergency." Corwin had made the decision that the hospital should experiment with the possibility of using a double ventilator, which set off real concern in the anesthesia department. "Then I get a call: 'Is it ethical to do this experiment?'" Prager was under the assumption it had come from New York State and Cuomo. "Look, [they] can say all kinds of things," he said, "and that doesn't mean that it's ethical. So I called an emergency meeting of the ethics committee."

In Brooklyn, learning of the directive to experiment with two patients connected to the same air source, respiratory therapist Felix Khusid was apoplectic. "I heard about it and I thought: *What? Experimenting with the lives of COVID patients who are struggling to breathe? Is this Frankenstein's lab?*"

10

On March 27, the first sounds of applause could be heard faintly in Queens, starting in Jackson Heights. The prompt for the somewhat ad hoc appreciation for the health-care workers were hashtags (#ClapBecauseWeCare and #JacksonHeights #Queens) and phone calls and e-mails, and then there it was: Out the windows of their houses, cherry blossoms visible below, came the clapping from scores of homes.

Within thirty-six hours, the nightly celebration of thanks would become a ritual—town houses on the Upper East Side kept pots and pans by the front door to bang while catching a glimpse of neighbors. But the clapping would not camouflage how grim the city had become. A reporter who had showed up at Elmhurst Hospital was warned away by an EMS driver: "There are people in beds all over. They don't have enough space here." NYC Health + Hospitals, which operated the public hospitals in the city, was reporting Elmhurst was "the center of this crisis"—thirteen people had died there in one day alone and that number would soon double despite medical workers from elsewhere sent to Queens to help out. Even at Columbia, it was bad; Craig Smith's daily letter informed the world that the number of New York-Presbyterian coronavirus patients on ventilators had doubled in the past three days.

"New York State Death Toll Tops 400." The day before, at his daily press briefing in Albany, Andrew Cuomo stated the obvious: "This is really bad news," he said. "That's the worst news you can have. . . . I don't want to sugarcoat the situation. But easy times don't forge character. It's the tough times that forge character. And that's what we are looking at right now."

Cuomo's response to the latest data was hard-hitting: He invoked emergency powers and took funding away from the state agencies and the state legislature, predicting that the lockdown could cost the state fifteen billion dollars, and (it went without saying) they could not be trusted to prudently prioritize and allocate. Yet he also shared a general inconclusiveness about whether the state's strategy was working. "We closed everything down," he said, almost free-associating as he continued. "That was our public health strategy. I don't know that you would say, 'Quarantine everyone.' . . . Young people quarantined with older people is probably not the best public health strategy." He went on, that day and many of the next, tossing *maybe*s and *maybe not*s to his viewers, viewers who, no matter who they listened to, be it the CDC, the DOH, the governor, the media, their doctor, their aunt in Albuquerque, or their cousin in Cleveland, had many of the same uncertainties. Or, for those taking their cues from Facebook, Twitter, and the Oval Office, fatal certainties.

On March 31, Cuomo's younger brother, CNN anchor Chris Cuomo, feverish and coughing, announced from his home in the Hamptons that he had tested positive for COVID. It would take months for Albany's *Times-Union* to announce that the governor had ordered his own department of health officials to take a state car to Long Island to test his brother and his entire family. Eleanor Adams, still working for the state out of New Rochelle, had initially refused to break ethical guidelines, but she was threatened with the loss of her job if she refused, those close to her said. She was put in an untenable position at the height of the pandemic, when her expertise was needed, and it just wasn't worth the battle against the governor when so many people were dying. Cuomo's hypocrisy would come back to bite him.

That much of what Steve Corwin was doing was behind the scenes made his physical absence even more of a sticking point for many. "A good leader would have been walking the floors," ICU attending Bradley Hayward complained. "You are on a news briefing every day for the hospital saying PPE is effective and a surgical mask is enough even though we are taking care of colleagues that are literally dying of this because of the PPE issues. And you will not even come to the ICU in your PPE to show us you believe it? They did not do that. It was beyond insulting. Many times we were told the PPE is fine and it is safe. Then we thought, *If that's the case, why aren't you here doing this?*"

Hayward later understood that the level of outrage he was experiencing toward the corporate side was a coping mechanism for an unprecedented situation. There was an overwhelming outpouring of support from the hospital's department of medicine, exemplified by critical-care pulmonologist Fernando Martinez and chair of medicine Tony Hollenberg quietly appearing on the floor every single day, sometimes twice a day, to round with Lindsay Lief and Hayward and the other ICU attendings. And right across the hall was critical-care director David Berlin, whose upbeat sense of mission, of what it meant to be on the front lines of a medical mystery, was its own form of inspiration.

Martinez, who had come from the University of Michigan, where he'd run the lung transplant program, had always understood the need for collaboration across the hospital and for his ICU directors across specialties to form a team. The hierarchies of NewYork-Presbyterian with its command structure—medicine department separate from the corporate side—took deft navigation, a particular skill of Martinez's acquired by necessity.

Martinez's mother was able to flee Cuba, taking her children with her, in 1968. Martinez and his twin sister were ten. Two older sisters had been drafted to work in the brutal sugarcane fields by the Cuban government as part of their Communist training. One day, when they still lived in Cuba, Martinez's mother got a call. Her daughters, with their red hair and pale complexions, were seriously ill from sun poisoning and dehydration from the inhumane demands of cutting rows of cane with a machete. His mother borrowed a car and drove hours to the fields, where a foreman pulled a gun on her. "I don't care if you shoot me, I am taking my daughters home," she said. At the airport later, his mother sobbed when she saw her husband standing on the roof of his car waving. "Why isn't Daddy coming with us?" Fernando asked his sister. They moved to southeastern Georgia because of a family connection while their mother mastered English and got a license to teach. Martinez's father was allowed to take a vacation in Spain, where he applied for asylum at the American embassy. All of which, Martinez implied, made him understand as a teenager the need to deal with whatever life hands you with the most delicate diplomacy. As the pandemic rolled into New York, he made a decision "to spend as much time as I could in all of the ICUs trying to listen to the nurses and doctors and understand their fears—I know fear."

"How is it?"

Lindsay Lief's husband, Jake, texted or called her every night and asked this. Her answer was always the same: Horrible. She would summon every bit of discipline to keep from weighing Jake down with what she was seeing, the amount of death and illness that was taking over the hospital. Sometimes, even with the one person you were supposed to be able to tell everything to, there was nothing to say; sometimes, even with the person you most want to hear from, it's better not to hear anything. But then there were the nights when Jake's phone would light up at 3:00 a.m. And there would be Lief, sobbing. The guilt and anguish she felt about being away from her boys caught up with her in these sleepless nights.

After catching up with Jake on the details of life upstate, she would switch to FaceTime with her boys to go over their homework, as if she didn't have a care in the world. Her mother would text her several times a day from Philadelphia to find out when she was home safely.

Lief had asked her mother, an executive coach, to work her contacts and try to come up with more donated N95s.

Jake and Lief had employed a nanny for the kids as she did her hospital shifts and he worked on projects to educate children in the townships near Port Elizabeth, South Africa. He rushed back to New York as the pandemic began to shut down the city, hoping to stop in London to visit the offices of his NGO, but Lief called him: "You better come home. This is getting bad."

On her sleepless nights, Lief turned over and over her decision to send Freedom and Madiba upstate with Jake. In early March, it seemed obvious, like so much else: Jake had already heard from his friends working at other nonprofits that the city was getting close to being on complete lockdown and that within days, de Blasio would close the schools. Jake had convinced his parents to rent a small house near Hudson, just ninety minutes from the city, where they could help their boys with their schoolwork during the day for the few weeks the crisis would last.

In her heart, Lief wasn't sure about the plan, but in her head, there were no doubts. Her time in the ICU had imparted a lesson about not waiting for things to happen, and as a result, she had a good sense of when it was time to take action. Now was the time.

The night before Jake and the kids went upstate, it was so balmy that Jake and Lief were able to take the boys to a local outdoor café. The next morning, Jake and the boys left. Their departure was so hasty that when it snowed in Hudson the next week, Jake realized the kids had left their winter coats behind. (Lief had them sent.)

The Liefs had rented the house for one month; that became three.

Lindsay Lief's sister, Liz, was constantly worried but tried not to show it. In early April, Liz got COVID and did not tell her sister so as not to add to the worry load. Almost every day they texted back and forth.

Lindsay: *From Jake:*
Madiba says out of
nowhere "maybe Mama
will meet me in Maine for
my bday. If she does I
don't need any other
presents . . . but will need
a cake still. mama and a
cake."

Liz: *I'm so sorry. How are*
you doing? Or, how were you
doing before that text?

Lindsay: *Before the text*
okay.

Liz: *ok, Well, that's something*
He's going to be ok, He is/will
be sad but he is going to
get through it and so will
you. He has Jake and his

grandparents. It's just hell
between now and then/m I
just feel so sad.

Lindsay: *Occupying*
someone else's body.

As grueling as the separation was, in retrospect, Lief said, "There wasn't a question that it was the right thing to do. They were six and eight, and it was very easy to send them away because it was so obvious what was happening. It wasn't like we were ambivalent. There were no tests available for the doctors at Weill Cornell, not for a long time—the danger was real."

The stress on the attendings in the unit was obvious very early, however. As COVID patients began to code, one attending became convinced she was responsible for a death because she had not put on her PPE fast enough. She had just returned to 5 South, which had yet to be overwhelmed—only 20 percent of the ICU had COVID patients—but learning the cumbersome PPE procedure and then having to actually garb herself took two extra minutes, and by the time she was fully gowned, the patient was gone. "It wasn't even clear that this patient had COVID, but I blamed myself," the attending recalled. "I just lost my shit. We didn't know why he had died—was it because we were two minutes late intubating him?" The overcome attending began to bawl when Lief came over. "Lindsay was so calm. 'You need to go home. I am here. You can't be a doctor right now. You are utterly incapable. I need you to see that and to get out of the hospital.'"

11

On April 1, as a sense of catastrophe overtook the city, COO Laura Forese delivered a calamitous briefing that stunned and profoundly offended the NewYork-Presbyterian community.

From a boardroom at Weill Cornell, a portrait of NewYork-Presbyterian founder (or at least his hand) visible behind her, Forese appeared with the HR head next to her. No agendas or outlines accompanied the daily briefings, so those viewing had no clue what she was going to talk about, but the usually cool and unruffled Forese looked strained.

Steve Corwin and Forese had been receiving numerous letters, cards, and messages from the besieged NewYork-Presbyterian back-office staff begging for help and decrying the lack of support from above. Now Forese asked those who had been writing that they felt unsafe and "disrespected" to stop immediately. "The notion that we are disrespecting you because we are saying you are part of the team and may have to come in is incredibly dispiriting." Forese's mouth visibly tensed. "You are here because of the work that NewYork-Presbyterian does. You do not work for a tech company. You do not work for a finance company. You work for a hospital and a health-care system. Please, for you and your families, stop sending e-mails, cards, and letters saying that we are disrespecting you. If you feel that way, we can understand that. You're entitled to your opinion. It raises for us whether you in fact want to keep working for New York–Presbyterian."

It was a confounding moment. Forese, who earned $4.5 million a year, appeared to have little understanding of the pressure that the hospital's back-office employees were under. Even her outfit put her at a remove from the rank and file: a gray cotton sweater with a single, cartoon-like hand-painted black flower below her left shoulder—the right fashion choice for a Southampton summer dinner but not for an all-hospital briefing in a week where one tabloid horror headline piled on top of another. Already there had been 20,011 cases and 289 deaths in the city. Tom Kato was struggling for his life at Columbia; emergency department doctor Chris Belardi was on a ventilator in 5 South; and Mount Sinai's assistant nursing manager, Kious Kelly, had died of COVID after testing positive two weeks earlier.

Forese's dismissive address did not go over well, but it was not without reason. In her view, she was trying to treat all the hospital workers—both frontline and back-office—equitably. "It was a reaction to 'How dare you?' We're getting people's families writing to us saying, 'How could you put my loved one at risk?' What's in your head is, it's the doctors who are working thirty-six hours and the nurses who have to come in, who are worried about their families," she later explained. "You're a back-office person." However, there was a larger reality at hand.

On Friday, March 27, Andrew Cuomo gave his daily press briefing at the Javits Center. The gargantuan facility had been converted, at a cost of twenty million dollars, to serve as a field hospital to take a huge load off the city's hospitals, but it remained virtually unused, as the federal government refused to allow COVID patients to be treated there. In partnership with Mount Sinai, Samaritan Purse set up medical tents in Central Park, but tents were not hospital rooms. (A Queens paramedic later described the effort as "like battlefield triage.... We're pretty much bringing patients to the hospitals to die.") On the *Today* show, the mayor announced that soon "every one of New York City's twenty thousand hospital beds will have to be an ICU bed and will be taken by a COVID patient" when the number of cases reached 42,000. The Brooklyn Hospital Center pulled out a forklift to haul the dead bodies that could not be taken to funeral homes—there was no room. But Forese and others at the top of NewYork-Presbyterian had a different capacity crush in mind, which was part of the reason for her address. Later, she would reiterate she was referring to back-office staff requests to stay home, not to those on the front line. Yet she was also speaking to future patients, their families, and the fate of NewYork-Presbyterian itself. The fear of the virus was second only to the fear of litigation. Every doctor knows that getting sued for malpractice is not an "if" but a "when," an inevitability of doing their work within an ecosystem of imperfection, uncurable cases, and a very American reflex to sue when discontented. To be sure, actual malpractice existed, but the inevitability of frivolous lawsuits by heartbroken patients and their families was accepted as par for the course. A jury might more easily be swayed to decide in favor of the patient if it could be shown that, say, a hospital had not provided enough nurses or doctors to make sure the patient received the care they deserved. However, if the hospital could claim it did have a sufficient quantity of doctors and nurses, it had a much better chance to defend itself. Given the number of COVID patients that overwhelmed hospitals had admitted and the number of patients who were already in the hospitals suffering from other maladies, there was a potential for astronomical malpractice awards that could bankrupt the hospital.

So all the executives had to play a shell game, had to say to the world, "Yes, we have enough people. Yes, we are short of some supplies, but the people who are taking care of you have what they need. No, employees aren't claiming they don't have either of these things.

Well, not after that first, tough little stretch—really just a few weeks, when you think about it. After that, such concerns went away. Now, at those *other* hospitals . . ."

The wonders of modern medicine had raised the expectations of patients that everything could be cured. As it was, NewYork-Presbyterian was hemorrhaging money; the expensive surgeries and procedures that covered the costs of treating other patients had evaporated thanks to COVID. The hospital was fighting for its life, and while it wasn't the first casualty, this particular war on COVID inevitably sacrificed some truth.

The briefing was to the two thousand back-office employees who worked at the hospital corporate headquarters blocks away from the frontline staff. You needed a passcode to watch it. Even so, the fact that it was, as Forese pointed out later, "for the back office" did not explain her unfeeling and threatening tone toward those who were terrified to come to work in a city locked down by a pathogen killing thousands around the world. It seemed unimaginable that the feelings of "the back office" would be dismissed by a lavishly compensated corporate leader. The seismic pressure on Forese as she dealt with exhausted doctors and frontline workers, morgue trucks, and a lack of PPE and ventilators clearly overwhelmed her; she appeared to snap.

Forese's comments ricocheted through the hospital. The hashtags #firelauraforese and #where'sLaura sped through social media. "Someone was pissed because it was [directed] to the back-office group only," Forese explained. "To say to them, 'You have a different set of issues.' And we were starting to want them to come into the hospital and do some work there. Someone was unhappy with me and . . . posted it as though it was to doctors and nurses. And it wasn't." A meme circulated of Forese demanding that the NYP employees stop sending letters intercut with scenes from the 2005 film *V for Vendetta*, Laura Forese contrasted with the über-evil High

Chancellor, played by John Hurt as he channeled Hitler and British fascist Oswald Mosley. *Tonight, what we need is a clear message to the people!* And from Forese, repeating from her back-office briefing: "If you feel that way, we can understand that. You're entitled to your opinion. It raises for us whether you in fact want to keep working for NewYork-Presbyterian." *Tonight, any protester, any instigator or agitator, will be made an example of!*

However horrific the strain on her, Forese became the proxy for the fear cascading through the hospital.

The call came to Dr. Kerry Meltzer on her fourth day in general medicine. The scheduling for the residents had vaporized as COVID took over Weill Cornell, and she was now on night float, stationed in a workroom with ten computers and ten people with no plans to be home before breakfast. All that month, they had been watching CNN, hoping for some good news anywhere, but coverage was predictably grim. One resident would pull up the Johns Hopkins COVID projections on her computer screen and watch as the model showed infection cascading through the Northeast and seeping toward the middle of the country. "Oh my God," the resident had blurted when it first became clear what was going on: *exponential growth*. Now she just looked at the splotches of scarlet dots filling the states, the function fed by dysfunction.

In the first weeks, there was an excitement, but the patients just kept coming, and the step-down units and pop-up ICUs had patients who were sicker and sicker, their odds of survival lower and lower. The halls of the hospital swarmed with scores of urologists, dermatologists, and retired gastroenterologists who had volunteered to pitch in or who had been hired to help. Meltzer spoke to families on iPhones and iPads, often bearing the worst news. The residents traded stories of anonymous fathers and mothers saying their final goodbyes to their children on iPads and of babies cooing in their mothers' arms as fathers slipped away.

And all through the day, the residents, nurses, and attending physicians spoke with families on FaceTime: "We are doing everything we can, but there hasn't been a change. I don't have anything to report."

On April 2, Meltzer's phone lit up; the screen said *Mom*. She had talked to her mother less than two hours before, at 6:30 p.m., right before she started work. Why was her mother contacting her in the middle of her shift?

Can you please call? her mom texted.

I'm really busy, can it wait?

And she said, *It's important.*

That morning, Meltzer's sister Maeve had texted her to tell her that she loved her and was so proud of her. Dr. Meltzer called her sister back as she was walking to the hospital for the night shift. The message went straight to voicemail.

The clamor of patients around her and the constant beeping of the ventilators made it hard for Meltzer to hear her mother on the phone, so after she called, she ducked into an empty room. Her mom said, "Maeve and Gideon have been in an accident. The Coast Guard is out looking for them."

Meltzer rushed to find her supervisor.

Maeve and her husband, David, a human rights lawyer, lived in Washington, DC. They had taken their three children to Maeve's mother's house on the Eastern Shore of Maryland to quarantine after lockdown. Maeve and David told the kids that this would be an adventure—a summer camp where they could be outside all day. For Maeve, the inventor of elaborate treasure maps for her eight-year-old, Gideon, and her seven-year-old, Gabriella, the idea of the Chesapeake Bay retreat was idyllic. Here, the bookish Gideon could curl up in his upstairs bedroom for hours with his books or, his father claimed, decipher the secrets of the stock market. And Gabriella could run maskless by the shore, not worrying about a pathogen.

Maeve had always put her heart and soul into her work, but she had made it a priority since day one of motherhood to spend time with her children. Getting home after a thirty-hour flight back from Asia, where she'd been on a global health initiative, she would go straight to the family pool and dive in. She planned last-minute New Year's Eve parties on cross-country flights while reading a book to her youngest child, Toby, on her lap. A tomboy and an athlete (she had run the Boston Marathon), Maeve made sure to get her kids outside to run, swim, and paddle.

On the afternoon of April 2, she and Gideon were playing kick-ball when the ball was blown into the water. Maeve insisted they should retrieve it and jumped into a canoe at the dock, Gideon right beside her. Suddenly, the wind whipped up and they got caught in a strong current; Maeve and Gideon could not paddle fast enough to get back to shore and were swept into the open bay.

It had been Maeve who pushed Kerry into medicine from the time she was in high school, talking to her about global medicine and what was achievable. Maeve's expertise on vaccines and her dedication to global health had inspired her career, as had her mother's time as lieutenant governor of Maryland, where she focused on the state's health-care challenges. Maeve's work in the Obama administration had inspired Meltzer to take a course in health-care policy in med school and to understand Medicaid expansion and Obamacare and how it truly affected the care of those who needed it most, especially the undocumented. One year later, Meltzer had started her residency at Weill Cornell.

It had also been Maeve who continued to take their uncle's hours-long hectoring phone calls about vaccines, who resisted the impulse to slam the phone down when he insisted she look at his lunatic

PowerPoints and "proof," despite Kerry's admonitions that he was robbing Maeve of her time with David and the children.

Not that she was shy about letting her views be known; the previous year, Maeve had taken him on in *Politico* with a fierce policy piece she coauthored with her mother and her uncle Joseph Kennedy II. (The headline was "RFK Jr. Is Our Brother and Uncle. He's Tragically Wrong About Vaccines.") As always, when dealing with the prickly Bobby Jr., they pushed out the pro forma: "We love Bobby. He is one of the great champions of the environment. His work to clean up the Hudson River . . ." But, they wrote, everything he had done since had produced "heartbreaking consequences" and was in direct opposition to the massive public health campaigns run by their great-uncle, who, as president, had urged eighty million Americans, including five million children, to get the Salk vaccine, which he called "this miraculous drug." The same fierce passion was brought to childhood vaccine mandates by Kerry's great uncle (RFK Jr.'s uncle), Massachusetts senator Ted Kennedy, who opened hundreds of community health-care centers in inner cities and rural areas to administer vaccines.

"Teddy was like a grandfather to me," Meltzer reflected, "his passion for health-care policy. I was always interested in science and how the body works. I grew up in a family where you try to make the world a better place." And now her uncle Robert F. Kennedy Jr. was out selling a line of anti-science that Maeve and Kerry and their mother could not ignore. "On this issue, Bobby is an outlier in the Kennedy family," Maeve and her mother and Maeve's uncle Joe wrote. "Those who delay or refuse vaccinations, or encourage them to do so, put themselves and others, especially children, at risk." That Maeve would still take his calls was a testament to her respect for family and to her faith.

And now, the unimaginable: The curse of the Kennedy family—a phrase that made Dr. Meltzer cringe and that she knew full well would be trotted out in the media—had struck again. For twenty-six hours, the Coast Guard, with every helicopter and boat that could be summoned, scoured 2,700 square miles of water. It was another three days before Maeve's body was recovered and another two days before an underwater diving team found Gideon's body.

For the next three weeks, Meltzer and her husband, Max, remained in seclusion. They helped take care of Gabriella and Toby, who could not understand where Gideon and their mother had gone or that they would not be back. Then Meltzer returned to the hospital. "It is what Maeve would have wanted," she said. "To put aside my private grief for the larger good."

On Meltzer's first night back at the hospital, Stephanie Pagliuca was the resident in charge, and sensitive to Meltzer's tenderness. "I tried to be as normal as possible because no one wants to feel different," she remembered. "But I was so aware that conversations about death and patients' situations were going to be a lot harder than usual." The pair were next to each other at the desk when a code call came in. "I said, 'Do you want to take a break?'" Before getting an answer, Pagliuca took Meltzer's phone, which served as the hospital's pager system. She wanted Meltzer to understand that it was okay to step away again.

13

Hoping that ignorance might be bliss, the comms department of NewYork-Presbyterian had been ignoring Columbia University's department of surgery chair Craig Smith's letters, but thousands outside the hospital found their way to his daily updates. "Dr. Smith's emails are Winston Churchill's radio speeches of this war," the *Wall Street Journal*'s Ben Cohen would write two weeks after his first letter appeared. Smith declined to speak to the *Journal,* saying only, "I'd rather let the written messages to my colleagues speak for themselves." Smith was an inside player and internally was well known for an iron will when it came to maintaining his power as chief of surgery. Part of that was by conveniently projecting a modest persona, avoiding the tall-poppy accusation; he did that now with a masterly display of performance humility: "I should also state something that I assumed was obvious: the target audience for my updates has always been the Department of Surgery family. That people outside the family find value in some parts of the message is a welcome bonus, and perhaps a reminder that even surgeons are human ... we struggle with many of the same issues that perplex the rest of the world." *See,* he seemed to be saying, *any old doctor could have written this stuff. And we're all human!* But heart surgeons were not known for that "any old doctor" conceit, and if there was a heart surgeon who knew everyone should listen to him because only he was great enough to express what needed to be said, it was Craig Smith.

Five days later, Smith considered the need for a larger perspective, describing the anxiety of a moment when repairing a minor bleed in heart-valve replacement. "All is very routine until the back of the heart starts to bleed; it's coming apart . . . I'm not ashamed to admit that my first reaction, 100 percent of the time, is crippling anxiety and self-doubt. Can I put Humpty together again?" His point was that when things were going wrong, you had to keep your focus and cool. "Back to this reality, we can expect the vast majority of COVID patients to do very well. Even most of those who go on ventilators survive, but not by chance. They survive because we don't give up."

In the third week of March at Columbia, the anesthesiologist Steven Miller was running in the circular entrance driveway of Columbia Medical Center, looking for a red Toyota station wagon driven by some graduate students he had never met who had come up with a way to save dozens of the desperately ill who needed an immediate ventilator. Around his neck was his last N95, attached with a lanyard hook to his hospital badge. He would use that same N95 for a month.

The whole thing had started a few days before. Late Friday night, Miller was still at the hospital, trying to ignore the TikToks that were coming from his wife—the "bored housewife going mad" as a running joke between them went—when his phone lit up. It was Nat Stern, the head of supply. "Dude, I have good news and bad news. . . . The good news is I have a lot of ventilators coming from FEMA and the Reagan-era stockpile—and you and I are going to figure out how to distribute them through the hospital." That was good news indeed. "And the kind of good news but less good news," Stern informed Miller, "is that they are still in their boxes and we don't know if they work or they have parts."

Stern and Miller would learn that most of the ventilators had been purchased between 2006 and 2008—they were already, at best, twelve years out of date. On the loading dock when the ventilators arrived, the supply team and Miller saw that many had missing hoses and missing parts. In an oxygen-saturated atmosphere, hoses that did not fit perfectly could cause the ventilators to burn up. What to do?

The Columbia graduate engineering school had a team of students who had spent their lives studying air filtration and quality management, and Miller reached out to them immediately. These days, his introductions often began awkwardly. As soon as he told people his name, inevitably he would see that look cross the listeners' faces—*Stephen Miller? The Trump guy who hates immigrants?* Steven Miller desperately hoped that Trump and his cabinet of third-raters and sadists and grifters would vanish quickly so he could reclaim his name.

"They had already volunteered to do whatever they could do to help us," Miller said. "They don't like sitting idle."

When Miller explained to the grad students what he needed, the reply was, "Not a problem. We can run them off on our three-D machines." The students asked Miller how long he wanted the hoses to be. "I said, 'We want from six feet to twenty-five feet.' They scrounged whatever they could find—tubes of all different colors, shapes, and sizes, some flexible, some metal, whatever was appropriate and safe and compatible with oxygen—and just started retrofitting." And it wasn't just tubing; another team started making filters off their 3D printer. All of it, the students told him, could be ready in twenty-four hours if nothing went wrong on their end.

Within a day, Miller was running to the driveway of Milstein to pick up the hoses. Moments after Miller arrived, there was the red Toyota. The engineering student at the wheel cracked his window and shouted, "I'm staying in the car! I will pop the trunk." And out came boxes of miracle rubber tubes fitted to the exact specifications the ventilators required.

14

As the pandemic entered its third week in New York City, the mounting desperation was palpable in the streets, and there would be days to go before there was any real sign of a peak. On March 31, New York City recorded there had been one thousand COVID deaths. The flaneurs of New York shuffled joylessly in the middle of deserted streets, ready to dart away from anyone approaching, a maneuver that was called the coronavirus swerve. At the Central Park reservoir, runners began to appear in masks. Near the reservoir, the Central Park patrol used bullhorns to shout, "Six feet apart! Six feet apart!" There were, however, a few signs of New York City's indefatigable spirit. A singer-songwriter and part-time rabbi named Steven Blane appeared with his guitar every day at the same location, near the path that led to the Metropolitan Museum of Art. There was nothing casual about his urgency to perform for his daily Facebook upload, singing with dazzling brio and no audience. Every day, Blane had a new riff. After the passage of the trillion-dollar COVID relief fund, Blane rose to a new level: *A trillion or two for a virus / Won't get you too upset / Especially when that virus is something you can get.*

As the weather warmed, clusters of children out with their mothers on the north field by the reservoir chased one another through a grove of blooming cherry trees. They too shouted, "Six feet apart! Six feet apart!" Spring came early to New York; the forsythias had

burst into bloom. Throughout the city, the parks and playgrounds
shut down by the mayor were as desolate as the traffic-free streets. In
the silence, actual birdsong could be heard. Many observed that the
sound was strange and discordant, as if the birds were mimicking the
incessant sirens.

At Columbia University Irving Medical Center in the emergency
department, they called it the "bad-news chair," and when he wasn't
running around trying to save lives, that was where Cleavon Gilman
sat and made calls he'd never wanted to make. And by now, he had
made many of them.

Gilman recalled, "I had elderly patients whose blood oxygen levels were extremely low, with trouble breathing." For some of these
patients, their blood work showed high levels of a protein, troponin,
that is released after a heart attack. "I was like, 'Oh my God,' and I
would call the patients' families and arrange for them to connect with
their loved ones because I was very concerned they would pass away
soon." Gilman said there were times when patients would pass away
within minutes of speaking with their families. "That was how quickly
the virus had an effect on their heart." All the while, "we were battling
the misinformation from the Trump administration downplaying the
virus. . . . Imagine being at war in Iraq and you don't even have the support of your president." It wasn't just that Trump was not providing adequate aid because he considered New York enemy political territory;
it was that his groundless assurances and political slant were leading
to the spread of the virus. "People were talking about going to spring
break. It felt like . . . 'What am I doing out here? What's going on? Am
I seeing the same thing?' And I just thought the politicization of masks
and social distancing downplayed this virus. . . . This virus is horrible,
the way it robs people of their life. . . . We are actually dying from a
virus that the president and the Republican Party is just downplaying."

All of this—the disinformation, the lassitude, the overconfidence, the ignorance—left him feeling "like I had an obligation to warn people about this deadly virus, and that's why I took to social media." First on his Facebook account, then on Twitter, he posted information about how to protect oneself from infection, debunked the garbage science and claims that the virus was a hoax, and told his followers about what was going on in the hospital. He also tried to humanize the tragedy in a way that few others were doing. COVID had exploded so quickly that it had almost entirely become a story of numbers: how many ventilators, how many beds, how many infections, how many dead. Later, after Gilman had left New York, he posted captioned photos of his Arizona patients who had lost their lives, and he would continue honoring the dead in the coming months. There was twenty-two-year-old Aimee Ayala, who died of COVID shortly after giving birth to her baby girl; the post was accompanied by a photo of the new mother, oxygen tubes attached, eyes closed, the baby resting on top of her chest, balanced there by the hand of a nurse or doctor. There was twenty-one-year-old Tayra Rangel, a student at Kennesaw State University in Georgia, smiling at the camera, denim shirt over a mustard-colored sweater, whose family had been planning for her graduation and were now holding her funeral. Nearly two years later, he continued sharing stories, such as that of eighteen-year-old Sara Golembiewski of Westlake, Ohio, who was the only one in her family who got vaccinated and then watched her father, mother, and aunt all die two weeks after they'd gathered for Thanksgiving. And there were hundreds more. Gilman posted on a daily basis, a cascade of grief that broke through not only the abstract coverage and political assessments but the detachment of some of those in the executive suites.

As his following grew from a few people to a few hundred to more than 100,000, some worried that NewYork-Presbyterian, still upset about Matt McCarthy's *Squawk Box* incident, would tell Gilman to pull the plug, but it didn't. "I didn't get any pushback from the hospital. I was just telling people what I was seeing with the patients." And perhaps he just didn't have the extra time to complain about the hospital; he needed that time to sit in the bad-news chair, to again and again call husbands, wives, grandparents, and children to tell them that the person they loved so much was gone.

"I had to create a spot," he explained. He positioned an ordinary, no-frills desk chair in a hallway where he would have the space to stretch out his legs. "The first thing I say is 'Hello, I'm Dr. Gilman. I'm calling you about so-and-so,' and I think they know; they always know when I call them. And then I just give them a picture of what the situation looks like, how sick their loved one is, and, 'We've tried everything we can do, but unfortunately it wasn't enough.'"

It was standard for residents to be lectured about how to deliver bad news, and some of Gilman's colleagues were looking on the internet and other sources, trying to figure out the best way to handle such sad exchanges. Concluded Gilman, after you did it "twenty, thirty times, you get a bit better at it." But a "bit better" didn't mean it was "much easier."

"You know what's the hardest about anything? It's the hardest when the person is on the phone and it's translated and you have to do it twice . . . the person on the phone is translating from English to Spanish, and then you hear that cry twice. That happens a lot out there."

Gilman called about three families per day to tell them about their loved ones passing. "I was trying to protect people as well . . . one thing that happens when a person dies from COVID early on, friends and family would gather with their loved one, with the widow, or the survivor, and so people who do that, and of course the survivors, would usually be COVID-positive, and so a few weeks afterwards, you would have another family member in the hospital who dies from the virus as well."

There was a mirror of his experience in Iraq. "I find the busier times of being in the ER to be the easiest, but when it's quiet it's just very hard because you're just up there alone with your thoughts." For everyone on the floor, the whole thing could seem unreal, and yet nothing had ever been more real.

"You know, it's not normal to see people die every day. It's not normal to also work twenty-four hours and be under that constant threat that you're going to infect your family. . . . That's a lot of stress to bring on. Here I am, working hard, putting my life on the line, my call of duty, protecting my country, doing everything I have to do, and then my fiancée is like, 'Well, let's get out, let's take a walk in Central Park. You've been working very hard.' And so we go out, and people are just laying in the sun. I'm like, 'What?'"

In Brooklyn, on April Fools' Day, Susie Bibi's running COVID jokes stopped making Reuben laugh. All that month, exercising in her basement and walking to Coney Island with her friends, she could not stop coughing. "I must have COVID," she said, laughing. "I kept telling everyone as a joke, 'I bet I have COVID,'" she said. "It was, 'I think I have COVID. This could be COVID.' I didn't know if it really was COVID because there was no way to get a test." Then she and her husband heard that one of the doctors in the community had somehow secured PCR tests and was running them in his parking garage, an example of how wired the Syrian community could be. "We drove down to Foster Avenue, and the nurse came downstairs from his office. We stayed in the car. She had a clipboard. We both took the test and they said, 'It will take a few days to process.'" It was a moment in New York where the few tests available required going to a tent set up by the city or hoping the urgent-care clinic had not run out, and here was a private doctor who had worked the machinery. "I kept calling all of my friends saying, 'Has anyone taken this test? Does anyone know about it?'" None of her friends had.

But this was Brooklyn. "There's a guy for everything," Reuben Bibi said. "He had an office upstairs but wasn't allowing anyone in. . . . So you would call him when you were in the garage. His nurse would come down. You would literally roll down your window. Swab. Go to the other side. Swab." Susie Bibi felt as if she were in an episode of *Seinfeld.*

"I had no other COVID symptoms. No fever. No chills. No lethargy. I was exercising. I had my smell and taste. I only had a cough—a very long and weird cough." By Friday, her oxygen levels had dropped. A close friend said, "You should go to the hospital now, before Shabbat, so you can be home by sunset." All of Bibi's children had been born at Weill Cornell. She was advised that it was the best place for COVID—the other hospitals were jammed. Her husband called the Jewish private-ambulance service Hatzalah. Susie Bibi learned from a text while she was in the ambulance that she was positive for COVID—and so was Reuben.

Arriving at the hospital, Bibi walked into bedlam. "I was in the ER and they gave me oxygen with a mask. There were so many people, it felt like chaos. They couldn't really pay attention. Someone said they were going to try me on oxygen for a day or two to see if that would work. . . . I texted Ruby and my sister: 'Get me out of here.'" She told the attendings who would see her, "'I am very fit.' . . . I remember thinking, *I have to let them know I am not weak. I have to tell them that our family had donated to the hospital so they don't leave me in the basement.* I said to them, 'Really, I am very fit. I'm like a triathlete.' Then they write that in the notes everywhere I go. I hear them say I am a triathlete. 'She's a triathlete! She's a marathon runner' . . . even when I was discharged. I have never run a race in my life. I am not a runner. But I was all muscle—a hundred and seven pounds. Not one ounce of fat." April 3 was one of the peak days at Weill Cornell. There was no room in the ICU, so they moved her to the third floor to one of the temporary rooms. "Ruby and I were texting back and forth, 'How are you feeling?'

'They're not helping me.' 'Please text the nurse.' 'They're not answering me.' 'They're leaving me alone.'"

"So I called the nurses' desk to see what was going on, to try to get her some kind of service," Reuben Bibi later recalled.

On Monday, April 5, the pulmonologist Kapil Rajwani walked into Susie Bibi's room. "'Do you think I need to be intubated?' she asked. She was very uncomfortable. Her oxygen had dropped into the seventies range," Rajwani said. Bibi texted a friend, but she told Rajwani that she was very fit. Rajwani's team called her husband, who had a daily 4:00 p.m. call with the doctors. "From the day they took her, I thought she was mismanaged. Everything was crazy. They won't let you make phone calls to them. They won't let you come in." (The hospital had instituted COVID protocols weeks before.) "She's just like another number. It's like you're in a warehouse. She's a number." He remained very focused, although he was in turmoil. At the same time, he had been speaking to his friend, the son of Stanley Chera, the real estate mogul who was as private about his life as the Bibis but who also was at Weill Cornell, stricken with COVID. As it happened, in the White House, Trump was concerned about Chera and began to talk about him in his daily briefings. A leader in the Bibis' community, Chera had become a billionaire by expanding Young World, his family's Brooklyn children's store. He had helped Jared Kushner's father sell his retail properties at 666 Fifth Avenue and had hosted a fundraiser for Trump in 2016, personally donating hundreds of thousands of dollars to his campaign. Chera's Crown Acquisitions had a global footprint, but Chera operated, as did the rest of the community, as if he were invisible. When COVID swept New York, Trump told Chera and his wife, Frieda, to leave Brooklyn immediately and move to their house in the Syrian-Jewish seaside enclave of Deal, New Jersey. From the White House, Trump talked about his condition. "When you send a friend to the hospital and you call up to find out how he is doing—it happened to me, where he goes to the hospital, he says goodbye," he said during a White House briefing the week Bibi was placed on a ventilator. "He's sort of a tough guy. A little older, a little heavier than he'd like to be, frankly. And you call him up the next day: 'How's he doing?' And he's in a coma? This is not the flu." Later, when Trump was taken to Walter Reed Hospital, he was reported to have asked his doctor, "Am I going to wind up like Stanley Chera?"

As Bibi was placed on a ventilator, Chera struggled for his life one floor below.

Later, when they discussed how the hospital was able to save itself despite its budget being torn to shreds, the supply team would marvel about one woman in New Jersey. At NewYork-Presbyterian, supply executives Anand Joshi and Scott McClintock had stopped sleeping—they needed those hours to keep cold-calling every medical supply company in the tristate area looking for hoses and parts to fix the broken ventilators coming from FEMA and New York State. "Often we wouldn't even know they were coming," Joshi said. "A truck would just back up on our loading dock and dump these broken machines out." Even when something did arrive, it wasn't necessarily usable. The ventilators coming from the state were often absolute trash, most of them missing parts.

Enter Lisa Stoia, a divorced mother of three who had been trying to keep Ronco Technical Services, her small medical-equipment company in Hillsborough, New Jersey, going through the pandemic. That reality explained how she happened to be in her office on Sunday, April 5. Stoia was scrambling to get her application in with the rush of other small-business owners looking for a slice of the $349 billion Paycheck Protection Program that Trump had signed into law a few days before. (Trump himself would try to tap into the program to get money for his hotels.) Without some PPP funding, Stoia could not survive.

When she arrived at her office in an industrial park, she saw a light blinking on her phone. "There was a message from Scott McClintock from NewYork-Presbyterian, saying he needed to speak with [me] urgently about supplies," she recalled. "*Wow,* I thought, *NewYork-Presbyterian. Are you kidding me?* I had never heard from them. This was like getting a call from the White House." Stoia called back immediately.

McClintock answered on the first ring. "He said, 'We know of your reputation helping supply some of the labs. We are in extreme trouble.'" At first, Stoia had a hard time processing the desperation in his voice. NewYork-Presbyterian was in extreme trouble? The number one hospital in the city? "I said to him, 'What can I do to help?' My office is connected to our warehouse. I asked him, 'Do you need rubber hoses? Ventilators? Do you need centrifuges? Let me walk into the warehouse and show you what I have.' I walked into the warehouse and FaceTimed, showing him our shelves of supplies. I said, 'We have loaners. The inventory is huge.' I went through all of our hoses. . . . The green was for nitrogen, the black hoses were for nitrous, and the yellow hoses were for medical air. 'Those are color-coded but you can take what we have and use green electrical tape and mark them for oxygen.' . . . I had rolls of medical hoses that fit a standard ventilator."

Although Stoia had never met McClintock, she could sense how stressed he was. "He said, 'I will take it all.' He needed more oxygen meters and regulators. I said, 'I don't have them, but I will work the phones for you to my people.' Then I tracked down a large manufacturer, who told me that they would need a confirmed purchase order from NewYork-Presbyterian. I got a confirmation in ten minutes and called them back, and they had already sold what they had to a competing hospital. I was so angry that I went on LinkedIn and found the key executives at the company and spoke to HR. My brother had worked there a few years before and had died while he was there. Within hours, the man who rescinded my order called me back with massive apologies. 'I don't know how you did it,' he said, 'but my boss wants you to have that order.'"

It took her until Wednesday to load her car and assemble everything the hospital needed—essentially most of her inventory. She decided to make the delivery herself in her own SUV. "I did not want anyone from my company possibly getting infected. My technician came over and helped me load all the boxes of hoses. I drove to Secaucus, where the hospital had its loading dock." Driving in, Stoia said, she thought "it looked like a science fiction set. Everyone had on goggles and masks and shields. There were eighteen-wheeler Stryker trucks loading massive numbers of beds and dozens of people in full PPE unloading and loading. It looked like the end of the world." It was also a hot zone.

Stoia texted McClintock to see if they had questions. "They were asking me the status of some of the equipment and how to use it. This was all me doing it. I told my children not to come near me. They are twenty-one and nineteen and seventeen. I told them I was doing this on my own. They wanted me to be safe. I wanted to put the clothes I was wearing in a trash bag. Everyone was so under the gun."

Stoia had been raised by a single mother from Puerto Rico. Drilled into her from the time she went to school was the idea of mission. She deeply believed that "we cannot question who needs help and when. You need help, you need help," the same Catholic-school sense of mission that had inspired Matt McCarthy, Xenia Frisby, Rosanne Raso. And Lisa Stoia had helped.

15

In April, one week into his return to New York, Jay Varma had come to a simple conclusion. "I was like: Holy shit—there's no plan to get us out of this."

Once he'd been told by his wife to come back from Africa, Varma had contacted CDC headquarters in Atlanta and said, "Well, New York is calling me." Varma's boss pointed out that the CDC was funded by the United States and that if New York wanted him back, he should get back.

The CDC arranged his travel. Over the next two days, Varma packed up, sold his car, and did the usual, frantic running around trying to make sure he had what he needed and wasn't taking anything he didn't. He put the cats in their carriers and drove them up to New York because the airlines would not allow them to fly. When he arrived in New York with the felines dazed but unscathed, his daughter burst out, "How could you have treated our cats this way?" But, like her father, they'd made it.

Three days later, deaths peaked in New York.

What Varma had quickly discovered—the "holy shit"—was that the city was in panic mode. "They had not planned to set up a massive testing," Varma said. "The health department, for some reason, had not thought past stay at home and shelter in place. They hadn't thought of an exit strategy." It seemed to him that their entire plan was to keep people apart and wait for a vaccine, not knowing when (or even if) one would arrive. "They weren't thinking ahead. . . . They were like, 'How do we dig ourself out of the mess we're in today?' They weren't thinking about 'How do [we] accelerate ourselves out of that mess? And keep [this] mess from happening again?'"

Varma understood the mindset, even if he disparaged it. To him, it was like being in a field hospital during a war where you had ten people bleeding out and you had to treat them right then and there or they would die. How could you focus on stopping the war? But if you didn't focus on that bigger issue, ten more patients would show up, and ten more after that, and ten more after that, on and on.

If part of the problem was a lack of vision, another part was budgetary. Said Varma, "People in public health are traditionally used to saying, 'Well, I would love ten dollars to solve this problem, but I'm only going to ask for one because there's no way they'll give me more than one. And even then, I should probably only spend seventy cents of it because I'll probably need that thirty cents for the next.' They operate on this notion of scarcity. And this is what doomed HIV response in Africa twenty years ago."

It made no sense to him that military officials could say they needed, for instance, a two-billion-dollar fighter jet when they didn't—that they could in fact say they needed a hundred of them—and they'd get the money, but those in public health resigned themselves to asking for (and getting) a fraction of what was essential. As he saw it, that was exactly what was going on with the health department. "They were like, 'There was no way we can build a system to test people every day,'" Varma lamented. "'There's no way we can investigate and interview all those people. And there's no way we could find all their contacts.'" And as a result, they had stopped contact-tracing in March, right when the virus was charging through the New York metro area. "So they don't even know who's getting infected. All they know is who's dying." But when he asked whether the health department was working on getting a testing program going, the response was that there were no reagents for tests anywhere in the country, and that probably wouldn't change for a year, so it was pointless to put too much effort into something that wasn't going to happen.

And that was just the city; Varma found the state even worse. "I mean, that was a disaster," he said. "I mean, it was impossible to work with them." And since the New York City health department had no authority to override the state, even if the city had a bright idea, it could promptly be suffocated by Albany.

On April 3, Cuomo signed the Emergency or Disaster Treatment Protection Act, which granted qualified immunity to hospitals, nursing homes, and physicians from civil and criminal liability arriving from decisions, acts, and omissions occurring from the beginning of the emergency declaration, March 7, through its expiration. Kenneth Prager, the chair of the hospital's medical ethics committee, tried to re-create the complicated and almost incomprehensible legal jargon. "The executive order covered liability stemming from the care of individuals with or without COVID." It did not excuse intentional criminal misconduct or gross negligence, "but it makes clear that 'acts, omissions, and decisions resulting from a resource or staffing shortage' will be covered." All of that was great, but there was one big hitch: "it did not protect triage doctors who went against the clearly expressed wishes of family or patients," Prager explained.

A few weeks earlier, 5 South's Brad Hayward had written to medical ethicist Joe Fins: "I just want to be clear for what to expect when I'm faced with the same moral dilemmas tomorrow. The nurses, the PAs, and the young faculty and fellows have to continue to make these extremely difficult decisions and deal with the repercussions legally, ethically, and morally alone then? I just want to be clear that's the directive that we have." Taking the liability issue (mostly) off the table didn't make the moral dilemmas vanish.

Hayward found himself unable to hold back. "I said [to Joe Fins], 'Isn't this why you went into ethics? I don't understand. I don't understand what exactly you came into this hospital to do. And I don't know how you sleep at night. I don't know what the ethics are of the situation we are in, but I know what you are doing is unethical.'"

Fins understood Hayward's anger and was equally upset. "I found this state official in his office at 10:00 p.m. at night. And I said, 'Are you telling me that if a brain-dead person comes into the emergency room and the family wants them resuscitated, the doctors will be prosecuted if they don't do it?' And he said, 'Joe, I have to sleep on that.' And I was like, 'Well, I can't sleep on that because we have to make these decisions right now.' . . . People were under enormous stress. . . . I didn't want to give any advice that would put the doctors in legal jeopardy."

Katherine Fischkoff, a general surgeon, was one of the ethicists. Her sense of things was, as one might expect, different.

"New York State, in 2008, after the flu epidemic, put together a set of published guidelines for ventilator allocation," she explained. "So there is an existing set of guidelines for how to triage critically scarce ventilators." One of the problems was that some of those who were so desperate for advice had apparently not looked at the guidelines, which, she said, could be found with a simple Google search.

That report—"Allocation of Ventilators in a Public Health Disaster"—had appeared in the March issue of *Disaster Medicine and Public Health Preparedness*, a quarterly journal of the American Medical Association, so it hadn't exactly been buried, though the lack of an epidemic in the years before COVID hit had made a good number of doctors and nurses unaware of its existence. The report stated that decisions about which patients should be put on ventilators needed to be based on the chance for recovery, and no underlying variables, such as a patient's age or preexisting health conditions, should change that equation. In an interview with the *New York Times*, Tia Powell, a renowned bioethicist who was one of the lead authors of the report, said, "We are not interested in quality of life. We are just interested in whether you are able to survive this particular crisis."

"The truth was," Fischkoff said, "the ventilators were never the problem. It was the ICU beds and dialysis machines, and nurses, and where we were going to put them."

She explained that "early on we had met about allocation guidelines to try to say, 'We need a plan before things get crazy.'" Those guidelines, she insisted, were not restricted to one resource. "Those guidelines could be applied to any scarce resource. It doesn't have to just be a ventilator. It can be an ICU bed or a dialysis unit. The idea was that you would save the people who are most likely to be salvageable. A normal life, we have sort of a first-come, first-served model, where whoever walks into the emergency room, you get treated in whatever order. But here, the question was, if you've got, like, five people all at once, what are you going to do?" But, as she and everyone in the hospital were realizing, treating COVID was a nightmare of imperfect information.

"The ethical basis of these guidelines was to try to save the people who you think you can save. The real problem with that is that nobody knew anything about COVID. So the idea of knowing who would survive was pure guesswork. So you would say, 'I'm sure an eighty-year-old person would do worse than a forty-year-old person'—so that made sense. But this was like . . ." Even when it seemed like there were regularities, they might be discredited come the next study. "We always talk about ethics coming from facts," she said, "and we didn't really have any facts."

One particularly misleading study came out in April. Northwell published early data on COVID patients "and they reported an outrageously high mortality rate. Essentially they said eighty percent of people who went on ventilators died." Eventually, Fischkoff explained, they had to publish a correction, but until then, if you didn't do your own research and analysis, you would have believed that 97 percent of patients over sixty-five who were intubated died. "We looked at that and we thought, *Why are we putting anybody over sixty-five on a ventilator?*

That's crazy. But of course, when you looked into the data, you saw that was not a reflection of the truth—and that was really dangerous."

Given that there was so little to go on, the ethicists tried to create a sort of scoring system. "Ultimately, the truth was, we just kept expanding and expanding and expanding, but we never actually had to activate our triage plan," said Fischkoff.

Did anyone read the guidelines? Sometimes Fischkoff and the other ethicists weren't sure. She would get calls from doctors saying, "This woman is eighty-five and she's kind of doing okay, not great—do I really have to intubate her? The daughter wants us to do everything, but there's no way . . ." These doctors knew it was a waste to put these patients on ventilators, but their hands were tied unless Cuomo got rid of the state requirement that you were not allowed to withhold or withdraw care over the objection of a family member or patient. Still, Fischkoff insisted, "We didn't really have a leg to stand on, because we had ventilators and we found beds for people."

Yet even if that was true, there was the question of how much time and attention was being taken away from patients who had a better chance of survival. That too was a fact, but there was no way to test it.

Eventually, the 5 South team gave up. "We made the decision that the ethicists were not a helpful group to us—and we stopped consulting them. We had to make these decisions ourselves. And live with it—and have to accept the legal consequences that come with it. I don't regret anything that I said—or did. It would have been nice having the hospital back us up in those decisions but they did not do that. That was very frustrating," Hayward said.

At Columbia during the height of the surge, there were twenty-four operating rooms converted into ICUs with two turbines, each at full velocity. Not only did they crowd the hallway, which affected everyone's ability to navigate the corridor, but the sound from the system was overwhelming; it was like sitting in the engine of a jumbo jet. "The idea was that if a patient could cough and somehow dislodge a tube—God forbid—the staff would be unprotected. You could re-filter the air in the small rooms in eight minutes and in the large, fifteen minutes. Everyone was roasting alive. The fans were blowing. It was like standing in an airplane hangar. The sound is deafening. And while you are taking care of the patients?" So he wouldn't pass out in the heat, anesthesiologist Steve Miller wore his only N95 on a lanyard around his neck. "The PPE was hot and sweaty . . . you didn't want the staff in the rooms for a long time. . . . We would keep ro-tating them in and out," he recalled. "We kept our masks on leashes around our neck. . . . Two people would remain in the room and then swap out . . . and then we would come out and put in all of the notes on the computer." Still, there was a coming together. "'Who can help the nurse? Who can empty this drain?'"

Miller had plunged into caring for the COVID patients, and, like so many of his colleagues, he was beleaguered professionally and emo-tionally. He and the residents and the other attendings found them-selves in ICU units where the patients weren't just sick, they were "stupid-sick." The residents had never seen an infectious-disease out-break like this—nor, for that matter, had any of the attendings. "It was, 'Holy crap. I will deal with my own psychology later,'" Miller said. "There was shit that needed to be cleaned. There were tubes that had to be drained. Forty patients a day with a rectal tube—and we had nine hundred tubes. At the height of it, there was a shortage of body bags."

Fischkoff had stopped doing operations in mid-March when the ORs were shut down. Those rooms were incredibly valuable real estate in a hospital starting to overflow with patients, and it was decided to convert them into ICUs.

For Fischkoff and nearly everyone else, wearing PPE was

cumbersome and oppressive. It was incredibly hot—"That was the worst part about it, was the layers and wearing mask on top of mask, and the face shield—walking up a flight of stairs, you thought you were going to pass out." The face coverings and noise made it hard to understand what anyone was saying. The masks were also uncomfortable. "We put on a barrier cream or there'd be a tape kind of thing you could put to keep your skin from chapping," she said. "It was annoying, because one day there was one type of mask, and then the next day those were gone and it was a different one. We had tons of donations of things. So you would just like grab what you got. But just when you got used to something and you figured out how to stay comfortable . . ."

Fischkoff's group oversaw the operating-room ICUs (ORICUs) and then some of the standard ICUs. She also spent time in one of the cardiac ICUs. Normally, the supervision would have lasted a week. "But in the ORICUs it was too much. You couldn't do seven days in a row. So we switched it to, you know, three days, four days, and then some nights, and that kind of thing. We bounced around a little bit. I think it was hard to do one thing for too long."

No matter where Fischkoff and her team bounced, two things were the same: the patients were suffering and dying from COVID, and it was becoming impossible to keep the rooms as clean as they needed to be. If you had limited PPE, were you going to give it to the cleaning staff or the doctors and nurses? Would the cleaning staff even want to come into the rooms, given the risk?

Then there was question of *how* to clean the rooms. "The ICU room usually gets cleaned once a day—the disposal and the garbage several times a day," Miller explained. "And that is with one patient. What happens when you have six?" Or, in the case of the less-endowed public hospitals, twelve or fourteen? "The problem was that COVID could cause a patient to have massive diarrhea. You have six patients who are incredibly ill, with massive amounts of stool, and then you have to have the patients cleaned and changed. You had to be nose-blind. And the entire team, our residents and medical students, would take turns. You would routinely have an attending physician, an anesthesiologist, a nurse, and a medical resident to help clean up a patient. It wasn't about whose job it was, it was about what did this patient need?"

Nothing seemed too much for Andrew Knapp, the anesthesiology resident who was called "the gentle giant" by Miller and who had taken on every possible job in the overwhelmed ICUs without a whisper of complaint. There he was, whenever Miller seemed to need him, cleaning waste, dumping sharps, changing sheets, cleaning bed after bed. No matter what needed to be done, Knapp was there. At six-foot-five, Knapp towered over Miller, but he seemed always to be in the ICU ready to help prone a patient on a vent by moving them oh so gently when they were attached to so many machines. "There Andrew would be, night after night, sometimes just doing everything. We were short of staff. Clean the patient, fine. Take the garbage, fine. I relied on him for everything. He was just there, by your side. The care he gave the patients. He could turn them in the bed and it would be so effortless."

Knapp did not even seem to notice when the dead were not picked up for hours at a time, so overwhelmed was Victor Holness, the morgue attendant at Columbia, who had started his career at the *Village Voice* as an illustrator but who had dreamed of being a funeral director since his father died when he was eight. Holness worked closely with Gabrielle Clarke, the head of the transporters, responsible for taking patients from their rooms to procedures, and also taking the dead to the morgue. Clarke, a native of Trinidad, had a degree in anthropology and had spent years working in catering at Marriott hotels in South Carolina. She was drawn to hospital work because of her desire to take care of the sick—and moved jobs at Columbia from food service to managing 120 transporters. As it became known there were COVID patients at Columbia, Clarke's team "was in panic mode. Everyone was hoarding PPE. . . . We had constant meetings. I had one employee who would turn down every job. He would say it in front of everybody.

'I have a sick mom . . . two kids at home.' And he couldn't take the chance to treat COVID patients. And I had another employee who said, 'The hospital doesn't care about us.' He said, 'We go to the emergency room and everyone has shields, and everyone has goggles. And we have nothing.' I walked into the ED and I saw that he was right—everyone in the ED had PPE and gloves and masks. And I had to take this up to my supervisor." And then suddenly, Clarke recalled, "There were hundreds of patients, and the transporters were running out of equipment. It was too much for them."

It was too much for Holness and the morgue as well. By the last week in March 2020, scores had died at Columbia and the Allen, and hundreds more would die that spring. "Normally we have room for ten. I would say no more than that. And I had no room. I had a call from someone at the Allen who said, 'I have another morgue for you, but it's not very nice.'" Holness found himself in the basement morgue at Columbia medical school, which had been used by generations of medical students. The acrid smell of embalming fluid exacerbated Holness's chronic bronchitis. "It was like a monster movie. They kept the donated bodies for the medical students to dissect on racks like at a dry cleaners. There was no ventilation. I said, 'I am not going to go in there.' And they said, 'You have to.'" The bodies were brought in and there was no ramp to help us. Then we ran out of space there as well." When word circulated in the hospital that the morgue was overwhelmed, a psychologist working in an upstairs lab came down to help. But every protocol Holness had been trained to use—systematically identifying patients in their body bags—created an even greater sense of fear inside the hospital. "You can't open that body bag," a nurse told Holness as he tried to confirm the identity of someone who had just died of COVID. "You absolutely cannot," she said. "I will give the identity." And that was that.

In the days leading up to Easter, Craig Smith had begun to hear about the appalling conditions in one of his hallowed shrines, operating room 22—not only things like overflowing garbage, but a shortage of nurses who were calling out before the holiday. Then came the news that an anesthesia resident had turned whistleblower and prepared a lengthy e-mail describing the Stalingrad-like conditions that had taken over the arena of Smith's decades of historic operations. The e-mail and the attached hastily snapped iPhone pictures buzzed through the department of surgery and were somehow forwarded to the *Wall Street Journal*. "This resident stewed about it and stewed about it," Smith said. "I saw the pictures—and they were shocking."

As the chief of surgery, Smith had been kept informed of the situation by the leaders in his department, among them Beth Hochman and Katherine Fischkoff, whom he particularly admired. The day after Easter, Smith went with Hochman to check out the situation for himself. "Well, I see OR twenty-two is getting a fair bit of use," he said to Hochman with his characteristic "man of few words" restraint. The flat tone was misleading. "I really lost it," Smith recalled. "I usually don't get angry, but in this case I took it all the way up to Laureen Hill."

Smith's operating room was understood to be a sacred space in the hospital. Everyone who knew him from his earliest days at Columbia knew exactly what he had pioneered and advanced in this theater. What drew him to Columbia as a resident was that the hospital was one of only three centers in the country that performed heart transplants. "My career was staked in those early days of transplant. There was so much we really did not understand. I had done only nine operations, but I was among those who had done the most in the world at that time. So my assignment was to start heart/lung transplant here, which was a suicide mission, partly because immunosuppression was not well understood and also because—as remains the case—obtaining an organ was never a walk in the park.

"You would go to get a donor organ," Smith remembered, "and

there would be an ambulance ride to the airport—Teterboro—for a private plane. You would land and the police would be waiting there on the tarmac and you would run to another ambulance and you would take off going a hundred miles an hour. They would take you to the George Washington Bridge—not far from the hospital—and there would be the kabuki theater at the bridge where the Port Authority guys would peel off racing through the open tollbooths hoping you didn't hit someone. The bridge would be cleared and then the New York police would take over. It was pretty exciting. The attendings were asked to do this—and there was a lot of taking chances and running off the ice on the runways."

As this was going on, Smith would be washing up and making sure all the necessary equipment was ready. "The call would come at three a.m. and we would show up and sew in the heart . . . we were figuring it all out. Now it is so much more figured out."

That meant the chaos he saw in his beloved operating theater hit him hard. His letter to the department of surgery was a masterpiece of clipped condescension: "We must create vacancies in our ICUs. Desperately ill patients with a poor chance of survival necessarily preoccupy us, but they represent where the puck is now, not where the puck will be.

"At the risk of mixing metaphors, and overwhelming poor Balto, I'll mention that only a spectacular lead dog can take his team through blizzard headwinds, in white-out so complete that the musher can't see his dogs. There are other relevant parallels—the 674-mile serum run was accomplished not by one team, but by 20 mushers and 150 sled dogs. A storm in Alaska early in the relay subjected teams to temperatures ranging from −50 to −70, killing some dogs, and freezing hands to sleds. While the dogsled teams mushed on to Nome, the same storm swept East to New York, delivered 27 inches of snow on Manhattan, and nearly froze the Hudson River. Don't all momentous stories drop their curtain in New York City?"

"We made a conscious decision very early on that we were going to take care of everybody," Katherine Fischkoff said. "We were just going to do what it took to take care of everybody. And we knew that meant sacrificing quality." It had been a utilitarian decision, and everyone understood there would be trade-offs. "We knew that meant more patients per nurse and more patients per resident. And we knew that meant that the trashes were going to fill." But, she acknowledged, "When you see it in action, it's obviously different . . . unless you'd been in an Ebola camp or something, how would you have ever seen or known anything like this?" It was, she said, "shocking and dehumanizing to see." But there was "a hierarchy of what needed to get done . . . we had to get them a bed, and that's all that mattered. Then, when we started to see that things were just building up—like the sharps containers were flowing over—that got addressed. We weren't going to leave them on the street like they did in Italy."

"We had twenty-four to twenty-six anesthesia residents . . . just over a hundred residents," said Miller. "Another twenty to thirty fellows, twenty from pediatrics. They were all helping take garbage out of the rooms. They were helping suction lungs, giving breathing treatments . . . we were so short of staff, our respiratory therapists were training our pediatric anesthesiologists! They were being trained to be junior respiratory therapists . . . suctioning and cleaning and using nebulizers. . . . A lot of times there was drool and vomit. They are in the room to clean the breathing tubes—and to suction out the air to brush their teeth."

"People were not laying in filth. Everything just was a little slower and a little more difficult," Fischkoff said. "It wasn't that nobody noticed and nobody cared. It was just that we were so busy getting ventilators into the room." And, she felt, it was about more than just the trash cans: "Understand that the residents were repurposed. They were doing things that they weren't comfortable with." That discomfort would soon go public.

And what was the greatest risk—a garbage can that needed emptying or the patient in front of you? "Was it even safe for a surgeon to do a tracheotomy procedure?" Miller wondered. "Was it safe for a surgeon to be face-forward during these procedures? We said, 'Let's be safe.' So we delayed some of them . . . tracheotomy helps you get better faster—delaying does not."

On top of it all, through the entire city and in every hospital, there was still no absolute data or certainty about how contagious the virus was. "When you go into medicine, you know that you are going to be taking care of people with infectious diseases, but in this case, we were learning new aspects of the disease every day," Miller explained. There were constant conversations and exchanges of anecdotes that might or might not have been significant, but hard data was scarce.

"One of the more extraordinary aspects about Columbia is that there are physicians from all over the world and many of them live in this community in Washington Heights or the Upper West Side. The larger staff were watching their friends and neighbors get sick and they got scared," Miller said. Laureen Hill would walk the halls speaking to everyone she could, explaining that the filter pressure made it almost impossible for anyone to get infected—but the cleaning staff and construction crews were equally concerned. Head of construction Edo Volaric told his team installing all the new walls and machinery, "The doctors will be in the room with you if you feel better. . . . You will be forty feet away [from] someone with the virus. You are not at risk." When Miller was in the room with the construction crew, he would take off his PPE and his mask. "I would do all of my work there to convince them they were safe—they could do it wearing masks and shields, if I could do it with nothing. . . . I didn't tell my wife about that! But we knew we were scientifically safe. . . .

Hill had bought the most expensive and highest grade of filter that you could get. If we had had more time, we would have figured out how to make them quieter."

Throughout NewYork-Presbyterian, the focus remained on getting ventilators. The hospital system was calling in every unit it could find, including the LTV ventilators that looked like military machinery and were meant for patient transport in medevac helicopters and ambulances and for home care. There were ventilators that had been borrowed from all over the city; engineering professors had been pulled in from Columbia University to consult on how to repurpose anesthesia machines to ventilate patients. Many of the Zoom calls focused on the physiology and supervision. Given the noise and the heat and crowding, they couldn't hear the vent alarms, so how could they monitor the patients? And what about that idea of patients sharing a ventilator—possible?

As it turned out, someone in Brooklyn had a very strong opinion about that one.

Hey, buddy, it's Felix.

Miller always looked at his phone when it lit up with a text from Felix Khusid, which it did about six times a day. One of Miller's jobs at Columbia was anesthesia director for the respiratory therapy group, and he and Khusid had known of each other through the chain e-mail correspondence about ventilators and anything to do with respiratory therapists. They would later laugh and say, "When this pandemic is over, we will finally meet—you owe me a dinner," but now, as crowds of patients surged into the EDs, when Miller and Khusid spoke, it was all business, often Miller tapping into Khusid's encyclopedic knowledge of ventilators. (Khusid was so obsessive that he knew the serial numbers of some individual units by heart.) Miller had heard of Khusid's basement Wunderkammer, the collection of ancient machinery that crowded his subterranean office, and he had promised to visit, but he knew he would have to endure yet another Khusid barrage about how "the enterprise" had to immediately train a Magnum Force to use Forrest Bird's VDR—a high-frequency, percussive ventilator that is tricky to master. He kept two in his equipment room in Brooklyn, ready to go. They were already using them at Long Island Jewish and in London, so why not at NewYork-Presbyterian?

On March 6, Khusid had received a text from Robert Guimento, the president of NewYork-Presbyterian Brooklyn: *Could you come to see me?*

When Guimento's message arrived, Khusid had worked a hundred hours without stopping for more than a nap on his office chair. His wife was recovering from COVID, and he had a list of food he had to pick up for her before he went home to Coney Island: borscht and chicken and Gatorade. All around him, he saw one desperate patient after another on stretchers in the halls waiting for a bed. But, knowing his wife could make it a bit longer without dinner, this meeting took priority.

In his thirty-one years in the hospital, Khusid had met Guimento on only two other occasions. ("We are RTs—not the fancy people in the upstairs offices," he explained.) Khusid was vaguely anxious as he headed upstairs. Had he broken a protocol that he was unaware of? When he walked into Guimento's office, he tried to make a joke. "Should I clean out my museum?"

Guimento smiled. "No, Felix, just—we are very aware what is going on with your group. What can we do to help you?"

Khusid tried to contain his excitement. "I need nothing," he said. "But for my patients, we are desperate for help. We do not have enough RTs [respiratory therapists]—we are overwhelmed."

"Done," Guimento said.

Khusid did not believe him—what did that even mean, *done?*

Queens was overrun and Lower Manhattan resembled Elmhurst. Still, he thanked Guimento and left.

Once home, Khusid told his wife, "I will believe it when I see it."

Forty-eight hours later, ten travelers (as floating hospital staff were referred to) appeared in the RT offices. "I will remember this day my entire life. They were all greeting me by name: 'Hello, Mr. Khusid.' 'Hi, Felix,'" Khusid recalled. "I turned to my supervisor and said, 'Emma, are they all ours?'" Guimento had assigned ten new respiratory therapists to his team, and they were a godsend, completely changing the equation. Now he wanted to return the favor.

When Miller saw the text from Khusid, he was not expecting to hear about the Felix-1, as it would later become known, a concoction of plastic and tubes and wiring Khusid had put together.

I have something new here, his text to Miller continued. *I have a face vacuum. It is literally vacuuming faces.*

Working past midnight in late March, Khusid had taken parts from his storeroom—a tube here, a motor there, and a bucket-shaped piece of plastic—and built a device that delivered high-flow oxygen via nasal cannula to a patient while also creating an area of negative pressure (essentially a vacuum) around the patient's face, preventing the spread of droplets. "It looks like a face TV!" he told Miller. It was inexpensive to put together, and if it worked well, it would allow hospitals around the world to treat COVID patients with high-flow therapy even if a negative-pressure room was not available—and avoid intubating them immediately and putting them on ventilators.

Khusid sent Miller a video of the device. "I said, 'That's hilarious—and genius.' We started putting them together . . . they were cheap and easy to do." They looked weird, Miller said. "But if it conferred extra protection to our staff and it didn't hurt the patient, they were worth it."

The very fact that a respiratory therapist in Brooklyn was working through the night to come up with a device to keep the medical team safe was a miracle.

Andrew Cuomo's daily briefings were both reassuring and frightening. It was heartening to see a leader who was actively and directly engaged, a commanding and authoritative force who listened to doctors instead of dismissing them. But it was chilling to hear him talk about the projected numbers—the forty thousand ventilators that would be needed, the colossal body count to come, and so forth. These figures had been calculated by a group from McKinsey as well as from other modelers, briefly, and they appeared to influence one of Cuomo's most destructive decisions: to send hospitalized COVID patients who'd come from nursing homes back to their facilities, despite inadequate protection, given the predicted deficit of hospital beds and ventilators. Later, Cuomo and his aides attempted to cover up the damage by keeping around four thousand deaths off New York's total count. Ultimately, Cuomo paid a price for his missteps—though certainly not as heavy a price as those infected in nursing homes due to his fatally flawed decision.

All that was to come. Back in Princeton, researcher Nathaniel Hupert, with no political skill set and no levers in the state, was desperately trying to get New York State's COVID-19 task force and the city's department of health to at least *discuss* what he was seeing: that by his calculations, New York's numbers were not skyrocketing, they were peaking. Where McKinsey saw *Apocalypse Now,* his group at Cornell saw hope—a flattening of the curve long before anyone else called it.

In desperation, Hupert sent an e-mail (identical to what he'd sent the state and the city) to a series of his medical school deans and department chairs, including Augustine Choi, Fernando Martinez, Roy Gulick, and his boss, Rainu Kaushal, as well as to the head of Weill Cornell's Center for Global Health, Monika Safford, who had welcomed him to her team way back when. Although written with scientific restraint, his message nonetheless was worrisome.

Dear leaders:

Please see attached figures.

There's a possibility that by taking the NYC-wide figures, which are being driven by the Bronx, Queens and Brooklyn, that the models may be over-estimating. We have no data on actual PUI cases for COVID, but the attached shows influenza-like illness reporting, which has been in place a long time in NYC. It shows the January peak of flu, then the second peak in March, which is in all likelihood COVID. It shows a 4 day pattern of decline in the last few days. We need to watch over the next several days, but if it continues the interpretation could be:

1. We are seeing micro hot spots currently not incorporated into models being used to project apex of surge for the whole city, which could lead to citywide over estimates; these hot spots were apparently also seen in China after initial "stay home" policy, which WHO says also led to a temporary increase in transmission within households (was on the phone with them this morning). When they changed to isolating mild cases and quarantining contacts, they contained effectively.

2. We may have "bent the curve" in some (UES?) but not other (Queens?) neighborhoods

3. The micro hot spots may be burning out rapidly

4. Very hard to know where the apex is under these circumstances, but may actually be right now in some areas of the city

Hupert desperately hoped his numbers would be made public. He had already reported his findings to the city's department of health, warning discreetly that "if you feel the need to go public with modeled numbers, our only hope is for scientific rigor to make much more contextual models that make smaller-area projections. . . . This requires looking at e.g. individual hospitals and neighborhoods, and ideally with demographic factors such as household composition, etc. that might control infection rates. That requires much more complicated models than anyone has now." And what had that gotten him? A request to shut up, that's what—a DOH official asking him to "consider the impact your words are having on our response" and saying that the "communication that you have been expressing does not align with information we have of real-time response efforts that we are working to support." In other words, the state was committed to McKinsey's ten-million-dollar projections.

Besides contributing to Cuomo's nursing-home crisis, the inflated estimates generated by McKinsey and other modeling groups had, several public health experts later suggested, pushed the city to build a fifty-two-million-dollar hospital at the Billie Jean King National Tennis Center in Queens. There was a true division of opinion over whether the field hospitals would be a help. In the third week of March, Cuomo called Nathaniel Hupert to ask whether he thought they were a good idea. "I told him yes," Hupert recalled. The city was overwhelmed with cases and the hospitals were close to the breaking point. Who knew how long it would last? Even if the field hospitals took auxiliary (non-COVID) patients, wouldn't any extra bed be a help? That is how it looked in the last days of March amidst a barrage of dying patients. The facility had hundreds of beds and was staffed with doctors from all over the country who were being paid as much as $732 an hour. However, the city's bureaucrats, the *Times* would later report, decided to prevent anyone who had a fever—a hallmark of COVID—from being treated there. Although meant to relieve the horrendous overcrowding of Jamaica and Elmhurst hospitals, the city allowed it only two ventilators. "I basically got paid $2,000 a day to sit on my phone and look at Facebook," nurse practitioner Katie Capano told the *Times*. The center remained open for a month, and in all that time, it took just seventy-nine patients.

This farce was repeated all over the city, perhaps most ridiculously in the saga of the U.S. Navy hospital ship *Comfort*. The ship carried a thousand beds and was presented by officials as a godsend for a city running out of space for its infected. The hype for the rescue mission was so great that the ship had been personally seen off from its port in Norfolk, Virginia, by Trump himself. Ivanka Trump touted its arrival with a tweet: "This great ship is a 70,000-ton message of hope and solidarity to the incredible people of New York." From there, it immediately went downhill. The federal government and the state had paid thirty million dollars for the hospital ship, but because it specifically banned patients with COVID, as well as forty-nine other conditions, and had a thicket of bureaucratic procedures and regulations that made it difficult for non-COVID patients to be allowed on board, the entire exercise was a humiliating failure.

Hupert was operating on a narrow ledge. The warnings of his early mentors that modelers were always at the bottom of the funding food chain had proven true, but recently the bottom had fallen out—his funding had been cut, and the medical school in January had told him he needed to clear out his office until he could pull in another research grant. But Fernando Martinez and the chair of medicine Tony Hollenberg optimistically took Hupert at his word. "If this holds out, it would certainly be good news. Hollenberg and I were just walking through the units and any good news would be appreciated on the front lines." The dean of Cornell's medical school, Augustine Choi, had not had time to focus on Hupert's predictions in the first days of March, but he now wrote to him and Monika Safford: "Great work Monika and your team." Martinez began to call Hupert "the ICU whisperer."

On April 19, Andrew Cuomo belatedly discarded McKinsey's figures and announced, "We have flattened the curve." An aide to the mayor who had helped ram the fifty-two-million-dollar tennis-center hospital into being now pivoted nicely. "The alternative space has been less needed than we expected it to be because we broke the curve, thank goodness."

17

At Columbia, for weeks in late March, emergency department head Angela Mills had been so ill that those close to her urged her to go to the hospital. The hacking cough and shortness of breath had been compounded by a bacterial infection, but she stayed on Zoom calls from her Midtown apartment sometimes fifteen hours a day. Finally, she went to the Columbia ED; she was admitted and put on oxygen. Her vice chairman called her. "Angela, if you don't get off that phone, I am coming to your room and taking it away."

She stayed for just two days and forced herself back to work soon after. Columbia was so overwhelmed that Mills was working in the ED. One day, she got a call from a number she didn't recognize. "He introduced himself as Lorna [Breen's] brother-in-law and said that she had given him my number. He said that she wasn't acting like herself . . . that she couldn't get up out of her chair or get dressed and do anything. At some point, she stopped answering their calls. And so they were worried about her. . . . They thought they might call 911 and have the police go check on her—and they asked what I thought. I said, 'Listen, I'm very happy to go check on her.'"

Mills went to Breen's apartment. Another friend of Breen's, a psychiatrist, also arrived to drive her to Virginia. Breen was on the phone with her mother, a psychiatric nurse, who was, according to someone close to the participants, doing everything that she could to keep her on the phone. Mills would tell the *New York Times* that Lorna always had a glimmer in her eye, but now there was no glimmer. People who knew her well remarked on her exquisite taste in clothes, how perfectly turned out she always was. What had happened to this tall and commanding doctor?

Breen's family and friends were deeply concerned. They had good reason to fear that she might want to hurt herself.

On the day Breen's sister and brother-in-law reached out to Mills, Feist was trying to understand what he had been seeing as a health-care executive—the stress that caused doctors and nurses to have a suicide rate that is twice the national average. The CEO of the physicians' group at the University of Virginia, he would learn of the long hours and the strain from the donning and doffing of PPE (a term he had never heard before the pandemic) and the low staffing and the exhausting billing procedures that led doctors and nurses "to just stop caring. . . . You are exhausted and you can't sleep. All of these things . . . Add COVID, and what you get in a certain subset of the health-care population is repetitive trauma."

He would come to believe, as would his wife, that Breen's harrowing time and exposure to the chaos and overwhelming, uncontrollable horror of COVID not only gave her the disease but also triggered her to break. The word Breen used to describe what was happening at the Allen was *Armageddon*. She would call during the day and tell her sister and brother-in-law "that people were dying in those chairs in their very small emergency department. That there was not enough in-wall oxygen, which has a longer life than the handheld tanks. And so there were patients that were on handheld oxygen, sitting in those waiting-room chairs that you saw, but they didn't realize that these oxygen tanks were expiring—and so too were the patients when the oxygen ran out." Breen told her sister and brother-in-law that they could "not get the patients out of the chairs fast enough," because they were completely flooded with patients. "They were waiting in ambulances outside, and it was just a big operational Armageddon."

Angela Mills was worried, and the situation was almost as acute at Columbia. "It was clear from an infection point of view there were no barriers, there were no rooms. People just were strewn everywhere, in hallways, on stretchers, gurneys, anywhere . . . chairs and anywhere there was space to put patients, we were putting them and there was just no . . . it just seemed like there was no end in sight. Patients would keep coming and they were very sick. The hospital was full. They weren't leaving the emergency department and there were no backups," Mills said.

As long as Breen had been at the Allen, Jennifer and Corey Feist had never visited the midsized hospital, nor did they know that the Columbia soccer field that would become a field hospital was adjacent to it. Breen had returned to the ED on April 1, before the plans for the field hospital were announced, before the PJs, the retired Air Force military medics, appeared to construct it in only five days. They had tried to reassure Breen: "'We know help is coming.' And she said, 'I don't see any of that help.'" On the same day Lorna returned to the hospital, the Samaritan's Purse tents appeared in Central Park. In bed with COVID, Breen would sleep for hours. Corey and Jennifer sent her a pulse oximeter through Amazon so she could monitor her oxygen levels.

Feist had long understood that being a doctor was Breen's calling. "She would call us and say, 'Hey, I am going to India in forty-eight hours because they need to train people on CPR over there,' and she would just get on a plane and fly off. . . . Once, in the Denver airport, she saw someone turn blue and she jumped the walkway, did a face-plant, and then revived the individual. . . . On another occasion, a bicyclist who had been cut off by her cabdriver came around and punched him. Lorna went right into this mode of taking care of him and did an assessment on the driver in the middle of traffic."

On the ski trip, Breen had been in direct touch with the Allen hospital, trying to help them manage patients remotely. Breen told her sister she was convinced she'd get COVID on her return. Before she left, she told her team, "'It is not the person who has all the COVID symptoms that is going to get you sick, it is someone who seems asymptomatic.'... She was trying to get a system in place that would protect them." Breen was braced for how bad the pandemic could be. She was close to Craig Spencer, who had fought Ebola, and she had watched her six-year-old nephew fight for his life at the ICU in Virginia during the H1N1 pandemic.

Angela Mills has been reluctant to speak about what happened inside Breen's apartment when she went to check on her. When Breen's friend, the psychiatrist, arrived to drive her to Virginia, there was a palpable sense of relief. Breen's friend distracted her with talk about her cat and who would take care of it. Mills offered to help Breen in any way she could and mentioned treatment options at other New York hospitals where she had friends on the medical team. "I can call and get her in anywhere," she said, according to someone close to the participants. "You tell me, and I will make it happen." It would be the last time Angela Mills would ever see Lorna Breen. Mills reassured her that she'd be able to return to the hospital and resume her MBA studies, but Breen, according to Feist, had become convinced that her career in medicine was over. There was little Mills or Feist or Breen's sister could do or say to convince her that the exhaustion and trauma she was experiencing had altered her thinking—and that she would be able to return to the profession she loved. The plan had been for Breen's friend to drive her to Baltimore, where her sister could pick her up. Feist later recalled that in the car Breen seemed so altered, she could not speak. "Where do you want to stop for something to eat?" her sister asked her. "Wendy's? Burger King?" Breen could not answer. It is almost impossible to imagine the fear and powerlessness her sister experienced seeing her adored older sister in such a trau-

matized state. There was no question for her about the right thing to
do. The Feists immediately took Breen to UVA University Hospital's
emergency department to be evaluated for PTSD.

There was no doubt in Jennifer Feist's mind of the inordinate
stress her sister was under. When Breen returned to work on April
1, she called her sister to talk about the chaos, according to the *New
York Times*. "Just baffled and overwhelmed," she wrote a friend the
following day. The new protocols seemed unwieldy to her—the desperately ill who were taken to an ICU unit were still under the ED's
authority. Breen felt compelled to oversee all of the cases. "I'm totally
lost," Breen wrote a colleague. "Trying to get up to speed." The ED
was admitting three times the number of patients it could accommodate. One man, the *Times* would report, had seemed stable enough
to transfer to a different unit but was found dead in a chair, his skin
already discolored. Breen became overwhelmed by the statistics. On
the day she returned to work, eight hundred died in the city. In her
emergency department, almost one quarter of the COVID patients
would die. One week after her return, her colleagues began to notice that Breen seemed in a state of mental chaos. She was trying to
re-order many wrongly recorded Epic notes that her staff, trying to
master the hospital's new electronic system, had entered incorrectly.
"I'm drowning right now—may be AWOL for a while," she said in a
message sent to her Bible study group.

As the pandemic began, Columbia had set up a psychiatric
service—CopeColumbia—for the frontline staff, but Breen had been
too busy to register. Feist believed she felt a lot of pressure from the
"shadow curriculum," the need to be the toughest of the tough out of
medical school. Lorna's particular fear was showing any weakness at
all. She was terrified, she told her sister, of the repercussions of taking a psychiatric leave; when she was admitted to the hospital—her
first known mental health treatment—she worried it would affect
her medical license. Mills and the Feists assured her she was wrong,

but Breen believed that unless she strictly followed the code—"This is what you signed up for"—she would lose her career.

The next day, Mills arranged to have Breen put on medical leave. "I was relieved that she had gotten to Virginia without harming herself. And I felt good that she was getting help. I felt really hopeful. I said to Jennifer, 'Should I reach out to Lorna?' And she said, 'No, no, no, she's getting treatment.' I feel terrible guilt that I never reached out to Lorna directly. I kept texting Jennifer to say, 'How is she doing?' At some point, Lorna went home, and I said, 'When she's ready, let us know. Or if she needs anything, just let me know.' Then, the next thing I know, Corey's calling to tell me the tragic news."

Lorna's ten days at the hospital seemed to help her. She went running and was planning to resume her MBA studies. She was staying with Corey and Jennifer, subdued but seeming to improve. One day, Jennifer was in the bathroom, unaware that Lorna was in the kitchen. When she came out, she saw Lorna on the floor. They rushed her to the emergency department, but they could not save her. Feist, fiercely protective of his family's privacy, refused to disclose any details about what actually happened in the last hours of Breen's life.

When Feist called Mills to tell her, he was abrupt, clearly in shock. He did not want anyone to know she had committed suicide, Mills said. He said, "Please protect her." Mills crafted a careful statement stating that Breen had "died unexpectedly." She did inform Laureen Hill and her bosses of what had actually happened, then she called an emergency Zoom meeting to let people know Breen had died. "The assumption was that she had died of COVID. . . . Everyone was in tears. It was the hardest thing I have had to endure in my professional life. Some of the group were so angry—they felt COVID had killed her, and that she was working so hard and that's what killed her. Others were just so sad and crying. People kept asking, 'How did she die?' And I had to say, 'I am so sorry. I can only share what the family asked me to share.' No one knew it was a suicide. The next day one of my faculty called me—she does a lot of media . . . and she said, 'You know the *New York Times* is getting ready to break a story that Lorna's death was a suicide.' I called Corey. He said, 'I am on the other line with them trying to tell them not to run it. Lorna's father told them.' At that point, I called another emergency meeting. I didn't want for people to read this in the *Times*. I thought that would be terrible. Five minutes before the meeting, the *Times* broke it. A few on my faculty had actually already seen it." The news of Breen's suicide made front pages around the country and the world, exposing the reality of the medical front lines, the desperate psychological pressure doctors and nurses endured to save lives, and the fragility of the system they believed would protect them. Later, Corey Feist would come to understand that the level of trauma that Breen experienced—even in the nine-day period she was at the Allen—could resemble that of war reporters and combat troops who had endured months on the front line. The unraveling psychological state of doctors became, for the Feists, a crusade that would result in their establishing the Dr. Lorna Breen Heroes' Foundation and, almost two years later, the passage of the Lorna Breen Act to protect doctors and frontline workers in similar circumstances.

The suicide of Lorna Breen became a tipping point, the moment the hospital began to understand the level of PTSD the medical staff was suffering.

They needed some good news—and soon they would get it.

18

Why could no one hear Dr. Tomoaki Kato?

You need to go now, right this minute. You have to get the plane. I have to warn Steve Corwin about the hospital. Where is my phone?

On the road to Waterloo, close to Brussels, Napoleon commands 125,000 troops along a 175-mile front trying to capture the British army in Belgium. All the British treaties with France are under siege as Wellington moves toward Alsace-Lorraine. Napoleon is determined to fight to the last and is swept out of Paris with a hundred-gun salute. A coterie of observers are with him, including a small boat with the women of the court . . .

He sees the women on the lake and finds himself in a field near a castle as the boat goes by. He notices how tired and weary they look, all different ages. The youngest has the highest rank and the most splendid clothes. But he is seen, arrested as a spy, and taken to China, where he sits in a hospital watching an anthrax pathogen be created. The Chinese are modifying anthrax and getting people infected. He is allowed to go to dinner with a friend and has so much to drink, he loses his memory. The next morning he is on a flight to New York.

On the flight he starts to feel very sick and have real shortness of breath, gasping. He wonders if there is anyone on the plane who can assist him. There is one young woman who offers to help, but she is the one who poisoned him. When he lands in New York, the airline offers her a lot of

mileage. She says, "No, I don't want it." They say, "You can be a flight at-
tendant!" And she still says no. He knows he's met her before. She says she
was a doctor—maybe she wants to be like him? That is what he says to her.

And then he goes to the hospital, Weill Cornell, but it's in a tent.
He is in the tent, and there is another man breathing without any
machine. He is awake and speaking with people. There is a man from
the Middle East. He is bringing a cow and a goat to the hospital. He is
sick and so is his child. And then the infectious-disease doctor comes in
and takes them all to the hospital. He is still very sick from the poison,
and though he is discharged, he knows he has to get to another hospital.
Someone put this on social media—the plot of poisoning so many of
people with anthrax. He knows that some people at this hospital are
going to try to kill him.

The new hospital is even worse. It is in the middle of somewhere near
the water. It is in the Middle East, and the nurses require tips. They are
told, "You see this guy, you will get a tip." And that's how you got help.
He has to call Steve Corwin to tell him not to have this hospital in their
system. He has to get to him right away.

He calls for his phone. He shouts for someone to bring it to him, but no
one hears him. He has to tell Steve: This place is a danger, do not have any-
thing to do with it. He has not had anything to drink and he is desperate.
He says again and again, "OJ, OJ, OJ . . ."

Next to his bed in the ICU at Columbia Medical Center, Peter Liou
could barely make out what Tom Kato was saying: "OJ . . . O . . . J . . ."
And what in the world was all of this about Napoleon and the Battle
of Waterloo and needing to get to Antwerp, the foremost hospital
for poisonings in the world?

———

Why is Peter not leaving this very moment, as fast as he had gone to get a liver or a kidney from a child who had died in a diabetic coma? Go now, Peter. Go.

Tom Kato was waking up.

For days, Liou had been in the MICU trying to make out Kato's words.

Mercedes Martinez, the director of the pediatric liver and intestinal transplantation program, was with Liou when Kato was extubated and asked for OJ—orange juice.

Juice was out of the question—but maybe he wasn't asking for orange juice? His words tangled on top of each other, impossible to decipher.

Kato thrashed, still believing himself to be in Brussels on the fields near Waterloo. Later, he would be confounded by this hallucination; he had never studied French history and knew nothing of Napoleon or one of his greatest defeats, the Battle of Waterloo. Yet there he had been, in the nineteenth century, amid the pageantry of Napoleon and his men. There were other vivid hallucinations too. He had become convinced that the only man who could save him was a thoracic surgeon in Antwerp who was considered the greatest transplant surgeon in the world because of his delicate touch. But it was Napoleon that flummoxed him. Later, when he discussed those hallucinations with people who knew the relevant history, they were all stunned at how much Kato knew.

All of April, Liou ran from room to room at Columbia as one of Beth Hochman's copilots on the surgical SWAT team. During that stretch, he had been part of two hundred procedures. It was, for Liou, a time of wonder, amid the horror, at the way the entire hospital pulled together. "Normally everyone is so busy and competitive; we do not have time to help each other," he said. But now they did; the employees were from different departments with different specialties, but they were also the embodiment of an institution that by saving patients was, in a sense, saving itself. Kato's doctor Marcus Pereira said that his survival became the hospital's as well. The wonder of his progress stunned them, despite the setbacks, such as a brain bleed that made him incoherent and hallucinations that altered his reality for months. ICU delirium, what Kato experienced, was a phenomenon that would come to be associated with COVID-19, brought on by hypoxia and sedating medication. That the altered reality persisted was also a part of COVID—it would take months for Kato to understand that he had not tried to call Steve Corwin. And he had not been an observer at the Battle of Waterloo.

Kato's wife texted Liou and Mercedes Martinez to ask why she couldn't be allowed to speak with him. One of the physician assistants was half Japanese and spoke with her several times a day, but they waited to have her FaceTime with her husband because of Kato's jumbled state of mind. When she and Kato finally saw each other, both wept, as Kato did when he spoke with Corwin.

Slowly Kato began to emerge, at first with so much agony it took him an hour and a half to reach his call button by the bed. "The very act of moving my hand was impossible," he said. "It weighed so much I could not move it." From his bed, he began to hear about the horror in the hospital; he watched several of Andrew Cuomo's prior briefings to understand what he had missed in the weeks he was on a ventilator. At night, he watched movie after movie. He resolved to spend the remainder of his life imparting his surgical secrets to his residents and vowed to stop forcing his transplant patients to eat the gruel of paste that was often given to them. "It was so horrible I rejected it and would never give it to another patient," he later said.

In April, Liou had started playing concerts for COVID patients on a baby grand piano in the hospital lobby. In the first days of May, he and the surgical SWAT team dedicated a concert to Tom Kato,

who attended in a wheelchair. Kato introduced himself to the assembled audience and told of being so thirsty he kept asking his nurses
for ice chips. He often said, "This is a whole new world." Tom Kato
had yet to walk—that would come a few weeks later—but with lyrics in his hand, he began to sing a song from, of all things, Disney's
Aladdin. With Peter Liou in his raspberry scrubs accompanying
him on the piano and a chorus of surgeons and anesthesiologists in
matching scrubs and surgical caps and N95s singing backup, he sang
the Tim Rice/Alan Menken standard:

A whole new world
A new fantastic point of view

19

At Weill Cornell, all that spring, Fernando Martinez had started rounding at least three times a day, spending as much time in 5 South as he could. One afternoon, he saw Lindsay Lief standing with Hasina Outtz Reed, an MD/PhD who had just returned from maternity leave. Reed, Martinez said, "was the smartest person I have ever met." Always unflappable, with three children under the age of six, Reed had spent years training and had career development grants from the NIH to fund her work on the link between lymphatic dysfunction and lung injury. "It is a niche area, but she is considered one of the world experts—she is a rising young star," he said. With her were two other MD/PhDs, Alexandra Racanelli and Jamuna Krishnan, both investigative scientists. Martinez was worried about their research careers—the Weill Cornell labs had shut down, so Racanelli's mice strains were gone, as were Reed's. Over a decade of Racanelli's work on how endothelium, which lines certain organs, becomes dysfunctional had been put on hold, as had Krishnan's research on the health disparity affecting African Americans with COPD (chronic obstructive pulmonary disease). Each had young children at home, and with their research on pause for months (it would turn out to be a year and a half), Martinez worried about their states of mind, especially since 5 South was now full, with more COVID patients arriving every hour.

"Hasina, how are things?" he asked.

"Fernando, don't worry," Reed replied. "You have four mothers here—we have it under control."

Or so they imagined, until the arrival of a young man.

At twenty-eight years old, Chris Kampel was not far in age from the mothers taking care of him. He'd had a thing for computers from nursery-school days. At the age of four, he was in the den in the family's shingled house in Islip, in the middle of Long Island, when a neighbor came to help Robert Kampel, Chris's father, deal with some new software that was crashing repeatedly. Chris watched his father—who was no beginner when it came to computers and software—fighting with his machine and then said, "I can fix it." Kampel asked, "How can you fix it?" Chris said he could. Kampel thought to himself, *Well, he can't mess it up any more than it is now.*

Fifteen minutes later, everything was working just fine. From that day forward, Kampel had Chris by his side as he started to build his own computers. After that, they moved on to chess. The family was comfortable—Robert worked at the Long Island daily *Newsday* in the collating department, maintaining the machine that put inserts into the newspaper. When Chris was ten, his parents divorced—and there was a lot of anger on both sides. He began to struggle with his weight—he was small, only five three, but soon gained thirty pounds. Chris and his sister lived with their mother, then Chris asked to move back with his dad. They became a club of two. Robert encouraged him to try for the best college possible when his SAT scores were off the chart. He was accepted to Rochester Institute of Technology in upstate New York, but ultimately decided to attend Adelphi University, where he met and fell in love with his fiancée, Sam Sportiello. All of which Robert Kampel told Lindsay Lief and Brad Hayward sometime during the weeks while his son languished in 5 South.

As COVID rolled into New York, Chris Kampel, by then an IT tech for Advantage, a private health-care provider with offices all over Long Island, was assigned the job of making sure the system could be managed virtually. In the first weeks of March, he commuted to Manhattan by train, without a mask. Sportiello had been worried that he was risking his life for his job. "This thing is really dangerous," Sportiello's mother had told her. "You and Chris need to stay home."

"You should not be doing this," Sportiello told him. "Everyone is staying home."

Then he did stay home.

"I am not feeling up to coming," Chris told his mother as her birthday, March 20, approached. They had remained close, and he worried about her health—Mary had stage 4 breast cancer and was getting chemo. Kampel decided that if he wore a mask and stayed in bed, she could safely visit him, and they could have some semblance of a celebration. But she first had to get there, and given her age, fifty-eight, and frailty, he didn't trust a car service. Rallying, he drove to her place and picked her up. He did all of this with his mask on.

Kampel and Sportiello were planning their wedding for September 2020. When he started to complain of a scratchy throat, she began to sleep in another room. "Put distilled white vinegar in boiling water, then put a towel over your head and breathe deeply," his father told him. Robert instructed Sportiello to make sure Chris did the steam treatment four times a day, but he didn't stick to the regimen and mostly just slept.

The day after his mother's birthday, Kampel had chills and a fever. He went to an urgent-care clinic, took a test, and was told to stay home and drink a lot of fluids until the results came back. The processing of tests in the city was chaos—getting a test and having it returned was about as certain as throwing a key across the lake. On the telephone, Chris told his father that the batteries in his thermometer were no longer working, but the last temperature he had recorded was 103. Then he lost his sense of taste and smell.

On the morning of March 27, he had a hard time breathing. "That is when he decided he needed a hospital," Sportiello said. Kampel recorded his wheezing breath and sent the sound file to a college friend who was now a nurse at New York-Presbyterian. "I can get you into Weill Cornell, where I work," she said. "That way I can keep an eye on you."

He thanked her and headed to his car. Sportiello said, "I said to him, 'Oh my God, you are driving into the city? Oh my God.'"

"Don't worry. I got this," he said.

"We FaceTimed in the hospital, but that was the last time I saw him in person, awake and alert."

Kampel parked his car in the Weill Cornell garage and texted Sportiello about the nurses coming and going from the ED. *I am scared,* he admitted.

To keep herself from being overwhelmed with worry, Sportiello spent the next few days scouring every inch of their apartment and waiting for his texts. At 7:00 a.m. on April 1, Kampel texted her, *I'm getting intubated. I love you so much.*

"I didn't know what that meant at first," Sportiello recalled. "So I was like, 'What? What does that mean? I love you too.' And then that's when I knew. 'Oh, shit, it's the ventilator.'"

In Brooklyn, respiratory therapist Felix Khusid had every right to worry. Ventilator-splitting had been done only twice before in crisis situations, most famously in Las Vegas in 2017, when a crazed assassin on the thirty-second floor of the Mandalay Bay hotel fired more than a thousand bullets into the crowd below. He killed sixty people and wounded more than four hundred, but in the panic that ensued, more than four hundred others were injured. Nearby Sunrise Hospital was inundated and quickly ran out of ventilators. Kevin Menes, the attending in the ED that night, remembered a study that a resident a year ahead of him had done on ventilator use in mass-casualty situations. That study said that if you had two patients who were close to the same size tidal volume (or lung capacity), you could connect both to a single machine and simply double the tidal-volume-output setting. It worked, but the patients in Las Vegas obviously did not have the ravaged lungs of patients suffering with COVID. The second ventilator-splitting trial had been done by Marcus Garrone, an ED doctor in Italy, but not enough time had passed to see if his approach truly worked.

Columbia's trial required the consent of two patients who had similar oxygen needs. Laureen Hill tasked pulmonary disease specialist Jeremy Beitler, a ventilator expert, to mastermind the experiment, but limited the trial to forty-eight hours—the maximum recommended by the FDA. "We're doing something that hasn't ever really been done before," Beitler told the *New York Times*. Although the hospital had yet to run out of ventilators, Beitler added, it was better to try the technique now instead of "when you have absolutely no choice."

There were those, like Felix Khusid, who strongly disagreed with the experiment and the concept behind it. Another dissenting voice was the editor in chief of the journal *Respiratory Care*, University of Cincinnati respiratory therapist Richard Branson, who had authored a study on shared ventilators in 2012. Concerned about the possibility of infections and the oxygen requirements if patients deteriorated rapidly, Branson declared to the *New York Times* that "the time to try an untested treatment not previously used in humans is not in the midst of a pandemic."

Yet there seemed no alternative to attempting something that until recently had not been considered. Still operating from McKinsey and other extremely high projections, Cuomo tweeted that the shortage of ventilators was dire; even after a shipment of four thousand came from FEMA, the governor warned, "Our single greatest challenge is ventilators." They needed thirty thousand, he said; they had eleven thousand. In the first days of April, headlines announced that New York would run out of ventilators by Easter weekend.

As it was, Khusid had other things to worry about. After the forty-eight-hour trial, Columbia published the results of Beitler's experiment but did not continue their use. The patients on the ventilators survived but were taken off the machine two days later. It was thought that the need for highly trained intensivists or respiratory therapists to monitor the shifting conditions of two patients on one machine made the shared ventilator impractical when thousands of patients were waiting.

20

However tasteless and, ultimately, harmless the Forese/*V for Vendetta* parody might have been, within days it had reached CBS News reporter David Begnaud, who tweeted out the inter-hospital briefing clip and then asked to interview NewYork-Presbyterian's executive vice president, Laura Forese. Surprisingly, she agreed to an interview, which took place on the morning of April 10. Wearing an elegant white suit, Forese seemed almost baffled by the response to her remarks. Begnaud might have been expecting a clean-up-the-crisis, fall-on-her-sword mea culpa, but Forese was having none of it.

In his lead-in, Begnaud added to what the *Wall Street Journal* and the *Washington Post* had already reported about the chaos in New York's hospitals and the reactions to the health-care workers "who have voiced concerns about coming to work during a pandemic." He cited Forese (identified as the CFO of "one of the nation's largest health-care systems") for "some comments to the staff that shocked some of them," then ran the clip of Forese, her lips pulled into a line: "Please, for you and your families, stop sending e-mails, cards, and letters saying that we are disrespecting you. If you feel that way, we can understand that. You're entitled to your opinion. It raises for us whether you in fact want to keep working for NewYork-Presbyterian."

"Do you regret the way you said it?" Begnaud asked in a follow-up.

Forese then made it worse. "What I would say is we're committed to all of our team members, and I feel great respect for all of our team members, but I was trying to deliver a very specific message to a team that I was clearly trying to rally."

"But for some people," Begnaud said, "they weren't rallied. They were offended." Begnaud waited for her response, and when he got it, there was little sign of empathy or regret.

"What I would say is the vast majority of people responded very positively to who we are, to what we do, our mission. And, in fact, after that video, we got a lot of people coming forward and saying, 'We are part of this team, that's why we work for NewYork-Presbyterian.'" It was an account that many in the hospital system later thought was absolutely preposterous.

The ever-upbeat *CBS Mornings* anchor Gayle King seemed nonplussed after Begnaud's interview. At home wearing oversize glasses that magnified her surprise, she said, "David, eyebrows raised just a little bit with that exchange. . . . I'd like to think that I know the message she was trying to send, but it didn't come out the way maybe she was hoping. You know what? I think coronavirus is a vicious—"

Just then, the Zoom broadcast glitched, though Begnaud continued. "I was just saying, a lot of doctors who are on the front lines are shocked by it . . . but look, I appreciate her coming forward and stating her point. I think, Gayle, one of the most important things to say is the doctors keep working and we keep hearing: This is a war. The frontline soldiers in this war are people who wear gloves and scrubs."

"You know, nobody is immune from this. I get that, but it just seems to be a double punch and even more hurtful when the people who are on the front lines risking their lives for strangers end up losing their lives in the meantime. That's very tough," King said.

"Thank you, David. I'm surprised she talked to you," King said in her closing. Not long after, the CBS interview with Forese virtually disappeared from the web. From a chat room of doctors and health-care workers, someone registered under the username "u/superfan 14" posted, under the header "[Serious] NYP Admin Scandal Being Deleted Internet?," "Can no longer find the CBS video in response to her video and all of the reddit threads have been deleted or shut down. Is NYP really paying to have all of this scrubbed?" That comment rocketed through the NewYork-Presbyterian system too, but the video remained buried.

21

On April 23, Dr. Perry Cook, a hematologist/oncologist at Brooklyn Methodist, was taking a break with some colleagues in the doctors' lounge, where the TV was always on. He looked up to see the president in a blue and white tie say nonchalantly, "Supposing we hit the body with a tremendous—whether it's ultraviolet or just very powerful light. And I think you said that hasn't been checked, but we're going to test it? And then I said, supposing you brought the light inside the body, either through the skin or some other way." He turned toward the White House Coronavirus Task Force coordinator Dr. Deborah Birx, who twisted her face into a grimace. "Right. And then I see the disinfectant, where it knocks it out in a minute. One minute. And is there a way we can do something like that, by injection inside or almost a cleaning. Because you see it gets in the lungs and it does a tremendous number on the lungs." Birx, who had worked with Barack Obama on the AIDS crisis, stared at her shoes.

"What the fuck is he talking about?" Cook shouted as his colleagues erupted. "The response was unrepeatable," he told me. "There would be jeers." In the hospital, there were also disputes. "We had doctors who stood up for Trump. They would say, 'It's not his fault. You can at least give him that. This pandemic would have happened without him,'" Cook said.

22

May 6, 2020

Dear Colleagues,

Today is Nurse's Day. This year it should have been combined with Mother's Day and Father's Day, because nurses have been that important in our battle with COVID-19. In an earlier message I compared nursing to the thickest part of a dam, where the pressure is greatest, the part that prevents drowning and devastation by not breaking. It was the absence of nursing expertise that concerned me the most in the ORICUs during the worst of the surge. We had master planners, and MDs aplenty covering the top half of the dam. At the nursing level we had a few trained ICU nurses and large numbers of OR and PACU nurses doing things they had never been trained to do. Yet learn they did, and do they did, for our patients. This week I received an email from one of my regular OR nurses: "It is truly amazing what has been done in the ORICU—I am simply blown away by the teamwork. . . . These last few weeks have been life-altering. I wish I had not missed two of them while out ill." She ended with Bob Marley: "You never know how strong you are, until being strong is the only choice you have."

Craig R. Smith, MD
Chair, Department of Surgery
Surgeon-in-Chief, NYP/CUIMC

23

In May in Briarwood, Queens, twenty-three-year-old Benedict Harvey was waiting to see if he had gotten off the wait list to attend Cornell's medical school. His entire life, he'd dreamed of being a doctor. For months, he had been living the horror of the pandemic. His father, 5 South's Ben-Gary Harvey, a pulmonary and critical-care specialist, sounded strained on the telephone in the rare moments he could leave his patients.

Ben-Gary Harvey had been spending long hours caring for Susie Bibi and counseling her husband, Reuben "Ruby" Bibi, trying to come up with something that would treat the unimaginable level of destruction that COVID had caused in her lungs. At the moment, she had seven tubes in her chest to keep her lungs inflated, and in May, when her grown children came to the ICU to see her, Brad Hayward told them, "There is almost nothing we can do for her now. Her lungs are so destroyed. We don't see her pulling through." Her husband was furious that Hayward had told his children that their mother was close to death ("That is my responsibility, not his," he said), but his anger did nothing to change her situation.

In fact, nothing seemed to be helping. Reuben Bibi had desperately attempted to get her a lung transplant—even found a specialist at Mass General who was willing to operate on a COVID patient—but

Hayward told him that she could not survive the trip. It seemed there was nothing to do but hope for a miracle.

But then Ben-Gary Harvey had a miraculous idea.

Harvey was meticulous about guarding patients' privacy, and he never mentioned his plan to his son Benedict or his former wife, Benedict's mother, who used to be an ICU nurse at Jamaica Hospital and had now been deployed to the ICU of the large public hospital fifteen minutes from her house. She too preferred to keep her experiences to herself. She would return home at night, dry her two N95s on a heater, and, in the bathroom, take off all her clothes and scrub down. "She was terrified she would give us COVID," Benedict recalled. She was terse when her son asked her about her day. Benedict knew full well about the forklifts for bodies, the drowning of hospitals, the endless alerts, so at home "we would have Pavarotti's *Three Tenors* going and try to focus on the music and small talk," Benedict said, before his mom would have to head back to the hospital.

Benedict Harvey always struggled to understand his father's formal detachment, which at times felt callous and dismissive. He refused to tell Benedict or his brothers what he did, but he would snap at them, "You have no idea what I do. None." That partly changed the summer of 2017, before Benedict's final year at Cornell University. "I shadowed him as his intern from morning until night," he said. Benedict had already decided he would follow his father into medicine, but now he was able to see what went on in his father's professional life and got some insight into the lives of all the doctors and nurses he had known as family friends while growing up.

People who worked with Ben-Gary Harvey also struggled to understand his obdurate nature, but his skills as a research pulmonary critical-care specialist were almost unmatched, his work hours ferocious, and his study of every aspect of his patients' cases thorough.

Ben-Gary Harvey's ascent at Weill Cornell was so far-fetched, he rarely discussed it, not even with his colleagues, who wondered about his background but respected his aura of formal disengagement. As a child in Colombia, he'd had to say goodbye to his mother when she moved to New York to take a job in a Bronx clothing factory. Before leaving, she had tried to explain to her seven-year-old son that she needed to support him and his brother, and while she was in America, they would need to stay in Barranquilla, being passed from place to place. "It was very erratic," he recalled. "I was very unhappy a lot of the time." All he knew of his mother's life in America was that she was "sewing and sewing and sewing and sewing."

Harvey's father, a native of Trinidad, had long since abandoned the family, but his mother sent money to keep Harvey at an American school in Colombia even after he was dispatched to a village where older relatives were constantly asking the twelve-year-old to go grocery shopping and help with cleaning in a home where seven people lived at any given time. "All I wanted to do was my schoolwork and play soccer," Harvey said. His mother came to the rescue. When Harvey was ready to start high school, he was allowed to move back to his hometown and attend the American school. He studied English for the first time and when he graduated, decided to pursue medical school in Barranquilla. His mother paid his tuition and made sure there were helpers in the house to cook and clean so Harvey could focus on his studies. In medical school, he truly fell in love with the idea of saving lives. When he graduated, his mother insisted he come to America. "If you don't come now when I can bring you, you will never be able to come in as a citizen." His first stop was a community college in Queens, where he studied English and prepared for his exams. He took the tests on consecutive days and then had to find an internship. Harvey borrowed his stepfather's car and drove from hospital to hospital, leaving a letter and résumé at each one. "I had heard of Cornell Medical School and parked on Sixty-Eighth and York and walked into the fourth-floor office of the department of medicine. The secretary looked at me and said, 'You don't have a chance of ever getting in here. Don't even leave your résumé.' That was what she told me. She was quite a tough lady. She wouldn't let me talk to anyone who was there." Nevertheless, walking around the hospital, Harvey thought, *I like the looks of the people here. This is where I want to be.*

It was not to be; he spent a year at Jamaica Hospital, where there weren't enough technicians to accommodate the hundreds of patients. "I was running all day long—doing IVs, EKGs, drawing blood, taking care of the emergency room—and then exhausted and up all night. The residents would come and yell at you. It was crazy. Total abuse." He transferred to a hospital in Brooklyn, an academic center run by the state, for the final two years of his residency, but always believed the chaos at Jamaica Hospital prepared him for the ICU.

Harvey waited to share that story with Benedict until he was applying to medical school. "I knew I wanted to be a doctor from the time I was five," Benedict said. "When I was growing up in Queens, we had an assembly at my school, and I said, 'I will be a doctor.' I didn't even know what a doctor was." At home, "the only conversation we had seemed to be medicine."

Actually, not the only conversation. "If you work hard enough and just keep working, the color of your skin will not matter," Ben-Gary told Benedict all through his years at his Queens Catholic high school in Jamaica. "There will be many who treat you differently because you are Black," he said. "But that is their problem—not yours." Of course, like any parent of a Black son, Ben-Gary knew "their problem" could lead to terrible things. He had for years had "the Conversation," telling his sons about the need at all times for caution if stopped for a traffic violation by the police—even in Queens.

Benedict's grandmother always told him, "There is nothing you can't accomplish if you put the work into it," but she also warned him about the risks of being a young Black man. But that was true for an older Black man too, even a brilliant pulmonologist at NewYork-Presbyterian. Harvey had devoted his life to studying the lungs, but when he thought about his sons and the odds, easy breathing was sometimes impossible.

In January 2019, Harvey had been assigned to work on a device called the Zephyr, a tiny valve that could be placed in an airway to improve airflow. It had been studied for over a decade but was not approved by the FDA until 2018, and soon after that, Harvey was tasked by Weill Cornell with trying it for COPD, which is characterized by emphysema and bronchitis. The Zephyr Valve is designed to let air flow one way—out of the lungs.

Thinking about Susie Bibi, Harvey wondered, *What about the Zephyr Valve?* As far as he and everyone else in the hospital knew, nobody had ever tried it on a COVID patient.

For weeks, Harvey went back and forth with Lindsay Lief, Fernando Martinez, Hasina Outtz Reed, and critical-care director David Berlin. Bibi's lungs had multiple pneumothoraces (areas where parts of the lung had been damaged and collapsed), and she had seven tubes in her chest to keep the lungs inflated. Harvey estimated that 60 percent of the air flowing into Bibi's lungs escaped through a fistula, a hole that had been caused by COVID. Most of the air would escape through the chest tubes, which kept her lungs collapsed. "If I can figure out where the hole is," Harvey reasoned, "I can insert valves that will prevent air from going into the diseased part of her lung." He was pretty confident that valves might work; a bunch of things had to go right for it to be perfectly implanted, but in theory it might work wonders. There was one huge problem, though: He could do nothing without a CT scan of her chest so he could see exactly what was going on in her lungs and determine where to place the valve, but he had been told in no uncertain terms that taking her to the CT machine might kill her. No matter how hard he tried, Harvey had no success convincing the other attendings to help make Bibi's CT scan happen—they didn't want to risk it.

"Well, somebody has to have the guts to move her," Harvey told his colleagues.

But everybody thought she was too sick.

As it stood, each tube in Bibi's chest was connected to a separate suction device; that meant they needed seven portable devices before they could even consider moving her. Harvey pulled in the critical-care nurses. "I said, 'Can you just get all the portable options that you need from the hospital? Go floor to floor, find them, because I need a CT scan.'" Harvey knew he had only a narrow window of time; Bibi was deteriorating quickly, and soon they would lose the chance to try the Zephyr.

Harvey was scheduled to be the attending on 5 South the following Monday, at which point he would have the authority to order a CT for Bibi—and that's exactly what he did. "On Monday, I said, 'Susie Bibi is going for a CT scan today.' Everybody thought I was crazy. . . . There were a lot of people involved. We now had collected enough portable suction devices to move her. Each different chest tube required suction equipment. We got her to the CT scan before she decompensated—and she survived it." Against the expectations of his colleagues, step one was complete.

Scan in hand, Harvey studied it again and again. He told the nurses and the pulmonary fellows he thought he had located the most diseased area of the lung. Standard operating procedure (literally) said the next step was a bronchoscopy, but that was out of the question. "A bronchoscopy would have involved using a camera through the tracheostomy tube she was breathing on," Harvey explained, "instead of putting a camera through a new tube, which would have lessened the air supply." Was there another way? Harvey thought there might be. He called her husband to explain what he wanted to do in the procedure and get his sign-off. "It is a risk, but I think I can get into her lung very quickly through her vocal cord and put a balloon in with a camera, and if I am right, the air leaks that we see will stop," he told Reuben Bibi. The type of balloon he would use was not the sort you'd find at a birthday party; it was a tiny catheter called a Fogarty Balloon, the same kind that vascular surgeons use. Guided by the CT scan, Harvey was able to insert the balloon in just the right spot—in the middle lobe of Bibi's right lung. The procedure lasted less than five minutes, and to his surprise and relief, it worked on the first try. The balloon inflated and the air leak stopped. He called Bibi's husband to get his consent and then inserted the valve.

The two men had developed a certain rapport. Harvey was truly astonished by Reuben Bibi's focus and calm. He was at the ICU with his wife almost every day, keeping meticulous notes about every procedure. Often he would speed-dial her cousin Jack Hidary, an early partner of Google founder Sergey Brin and an expert on quantum physics. Hidary—who staged a brief run for mayor in 2013, promising Google Glasses for every New York schoolchild—had a platoon of experts in medicine and science who were weighing in on Susie Bibi's case, but Reuben Bibi had come to trust Harvey's clinical intuition, regardless of what those experts were saying. "Go ahead," he told Harvey. Harvey assured him that he would be implanting the Zephyr Valve himself. Pulmonary fellows typically handle the bronchoscope, or camera, but in this very special case—the first time a Zephyr Valve would be used for COVID at Weill Cornell—Harvey would be in charge. "I won't involve any of my fellows," he said. "I will just place it and come right out."

The procedure was scheduled very early the morning of July 8, in case something went wrong and he had to repeat it. Reuben Bibi stayed home, perhaps feeling that his presence down the hall or even on another floor of the hospital might distract Harvey when he most needed to focus. This was his wife's last chance. The whole point of using valves was to avoid invasive surgery, and in any case there was no way they were going to open up Susie Bibi's chest. As a result, the valve would have to be delicately placed. Focused on the procedure, Harvey asked the nurses observing the monitor what they saw.

"Suddenly, everyone was saying, 'The leak stopped!' and I said, 'Are you kidding me? The leak stopped?' You are talking about more than fifty percent of the air we were giving her. And I thought, *Wow. Why didn't we try this earlier?*"

Harvey came out of the room, talking to himself—*Why didn't we try this before?*—and called Reuben Bibi.

"We got the balloon in and she tolerated the procedure," he told him. Only one valve was needed to prevent air from leaking out through the damaged parts of her lungs into the chest cavity, which would facilitate getting Bibi off the ventilator. They'd said she wouldn't survive the CT scan, and she had. "Everyone was telling us that she could die, and she didn't," her husband said. Still, it was his choice: Try the Zephyr, which had never been used before on such a patient, or not? A mistake could have killed her.

"The next day we got an X-ray and then another X-ray, and day after day, more pictures," Harvey said. "We were like, 'Oh my God—this is big stuff.'"

Almost immediately Bibi's lungs started to get stronger. "One of the most rewarding things," Harvey said, "was we now felt we might be able to get Susie Bibi off the ventilator and save her life." They lowered the pressure on the ventilator, and she held. By now, she was officially Harvey's case. Finally, he said, "Okay, she's ready to be weaned off the ventilator."

On July 28, in her hospital room overlooking the East River, Susie Bibi came off the ventilator. She'd still have to breathe through a trach, a tube in her neck connected to the windpipe, but it was a major milestone in her recovery. As she began to breathe on her own, the doctors and nurses who had been worrying about her for months started to cry. It was almost impossible to believe that she had been on a ventilator for four months—and lived. "Everyone was excited and emotional because we thought she was going to die," Harvey remembered. "Everyone was telling me congratulations, but the most important thing was about risk—are you willing to take it?" He had been, and for the first time in a very long time, it was possible to imagine that someday, Susie Bibi would be back in Brooklyn, enjoying her morning aerobics class.

Nine minutes, twenty-nine seconds. Those on 5 South knew better than most precisely what would happen if someone's breathing was obstructed for that long, but nobody needed pulmonology expertise to understand what had happened to George Floyd.

Seven days earlier, Floyd had been brutally murdered by a white Minneapolis cop who had a history of using excessive force. Now, looking out the windows, the 5 South team witnessed something extraordinary: Thousands of NewYork-Presbyterian employees— doctors, nurses, residents, housekeepers, attendings, specialists—at every NYP campus, all taking a knee. At Weill Cornell, the driveway at East Sixty-Eighth Street was hidden by a wall of employees kneeling in scrubs and white coats, fists in the air.

New York and many other cities in the country were rocked by massive demonstrations on June 2 and beyond, but while much of the focus was on police brutality, the protests at hospitals all through the city and the country were about something more. For years, Steve Corwin had been obsessed by health disparities, and in a message he sent to all employees the day after Floyd was killed, his voice vibrated with revulsion. "NewYork-Presbyterian has stood up to the coronavirus, and now it will stand up to the virulence of racism," he said.

On the morning of May 26, Veronica Roye's mother was home in

East Harlem watching the local evening news. She called her daughter: "Did you hear about this guy that was killed?"

She hadn't. Back in New Jersey, Veronica Roye, working in liver-transplant outpatient care, had been taking a break from social media and TV for her sanity. "It was just COVID all the time, and I couldn't take it," she said. She told her mother, "No, I'm on a news break. What are you talking about?"

Roye's mother told her what had happened, but it wasn't until later that day that she broke her fast, turned on her TV, and stared in shock as she watched a Black man so casually murdered, while no one did anything to stop the cop doing it. "It was Derek Chauvin's hand in the pocket that got to me," she said. "The casual cruelty. You have a man calling for his mother and saying he can't breathe—and this man does nothing to check on him."

Overcome with sadness and revulsion, Roye reached out to Nicole Golden and Monica Nelson-Kone, close friends who worked with her on liver transplant patient care. They spoke again and again through that afternoon and the night—a three-way conversation from Mahopac, New York, to Brooklyn to New Jersey that was familiar but, because it was during quarantine, different. "None of this is new to us," Roye said. "We talked about how Black men get killed all the time. But everyone was home—and they got to see it." Over the next days, what started as profound sadness turned into outrage.

On East End Avenue, Steve Corwin was as outraged as he had been since the Charlottesville horror of 2017, when neo-Nazis and white nationalists took to the streets to (ostensibly) protest the removal of a statue of Robert E. Lee. "Jews will not replace us," protesters yelled. A car driven by a white nationalist rammed into a crowd of counterdemonstrators, killing a young civil rights activist. "I have to talk about this," he told his wife, Ellen, the weekend after Floyd was killed. For the CEO of New York-Presbyterian to jump into the fray struck several at the hospital as risky. "There was a worry that I was getting out of my swim lane," Corwin recalled. The hospital would soon engage in a fierce internal struggle over race disparities that had enraged hospitalists in Lower Manhattan, who circulated a petition in early April decrying the lack of nurses. "The ratio [of patients to nurses] was five to one as opposed to three to one at Weill Cornell," the petition said. Corwin would dispute their assertion. "This wasn't race—this was because we were overwhelmed," he said, pointing to similar numbers at Columbia. Still, the hospitalists did not agree— and they would take their case to the *New York Times*. But by the end of May, the petition—and the larger story—had yet to be published. Despite the potential risks to their careers, the doctors deeply believed they were acting in the best interest of their patients. The petition might call attention to the urgency of their situation. Why weren't there better resources spread through the system? The diversity issues among the privately insured and those on Medicaid would become an ongoing debate simmering all spring.

At Roye's son's school in Maywood, New Jersey, an e-mail went to all the parents expressing shock and empathy over the Floyd murder. "I sent them an e-mail back saying that for four years, since he was in middle school, we've learned about the Holocaust—four years in a row. One way the school can start to bridge that divide is to break up what we are teaching our children. The Holocaust is important, but by showing them so much of it and not showing them anything about slavery, you are not showing them the same empathy toward Black people. And when they get older, and they don't know about slavery—you have failed them." She took a screenshot and sent it to Nelson-Kone and Golden.

She was more impressed with what Corwin had said about George Floyd's murder. They had not heard anything like that from their own department, Roye explained. "We wanted to thank Dr. Corwin for actually having the courage to say something here. To say it from a position of white power and privilege. I said, 'We need to thank him.'" The trio sent him an e-mail and told him that they would love to meet. Corwin responded the same day, and within two days, Roye, Nelson-Kone, and Golden were meeting with him on Zoom.

For their conversation with the CEO, the nurses had prepared a six-slide PowerPoint presentation on the disparities in health care, and especially liver transplant, including data concerning the waiting list. Then the talk turned to income and pay disparities, including the unfairness of not being considered for special assignments and management. Roye talked about the experience she had had at the Weill Cornell PICU that caused her to leave the hospital, that the Black nurses who rotated through the unit had warned her of the subtle and overt racism, the excessive politeness and condescension, the failure to promote the most experienced Black nurses, and in graduate school, the singling out of Black students who walked in late to a lecture, even though most of the Black PhD nurses were working part-time or had families. Corwin listened intently and made it clear to her that he completely supported their proposal to increase the number of Black patients on the waiting list for liver transplants and encouraged them to do more outreach in the neighborhoods. He understood how glacial progress could be through the New York-Presbyterian system—department heads passing the buck, supervisors feeling threatened by the Black nurses' moxie. But nothing could succeed, he told them, without trying, and navigating the egos of those who made the decisions could not be his responsibility.

The trio had debated whether to include the final slide, which discussed the terms of race and gender politics that they believed were imperative to explain to a white CEO: "microaggressions" and "white fragility," "retention" and "retrenchment." They were afraid of Corwin's reaction. "It could be career suicide, but we decided to put everything on the table and let the chips fall where they may," Roye explained. "Either he's going to like this slide or he's going to be super-offended by it," Roye had predicted. But Corwin lit up: "That's *it*," he said. "This is *exactly* what I am talking about." He added, Roye recalled, "It is so hard for white people to grasp what this is."

Corwin, close to the pulmonologist Carlton McGregor, the only Black resident in his residency class, began to think about those years and what he had missed by not talking to him in a deep and profound way about what he was experiencing. "I learned so much from him, but in all the time we were in training, I never asked him about his life or his background or what he had to go through to get into Columbia. It was not done in 1980. And it should have been," Corwin said.

Corwin told Nelson-Kone, Golden, and Roye that he had friends who were saying, "Why are you getting into this?"—the implication being that the identity politics of race could ensnare the hospital in charges of a white-savior complex or, worse, paternalism. Roye understood it was complicated territory to navigate. "With words like *white fragility, implicit bias*—these are the terms that could cause people to be reactive." Roye recognized that "all of us have bias but if you start from that place people can move forward. I think he was very honest with us about this in ways that we weren't expecting him to be," Roye said of their discussion with Corwin. "We had no idea how this meeting was going to go. At the end, he said, 'I want to see this slide presentation come to life.'"

Almost immediately, Corwin told them that he had made a decision to shut down the dilapidated AIM clinics, where Columbia residents had worked for a decade, because of the medical care. "No more separate but equal," he said.

Corwin connected them to Julia Iyasere, who was in preliminary conversations to establish a new all-hospital center for health justice—a fifty-million-dollar foundation that would be financed by Bridgewater founder Ray Dalio. Roye, Golden, and Nelson-Kone were elated—they could finally get to work on reaching out to the community to help with liver transplant and education. Their next weeks saw meeting after meeting at Columbia with the department heads and the medical director for liver disease, Lorna Dove, who was Black. They tried not to be concerned when Dove told them she thought their PowerPoint slide on "microaggression" showed a lack of sensitivity about how it might be perceived. "I never thought it was disrespectful. I'm sorry [Veronica] thought that," Dove said. "What I might have thought was that people can become sensitive when you talk about 'microaggressions.' But I never said it was disrespectful. I do not recall saying that."

From the hospital, Corwin had been deeply engaged in the issue as the massive protests overtook the city, but, what upset Roye, she later said, was that the Columbia School of Nursing did not send a single e-mail expressing compassion to Roye and the other Black nursing doctoral candidates, even as other institutions weighed in. "I took it upon myself to actually e-mail them, and I made it known that just because you only see a few of us in the room doesn't mean that this is not a collective global issue. At the height of the COVID surge there had been a massive outpouring—we were all in it to fight COVID, but now you need to let us know that we are all in this together when it comes to racial reconciliation and what's happening in America now. And so they apologized."

"Our professors—all white—spoke with us on a regular basis and during COVID," Roye said. "They acknowledged how stressful that situation was. Why didn't they do the same thing after George Floyd?" To her, it was "white awkwardness. We can't talk about things openly and honestly. We don't want to make white people feel awkward [if] we say what we need to say."

Weeks passed, but the policy plans she had lobbied for kept getting put off. Roye wondered if the lack of progress was coming from Columbia or from the corporate side. "I began to feel that my department was looking at the three of us like we were troublemakers," she said. But around the hospitals on every campus, uncomfortable conversations that had "once never happened" began to happen organically all the time, said Columbia trauma surgeon Beth Hochman. While it sometimes seemed like everything was now out in the open, that raw honesty was not always appreciated. Roye no longer felt the slightest reticence discussing obvious differences. ("A white nurse could become angry and it would be forgotten about. The Black nurse would be told, 'This is inappropriate behavior.'") But she was upbraided because at one Zoom discussion, she talked about feeling invisible. It was almost as if some on the call felt like they'd heard her complain about it and didn't need to keep hearing it when they were trying to be better. "I feel like it's one of those annoying bugs that you keep smacking and wanting to go away. But they won't go away. I feel that we are the bug. We are the bug, we just won't let it go. And if it hasn't changed much—it will just become more hidden." And here Roye's dream project was pushed to Lorna Dove, who would have to figure out how her department could get it funded.

Later, Dove would say she believed the impediment to realizing Roye's plan was money: Who was going to finance the Black Liver Transplant Project, with its projected community centers? For the department head, Roye was "very conscientious, very confident, very honest and self-motivated. You could just give Veronica a project and then she would go forward with it." Dove, who grew up in a small town in North Carolina, where her father started his career as a garage mechanic, had been at Columbia since 2001 and was used to the labyrinth of grant applications that every new project required. Dove has not given up on trying to find ways to make Roye, Nelson-Kone, and Golden's project a reality. It has taken over a year and a half, but how to fund the Black Liver Transplant Project is still being discussed.

24

In June, 5 South was ready to implode. The New York-Presbyterian corporate side had sent thousands of umbrellas to its teams, each with a message that said, *For all of the bravery you have shown.* In the ICUs, still overwhelmed with COVID patients, the umbrellas became a symbol of a shocking lack of empathy. "We are struggling to pay three-hundred-thousand-dollar medical-school bills and they send us an umbrella?" an attending said. By now, no one watched the daily hospital briefings. "They were like out of *Veep*," one of the attendings said. "If I sit there for twenty minutes, who is going to take care of my patients?"

The strain on Lindsay Lief had become almost unbearable. Her sons were still up in Hudson, and there was no sign they could come home. A few weeks earlier, when Lief finally felt as if she was collapsing, she had to prevail on a friend at Memorial Sloan Kettering Cancer Center to get her a COVID test—Weill Cornell would not provide them. At 5 South, the nursing director, Anthony Sabatino, was constantly lobbying to get his nurses tested at the hospital, but the doctors were also not provided tests. "We couldn't get tests to see our families. We couldn't get a test to come back when the test was required to go to work." Sabatino would be told, "We can't accommodate that."

Finally, Lief was able to see her boys. Jake drove down to pick her up for a three-day weekend.

The next morning, when Jake arrived, he recalled, "I was stunned when I saw her. Exhaustion and grief was etched into her face," he said. "It was as if she were occupying someone else's body."

In early June, the city was beginning to plan elaborate opening schedules—the phase 1 of small groups being able to gather, the phase 2 of picking up curbside purchases with temperature checks and masking required before anyone would be allowed inside; there would be a limit placed on the number of customers allowed to line up outside the doors of department stores. As of June 1, New York had suffered more than 200,000 COVID cases, the highest number of any city in the world, and restaurant closings had significantly added to the city's 100,000 lost jobs. With that in mind, there were plans to permit New York's restaurants to set up tables in the streets, blocked off with wooden fences or some other hastily conceived barricade. The quickening of hope, however, was having a paradoxical effect on Lief and her team: Opening up inevitably meant things were going to get even worse, and they were already working twelve-hour days, if not longer. Chris Kampel, the computer whiz from Long Island, had been on a ventilator for months and was struggling for his life. While the fact that Tom Kato had pulled through on ECMO at Columbia electrified the hospital system, they'd all seen enough by now to know there was only so much hope to be had. Lief's boys would get on the phone with her and try not to cry.

On Long Island, Robert Kampel had learned of a Chicago doctor who might be able to perform a lung transplant on his son. "The Five South team was doing everything to get Chris ready," he recalled. "He was on a vent but the thought was, he is twenty-eight—he might be able to survive it." Brad Hayward reached out to Robert, Chris's father, and to Sam, Chris's fiancée, to have them come see Chris, to see how he would react to their presence in the room. "We think it might help if you were here," he told them. "It might pull Chris into a different dimension." And it did. Robert grabbed his hand and spoke in a loud voice. "Focus on me," he told his son, and then asked some yes-or-no questions. Chris shook his head in response. "He wasn't in that twilight anymore," Robert said.

When Sam saw Kampel in the hospital for the first time in person, she was convinced that he knew she was there. The nurses gave her an iPad to FaceTime the family; Chris's stepbrother Gregory ribbed him about his new beard. "I think he lifted his head to show him the beard, to shake it a bit to let us know he was aware," she said, although he was still sedated.

Still, after the visit, Chris seemed to rally. Hayward and Lief decided they would try to give him a tracheotomy. This was an enormous step—a trach was one step closer to being able to breathe on his own. Robert was elated when an occupational therapist was able to get Chris to identify playing cards. *He's coming out of it . . .*

On every shift, Judith Cherry spent time with Chris. The nurse, who in the early days of the pandemic had effectively saved 5 South by finding PPE hidden away in closets and cabinets, called Chris "my baby" and hovered over him as if he actually were her son. Cherry had gotten to know Chris before he was intubated and was charmed by his easy charisma—the word she used—even though he was so sick. Cherry's own sister had died of COVID in March, three days after her husband had caught COVID in a rehab facility. The staff there had sent him home without telling him that he was infected. "They just let him go right back home and did not tell my sister. She was just seventy and caught it immediately. They were both so sick—and they went so fast."

And they were still going so fast. For every Susie or Chris, you had scores of others whose ICU stays were brief and brutal. A few months earlier, speaking with Kelly Griffin for Ron Suskind's oral-history video project, Lief, worn out and in a T-shirt, wept. "It is too much," she said. "And they are so young." Griffin, in the blue turban her mother made for her, said, "This disease . . . the people are so sick . . ." Her exhaustion made it almost impossible for her to speak. "I haven't slept in a month," Lief said. "And then I went home and didn't take any medication and slept nine hours . . . and then you go to the computer and you look for the young man you were taking care of, and there are so many you can't find him and you realize that you don't even know how to spell his name—and he is gone from the computer. Just in that time you were asleep."

25

July 2, 2020

Dear Colleagues,

Some of my readers will remember that I anonymously quoted "one of my regular OR nurses" (repeated below) in my May 6 Update. Her anonymity matters less now. Renee French died suddenly and unexpectedly at home on May 19. . . . To me, she was a great OR nurse. I was asked to say a few words (below) at her memorial service today.

During the worst of our COVID surge, Renee French was one of a large number of OR and PACU nurses thrown into the ORICUs, supported by a few skilled ICU nurses and a host of MDs with various levels of expertise. Renee and her colleagues were asked to do things they had never been trained to do, overnight. They learned fast, under appalling conditions, and saved many lives. Renee caught the coronavirus but returned to work two weeks later. Renee sent me a few e-mails during the crisis. They ranged from practical through affirming to celebratory, with pictures of thumbs-up patients leaving the ICU, or fields of Antelope Valley wildflowers.

On Sunday, May 24, the *New York Times* attempted to list each of the 100,000 people who had died of COVID-19, beginning on a front page entirely filled with fine print. An endearing feature of the *Times'* 100,000 list was their attempt to capture in a few words something indelible about each person. Not an easy task. According to an unproven legend, Ernest Hemingway was having lunch with writer friends at the Algonquin, and bet each $10 that he could tell a whole story in 6 words. He scooped up the money after passing around a napkin on which he'd written "For sale: Baby shoes, never worn." The *Times* didn't do badly, no doubt with plenty of help from family and friends. Matching Hemingway's 6 words is "Retiree determined to spoil her granddaughter." My 4-word favorite is "Could make anything grow." "One-man army" excels in 3 words. Measured by impact per word, nothing matches "New father," describing a 22-year-old Oklahoman. Such poignancy obscures how many names were kept off that list by the bravery and resourcefulness of most of you listening today. You helped 80% of our admitted patients survive. Renee French was one of you. At this memorial service, Hemingway could have said "Renee put others ahead of herself." We can remember that.

Craig R. Smith, MD

Chair, Department of Surgery

Surgeon-in-Chief, NYP/CUIMC

At Weill Cornell, as Chris Kampel fought for his life, his father frantically searched for a solution. At his job at the Northport Veterans Hospital, Robert Kampel asked every expert he could find what they would do if Chris were their son. He believed that Chris had been intubated improperly—that the inordinate amount of pressure that had been given him during the procedure had blown out his lungs. Now, he figured, the only possible way to repair the damage was for him to get a lung transplant—a procedure rarely done on a COVID patient, though it was being talked about. Still, Hayward and Dave Berlin made the calls to see what was possible and then filled out the needed forms to try to move him to a hospital in Chicago that was willing to take the chance. Among the many difficulties: Chris had to be put on ECMO for the flight, and if something went wrong, he would be thirty thousand feet above whatever hospital was nearest. When Chris's mother learned of a doctor at Mass General who had done a lung transplant on a COVID case, his father allowed himself a few days of real hope. "Massachusetts was a lot easier to get to from New York," he said. "He said he could do it. It would be a lot safer than flying at that point." So, again, the attendings did all the paperwork to move Chris.

It was not to be. At one in the morning Hayward called Robert: "We're losing your son. You need to come right away." Chris had been on a dialysis machine 24/7, but his kidneys had started to fail. "Chris is not going to make it," Hayward told Sportiello and Kampel.

Kampel had made Hayward promise to call him if the situation got worse. "Do not let my son die alone. You let me know, I will be there in an hour." He went to get Mary, and they raced into Manhattan. "It took us forty-five minutes," he recalled. "It usually takes two hours."

They arrived at the hospital at 3:00 a.m. and were there with their son all that night and morning. Remarkably, he stabilized, and a sliver of hope returned. Robert still thought that Chris might rally and get a lung transplant. He reached out to the CEO of Chris's parent company, Emblem Health; the CEO promised him they would pay for everything—the most important thing was saving Chris.

Then, another setback: a fast-moving fungal infection swept through his body. Again, his kidneys started to fail. Robert said, "At that point the Chicago surgeon backed out. He said, 'He will die before he gets here. I hate to tell you this, but it's over.' 'What do you mean?' I said. 'If I open Chris up, he will die on the table—that is how fast it will spread. There's nothing more we can do for him.'"

There was nothing more that 5 South could do for Chris Kampel either.

Judith Cherry was overcome. "We prayed in every language and in every religion. We all were desperate for a miracle. I was so attached to him—he was my baby. All of these months, we just prayed and prayed."

One week later, Robert was at a friend's house when the hospital called. "Come right away," Hayward instructed him. Robert and his new wife, Jennifer, picked up Mary and Chris's sister, Erica. They sat with him all night, waiting for the moment, but Chris stabilized again. Robert got home at 6:00 a.m. and went to sleep. Forty-five minutes later, the telephone rang. "It is definitely today," Hayward said. Robert rushed to the hospital with Jennifer, and they stayed until 5:00 p.m. the following day. Chris was still alive when they left.

The next day was Monday. Dr. Hayward called again. "Chris's numbers have dropped," he told Robert. "This will be the last day." Mary, a born-again Christian, rushed to the hospital with her pastor. Robert took his wife. Sam came with her mother. They played Linkin Park, Chris's favorite band, on Robert's iPhone. When Chris was sixteen, Robert took him to a concert. One ticket was available by the stage. "Chris said, 'You are going to let me sit alone.' And I said, 'God, yes, you are sixteen.' He took that ticket and took off. At the end of the concert, he said, 'You guys couldn't have seen everything I got to see.' That's how close he was." Those were the sort of memories a father would have of his son, a small moment together, nothing that changed the world but something that brought him happiness. That night, all had been right in the world and he felt like it might be forever.

At the hospital the last two days of Chris's life, Robert felt that his son's spirit had already gone, that the machines were just keeping his body alive. He berated himself for not going to his house in March and forcing Chris to try the folk remedy that he believed had saved a colleague. "Sometimes these old remedies are better than modern medicine," he said. But he could see how overwhelmed the doctors were at 5 South, how exhausted they were from trying, and trying, and trying. "They were up days and days and they had nothing to really help these patients," he said. "They still don't know how to treat this, really. This was worse than a war. No one had ever had to deal with this before—and we were the epicenter."

On July 13, 2020, Chris Kampel died. He was only twenty-eight years old.

Robert and his family had been in agony for months. But there would be no relief.

"You can't get over this; you are not supposed to bury your kid."

26

It was way too early to declare a victory of any kind, but that did not stop the endless self-promotion and grandiosity coming from all sides. Of all the acts of hubris and desperate brand-hyping that summer, it was hard to rival Cuomo selling the memoir of his pandemic-leadership genius to Crown, a division of Penguin Random House, for a staggering five million dollars, vaporizing Cuomo's image of unassailable public servant and transforming him into something closer to the man in the White House, who saw government service simply as a means to private gain. But while Cuomo's tone-deafness was big news, few people noticed another major player in the war on COVID. Michael Dowling, the ebullient Irish former professor and state official now running Northwell Health, was publishing his own book. Dowling's book, quickly crafted by Northwell's in-house journalist, was titled *Leading Through a Pandemic: The Inside Story of Humanity, Innovation, and Lessons Learned During the COVID-19 Crisis*. The book cover featured Dowling in full PPE—face shield, surgical cap, and mask—with his hands in blue nitrile gloves clutching the pale but perfectly manicured hand of a white patient in bed. His fellow author Andrew Cuomo blurbed Dowling's digest: "A clarifying, must-read in these uncertain times." Dowling, for all his showmanship, had a much larger understanding of the importance of the need for public information about the mission of his hospitals than the book he rushed out suggested. The hit 2020 Netflix reality series *Lenox Hill*, a compelling inside look at Northwell's hospital on Manhattan's Upper East Side, had been a Dowling project. But he will be remembered most of all for a risky corporate decision: As COVID overtook New York City, Dowling allowed the director Matthew Heineman, nominated for an Academy Award for his 2015 film, *Cartel Land*, to take a small production crew into an ICU at Long Island Jewish Medical Center, despite all of the HIPAA restrictions. Somehow Dowling found a way to make it possible for Heineman to produce the harrowing *The First Wave*, released in the fall of 2021, while still observing HIPAA protocols.

All over America, hospitals continued to threaten doctors who spoke out. Columbia's chief resident Cleavon Gilman, who had comforted grieving families from his bad-news chair through the New York surge of March and April, now had more than 160,000 Twitter followers. In June 2020, he left Columbia Medical Center for a job at Arizona's Yuma Regional Medical Center to work in a rural community. In November 2020, appalled by the tsunami of COVID cases now in Arizona, he tweeted: "Just got to work and was notified there are no more ICU beds in Arizona. What happened to the 175 beds??? We likely don't have nursing to staff them." His tweet would receive more than 78,000 likes, but the next day at the hospital, he was told not to return to work. Gilman told the *Washington Post*, "All I know is this hospital is trying to crush my voice, they want to silence me and they want to financially hurt me. This is all so wrong." Almost immediately, Gilman received a call from the newly elected president of the United States, Joe Biden, and was quickly reinstated. But despite the burnout and disaffection of so many frontline workers, there has been little change in the corporate communications policies of most hospitals, including NewYork-Presbyterian. One year after the first surge, Brooklyn Methodist's veteran hematologist and oncologist Perry Cook, who had watched Donald Trump in the doctors' lounge in April 2020 as he suggested America should try bleach to cure COVID, published an op-ed in March 2021 on the difficulties he experienced obtaining the highly effective monoclonal antibodies treatment for his patients. "We Have a Lifesaving Treatment for Covid-19. Why Is It So Hard to Get?," the *New York Times* column bannered. The next day, he received the now predictable response from the corporate office, accusing him of HIPAA violations and a follow-up threat about his employment. Cook insisted that, in his opinion, no patient was readily identifiable and that the public had a right to know about the efficacy of the treatment. The hospital disagreed.

In July, Ellen Corwin answered her door to find an enormous package from the governor's office. It was a huge poster adapting graphics from Cuomo's daily briefings to show how New York, under his impressive leadership, was now trending in a positive direction. "I turned to Steve and I said, 'Are you kidding me? Am I supposed to hang this thing?'" The governor's posters were as misguided as NewYork-Presbyterian's umbrellas, but in the summer of 2020, comms offices around the city were trying to gin up every bit of political capital they could, no matter how flimsy the base.

Then, on the same day, another delivery from Cuomo's office in Albany arrived on East End Avenue. This time the box contained a wooden plaque with a genuine N95 mask mounted on it.

Okay, Ellen thought. *What are we supposed to do with this? Like, thank you? Is this a thank-you for something? For what? Getting through this thing . . . I don't know.* She turned to her husband and, referring to the N95, said, "Maybe we could use this in an ICU. Someone around the country may need this." But she found that the mask was stapled and glued to the plaque, and when she tried to remove it, the whole thing fell apart. "Frickin' N95 mask stapled to a piece of wood," she said, groaning.

Locked down in full quarantine until June, the Corwins had not seen their children since March. But in July, the family finally reunited in Sag Harbor. Corwin's younger son, Joe, worked with Ken Raske at the Greater New York Hospital Association, but he was also studying for his master's degree in public health. Phase 3 of the Moderna mRNA vaccine trials had just been announced, but the timeline for the vaccine's approval by the FDA had already become a political firestorm. In May, hoping to distract from the virulent spread of COVID-19 through the country, Trump held a Rose Garden event to hype his administration's efforts to fast-track a vaccine. "We're looking to get it by the end of the year if we can, maybe before," he said. "Good numbers coming out of States that are opening. America is getting its life back! Vaccine work is looking VERY promising, before end of year. Likewise, other solutions!" Trump tweeted. Almost immediately, there was pushback from the country's vaccine experts. "I think it is possible you could see a vaccine in people's arms next year—by the middle or end of next year. But this is unprecedented, so it's hard to predict," Dr. Paul Offit, the frequently quoted director of the Vaccine Education Center at the Children's Hospital of Philadelphia, told NBC News at the time. Anywhere from six to eighteen months, said Anthony Fauci. Unless there's a miracle. And already there was the predictable fusillade of criticism, this time that the vaccines would be rushed through without adequate testing so Trump could run on them in November.

Corwin was focused on the larger questions of who would trust these vaccines, especially given the corrosively politicized climate, and how to ensure that once the vaccines were deemed safe, mass inoculations could be enforced. If the explosion of the wearing of masks had set off a civil war of red states and blue states, what would happen with vaccines? Trump and his allies seemed unlikely to help, given their ongoing rejection of anything but the most superficial, and sometimes plain erroneous, strategies to slow the virus.

"You know, Dad," Joe Corwin said, "there is plenty of case law that already exists on this. These laws have been around since the turn of the century. Haven't you heard of *Jacobson v. Massachusetts?*" Corwin had not. Out came Joe's textbook, which he handed his father as they sat by the pool: Not long after a Rockefeller grandchild died of smallpox, an outbreak in Massachusetts in 1902 prompted the City of Cambridge to institute a regulation ordering all of its residents to be vaccinated. Henning Jacobson, a local pastor, had come from Sweden, where vaccines were required. He believed that he and his family had had severe reactions to the vaccine, which they took as children, and he refused to obey the new law, fighting all the way to the Supreme Court. Writing for the majority in a seven-to-two opinion, Justice John M. Harlan declared that the regulation in Cambridge was necessary "in order to protect the public health and secure the public safety." The following week, Corwin addressed the hospital staff on the larger legal issue and the case law that had been used in every public health crisis since the Swedish pastor lost his case.

27

In her masterwork *A Paradise Built in Hell,* author Rebecca Solnit featured the Rutgers sociologists Caron Chess and Lee Clarke, who coined the term *elite panic,* drawing on detailed studies. "Elites tend to believe in the venal, selfish and essentially monstrous version of human nature, which I sometimes think is their own human nature," Solnit wrote, citing the fears of looters descending on New Orleans during Hurricane Katrina (which did not happen) and the move to limit the spread of information—a fact that stymied much of the reporting during the pandemic surge, as those inside the hospitals feared for their jobs if they pushed out the reality of what was happening, even in the number one health-care system.

A bit of the curtain was lifted on July 1, when the *New York Times* ran a front-page story with the headline "Why Surviving the Virus Might Come Down to Which Hospital Admits You." For months, the paper's epidemic and hospital specialists Sheri Fink, Joseph Goldstein, Brian M. Rosenthal, and Sharon Otterman had fanned out through the boroughs, interviewing scores of frontline workers and analyzing public and private data to compare the level of treatment in public hospitals and the elite academic centers.

Among the *Times'* most damning revelations was the simple fact that during the entire spring of 2020, there were only fifty transfers of public patients to private academic centers—the wealthy nonprofits that have been "aided by decades of government policies that have steered money to them ... two-thirds of their patients are on Medicare or have commercial insurance, through their employer or purchased privately." In contrast, only 10 percent of the patients at public hospitals had private insurance, and there were five hospital beds for every 1,000 residents in Manhattan, but only 1.8 per 1,000 in Queens, and 2.2 in Brooklyn. And when it came to COVID, those numbers actually made things sound better than they were, because not only were there fewer beds per resident in Queens and Brooklyn, there were higher numbers of them who needed hospitalization than there were in Manhattan.

All of this was understood by the doctors—and those in charge—of NewYork-Presbyterian, but when the system was under siege in April, the need for hundreds of extra nurses with ICU training opened up a sinkhole in the effort to stem the COVID tide.

David Scales had arrived at Weill Cornell excited to work there. After Yale Medical School, his residency at Harvard found him at Boston's Cambridge Health Alliance, a community hospital where he was able to further his understanding of the dynamics that produced huge pockets of underserved communities. Scales had already worked at the WHO, writing his 2008 dissertation on influenza pandemic preparedness, and had lived among Syrian refugees to address their health needs. Among his other fields of academic concentration were sociology and medical interpretation. He was, in other words, a perfect candidate for Art Evans's team of scholar MDs and Cornell's pioneering work on global health.

What drew Scales to this branch of the NewYork-Presbyterian empire was the hospital's immigrant population. Scales, whose mother was a chemistry teacher and whose father was a biochemist and former Peace Corps volunteer, spent his childhood in Atlanta and, later, in Los Angeles, where his father managed blood samples for local laboratories, ensuring tests were done as accurately and quickly as possible.

Downtown, Scales divided his time between the small community hospital on William Street, which had no residents or fellows, and Weill Cornell, with its army of highly skilled residents on the medicine service. In early March, he was the second hospitalist assigned to work with Matt McCarthy on COVID patients. By the end of the first week, he was moved downtown as Lower Manhattan, without the space to build negative-pressure areas or construct pop-up ICUs, became truly overwhelmed. "We were put in a position where we were watching patients deteriorate," he said.

In frequent calls with the COVID teams and department heads, Art Evans, a professor of medicine who oversees hospitalists, said, "Tell me what it's like at Lower Manhattan." They would all respond, "We have a shortage of nurses. The nurses are struggling to see all of the patients. It's dangerous because the patients get confused and can't call for help. And we are having to do this and that, and we don't have a step-down unit"—an avalanche of "We don't have" and "We cannot do without" that all came down to a simpler "We need more help, please."

"And we would brainstorm and we would get more help down there—physicians and volunteers to go down and help, but couldn't get nurses and respiratory therapists," Art Evans recalled. So Scales and Devin Worster pitched in however they could—drawing blood, positioning patients, assembling respiratory equipment—but their efforts were just a tiny plug in a dam that was breaking. On a visit, Evans saw Scales troubleshooting balky ventilators constantly going off; although they had about twenty state-of-the art ventilators at Lower Manhattan, there were times when they had to resort to travel ventilators, the kind used by EMS, which had to be adjusted with knobs and buttons instead of touchscreens. They had access to intensivists in Pittsburgh who dispensed advice via iPad, providing a sounding board and extra safety net as they were extubating patients, as well as reinforcements from Cayuga Health Center in Ithaca, New York.

David Weir, a critical-care pulmonologist in Lower Manhattan, had sent his children to Singapore to stay with his sister-in-law. The next day, Singapore shut down all air travel—it would be four months before Weir and his wife were able to get special visas to reunite with their two children. The result for Weir, and his patients, was that he could spend more time in the hospital without the fear of infecting his family. The downside was the heartbreak of separation. Their youngest, thirteen months, did not recognize her parents when they came for her in July. But Weir felt lucky his children were safe in Singapore.

Evans was closely watching the situation downtown, concerned about the psychological well-being of Weir, who was sleeping on a mattress in his office. He was well aware of the idealism and dedication of the hospitalists who were drawn to the intimate lower campus with only two floors of patients, as opposed to fourteen at Weill Cornell. In Lower Manhattan, the nurses and security guards and environmental service people were a family unit, and many patients were homeless. Many of the patients were from Chinatown with extremely limited English, which added to the challenge.

Scales's time working with refugees in Jordan informed how he approached the catastrophe. Scales volunteered to spend most of his time downtown, as did Devin Worster and Nell Eisenberg, who had worked with Doctors Without Borders. Rounding with his hospitalists several times a week, Evans was struck by how the doctors had constructed safe zones for the nurses and staff. "They had put tape on the ground in the wards that went along the corridors and it was done so that you did not have to change your gown as long as you stayed on one side of the tape. As long as you stayed within the tape, you could go to the next room, change your mask and your gloves but keep your gown on, and then go to the next patient with COVID. And they had innovated this at Lower Manhattan, whereas at the main campus it was much more inefficient."

It was understandable that Lower Manhattan and Queens and Brooklyn were hit the hardest—at Queens, the ratio of patients to nurses could be fourteen to one, Elmhurst numbers—but at Weill Cornell, the construction crews were struggling to build temporary rooms in the gleaming Koch Center to make them inpatient-suitable and repurposing rooms for outpatients. But even those situations were better than Lower Manhattan. Hospital administrators were late in planning for the looming influx of patients. "We are going to put the first patient with coronavirus here," one hospitalist recounted to Scales, noting the hospital had careful procedures for how they were going to handle the first two COVID patients. "Well what about the third patient?" the hospitalist asked at one administrative planning meeting, and they were like, "We will cross that bridge when we get to it." A quick look in the halls told you that that bridge had been crossed a long time ago.

Back in late February, on a day when the weather turned exceptionally warm, Hupert took a bike ride around Manhattan. He came to work the next day and shared his impressions with Scales. "It was one of those days in the seventies," Scales remembered. "And Nathaniel said, 'It is so great to see everyone out . . . it is so sad to know that this will all be shut down in a few weeks and there will be no one on the streets.'"

"Cognitively, what he said was completely rational," Scales said. "And yet emotionally, I did not [get it]. This was before anyone else was preparing for this. Nathaniel felt a bit like Chicken Little. I wouldn't say I dismissed him at all. I knew exactly what he was talking about, but I didn't think it was going to be as bad as what Nathaniel was saying."

A few weeks later, on the day that Hupert tried to brief NewYork-Presbyterian's leadership on his projections, they met again. "He walked out of the room and just thought he felt people were dismissing his warning. Nathaniel was so baffled and incredulous. We were hanging out outside the hospital and he literally pulled out his laptop and gave us the presentation he had given to leadership and what was going to happen," Scales said. "And literally, me and the other people who were there were like, 'Wow, this is crazy. I can't believe they weren't listening to you.'"

And now it was too late. In April, hospitalists from Weill Cornell would walk into Lower Manhattan and be horrified. "It was clear that there was a real disparity in resources," Scales explained. The nurse-to-patient ratio was so imbalanced that everyone was affected—not only the patients who couldn't get adequate care, but the nurses, who were being worked to a state of collapse. "We need to either bring in more nurses or send the patients out," Scales told the hospital's leadership. "I'm freaking out because I'm watching patients decline because of the bad care they're getting."

Scales had, among all of his other accomplishments, done some radio journalism while in the Boston area. "I called up my old editor at WBUR and I said, 'What should I do?' I said, 'I know there are people talking to you. And Joe Goldstein from the *New York Times* is on this.' And my editor was fantastic. She said, 'What needs to happen right now? Do you need heads to roll? Because if you go public, heads will roll.' And we both agreed that was not a good idea in the middle of a pandemic." The bottom line was that they had to get better resources for the patients, and they could not wait any longer. By that time, Scales had been told that the nurse-to-patient ratio was one to fourteen in Queens and was almost certain to get worse.

In September 2021, *Annals of Internal Medicine* published a study that showed a correlation between the survival rates of COVID-19 patients and how overwhelmed hospitals were; the more swamped the hospital, the higher the patients' odds of dying. The mortality rates of the extended hospital system were not disclosed, but Scales said, "We saw it with our own eyes."

The hospitals had been caught unprepared, but now, the hospitalists believed, the focus of 2020 would become about damage control as trauma seeped through the system and the nurses' morale plummeted—more than twenty-two hundred patients would die in the NewYork-Presbyterian system. After the first wave, the resignations started, and by the fall, there would be dramatic changes in the nursing staff. Lower Manhattan and Queens and Brooklyn and all the hospitals had filled with traveling nurses and doctors, who'd arrive for their assignments just as things were starting to calm down. "We had plenty of traveling nurses but no one in the hospital. No one listened to us when we needed it. . . . It was traumatizing because we could not provide the level of care that we wanted to. . . . And so the nurses started leaving." Which of course made everything worse.

Scales's WBUR editor had an idea. "The best thing you can do is to write a letter," she advised. "You should write a bunch of doctors to sign it and then go public." At the height of the crisis, Scales and Worster drafted a letter and circulated it among their colleagues. Although the proposals were preliminary and never subjected to a rigorous review, the immediate response suggested they had touched a nerve.

April 11, 2020

Dear Dr. Forese and NYP Command Center,
We are doctors at NYP working on the front lines to care for patients and families during this epidemic. We are inspired daily by every employee who has risen to confront the countless challenges posed by this crisis and steadied by a leadership that is adaptable and responsive to the ever-changing needs

of our patients and staff. We are writing today because of our concern regarding the differential mortality rates in NYP hospitals and the impact that these differential rates have on access to life-sustaining care for communities most impacted by COVID-19. We hope to work together to address these disparities and provide equitable care for patients across the enterprise.

What we have seen:

- Mortality rates at Lower Manhattan Hospital (LMH) are more than twice as high than at the main Weill Cornell campus.
- We have undertaken an analysis (attached) that shows these higher mortality rates are not due to patients at LMH being sicker than those uptown. In fact, our data suggests the opposite, making the higher mortality rate at LMH even more concerning.
- Nursing ratios at LMH in critical care environments are often 4:1 or higher. We know the wealth of literature showing that rates of patient complications increase and patient survival decreases as nursing ratios increase.
- Governor Cuomo said in his daily press conference on April 11th, "All hospital beds are effectively ICU beds," alluding to the high level of acuity currently seen on medical floors. At LMH, the acuity on the medical floors is indeed high, yet nursing ratios are frequently at 5:1 or higher, especially at night.
- It is our understanding that other hospitals, such as NYP-Queens or the Allen Hospital, also have concerning nurse to patient ratios.
- We have observed similar issues with staffing of respiratory therapists, who are required constantly in emergency, medicine floor, and critical care settings at this time.

- We cannot say that nursing and respiratory staffing ratios are directly responsible for differences between the hospitals. We have seen firsthand, though, that these levels of staffing have resulted in unsafe situations for patients and delays in care.

What we believe:

- While all patients in New York City deserve the same excellent care, it is particularly incumbent upon us to ensure that all NYP patients receive the same standard of care, regardless of which NYP hospital they enter. We are united with NYP leadership in this mission.
- There should be efforts to minimize disparities in how care is provided and resources distributed across the enterprise.
- What hospital a patient goes to (or that EMS takes them to) should not be a choice that increases adverse outcomes, including mortality.
- We understand that difficult decisions about resource allocation must be made and mortality rates are likely to be unfortunately high; however, we believe decisions about distribution of resources should avoid perpetuating structural inequalities and biases that already exist in our healthcare system that lead to higher mortality rates for our minority, homeless, and other vulnerable patients.

Therefore, to ensure the goal of equitable care across NYP hospitals, we propose the following:

- Human resources should be distributed across the enterprise as equitably as possible. NYP should have a staff that floats with the ability to go where they are needed most on any given day.

- Specifically, critical care and medicine floor nursing ratios should be as equal as possible across the enterprise on a daily basis. If nurses cannot be mobilized, patients should be transferred immediately to reach the same degree of strain on critical care nursing.
- Similarly, respiratory therapists should be mobilized until patient ratios are equal across the enterprise.
- If the above cannot be accomplished, patients should be transferred from LMH and other satellite sites to WCMC until nurse:patient ratios are approximately equal across the enterprise.

We understand that efforts to increase nursing and respiratory therapist capacity are underway. We recognize the challenges in rapidly adapting to the ever-changing needs during a pandemic. However, we are concerned that, without immediate action, our most vulnerable patients will remain disproportionately at risk. We ask for action now to protect our patients and appreciate continued transparency in this process.

The letter was detailed—and perhaps too academic for the *Times* team, which ultimately referenced it as "a petition circulated by a group of doctors" at NewYork-Presbyterian's Lower Manhattan. But within Weill Cornell, it became a cri de coeur. In an extraordinary act of unity, twenty-five doctors signed the letter, compelled by what they believed was their moral duty to inform the public.

Almost immediately upon the letter's internal circulation, Scales received a call from the director of Lower Manhattan at the time. "He's like, 'Tell me more about this. What is this? I'm worried that people may get fired over this.' And he's like, 'Not even me . . . I'm not worried about me. But I'm worried about Art. And if Art [Evans] gets fired, we are fucked.' He's like, 'In the middle of the pandemic, that is not the person that we need to lose right now.' And he's like, 'Do you mind if I share this with Art?' And I'm sitting at my computer, and I get a Google request, *Art Evans would like to get access to this document. Monika Safford would like access to this document. Augustine Choi, dean of the medical school, wants access. Tony Hollenberg wants to get access to this document.*"

Scales grew concerned. Of course he had meant for the letter to be noticed by those at the top of the Weill Cornell hierarchy. But now it was actually happening. Scales and his cosigners had been told by one of the department chairs that the group could certainly go forward with the letter but also that "we are very concerned, based on our knowledge of Laura Forese, that it will not only not have the intended impact, it will actually have the opposite." Scales and the other doctors felt that if they got fired, that was one thing; given the demand, finding another job would be beyond easy. "But if NYP is going to take what we do," he said, worried, "and use that actively in some way that makes things harder for our patients and potentially hurts our patients, I mean, the ethics of that is clearly horrible. That is probably a bigger way to hurt us than to fire us." It wasn't clear what that sort of harmful action might be, but they all knew the political and media impact of further neglecting Lower Manhattan was insignificant compared to doing the same at Columbia or Cornell.

The downtown team had been having conference calls three times a week. In one of them, Art Evans brought up the letter.

"He's a man of few words because he doesn't need many," Scales explained. "He said, 'There's this letter and there is some discussion that it has been leaked to the *New York Times*. And there has been a concern that there might be repercussions.'" There were as many as eighty doctors on the call, all expecting Evans to switch into a sort of bullet-point admin-speak about why it was better to stay quiet and work within the well and wisely established practices and confines that helped make NewYork-Presbyterian great.

He did not do that.

Slowly, he told a story. As Scales recalled it, "There was a slave, whose name was Spartacus, and he led an uprising. And he described how the Romans came for Spartacus. He was about to stand up and say he was the leader when someone else stood up and said, 'I am Spartacus.' And another person stood up and said, 'I am Spartacus.' And then everyone stood up and said, 'I am Spartacus.' Then Art said, 'It is our job to fight for our patients. Gastroenterology doesn't do that. Cardiology doesn't do that. They are focused on the organs. We focus on the patients. If we don't do that, who will? And if NewYork-Presbyterian comes for us, then we will. If they come for me, if they come for anybody, then we are going to behave like they behaved for Spartacus.'"

Later, somebody made pins at Lower Manhattan that said I AM SPARTACUS. Scales still wears his. But Art Evans would have known something else about Spartacus, something that underscored the situation then and, perhaps, before and after. According to historical sources, Spartacus's rebellion ultimately failed. After the final battle, he was either killed or vanished, never to be heard from again, and six thousand of his followers were crucified. At the end of the day, no matter the size of the hearts of those who ran great hospitals and the virtuous convictions of those who worked on the other extreme, in America, the gelato floors would always come first.

28

Nathaniel Hupert had done what he could, and it wasn't enough. His numbers either hadn't been noticed or hadn't convinced those who needed convincing when they were noticed. But even if he had correctly identified the trend, one that undermined McKinsey, it turned out that the data he was using to run his models were more problematic than he had known. One of the primary data points he used when calculating the potential spread of COVID and its impact on resources was the prevalence of antibodies to infection in a population—the seroprevalence. On August 6, he wrote to an associate, confessing that "my modeling went wrong in looking forward for NYC in April." He had discovered the reason for this: For months, the New York City department of health had been posting numbers on seroprevalence—a measure of the amount of infection of a specific disease that shows up in group of people who are tested. But the numbers were not, in fact, representative samples of the areas—such as Manhattan and the Bronx—they were listed for. How could this have happened in New York City with all its scientific resources? The data posted on the health department's website did not present an accurate picture of how much COVID had been circulating in the neighborhoods; it simply reflected the infection rate among those who went to a health clinic and had their antibody levels tested. It turns out the health department simply did not have the personnel, supplies, or funding to give a scientific assessment of the COVID rates in the city's five boroughs, so it published the data it had on hand. When Hupert realized this, he stopped trying to make borough-specific forecasts altogether. Once he adjusted for this, it turned out that his modeling had been pretty accurate, but by then, the moment had passed.

In August, Pierre Saldinger, NYP Queens chief of surgery, stopped at a roadside farm stand. He wore, as always, a surgical mask. At the stand, he noticed that no one else was doing so. "I began to vibrate in ways that I had never experienced before." It was three months since the surge, but there was no reason to assume that meant COVID was over. Saldinger erupted: "Do you not understand the danger you are putting us all in?" The response was indifferent.

The discord he was feeling triggered an unpleasant April memory. In the ICU at Queens, Saldinger had witnessed the director of the unit trying to bring a patient back from the brink of death. The doctor spent six hours on his feet, restarting the patient's heart, removing fluid from his lungs, ordering meds, all with no sense of how much danger he was in. Late that night, in the parking lot, Saldinger saw the unit director sobbing uncontrollably in his car. In the weeks that followed, they did not mention it, but he noticed that from time to time, the director's hands would shake. "We will never come to terms with what happened in the hospital," Saldinger said. "The surgical residents who were deployed—it was like sending troops in to be slaughtered."

That same month, Jessica Forman, the physician assistant who had brilliantly helped run a pop-up ICU at Lawrence, found herself almost incapable of staying calm when patients from her practice called to ask routine Before Time questions, like "How much exercise should my husband get now that he has a stent?" She was a

PA; these were the sort of questions patients were supposed to ask. *But—really? With all of this? How about you just skip the gym for one damn day while I try to save this woman, that man, this child, that college student, this uncle, that high-school junior, this grandmother, that aunt, this junior-high student, this father, this mother, this grandfather, that granddaughter, this nephew . . . possible?*

It is well known that there is a three-to-six-month lag time after trauma before PTSD sets in, but in this case: "You could not use the term *PTSD*," JoAnn Difede said. "The trauma is ongoing. This is not post-traumatic stress disorder. This is ongoing stress disorder. It morphs and comes back again."

Difede, Weill Cornell's director of trauma studies, had reached out to Laura Forese in the first days of the surge. "We are going to be seeing a lot of distress," Difede told her. "The hospital needs to have a plan in place."

"We are already on it," Forese replied. Forese said she was open to feedback for her daily briefings. Difede homed in on the essence of how to stay in the present and not write scenarios for what might be coming. "And she said, 'We want to . . . make sure that you're giving people enough information, but also not projecting so far into the future and panicking everyone, right?' So it was, use language where you're understanding that this is evolving, you're understanding that this is scary, but you're optimistic about: 'We're still going to be here together, we're going to give you more information. We're going to be back tomorrow,' kind of thing. And it was that you want to give people enough so that they can keep going. . . . First what was in my head was *Uh-oh, what is this? What is that? That's not helpful to share?* And it was just great advice."

But the magnitude of what had happened inside the hospital in just seven weeks was incomprehensible to both Forese and Difede. "The hospital was essentially turned into a pulmonary ICU without the doctors and nursing staff who were trained to handle it," Forese said.

"Doctors are used to perhaps three or four patient deaths a month—this could be ten a day." For doctors and other health-care workers, those catastrophic numbers were only part of the cascading stressors—the isolation of families in lockdown, race disparities, income inequality, children out of school, jobs lost, and haphazard, conspiracy-driven federal leadership that threatened every societal norm. The hospital is a health-care system, but it is also a microcosm of class and caste that becomes its own country. By the summer of 2020, the anxiety set off by the spring surge rocketed through the hospital. "There was so much anger, it could burn the place down," Difede later said.

All things considered, Rahul Sharma, head of the Weill Cornell ED, may have had an easier time dealing with COVID than his brother in Queens did, but there was one case at Weill Cornell that had caused him profound anguish—and, in the end, profound joy.

Chris Belardi was an emergency medicine physician who worked part-time at Weill Cornell. In mid-March, he'd been treating COVID patients at an ED in Princeton, where he divided his time. One week after his exposure, Belardi felt so ill he thought he might need to be hospitalized. He was right. By the end of March, as the U.S. Naval Ship *Comfort* was heading to New York, Belardi awakened. He later recalled the moment. "I kicked my wife at 2 a.m. and told her to get the car."

His colleagues were astonished when they saw Belardi's condition at Weill Cornell's ED. The doctor who was known for his warmth and expertise—and for the fruit and honey he'd bring to work from his farm upstate—would be intubated days later. His condition deteriorated, and in a few weeks, he was close to death.

In April, Belardi's wife, Joyce, was home when Brad Hayward called. "Chris is not going to live through the day," he said, unaware it was her birthday. "Perhaps you should remember him the way he was." Hayward made clear she should come to the hospital if she wanted to be with him in his last hours, but he let her know how dire it was: Belardi's organs were failing so rapidly "it was not compatible with life."

And yet, incredibly, Belardi held on. Two months later, when he was off the ventilator, Joyce brought a cake to 5 South for his birthday and thought she saw his eyes open when she sang to him. Belardi would not remember. Drifting in a delusion, he drove his hospital bed through the halls and got stuck in a stairwell. As he began to return to reality, he was moved to another room where he could gaze across the East River to a power plant on Roosevelt Island and three chimneys that kept him anchored.

His memory would not return until late July. "The way cognitive function comes back, it's a very, very slow process," Belardi said. "It's not like you open your eyes and say 'Auntie Em! Auntie Em!'" Later, he recalled the faces of his nurses, but most of all, he remembered Brad Hayward. "We don't often see patients in his condition get better," said Hayward.

In early August, not long after Susie Bibi got the Zephyr Valve, New York City was beginning to come alive as well. Up and down York Avenue, construction crews were busily assembling what would become a constellation of outdoor dining sheds. Soon after, Belardi was transferred to the state-of-the-art rehabilitation center, the Baker Pavilion, where he spent the next three weeks. He was so weak, he could get out of his wheelchair only with the help of two people. Even sitting was utterly exhausting. "I was like a little kid in third grade," he said. "I couldn't wait to get out [of the chair] and get back in bed."

It was almost impossible to imagine that not long before he'd been standing for twelve-hour shifts. He'd been practicing emergency medicine for thirty-four years and had never grown tired of the noise, the alarms, the chaos. "I'd always have little butterflies in my stomach before I'd walk in," he said. But then he'd get an adrenaline rush and his senses became heightened—his eyes, his ears. "You have to think fast," Belardi said, "because you have to be ready to deal with anything."

At Weill Cornell, he would arrive to work at 3:30 p.m. Walking into the Sixty-Eighth Street entrance, he would look up at the Gothic arches in the entrance. "They are magnificent. They were always gleaming and lit up by the sun." Belardi would walk on the inlaid marble floors and "always think of the people who've gone before me." Weill Cornell was his cathedral.

About two weeks later, Belardi was able to walk 120 feet, a miracle. Then, on September 8, more than five months after being admitted to the hospital he'd known so well as a doctor and now knew as a patient, Belardi left Weill Cornell wearing his white doctor's coat, scrubs, and hospital badge to the loud cheers of dozens of his colleagues. He felt the sun on his face for the first time since March. It would take him another year to begin teaching again at Weill Cornell. "My gait is a little awkward, my speech is a little awkward, but my brain works just fine," he said. Belardi keeps the shoes he wore to his last shift in the ED under his bed, waiting for the day he can put them on again and return to work full-time.

At Columbia on September 15, the transplant surgeon Tomoaki Kato returned to action. That same day, a paranoid bureaucrat named Michael Caputo, the Trump spokesman at the Department of Health and Human Services, was unraveling after *Politico* broke the story that he and, it would later be reported, Ivanka Trump had taken it upon themselves to influence CDC COVID reports. A protégé of Trump crony and dirty trickster Roger Stone, Caputo was the kind of operative who had a tax lien posted against him and at one point took a job in Russia reportedly to help Vladimir Putin polish his reputation.

It was a different Russia that continued to linger in Tom Kato's mind, the Russia that defeated the Grande Armée back in 1812—

or a few months ago, give or take some hospital-bed delusions. As incoherent as those hallucinations were, though, what was going on in the outside world was almost equally surreal. Kato had returned intact from the Battle of Waterloo to find himself in a land of far greater madness: Caputo, the spokesman representing the cabinet department in charge of COVID-19, had accused the Centers for Disease Control of harboring "a resistance unit" that was plotting against the president, bolstering the COVID death toll in order to damage and, ultimately, destroy him, the *New York Times* reported. Caputo claimed that scientists "haven't gotten out of their sweatpants except for meetings at coffee shops" to plot "how they are going to attack Donald Trump next." And while this conspiratorial mindset (which had spread throughout the world of Trump supporters) easily connected disparate events and fictional occurrences, it considered links between, say, unmasking and higher infection rates complete and intentional fabrications. "There are scientists who work for this government who do not want America to get well," Caputo proclaimed, "not until after Joe Biden is president."

Kato had eased back to work doing a few robotic-surgery hernia repairs, assisted by his fellows. "I wanted to start with something like that because it wasn't so difficult. Three or four surgeons came to watch. It felt fantastic." Soon he was back to the big stuff, those twenty-hour life-and-death procedures that he still did better than anyone else. Kato hadn't fully recovered from his COVID ordeal—his shoulders were still sore—and in one of his first big surgeries (a patient with a rare liver cancer), a fatiguing second ten-hour procedure had been needed. Still, he'd known things would get easier, and they had. Veronica Roye encountered him in his first days back and noticed a change in his aura. "He has always been so respectful, but now he seems to realize how precious life is," she said. "He seems to be really taking a deep interest in all of us." Once, while Kato was making rounds, everyone in masks, he looked at Roye and said, as if merrily perplexed, "Is that really you?"

Kato's return, Roye observed, changed the molecules of the entire transplant group, perhaps one of the most competitive departments at Columbia. Now in the halls, there was a stirring, a nascent sense of welcome and concord, and Roye could feel the difference.

Even when Kato returned to life, it was far from guaranteed he could return to being a surgeon. The fact that he was alive and able to be in his world and do what he loved again pushed out the discordant thoughts. Mysteries remained, of course, among them how he got sick in the first place. "We were doing surgeries every day and nobody was checking for COVID," he said. "I thought that this was going to be New Rochelle only and not going to affect us. And just like that, there were suddenly hundreds of patients, and the information was so far behind. Trump lied? That is probably true, but then Governor Cuomo saying it was a surprise it came from Italy when the reports came from Wuhan, the animal-to-human transmission?" Like so many others, he had lacked the imagination to consider that he might not be able to control what happened. "I wasn't that worried about it. I thought, *There are problems—but we will protect ourselves.* My feeling was that it would finish in Wuhan."

The time Kato had spent trying to piece together what had happened in the months he had been lost to illness prompted him to think about the pivotal moments of what he thought of as his purest world— the operating room. He found himself thinking of that young, ambitious Japanese surgeon, newly arrived in America, without the language skills to get the subtleties across. The detachment of self-compassion thrust upon him when he was so weak that he could not move his hand or swallow a bite of applesauce made him understand in an entirely new way what his patients often endured—the loss of self, the need to pull into a place of reflection and acceptance and wonder that he was alive at all. He vowed that he would now share many of the techniques he had developed with his fellows while he had the chance.

In the weeks where his propulsive forward motion was on pause, so many scenes from his past ran through his mind. Arriving in Miami as a young surgeon, he had been berated by an attending who told him, "You are not capable. You are incompetent." Still, in the first surgery, seeing that things were going wrong, he had pushed the attending aside. The patient was coding and bleeding out on the table. It was a moment when the organ needed a hand massage and suction to get the bleeding to stop. As the surgeon was screaming, Kato stepped in and took control, possibly saving the patient's life. "The next morning, the surgeon said, 'This guy has good hands,' and that was the turning point of my fellowship life." After that, Kato recalled, "they all treated me so nicely."

As his time in Miami wound down, Kato prepared to go on to Paris for an extended fellowship, but he was convinced to stay. Shortly thereafter, he met with a patient in the hospital who had been turned down by Memorial Sloan Kettering. The surgeon came to Kato and asked if he would try a pancreas resection. "I was a young surgeon in Florida; no one knew me. It was really tough to challenge the Memorial Sloan Kettering opinion. And that surgery went really well and the doctor—an oncologist—sent all his patients to me that Sloan Kettering would not do." His workload became intense. "I made rounds from seven in the morning until late at night and did all my research and then took all of the organs out of one patient's body and put them all back in. And then I became very well known.

"If you go out of your algorithm, there is always a risk," Kato reflected. "But if you stay in your lane, you won't get in any trouble." But he had. How did he get COVID? "I will never know. . . . We were going into surgeries without any protection. . . . Soon after I found out that several patients I did surgeries on had COVID. If you are doing a transplant surgery on the body, the electrocauterization makes a smoke, and in the smoke was the virus . . . you can easily infect a lot of people in an operating room." Was that how it happened? "Doctors in other countries knew that the virus could be contained in the smoke. . . . We knew about asymptomatic spread. . . . But we never thought it would affect us."

The Gang of Four in China in the 1970s. Yeah, that sounded right.

Back in New York and trying to get massive citywide testing launched, Jay Varma had run smack into the gargoyle structure of a New York State Department of Health cowed by years of dealing with Andrew Cuomo. It reminded him of China in the early 1970s when a small group, presumably acting on behalf of Mao, horrifically devastated the country via violently inconsistent and suicidally reckless policies. Obviously, there were massive differences between the authoritarians who helped implement national madness like the Cultural Revolution and the clique running the DOH. But seeing a tiny group of powerful officials who he felt cared only about not angering their boss and as a result instituted disastrous policies made the comparison irresistible to Varma.

"There was a group that would just stamp orders 'Department of Health' as if it had been thought out," he said. "In fact, it was three people sitting around with some consultants from McKinsey." Varma had set up in Brooklyn at the city response center. "We were trying to figure out: How do we get out of this faster? The only way you could do that, basically, was to get the whole city tested." As he saw it, that meant getting the necessary working equipment and sufficient staff to test 100,000 people a day. "I said, 'We need to be interviewing everybody. We need to be contact-tracing them. We need to be quarantining them . . . This will be about a billion dollars.'"

Go ahead and do it, Varma remembers Mayor de Blasio saying. *I will find the money somewhere.*

Not so fast, said the city department of health. By now, de Blasio and the agency were weary partners locked in a bad divorce. After presenting his proposal at the DOH, Varma received a strange response: "We will start doing contact and case investigations when we get to less than three hundred cases a day." It was the complete opposite of common sense; you wanted to test when the numbers were going up. What was the point of testing if things were already moving in the right direction? But the DOH wasn't interested in hearing more from Varma. Separately, the city department of health told de Blasio, "We only have capacity to test those over seventy-five who are sick."

"That's the one percent of the population that does not need it," Varma said. "You just assume if they're sick, it's COVID." Once again, there seemed to be no appeal to common sense.

Not willing to give up, Varma hit up Columbia, Rockefeller, and Weill Cornell for assistance, but all of them took his proposals and retreated into institutional hierarchies and committees. However, in a seeming turn of fortune, de Blasio appointed a new city testing czar, Deputy Mayor Jeff Thamkittikasem, who was also the mayor's chief of operations. Circumventing DOH, Varma and Thamkittikasem went to Labcorp and Quest. "We were able to tell them, 'We will buy X amount for the next six months,'" Varma recalled. They found a lab in Texas that could deliver results via FedEx, but by this time, the delays in figuring all of this out pushed Varma to go to the city's lawyers with a request: Could they commandeer every lab in the city? Then, he reasoned, using public-interest law, he could staff up 24/7.

The health department, with deep technical knowledge about how this might work in New York, resisted. To Varma, this meant they still didn't think testing was important. Unwilling to surrender, he pulled in a former colleague from the CDC to help make the case. He also recruited another group to help: the NYC Economic Development Corporation, which might resist what Varma called the public health notion of "the anchor of certainty"—the already approved CDC protocols that had proved not effective, confirmed by cautious advisers from Columbia, Rockefeller, and Weill Cornell who did not want to veer out of the known. There was some debate about whether they needed to do PCR testing or the more speedy, though less reliable, antigen test, but overall, the EDC was supportive. Still, the DOH did not want to upset Cuomo, who saw de Blasio as a rival who needed to be put in his subordinate place, even if slapping him down went against public health sense.

All summer and into the fall, Varma and the mayor's team battled with the governor's office over testing as well as reopening indoor dining in the city. "We were opposed. All of the decisions were economic and political—not public health," Varma said. "There had been outbreaks in Michigan and Wisconsin. And we knew that a second wave was coming in the winter—that's what happens with respiratory viruses when everyone is indoors." They didn't want a complete reopening—quite the opposite. "We wanted a partial shutdown of the city. We knew that a shutdown of the city for some period of time would help us and that testing and tracing would help us." They wondered what would happen if New York shut down dining and fitness early? What would happen if you did it later? "We had four or five different proposals with modeling that showed we could save one thousand lives," Varma said. "My proposal was that we do a circuit breaker—just like in the UK." That would mean a relatively short but sharp lockdown to slow transmission. Varma thought the right period would be three weeks, specifically the week of Thanksgiving and the two weeks after. "Then the city opens and in come the vaccines after."

De Blasio agreed: "You are right. This is the right thing to do." The governor said absolutely not. As Varma saw it, Cuomo's rationale was that the only people who really wanted the lockdown were liberals—and they were already voting for him. That it was de Blasio supporting the idea no doubt made Cuomo all the more enthusiastic about rejecting it. But there were other more pressing concerns—the city was in dire financial shape. The office towers had emptied, and the restaurants and small businesses in Midtown and all over the city were struggling to survive.

The mayor had no choice. If he tried to do something the state hadn't agreed to, Cuomo's people would say, *We are going to take your testing away. We are going to control the vaccine supply. We are going to take away your PPE.* De Blasio could do nothing. Varma had to figure out another way to help save the city.

29

Is your name Susan Sofia Bibi?"

At Weill Cornell, weeks after she was off the ventilator at last, Susie Bibi, still confused, did not know who the tall man who kept coming to her room was or what he was looking for, but he kept peeping in and asking her that question. "Is he looking for me? Does he want to take me to the Baker Pavilion for rehab? That was all I was hoping for," she said.

She was afraid to answer him, fearing that he was going to take her away from the nurses she had grown attached to and put her on another floor—far from rehab and even farther from leaving the hospital.

I have instructions to take you to another room.

From somewhere in another dimension, Bibi heard his voice but could not process what he was saying. Another room? "I had a bad feeling that he was coming to take me to something called a step-down unit, which to me sounded like the dungeon," she recalled. "So then I go, 'Please, I'm not supposed to go. I'm not going anywhere. I'm staying here.' When he went into the hall, the nurses saw what he was doing and that he was coming to take me, and they said, 'You are not going anywhere.'" The man kept saying that he had instructions to move her. "And they said, 'No, this girl is staying here. We've been watching her since day one and she is not going anywhere.'

They all ganged up on him. Then they came to move me to a different room in the ICU. 'We are not letting you out of our sight. We are not letting you go.' And I got to stay."

It was October. She had been in 5 South for 164 days—five months. In addition to the ICU nurses, Bibi now had a private nurse.

"Do you know how many times this girl was on the brink of dying?" her night nurse, Denise Inacay, nicknamed "Mama Deb" said. Nurses would come into her room and ask, "Is she still alive?" "I think every nurse in that hospital had something to do with me," Bibi said. "They would come in and say, 'I took care of you three months ago.'" Bibi kept asking for Dr. Harvey, knowing that he was the doctor who had given her a second chance at life with his miracle valve, although she had no idea that she was the first COVID patient at Weill Cornell and perhaps in the entire country whose lungs had been saved by the Zephyr Valve. "I kept hearing his name: 'Dr. Harvey said so . . . Dr. Harvey this and that . . .' All I wanted to hear was that Dr. Harvey was on the floor because I felt like with him, I was going to make it . . . he protected a part of my lung that got attacked from the virus."

She was still in the ICU, but she was no longer intubated; she was trying desperately to get to rehab so she could attend her son's wedding on November 19. "He kept saying, 'Ma, you have to be there for me, just for a dance, the mother-son dance. I really want you doing that dance with me.' Now I am thinking: *This nutcase is asking me to do the mother-son dance!*"

Suffice it to say, dancing at a wedding in a few weeks seemed highly unlikely. Bibi still had a feeding tube that was making her extremely nauseated. "I was throwing up—from a feeding tube!" Her progress had been slow but sure, and the nurses' care made her feel safe. "Not long ago I was still going to the bathroom in the bed. It was disgusting. Nothing worked. I had a trach. . . . I was on so many half-paralytics. . . . I was loopy, which was good because if I had known how damaged I was, I may have gone into shock."

She knew the step-down facility had a much lower nurse-to-patient ratio and was grateful that each time an attending appeared at the door and suggested Bibi was ready to be moved out of the ICU, Mama Deb or Judith Cherry or Geraldine Epping would intercede. "We have brought her back from death four different times . . . and if you take her out of here, she will be right back. You cannot take her. She is not ready. She can't even take four steps without falling. She is our baby and you are not moving her," Judith Cherry said. "Everyone had died on my floor," Susie reflected, "but my nurses kept rooting for me." And now, until she went to rehab, they were keeping her for themselves.

Being transferred to the rehabilitation center on the fourteenth floor of the Baker Pavilion seemed an impossible goal. To get there, she had to display a minimum amount of mobility. Each morning, her walking teacher would appear on the floor and say, "How are you going to do three hours of rehab a day if you can't do one minute?" It was supposed to motivate her: *Let's just get that one minute down; anyone can do one minute. And then once you've done that . . .* It didn't work. "When she appeared at the door, I would panic like I was in high school," Bibi said. "I cried every time the girl said, 'I am the walking teacher.'"

Her days of intense workouts seemed so implausible that surely they were just a dream. "She showed me a countertop that was four feet from my bed. She said, 'If you can take the steps to get you there, then you can get to Baker.'" But Bibi could not move her legs off the bed. "I couldn't understand how they expected me to walk."

Bibi was given a special walker. "I would lean my body over like someone with MS. When I would take a step, I was so out of breath because my lungs were so bad. They were using the term *Bump it up* when they turned up the oxygen, so I used to keep telling them,

'Please bump it up,' because if they would turn it up, [it would] at least give me a little more power to get through a step. Until I could get through those steps, they would not let me go." Bibi tried her best, but even with the additional oxygen, she could not make it, and they wheeled her back to her bed.

But maybe if she kept trying. "I kept saying to the therapist, 'I have got to go to my son's wedding.'" And finally, she took the steps. "I was able to walk the steps and they accepted me."

At the Baker Pavilion, she was put through hours of exercise each day. When Bibi was in her medically induced coma, her hands were spread out flat. "I couldn't make a fist. My fingers had stopped being able to move. They had to try to massage the fingers. I couldn't hold a pen. They tried to say, 'Let's fold clothes.' They would say, 'We want you to be ready to go home.'" Once she could grip, the therapists brought out some weights. "It was one, two, or three pounds. I was used to doing fifteen pounds in each hand. So when I saw the weights, I said, 'Give me the three.' Well, my hand hit the floor when I held it. I couldn't lift it. Then I was down to one pound. *One pound*."

The damage was most severe on Bibi's right side. It was almost impossible for her to stand. "Really, I looked crippled." But she had come this far, and despite the weights and the walking and her posture, her "I have got to go to my son's wedding" became "I am going to my son's wedding." She had dropped to around eighty or ninety pounds and had to find something to wear, but she remembered that not that long before everything changed, she had bought a long black skirt and a black sweater with epaulets in a very small size.

And there you had it. One week earlier than expected, Bibi was able to leave the Baker Pavilion. "They said, 'Go home and enjoy the wedding.'"

Back in Brooklyn, she continued her rehab. She was taken to the wedding in an ambulance from Hatzalah. The medical attendants followed her as she walked down the aisle. "Everyone was crying.

It was a very small COVID wedding in Park Slope." Some of her nurses were there, trying to stay as hidden as possible, keeping her oxygen tank out of sight. They let in only a few people at a time in different shifts. "Walking down the aisle, I had my son in the middle, my husband on one side. I held on to my son." Her aides had told her that after she did the mother-son dance, they would take her home.

"It was like I was at my funeral, but I was alive," Bibi said. "They had all prayed for me. They never thought I was going to make it." Her nurses texted her that they couldn't believe she was at the wedding: *We are so happy*. And Susie Bibi was too.

30

How much compassion and silence did Kerry Kennedy Meltzer need to shut out the ranting tweets of her uncle? For years, Meltzer had tried to think of Robert F. Kennedy Jr. with as much forgiveness as possible, as did many who knew him. This school of thought usually went like this: The raging anti-vaxxer with piercing eyes and a jutting chin was once a nine-year-old who was swept into the grief and drama of America when his uncle's assassination turned the country inside out; the now shameless opportunist was once a needy fourteen-year-old whose father was gunned down during the 1968 California Democratic presidential primary. And he must be forgiven because he suffered under the mantle of being a Kennedy son in the America of 1968 as America imploded, the burden of living up to the cult of his father, Bobby Kennedy, needing to find endless social causes to convince himself that he was his father's equal. The family was a clan of fierce tribal loyalty, and there was no better example than Meltzer and Maeve taking their uncle's calls for years, putting up with his three-hour litany of garbage science with bullet-pointed lunacy, understanding how needy he was.

How had this uncle, who had gone to Harvard and the London School of Economics and law school at the University of Virginia, devolved into a carnival barker of crass conspiracies? Here was her uncle Bobby, again and again, his hand on his hip, plumping himself in front of any audience that would have him. His father had inspired audiences with his calls for justice and equality; the son tweeted outlandish conspiracy theories. He was the proud author of anti-science monographs and articles and wrote the preface of discredited scientist Judy Mikovits's book. (He would later publish a brick defaming Anthony Fauci.)

Meltzer still downplayed her identity as a Kennedy at Weill Cornell. But in November, Maeve's widower, David McKean, forwarded her something that enraged her. It turned out to be fake: a New Zealand right-wing political party was putting out an essay supposedly written by her uncle about the RNA vaccine, weeks away from distribution, but it was the spur that finally caused her to take action. Although her uncle hadn't written the essay, it was of a piece with her uncle's trajectory; he had spun off his axis, Meltzer believed. In America, nearly three thousand men, women, and children a day were dying. Everyone she worked with at Weill Cornell was exhausted and heartsick beyond measure. Here she was, surrounded by patients who most likely would have lived had they been given a vaccine, and there was her uncle in a mansion in Brentwood, married to the actress Cheryl Hines. Not to mention that he was also raking in a hundred and fifty dollars a head at his Malibu "health advocacy" fundraisers, daring his antagonists to take him on so he and his Children's Health Defense nonprofit—which had brought in around twenty million dollars in the past year—could take them to court as he had Facebook in August 2020, accusing the company of trying to "censor valid and truthful speech" and running a "smear campaign against plaintiff."

All through the summer and into the fall, Meltzer was in 5 South and the other ICUs, aware of the struggles to save countless COVID patients, many of whom died. Some of these deaths were marked by friends and family—she especially recalled the young New York City police detective who had not made it and whose colleagues lined the driveway to pay tribute to him—and others went unnoticed. She was in awe of the accomplishments of the hundreds of doctors and nurses and PAs who showed up and gave their all.

I'm going to write something, Meltzer decided. She talked it over with her husband, Max, her best editor. "I don't want a big media storm about this," she told him. "But he's putting people in real danger."

"What do you want to accomplish?" Max asked her.

"I want to try to save lives," she said.

"Do it," Max told her. "Now."

Meltzer called her mother and told her she wanted to take on her uncle on the *New York Times'* op-ed page.

"Go for it," Kathleen Kennedy Townsend told her.

31

So here it was, the miracle day for New York City, December 15, 2020. It was just past midnight, and on West Eighty-Fourth Street, Randy Subramany couldn't sleep. Jangly and overwrought, he checked his phone repeatedly, trying not to react to the previous text from his boss. *Still no word. Could be 5:30 a.m., or maybe 6:00?* He was confounded by what felt to him like absolute chaos. *How can no one at the hospital know when the first box of Pfizer vaccines will come? How can there be no tracking numbers or any sense if the box will come by UPS or FedEx?* This was what Lindsay and Brad and Craig and the other Craig and Steve and Anna and Xenia and Julia and Matt and the rest of NewYork-Presbyterian and New York and America and the world—this was what they had been waiting for, and it was harder to track than a pair of sneakers bought online with the promise of two-day delivery.

"Holy crap," Subramany said. He tried again to sleep. He hoped his voice was soft enough not to wake his wife, Elsa, but loud enough to command Alexa (two-day delivery): "Wake me at three forty-five a.m." He added another: "Alexa, wake me at four a.m."—just in case, and then set a pair of alarms on his Apple Watch and two more on Alexa.

Subramany's job—monitoring the arrival of hospital supplies at the loading dock at Weill Cornell—required precision, urgency, and, most of all, a surreal calm. Calm was, however, the last thing he felt in the early hours of December 15. The front page of the *New York Times* showed the thrilling image of yellow-shirted Pfizer workers packing vaccines in dry ice to keep them at 94 degrees below zero; three million doses fanned out across America, one thousand headed for his loading dock. "'Healing Is Coming': U.S. Vaccinations Begin," the *Times* banner proclaimed the next day.

But were they coming? Weather forecasts predicted snow, a nor'easter headed for New York. And then there was that lack of information, the sinking feeling that because nobody knew when the vaccines were coming, they might not be coming at all.

At 3:45 a.m. Subramany bolted awake, threw on his chinos, a gray sweater, and polished Cole Haan brogue boots, drank a double espresso, called an Uber, and headed downtown.

Subramany was the son of Indian immigrants from Guyana; his father had worked at a grocery store in the Bronx to support his family, his mother in the advertising department of Condé Nast. His dream was to be a doctor, but since medical school was out of reach, Subramany abandoned that goal and, at Columbia on scholarship, switched to public health and hospital administration. He had been determined to master the layers and complexities that could put him on a "leadership track" for the booming business of nonprofit hospitals—the labyrinth of strategic planning, branding, liability, reimbursements, state and federal regulations—and had nearly killed himself to be hired by the best hospital system in the city. He knew that if he could make it up the NewYork-Presbyterian ladder, he could earn a salary in the millions. And indeed, without meaning to, he had become one of those "challenge," not "problem" administrators that drove the Lindsay Liefs of the world crazy.

For days, the loading-dock team had prepared for this, but this was a delivery like none they'd experienced. Subramany had heard that a federal marshal would be riding with the driver, who was to be met by the hospital security team, itself under the command of a former FBI agent.

"What are you doing here so early?" Fernando Fernandez, down from the Bronx, was working security on the early shift as Subramany opened the darkened warehouse, looking for the lights. "Holy crap, it is cold," he said. All through the surge, Fernandez had worked as a transporter, taking the dead to the refrigerator truck being used as a morgue on the driveway at East Sixty-Eighth Street.

The vaccines were coming by UPS, they learned. At 5:30 a.m. a truck arrived, but it was from Cardinal Health; a disappointed Subramany was on the loading dock to meet it. An hour later, another truck pulled in, this one from D'Artagnan, a food supplier. There was still no definitive message about when to expect UPS.

Subramany alerted Fernandez and the entire security team to be on constant lookout for a brown truck. Unable to concentrate on anything other than the delivery, he paced on the tips of his toes near the freight elevator they would use to rush the frozen vaccines to the pharmacy department's subzero storage, and, a few hours later, into the arms of hundreds of emergency department and ICU team members.

The only good thing about the other trucks showing up was that it seemed to raise the odds that the next delivery would be the one they were waiting for, and on the loading dock, there was an increasing sense of joy. Four security men arrived, each in coat and tie, ready for a photo op, and the supply team's office manager, Mary Carrillo, appeared with a chocolate cake she had baked for the occasion. She set it down on the cart intended for the vaccine box, thought better of it, and carried it away.

No question, Subramany's title was impressive: director of supplies. Every catheter and pair of scrubs, every crate of surgical gauze, vat of saline solution, box of masks and N95s, ventilator, and bedpan was the responsibility of the 450-member supply team, which, in a year nearly all of those things had been in fatally short supply, meant that no matter how you put it, he was sick of the "challenges." As much as anyone at NewYork-Presbyterian, he wanted that UPS truck to pull up and unload its cargo.

32

That same morning, Ellen Corwin awakened on East End Avenue to see the nurse Sandra Lindsay on page 1 of the *New York Times*.

"There he goes again," Ellen Corwin told her husband. All that day, the picture of Lindsay getting the first vaccine in the city, posed in front of a sign from her hospital—Long Island Jewish Medical Center—populated news websites and trended on Twitter, and tomorrow it would be on front pages across America, just as Andrew Cuomo had planned.

Cuomo had told every hospital hoping to receive vaccines that it was mandatory they sign an NDA pledging total confidentiality. The NDA specified that the hospital could not let anyone beyond those involved know about that hospital's participation in the vaccination process, including all details of the arrival, storage, and distribution of the vaccine. The hospitals were told they could not reveal which campuses received vaccines, where they were stored, the brand name, or even the manufacturer's name, despite the fact that anyone who had read a newspaper, watched TV, or been online knew which company made the vaccine. In what the hospital chiefs had come to call "another Cuomo," the governor's office threatened to pull their licenses if they broke any of the rules.

By forcing their silence, Cuomo had allowed confidant Michael Dowling to monopolize the limelight. Long Island Jewish was part of the Northwell Health network and had basically been unknown outside of Long Island. Now all of America saw it as the vanguard in rescuing the nation from the coronavirus plague.

Steve Corwin was not concerned with publicity for NewYork-Presbyterian. What worried him was how to get shots into the arms of so many in the hospital who were vaccine-hesitant. As the UPS truck made its way to Weill Cornell (he hoped), he was home waiting for his first Zoom meeting of the day to review a PowerPoint on the hospital's strategy to attack vaccine-hesitancy in every community it served. Nevertheless, his mood was "lighter than [it] had been in months," Ellen Corwin said. He had already started to think about how NewYork-Presbyterian could work with the state to provide vaccine hubs, deploying hundreds of NewYork-Presbyterian volunteer vaccinators to reach the urban poor, some of whom would need to be convinced to get shots. He was formulating a plan to reach half of his own staff at the hospitals who refused to be vaccinated. The Zoom call was to discuss all of it—the forums they could run in the hospital, the way to reach out to the communities, and the possibility for transformation because the vaccines had at last arrived. What was that Churchill quote? "Now this is not the end. It is not even the beginning of the end. But it is, perhaps, the end of the beginning." Well, this felt like the beginning of the end. It was not.

33

Veronica Roye made it clear to Julia Iyasere and anyone else who asked her that she had no intention of taking the vaccine, and she had no problem letting everyone know why: The vaccine was coming from the Trump White House and that was all the reason she needed. She was not going to be experimented on.

"I am a Black woman," she explained. "I enter the room with that. And that is who I am." Roye knew it was a paradox that she was trying to push for Black organ transplants in the community, working against that race stereotype, while fearing the vaccine, but that fear was wired into her, even with her doctorate in nursing. She was not alone; in December, 40 percent of those working at the hospital said they would avoid the vaccine.

Roye still felt shut out. Although her medical director was Black, Roye viewed her as a possible impediment to her plans to push for more transplants for Black patients. She wondered if her outspoken personality was seen as a challenge to her boss's corporate patina. Had the attention she'd gotten from Corwin threatened those above her? It was true that she wasn't always the most delicate. "With all due respect, Veronica," her surgical director, who was European, said, "I'm a white immigrant, but I am protected in life under white privilege, and I need my Black colleagues to teach me." Roye found herself annoyed. *Here we go again,* she thought, *race and identity tribalism.* "With all due respect," she told him, "you are an educated man. You need statistics. You need facts. You know where to get them. I don't need to teach you what to do; you have to find that out on your own." Responding that way to someone who had seen her as a source of wisdom might be perceived as off-putting, but Roye had had enough.

Getting the shot would have been a challenge in the best of times for Roye, steeped in the long bad history of egregious medical experimentation on Black children, including in the not so recent past at Columbia. The episode, detailed in the distinguished anthropologist Harriet Washington's *Medical Apartheid,* had happened when Roye was still in elementary school, not that far from Columbia. Charisse Johnson, a mother living in Brooklyn's Bedford-Stuyvesant, was frightened that her young son would come to harm in her neighborhood filled with gang members and drug dealers. One day, a psychologist from Columbia rang her doorbell. She was offered $125 and a gift certificate for Toys "R" Us if her six-year-old son participated in a study. Harriet Washington later wrote that the study involved 126 children, most between six and ten, mostly Black or Dominican. The boys were given a drug—fenfluramine—and some had their other medications taken away, including those for chronic illnesses like asthma. The point of the experiment, congressional testimony would later reveal, was to measure serotonin levels, believed to indicate aggressive behavior. Johnson's older son was serving time in juvenile detention; the researchers were recruiting a cohort of boys who had siblings who had been arrested in an attempt to establish whether aggression was genetic. The night before the children were given the drug, all food was withheld, and the following morning, water was also withheld. The children were given the drug, and blood was drawn every hour. Almost immediately, many of the boys complained of severe headaches and light-headedness—no one had ever prescribed fenfluramine for children under twelve. The drug, one component in the diet drug Fen-Phen, could trigger massive anxiety attacks and a racing heartbeat. As part of the Columbia study, Charisse Johnson and the other parents were subjected to hours of invasive questions, and for years after the study, her son was stricken with headaches and anxiety attacks. Eventually, Johnson sued Columbia, and the outrage around the case, delayed for years in court, was part of an extended shameful history that lurked in the background for Roye and the few Black nurses who were getting their doctorates at Columbia. When the vaccine was announced and set to arrive on December 14, all of this inchoate and actual fear took over. She told her son, "I am not so sure. This is way too fast."

That Monday morning, Roye was home and looked up to see Sandra Lindsay, who was Black, getting the first injection from another Black nurse. Roye immediately viewed the whole thing as craven manipulation. "That made me so angry. I was so angry with the two Black women that were on that TV screen. I was like, 'Don't let them use you as guinea pigs. Why are you doing this? We don't know what this vaccine will do.'"

For Thanksgiving, Roye's fourteen-year-old son was with his father and grandmother. They all got COVID. "When he came home, I took him to be tested—positive. But his father felt okay, so he delayed [getting tested]. A few days later he developed shortness of breath. He had been in the hospital a decade earlier and had been put in a medically induced coma, so he was the last person ever who wanted to go to a hospital. But the shortness of breath turned into coughing and he began to cough up blood. They called EMS immediately, but he died in the ambulance."

All of this had been happening as Roye, working from home, was helping her son with remote school and trying to avoid the madness of Trump challenging the election results in every state. "It was all just too fast, and then to see this Black woman to be the first person to get it. It's like, 'Oh no, we are not just going to throw this here to Black people.'"

Upstairs in the Greenberg Pavilion, Kerry Kennedy Meltzer had her laptop open in her cubicle and was ready to hit Send on an op-ed she had drafted for the *New York Times,* later published under the head-line "Vaccines Are Safe, No Matter What Robert Kennedy Jr. Says." In it she wrote, "As a doctor, and as a member of the Kennedy family, I feel I must use whatever small platform I have to state a few things unequivocally. I love my uncle Bobby. I admire him for many reasons, chief among them his decades-long fight for a cleaner environment. But when it comes to vaccines, he is wrong." Perhaps this too would be part of a vaccination effort, in this case against the disinformation campaign waged by her uncle and his allies.

Matt McCarthy, in his office at the Weill Cornell Starr Pavil-ion, was elated. He could not have imagined a year earlier, as the first reports of the mystery virus were coming in from China, that mRNA vaccines could be on their way to the hospitals this quickly, but here they were, and he knew it was the game changer. In the early-morning silence, he said out loud: "Immunomodulator . . . immunomodulator." No, that wasn't right. He was rehearsing, over and over again, the words he would use when pitching a clinical trial of a possible COVID cure, only the second trial he had ever run on his own. Today he had to deal with the last-minute requests for the sign-offs from the internal review board at the FDA that would allow his trial for three different medications in combination to go forward. *Immunomodulator* was a mouthful, to be sure, but if this thing worked, a lot of people would get very used to saying it.

At 8:08 a.m. on the loading dock at Weill Cornell, Fernando

Fernandez shouted at a New York sanitation truck blocking the driveway, "Hey, move the truck! Move the truck!" He looked down the street, saw a brown UPS truck parked at the curb, and stared hard at the driver, who wore a leopard-print mask. Then he turned to Subramany and flashed a big thumbs-up. Within moments, the driver wheeled a cart with a single white box onto the loading ramp where the security and pharmacy team waited, snapping pictures on their iPhones, fighting tears. The UPS driver was so rattled he could type with only one finger. He told Fernando, "I thought the FBI was following me."

The e-mail came in the late morning for Lindsay Lief, Brad Hayward, Judith Cherry, Ben-Gary Harvey, and everyone on the 5 South team: "Starting at 1 pm, you are group A for COVID-19 vaccine."

The line of critical-care teams snaked past the murals in the converted children's wing lounge toward the elevators. There, Anna Podolanczuk, who had left the Allen where she had spent April coping with the scores of dying patients while breastfeeding her four-month-old, now had joined 5 South. The news had reached her that Lizzy Oelsner's lab had received a grant, and that Brad Hayward and his partner, Anthony, had reunited and would soon move back in together. Inside the vaccination site, attendings were taking pictures of themselves on their iPhones and immediately tweeting them out— the hospital had requested it. At Lawrence Hospital, Xenia Frisby was the first person in line to get her vaccine. Her daughter Ariadne was coming for Christmas—she now taught school in Queens.

It would take another ten days for Veronica Roye to change her mind and get a shot. Just after Christmas, her son said, "Mom, is Grandma going to be able to come see us?" "You know she can't because of COVID," Roye said. "How long is this going to go on?"

he asked. "I want to see my family." With his father gone, Roye suddenly realized, *I have to rethink this.*

Rethink things she did. Within a month, along with Julia Iyasere, Roye was appearing in churches and hospital town-hall meetings, trying to convince the vaccine-hesitant to get their shots. She had seen so much death and she knew she would see more of it in the months to come. Her concerns had not evaporated, and she remained alert to the racism that had marked more medical science than the Osler-types might admit. But some risks were worth taking. Some risks had to be taken.

Epilogue

Steve Corwin waited until the first surge was over to read Albert Camus's classic *The Plague,* an allegory set in Oran, Algeria's second-largest city. The narrator, the town's doctor, Bernard Rieux, navigates the uncharted horrors of the unexpected arrival of disease—the German takeover of France is the implicit pathogen—as his patients develop symptoms that have not been seen since the Middle Ages. Raymond Rambert, a journalist who comes to town to write about the Arabs and Berbers of Algeria, is trapped in quarantine; he is unable to convince Rieux to give him a medical pass that would allow him to depart, so he has to accept that this will be his new life.

But Corwin did not interpret *The Plague* as a wartime allegory. He saw a very literal reality in Rieux's coping with death and disease, and he identified with the doctor's larger vision. When Corwin reads, he marks passages he wants to return to by folding the corners of those pages. In his copy, he marked this section: "At that moment, I realized we're all carrying the plague, and we have to be as careful as possible not to breathe it upon each other." Most of his marks came in the final section, when Dr. Rieux senses that the plague might be lifting but notes that "the townsfolk were in no hurry to jubilate. . . . All agreed that the amenities of the past couldn't be restored at once; destruction is an easier, speedier process than reconstruction."

In late December 2020, Corwin made a decision: New York-Presbyterian Hospital would serve as a command center for the distribution of vaccines in Upper Manhattan. The hospital spent millions, deploying 1,100 of its own staff to revamp the Columbia armory in just five days. The election of 2020 was still being contested by Trump. On January 6, 2021, Corwin was in his office on a Zoom call with a trustee when he got a text from Ellen: *Are you watching this?* He turned on the news and watched as the Capitol was invaded by the swarm of rioters who desecrated everything he held sacred. Fear had seized him in March 2020 as waves of people came into the hospital with the coronavirus, but here was a pathogen with an even more pernicious variant.

"How could anyone not be changed?" Steve Corwin asked me in March 2022. The two of us were talking about the aftermath of the surge and all the hospital had gone through in the previous two years. The city was watching a new variant, BA.2, and bracing for a coming influx of cases. Only 65 percent of Americans had been vaccinated, and now a second booster shot was recommended. New Yorkers once again scrambled for protection. The new mayor, Eric Adams, had lifted mask mandates in public schools, and most restaurants had stopped checking for proof of vaccination. Vladimir Putin's assault on Ukraine had replaced the 24/7 coverage of COVID-19 on cable news channels. Congress warred over a fifteen-billion-dollar COVID aid package for testing and prevention, paralyzing badly needed programs around the country.

In August 2021, Andrew Cuomo, after a yearlong investigation of his cover-up of the number of people who had died of COVID and an ongoing series of harassment allegations, resigned in disgrace. The team members who had guided the state through the surge of 2020, including modeling expert and SUNY chancellor Jim Malatras, were gone as well.

Corwin and I had met for the first time in the summer of 2020 at his gray shingled farmhouse in eastern Long Island. Meeting in person was still unusual that August, but it was the first of many conversations to come. I wanted to understand what it would take to report what had happened behind the scenes during the surge of March and April at NewYork-Presbyterian. The project was daunting. How do you tell the story of a health system with forty-seven thousand employees? With so many hospital regulations, how could people speak truthfully without fearing they'd lose their jobs?

The Corwins live in a woodsy area not far from a historic Black neighborhood on the outskirts of Sag Harbor. That summer of 2020, Corwin, still very protective of his health, used his time in the country to read. Hypervigilant COVID protocols gripped the summer colony. Lines formed outside the gourmet grocery stores in East Hampton. Still fearing the droplet spread of COVID, people scrubbed their groceries at their doors or left them on tables in garages for twenty-four hours to avoid any possible risk of contamination. Guests brought individual snacks and their own utensils to friends' houses; the rich bought elaborate firepits for outdoor dinners. There was panic about using bathrooms or walking into a close friend's kitchen. Children were kept from engaging too closely with other children on playgrounds. Mothers brought Lysol wipes to clean slides and swings. When people got together, they pushed their chairs six feet apart and asked, "Is this far enough?"

By the summer of 2020, COVID had moved from New York City and overwhelmed the hospitals throughout America. The idea of meeting in person and not on Zoom seemed to carry possible danger, even when everyone wore a mask. At that first visit, I tried not to react when Corwin pulled his lawn chair even farther than six feet away from me. Although many were going to restaurants with outdoor seating, Corwin and his wife, Ellen, would not eat out for many more months.

We sat by Corwin's pool with a good ten feet between us. Corwin, a slim man with a walrus mustache, was determined to understand how the great academic medical centers of New York City had been caught so unprepared by the tsunami of the pandemic, but more, he was compelled to get an uncensored look at how it felt to be on the front lines, a reporter's account that might be read in the future. He was still trying to understand the cascade of horrors that had hit the hospital five months earlier. On March 3, when he learned that Lawrence Hospital in elegant Bronxville, of all places, had its first COVID patient, a lawyer from New Rochelle, he said, "I remember thinking to myself, *This is really going to be bad.* It was community spread. This guy had no travel history." The hospital was going to have to buckle up. "In the first days, the doctors in their meetings, there was a willful suspension of disbelief. You could not believe this was happening. And then: This is going to be a disaster. People had to get used to wearing masks. You wear them with patients who have to be contact-isolated. Suddenly, we had to assume that everyone who came into the hospital could be infected. Now what do you do? Do you call meetings to say everyone should be wearing masks? We were following the advice of the CDC and the infectious-disease people. We were in evolution."

Corwin realized they were completely unprepared, and he had to decide what to do next. "There were questions—how widespread would it be? How do we treat the patients in the hospital? What do we have to do? And that took us about seven to ten days to say,

'This is an all-hands-on-deck emergency.' We were inching up to it. And then Laura came into my office and said, 'We have to cancel all surgeries. We are not going to make it through unless we cancel all the surgeries.'"

He continued. "The panic was that we were going to run out of beds, that the ICU units would have no space. And there were some people who pushed back on it. The doctors were reacting. They were saying, 'Do we really have to do this?' And we were saying, 'Yes, we really have to do this.'"

By the end of March, the hospital had twenty-five hundred cases and not enough ICU doctors and nurses. That August afternoon in the garden, Corwin shared details of what he had seen: the two thousand doctors who volunteered to fan out through the hospital to help; how employees looked when they saw morgue trucks being loaded. In late March, Hilary Shaw, who was responsible for converting the gleaming York Avenue Koch Center into more ICU space, walked down the hall and passed a transporter bringing out another one of the dead; she broke down sobbing. Rick Evans, the head of patient services, had trained to be a priest and had been in a small New Jersey hospital during 9/11 when the bodies were ferried across the water. In late March, he was drawn to the hospital's driveway, where he stood not far from the morgue truck, his head bowed in silent tribute, as body after body of the dead arrived. All of these stories Corwin had heard and was trying to process. He was also grappling with the fact that no city, state, or federal government had displayed anything resembling leadership.

In August 2020, parts of New York felt like war zones. For weeks, the boutiques of Madison Avenue had been boarded up in response to the massive protests over the George Floyd killing. Earlier in the summer, a *New York Times* banner headline provided a ray of hope: "New York City Expected to Open June 8th." New York City Council Speaker Corey Johnson and the city council were hammering the mayor, at the request of the restaurant industry, to allow restaurants to open outdoor sheds in the city. In front of Trump Tower, on Fifth Avenue, BLACK LIVES MATTER was painted on the street. The murder of George Floyd had rocked both the city and Corwin. "I thought we would somehow be in a more advanced place by this moment in our history," he said. "And we are not."

He had spent the past weeks rereading Harriet Washington's monumental history of racial injustice detailed in *Medical Apartheid,* and he was shaken by the brutal medical experiments and outrageous disparities in the health-care system that had gone on for one hundred fifty years. As the surge ended, Corwin got the first call from Bridgewater Associates chairman Ray Dalio. "I want to donate fifty million to the hospital," Dalio said. Corwin pressed him to support one of the hospital's most urgent missions: addressing the health-care disparities in the country. Dalio agreed without hesitation. The same issues troubled him too.

Our first meeting, that summer day in 2020, was scheduled to last an hour, but it stretched long into the afternoon. When it began to rain, we moved into his dusty garden shed, rakes and hoses propped against the walls. It was an interesting venue for an interview with the head of a nine-billion-dollar organization, but it somehow fit the moment more than any grand drawing room could. To be invited inside someone's home was still out of the question then. What struck me that day about Corwin was his authentic desire to understand what had happened to his hospital in the broadest historical terms. He never failed to tell me the facts as he recalled them, and when others I needed to speak to signaled their fear of losing their jobs, Corwin picked up the phone and said, "You have my word. No one is going to penalize you for telling the truth."

He and the other New York hospital heads had spent months attempting to navigate a political atmosphere that did not resemble anything they had ever experienced. Hospital systems were denied masks, ventilators, and essential supplies if Cuomo's office had not approved the requests. This was in every way a dramatic departure from standard procedure, which authorized the state department of health to make these determinations. (By the summer of 2020, twenty-eight department of health officials had resigned.) Threats came in the middle of the night; once, in a screaming phone call from the governor's vaccine czar, Larry Schwartz, Corwin was told that NewYork-Presbyterian would be shut down if vaccines weren't delivered exactly as the state mandated.

Corwin had decided that the public's need to know what had happened inside New York City's premier hospital system took precedence over the rigid corporate communications policies. That conversation was the first of many over the next eighteen months.

It was unusual, to say the least, for the chairman of a health-care system to allow a reporter to explore his own hospital. I would later learn that there had been intense discussions of the wisdom of allowing me any access at all. Several people close to Corwin advised him against it, saying that any and all moments could be "taken out of context." That phrase, often used, always confounded me. Whose context? I had yet to learn about the gag order that was imposed by the hospital to silence doctors like Matt McCarthy, who had tried to alert the public about the testing chaos, and that had enraged many on the front lines and in the deans' offices of the medical schools. It was hard for some I met to understand why I was allowed access; it seemed a reversal of hospital policy. Doctors are notoriously the worst patients, and here was NewYork-Presbyterian's CEO essentially saying, *Put us on the table and examine us.* That Corwin was encouraging the hospital's doctors and nurses and techs and corporate heads to share their experiences with me seemed suspicious at first. Was this some sort of Trojan horse maneuver? What was I not seeing? We spent the next weeks negotiating the terms.

Once they were agreed to, I got to work. Chief strategy officer Emme Deland, the daughter of *New York Times* reporter and author Phyllis Levin, was tasked with finding a way to thread that needle: allowing me to get honest reports of events without censorship but also preventing the violation of the strict privacy laws of HIPAA. It was just one of many projects she was handling for the hospital throughout 2020 and 2021. She was also spearheading the launch of the Dalio Center for Health Justice. Corwin, Deland, and Julia Iyasere had made it their mission to bring real change to the shocking disparities of health care, searching out data to understand who was most affected and determine how that could be remedied. Deland, a master diplomat, has a rare gift of making whomever she is speaking with believe she is his or her personal advocate. The new center for health justice became her passion project. For the next year, she and Iyasere approached the issue on multiple fronts, accumulating data to understand the immensity of the problem in the city and nation.

That project became twinned with another one of her projects: effectively using the hospital when the vaccinations began. Despite complicated budget matters, by late December 2020, the hospital had arranged with the state's health department to become a center of vaccine distribution. It would spend another ten million dollars to help get New York vaccinated. "At first, there were plans for four different locations," Deland said. She was grappling with enormous issues in an atmosphere of total frenzy. "How do you dispense enough vaccines for everyone in the city?"

Iyasere and Deland were also struggling to address the cultural issues that made so many hospital workers hesitant to take the vaccine. Iyasere scheduled town hall after town hall; Veronica Roye spoke to Brooklyn church groups, as did Nicole Golden and Monica Nelson-Kone. "No one had thought about the last mile," Deland said. "That was clear."

In October 2021, Steve Corwin was startled to learn that Lindsay Lief was threatening to quit. Corwin had said repeatedly that Lief and the other ICU directors had "saved the hospital" by engineering ingenious ways to turn all of Weill Cornell into an enormous ICU, finding doctors and nurses, and putting in fifteen-hour days to cover the hundreds of patients who filled every room in the hospital. Lief had worked the phones, scrambled for ventilators, and accepted every patient she could. She was stunned to see patients from Queens coming in on ventilators with not enough sedation. The toll was great; on wellness surveys that were presented to the staff regularly, Lief's team scored the lowest in the hospital. As that report circulated and psychiatrists reached out to offer help, Lief's staff learned that they were being stripped of their small hallway and conference room—the only place the team had to gather. It was impossible for them to understand how hospital management had come to this decision. Finally, Lindsay had hit her limit.

On October 6, I came to the hospital to hear Lindsay speak to a group of pulmonary fellows about understanding the enormous corporate demands that are part of a nonprofit hospital's need to make money. Lief seemed strained in the meeting, as if she wanted to say something but held it back. As we walked to her office, she said, "I have had it. That room you were just in? This hallway? They are going to try to move in an entire group of physician assistants for a new transplant wing. We will have no place to meet except our cubicles." Lief had heard about, but not been sent directly, a bland e-mail from upper management—"three levels down from Corwin"—that said something to the effect of *We are looking to relocate medicine PAs from the fourth floor. We know you use a conference room on the fifth floor for meetings, and we would like to find a different location for those meetings.* The 5 South outpatient clinics were blocks away in a dingy space that was inconvenient, and now this?

Trying to stop this new order, Lief was working her way through the medical schools' hierarchy, bringing in the chair of medicine Tony Hollenberg and Fernando Martinez, but she was getting nowhere. I had never seen her so angry. *My team gave everything to this hospital and this is what we get? What was so outrageous about it was that it was sent to one person—the nursing director!* she texted me later that day. *And with the assumption that the decision was done. That they would just take that room without involving stakeholders or even knowing what is happening there.* At the hospital, I'd asked if she had tried to alert Corwin to the situation. Lief looked startled, as if straying from the carefully drawn lines of silos and hierarchies was out of the question. Mired in the world of medical-school committees, Lief was depleted and infuriated. When Corwin learned of the situation, he said, "Lindsay Lief is not quitting." And he began making calls. Within a day, the situation was resolved. But what would have happened, I later wondered, if the CEO had not intervened? Four weeks later, Lief was promoted to associate professor of clinical medicine, a job she had been hoping to get for months.

Earlier in 2021, the arrival of the vaccines in New York was thought to be, as Corwin repeated, quoting Churchill, "the beginning of the end." New York City was starting to come alive again. The financier Steven Cohen, owner of the New York Mets, announced at a press conference with the mayor that Citi Field, the Mets stadium, would be a vaccination mega-site for Queens residents. At the press conference, de Blasio played it for a win, donning his Mets cap. It was, however, a very fragile time. Nine hundred COVID patients were still being treated at NewYork-Presbyterian, and Deland and Iyasere were coordinating vaccine-education Zoom talks at churches throughout Washington Heights, Brooklyn, and Queens. Deland was visiting possible vaccine sites for the hospital, including the Brooklyn Botanic Garden and the Park Avenue Armory. The early sites set up by the state had massive technology issues. Anyone trying to schedule an appointment in the first weeks spent hours paging through calendar dates only to see *unavailable, unavailable, unavailable.*

On January 6, as Americans looked at their phones to see hundreds of rioters smashing windows at the U.S. Capitol and bashing police with American flags, as senators and the vice president were rushed to safety, the *New York Times'* Brian M. Rosenthal broke a story on page 1: Northwell Health, the state's largest health-care system, run by Cuomo's confidant Michael Dowling, the governor's liaison to all the state hospitals, had sued thousands of patients during COVID for unpaid medical bills dating from before the pandemic. (State-run hospitals had been ordered to stop suing patients over unpaid medical bills, and almost all of the major private hospitals had voluntarily suspended their claims.) A New York City hotel employee named Carlos Castillo who had been working only two days a week during the pandemic was suddenly faced with interest charges and a debt of over four thousand dollars from a seizure he was treated for at

Long Island Jewish Medical Center—the chosen site for New York City's first vaccine. Case after case of heartless dunning policies perpetrated by Dowling's hospital empire was cited by the *Times*. A Northwell executive defended the hospital's policies, saying that even with the stimulus money, the seven-billion-dollar hospital chain had lost three hundred million dollars that year. The next day, Dowling suspended the lawsuits, but the scandal reeked of an insider's presumption of privilege.

On January 14, NewYork-Presbyterian opened its vaccine site at the Columbia armory in partnership with the state. (By May, the site had vaccinated more than 200,000 New Yorkers.) Cuomo came to the opening and posed with Laureen Hill and Laura Forese, who had directed the five-day conversion of the Columbia track-and-field hub, an astonishing feat of hospital management.

The three-story redbrick neoclassical fortress across from Columbia–Presbyterian's laboratories was used by the army through the pandemic of 1918, the Depression, and two world wars. The city took it over and used it for a homeless shelter until the Armory Foundation renovated it and turned it into perhaps the most prestigious running track in the world. Now that armory, at a cost to the hospital of six hundred thousand dollars a month, would enter history again. In just five days, Forese and Peter Fleischut had turned the two-hundred-meter, six-lane, banked Mondo track into a seventy-two-station center with the capacity to vaccinate thirteen thousand people a day. NewYork-Presbyterian staff—heart surgeons, pharmacy students, residents, internists—volunteered to give the shots, as did Veronica Roye, who a few weeks earlier had finally decided to get her own COVID shot.

In the first weeks of January, I spent hours at the armory watching construction crews pulling up the yellow tape marking the lanes under a jumbotron and hammering together booths for the coming vaccinations. A sound system piped in Gloria Gaynor's anthem "I Will Survive" for the few runners weaving around the crews. I have never loved my city more. By now, the early-morning drive up Broadway to 168th Street and Fort Washington Avenue had become familiar, a tonic to what was happening in Washington, DC. As I drove through the campus of Columbia University, still shut down for COVID, I saw fruit sellers were back at the subway stop at 116th Street. The sidewalks were crowded with New Yorkers getting on with it; everyone wore a mask. At 155th Street, where Washington Heights started, the Dominicans played salsa music from their shops, the soundtrack that had replaced the seven p.m. banging of the pots and pans.

In the third week of January, I met Laura Forese to watch her make a training film for the NewYork-Presbyterian board. As always, she had arrived at 6:00 a.m., perfectly turned out, to give orders to her team. I found her with her laptop in front of her in a converted café, her team around her, as people who had made it through the website crashes waited in long lines for shots. Her concern that day was how to get the vaccines to the minority communities, and I heard her arranging for vans to pick up area residents and bring them to the armory. Was she worried, I asked, about the exhaustion and burnout that was now widely prevalent in the hospital? "Well, you hear that everywhere, but somehow in the titrate of time, this doesn't happen. . . . Our mission is too important." It was hard not to disagree. The mission to save as many lives as possible had driven everyone at the hospitals and against impossible odds.

On January 20, Joe Biden was inaugurated. Forese decided to turn the jumbotron on and show everyone what was happening on the

Capitol steps. On the immense screen, the forty-sixth president, the oldest in the nation's history, said, "Democracy has prevailed." A woman near me in the line broke down and sobbed. Cheers went through the armory, and vaccines were paused. The poet Amanda Gorman, in a coat the color of a buttercup, gave a moving and uplifting reading. "We are unfinished," she said. That day, Priya, a volunteer pharmacist, told me, "I was in the children's hospital across the street when COVID hit. We were making meds. We were working all night long. I had coworkers who were getting COVID. They asked us if we could fill in. You would go home to get a few hours of sleep and come right back. Everyone was keeping their distance. Two weeks ago, they sent an e-mail around: 'They are looking for immunizers. We are trying to open one hundred stations to immunize New Yorkers.'" And here was Priya, along with a thousand of her colleagues, registering, guiding the crowds, putting shots in arms, and monitoring the rest-and-recovery period every day.

Since the pandemic started, almost one in five health-care workers in America have left their jobs. As I write in mid-March 2022, it is two years since Laura Forese shut down surgery at NewYork-Presbyterian and the city finally closed. Almost one million Americans are now dead from the disease, a statistic that places the country after many others in terms of success of fighting COVID-19. The catastrophic policies of the Trump administration, many believe, led to a cascade of horrific consequences. (But Trump did fund the massive ten-billion-dollar vaccine initiative Operation Warp Speed, which he is rarely credited for.) The *Atlantic*'s Ed Yong cited a Morning Consult survey that found that 31 percent of current health-care workers have considered leaving their employers, while the American Association of Critical-Care Nurses found that 66 percent of nurses were considering leaving their professions as well. Around America, many hospital systems burdened by the loss of revenue during COVID furloughed their staffs. Others made so much money from the government's reimbursements that they are buying smaller hospitals to merge into mega–hospital corporations. Fifteen percent of NewYork-Presbyterian's staff have left, many disheartened by what they consider inadequate compensation for what they went through during COVID. The hospital, with a seven-hundred-million-dollar deficit for 2020, did not furlough anyone, but it paused hiring in many departments and made an attempt to bring the medical schools under the control of the corporate board. That move, intended to streamline conflicting budget demands, set off a fusillade of anger at Columbia among department chairpersons and soon imploded. You could feel the shortages of nurses in every department, and many of the nurses complained that they were unable to provide adequate patient care.

In October 2021, Veronica Roye announced she was leaving Columbia. Although she had earned her doctorate, a new position that had been created for her did not come with pay comparable to that given at other hospitals. "They think at Columbia that you will work for less because of the prestige," she said. Traveling nurses could now command eight thousand dollars a week. She reasoned that if her Black Liver Transplant program was stalled for lack of funding, why should she stay? Her father wasn't well and she wanted to take care of him. On several occasions, Julia Iyasere had reached out to her, emphasizing that there was a job waiting for her at NewYork-Presbyterian whenever she wanted to return. In Bronxville, Xenia Frisby, who had first felt the anger of the nurses who were forced into quarantine, was now working, what felt like to her, two jobs at the hospital. Once, rounding on a patient floor, she ran into the president of the hospital, Michael Fosina, who in the opening days of the pandemic had begun to collect every edition of the *New York Post*, knowing that he was about to witness history. "Xenia, I was looking for you. I'm resigning from the hospital. I'm leaving at the end of the year," he told her. Xenia recalled being incredulous at first. Fosina, who had been so sturdy and present during the catastrophe, was burned out? Then she realized that he looked weary and that she did as well. She thought, *These years have changed us.* At Weill Cornell, COO Kate Heilpern also resigned. Someone close to her had long-haul COVID and she too wanted more time with her family. Nathaniel Hupert took a sabbatical year at Oxford to work with Lisa White, the mathematics professor and modeler who ran the prestigious global CoMo Consortium and who had worked closely with him through the pandemic. The mission of the CoMo Consortium, which consulted with governments around the world, and Hupert's mission as well, was in part the ethics of modeling, training international modelers to consider every aspect of diversity in all of their data sets. Hupert was at Oxford when Cuomo resigned. Months later, the New York State Department of Health finally issued a lengthy report citing 4,100 deaths that had been camouflaged in nursing homes. Hupert continued to believe, as did many others, that the large modeling numbers Cuomo had relied on through the New York surge meant that "no expense could be spared to increase and preserve hospital bed capacity," which led directly (it seems) to getting people out of the hospital as quickly as possible, which (it seems) led to a lot of elder-care-facility residents being sent back to those facilities before they were known to be noninfectious.

From time to time, Hupert wondered if he had been wrong to send a lengthy e-mail to Steve Corwin in the first week of May 2020. It had been prompted by an interview Corwin gave to David Gelles of the *New York Times* in which he admitted, "Our assumptions around pandemic preparation were flawed." The interview was remarkable for its candor, but Hupert could not stop himself from sending Corwin a two-page e-mail detailing all the times he had tried to warn the hospital teams, as well as commending him for his leadership in pulling the hospital through. He wondered later if it had been career suicide, but he said, "I have just never deferred to those kinds of pressures." He believed, as he had once learned from a Harvard roommate, that a true leader follows the inspiration of Herodotus, the ancient Greek historian and geographer known as "the father of history" who penned every scholar's Rosetta stone *Histories,* a massive investigation of the Greco-Persian wars. "I felt, however odd it sounds, that Corwin, like Herodotus, needed to know as much information as he could get about what went wrong." Corwin never replied to the e-mail, and Hupert never forwarded it to anyone else at the hospital. Recently, I asked Corwin if he remembered getting it; he said he did not, but at that moment in the surge, he was getting hundreds and hundreds of urgent e-mails a day. "Nathaniel may have been a voice in the wilderness," he said.

But maybe he did read it, as the modeling expert Jim Malatras had in Albany, and just took action instead. Not long after Hupert sent the letter, Corwin implemented the first outreach to establish a center to prevent the same catastrophe from happening again. Corwin wanted to understand, for real this time, everything that Hupert and several others had been counseling all along. "What is the early-warning system? How do we know what's happening in other parts of the world and how do you let us know about what they are tracking? What are the connections we need for our own infectious-disease people working within the hospital? What are the connections to the supply chain?" After months of discussion with the epidemiologist Jay Varma and public health experts, Corwin brought in Varma, in the fall of 2021, to launch the Cornell Center for Pandemic Prevention and Response. More than three million dollars was committed to the first stage of the start-up. Corwin was determined to prevent New York-Presbyterian from being unprepared for a pandemic ever again. He clearly understood that the methods of Herodotus were the way to go.

For Corwin, the hospital was a theater; the dramas and the feuds often set the players at odds with one another, but all had found their way to saving lives. The true glory of the hospital was also the glory of the city and what it offered to those who wanted to achieve. Here, they all knew that the doctor performing tasks she had never done before might have grown up in a barrio or found her way to science because of how she was encouraged by the father, a garage mechanic. And however much strain they felt, what united them was what had brought them to medicine in the first place. They wanted to save lives. For all their feuds and endless *"We knew it first and why didn't you listen to me, why didn't you home in on that study from Japan or how South Korea prepared,"* et cetera, this was, as Laura Forese said at the armory, "a once-in-a-century event." And for that, no one can ever be prepared. Yes, there were warning signs, and many died needlessly, but there were also many who, despite expectations, lived.

After Thanksgiving, there was another event no one had prepared for: the arrival of the most infectious COVID variant so far, Omicron. At the time, the hospital was badly understaffed. In all of our months of conversations, Corwin had never used the word *disheartened* to describe his reaction as he struggled to lead the hospital through the pandemic. "We've been through hell and back," he said. "But what we also did collectively was extraordinary." And now they were being hit again. Omicron shut down the city; theater performances, weddings, and public events were canceled, and the hospitals feared another tsunami. "The third wave. You've got sagging morale and we have a ton of cases and huge staffing issues." The hospital was "recruiting like crazy, but it takes weeks to get people in place." Matt McCarthy texted me: *You know I choose my words carefully with covid. The next 4–6 weeks are going to be a disaster.* Then another: *I'm not worried about the influx of patients; I'm worried about symptomatic health care workers. We're already tight on nurses and it wouldn't take much to disturb the delicate equilibrium.*

———————

A few days before Christmas, most gatherings were canceled; on the Drudge Report, a skull took over the homepage with the banner "USA Fears a Million Cases a Day." Hupert canceled his visit to his family in New York. The campus of Cornell University in Ithaca, 97 percent vaccinated, shut down due to the outbreak. Hupert and his group were immediately asked to help with modeling by the British government, but not by his own hospital. On December 19, he texted: *I think it will be a short spike of cases, with new places in New York having clinical effect (my smart colleagues are looking at S Africa and seeing lots of protection from prior infection).* By the end of the next week, Hupert's prediction would be echoed by many others, and indeed, the spike dropped sharply by the end of January 2022.

In the autumn of 2020, shortly before Susie Bibi's son's wedding, a box arrived for the MICU staff. It contained dozens of red heart enamel pins with tiny zirconia and the words WE LOVE THE MICU. Reuben Bibi was so grateful for his wife's miracle recovery after four months on a ventilator that he had his jewelers make hundreds more pins for future members of the MICU team as well. Back in Brooklyn, Susie was slowly getting better and being treated five times a week for several hours with acupuncture to stimulate her immune system. In January 2022, she was able to travel to Aruba for ten days.

Imagine it is the fall of 1970, the first semester at Cornell Medical School. The quick young future doctors in their navy blazers, striped ties, and Weejuns are rushing to their first lecture. The word has circulated through Cornell that the renowned tropical-disease expert Benjamin Kean extracted a thirty-foot-long tapeworm from a patient and he is planning on bringing it to his opening lecture on tropical diseases. Everyone wants a seat but some are late and have to stand.

Kean, as always, is wearing a navy velvet smoking jacket, and he's brought his Westie in on a leash. No one can mesmerize the incoming class like Kean, the infectious-disease detective who saved the paralyzed larynx of Gertrude Lawrence at the opening of *The King and I* and who has among his patients lyricist Oscar Hammerstein II and, later, the shah of Iran. His genius at uncovering parasites—he identified the pathogen that causes turista, the classic traveler's digestive malady—made his lectures so crowded that Tony Fauci and Henry Murray, the latter eventually the hospital's tropical-disease chairman, sometimes fought over seats. Both will later say that it was their hours with Ben Kean that sent them down the chutes to their futures—Fauci to the National Institutes of Health, Murray to Cornell.

When COVID comes to New York, Murray finds himself strangely exhilarated by its mysteries; he is up again at 5:00 a.m. and racing toward East Sixty-Eighth Street as he did when he first encountered his generation's north star, Ben Kean. Scores of Murray's colleagues will find joy and gratitude in the armory, putting shots in New Yorkers' arms.

Among the lines Corwin encountered when reading Camus was this: "What's true of all the evils in the world is true of plague as well. It helps men to rise above themselves." The staff of New York-Presbyterian was evidence of such ascension. And despite the terrible losses, they won. They helped save New York. They helped save the world. And the vaccines worked, no matter what the anti-vaxxers said. Today, almost nobody who is vaccinated is at risk of dying from COVID.

Someday, Lindsay Lief will tell her boys more about what she did on 5 South during the desperate hours. But not just yet.

Acknowledgments

On the last day of August 2020, I was told to come to the Weill Cornell security office on the Upper East Side to get my hospital badge. It was the day I officially began the reporting of this book. After my picture was taken and the necessary forms filled out, I was given a red-bordered badge that allowed me to enter NewYork-Presbyterian buildings to conduct any and all interviews that had been scheduled. Weill Cornell holds a special place in my heart: My daughter, Casey, was born there when it was still called New York Hospital.

The badge is now framed and on my desk. After decades of reporting around the world, I consider meeting more than two hundred of NewYork-Presbyterian's staff, many of whom generously entrusted me with their life stories and their struggles, the most extraordinary experience of my career. My deepest gratitude to all who gave me the gift of their candor and, by doing so, underscored again for me what makes New York City the beacon of hope for the world. The story of those who struggled to save the lives of the city is, most of all, a story of New York and its astonishing inhabitants.

Many I interviewed had not yet shared with their families the terrors of what they experienced in the first wave of the pandemic of 2020. Many were initially hesitant to talk about what they had seen and felt as the hospital became overwhelmed by the desperately ill. Many chose to speak anonymously. I am immensely grateful for everyone's contribution.

Writing this book would not have been possible without the leap of faith and the conviction that a reporter must be able to gather uncensored, unrestricted information held by NewYork-Presbyterian's CEO Steve Corwin and chief strategy officer Emme Deland. The only limit they imposed on me was the strictest adherence to the laws that ensure the privacy of NewYork-Presbyterian's patients. I was not allowed to roam freely through the patient floors of the hospitals. All patients I interviewed had to sign a HIPAA release. Immense thank-yous to all at NewYork-Presbyterian and especially to Zee Feliz, who tirelessly reached out to scores of the people I wanted to interview who had agreed to reveal their identities.

There are many to thank at Flatiron; its publishing team's enthusiasm for *The Desperate Hours* has been overwhelming. Editorial director Zachary Wagman has been remarkable, unflagging in his loyalty and a fount of so many helpful suggestions. Through the frenzy of the last months of the editorial process, he eased impossible deadlines and always made himself available to talk about how to make the book better. A special thank-you to Bob Miller, Flatiron's president, and its publisher, Megan Lynch, who have also been magnificent in their support. And a special thanks to Elisa Rivlin and Diana Frost for their thoughtful legal wizardry. The brilliance of cover designer Keith Hayes, a publishing legend, in coming up with cover after cover to try to capture the essence of New York in crisis has been a wonder. Thank you as well to associate publisher Malati Chavali and to publicity director Marlena Bittner and marketing whiz Nancy Trypuc for so many ingenious ideas. Production editor Frances Sayers has been uncommonly patient as we pushed toward deadline, as have managing editor Emily Walters and interior designer Donna Noetzel, who magically produced a New York skyline for the title page. Thank you to Maxine Charles, who has made my life so much easier with her tech translations and editorial assistance.

It has been my supreme luck to have gone through the sound waves of life with my longtime friend and agent, Amanda Urban. We did it again during the traumatic months of the spring of 2020, as New York became the epicenter of COVID-19, speaking frequently about our fears and what we were experiencing during lockdown. Through those months, I stayed in the city and was often out filling notebooks. It was Binky, as her many friends call her, who suggested I try to capture the story of the New York pandemic through the lens of its greatest hospital system. Thank you, Binky, for insisting I take on what became a reporting experience of a lifetime. ICM's masterful lawyer John DeLaney spent weeks in the summer of 2020 making sure I could be guaranteed the freedom from the hospital's strict regulations to make my reporting possible. And thank you as well to ICM's Ron Bernstein for years of friendship and creativity.

I have had remarkable editorial and research assistance in the last months of this project. My unending thanks to Bea Hogan and Ben Kalin, whose indefatigable fact-checking under deadline urgencies has been stunning. Their long experience at the *Atlantic* and at *Vanity Fair* has enriched every page of this book. With her soft touch with sources and eye for telling details, and last-minute reporting, Hogan brought new meaning to the practice of fact-checking at its most nuanced and valuable. Observing Kalin's herculean dawn hours of texting suggestions at 3:00 a.m. has been an unforgettable experience. And a special thank-you to Michelle Memran, a longtime colleague at *Vanity Fair,* for putting aside her own work as a documentary maker to help organize the early stages of the fact-checking process. Ted Panken and Emma Warshow have been enormously helpful organizing my interviews and research. I am deeply indebted to Geoff Shandler for his spectacular editorial guidance. The son of a doctor, Shandler's reverence for those who dedicate themselves to saving lives has deepened every aspect of my reporting. And to Dr. Tracy Roe for her exquisite line edits ensuring that I would not miss any medical context.

Of all of those who trusted me to tell their stories, I am most indebted to the patients and their families who so generously shared their histories. Many who lost loved ones were still grieving. The pain and difficulty of speaking of those you've lost is unimaginable. The word *gratitude* seems woefully inadequate to convey my enduring thanks.

And to my closest friends, who have guided me through every book and most especially this one, there are not enough thank-yous to express my appreciation for our years of sharing our lives. You have read early drafts and enhanced every line with your impressions and suggestions. The joy of your friendship has buoyed me through the most difficult times as well as the happiest. And as always, none of this would have been possible without the love and support of my beloved Casey, and Josh, James, and Kat, and Adam and Ali. But most of all, it is Ernie whose love and indefatigable spirit has made this book a reality.

Author's Note

In writing this book, I was granted extraordinary access and cooperation by NewYork-Presbyterian. This was accompanied however by their unwavering insistence that this be accomplished with the strictest respect for patient privacy. All those with whom I spoke understood that I was a reporter working on a book. All patients whose personal health information appears on these pages signed HIPAA consent forms. Where doctors were describing their experiences with patients who had not signed such forms, identifying details were altered so as to convey the reality of their experiences but not the specifics of any particular patient.

Sources

All interviews cited below were conducted from August 2020 through April 2022. Any quotations or thoughts attributed to characters in the text were taken from their interviews with the author.

Chapter 1

Interviews: Lindsay Lief, Fernando Martinez, Anthony Sabatino, Steven Corwin, Bradley Hayward, Ellen Corwin, Jessica Barnes, Laureen Hill, Stephen Rush, Mary D'Alton, Roy Gulick, Elizabeth Oelsner, and Emme Deland. Articles and books: "New York Coronavirus Map and Case Count," *New York Times*, April 1, 2020; Ben Casselman and Patricia Cohen, "Unrivaled Job Losses Accelerate Across U.S.," *New York Times*, April 3, 2020; David Oshinsky, *Bellevue* (New York: Doubleday, 2016); Matt McCarthy, *Superbugs* (New York: Penguin Random House, 2019); Bill Bryson, *The Body* (New York: Doubleday, 2019); Julia Marsh et al., "Bedlam," *New York Post*, March 28, 2020; "Treated Like Trash," *New York Post*, March 26, 2020; "Fever Pitch," *New York Post*, March 30, 2020; Chris Taylor, "Tragedy, Loss and Hope: Overseeing New York Hospitals During a Pandemic," *Reuters*, February 11, 2021. Hospital information provided by Emme Deland.

Chapter 2

Interviews: Kang Liu, Xenia Frisby, Nathaniel Hupert, Donald G. McNeil Jr., Peter Fleischut, Steven Corwin, Daniel Barchi, Allen Schwartz, Lindsay Lief, Bradley Hayward, Tomoaki Kato, Jean Emond, Carlton McGregor, and Veronica Roye. Articles and books: William Grimes, "Ralph M.

Steinman, a Nobel Recipient for Research on Immunology, Dies at 68,"
New York Times, October 3, 2011; Sui-Lee Wee and Donald G. McNeil Jr.,
"From Jan. 2020: China Identifies New Virus Causing Pneumonialike
Illness," *New York Times,* January 8, 2020; Ethan Hauser, "The Headlines
After Dark," *New York Times,* January 3, 2021; Alice Su, "A Doctor Was Ar-
rested for Warning China About the Coronavirus. Then He Died of It," *Los
Angeles Times,* February 6, 2020; "Li Wenliang: Coronavirus Kills Chinese
Whistleblower Doctor," BBC News, February 7, 2020; personal text mes-
sages provided by Kang Liu; Austin Ramzy, "Japan Executes Cult Leader
Behind 1995 Sarin Gas Subway Attack," *New York Times,* July 5, 2018;
Carl Zimmer, "A Man From Whom Viruses Can't Hide," *New York Times,*
November 22, 2010; Michael Lewis, *The Premonition* (New York: W. W.
Norton, 2021); Steven Brill, "Bitter Pill: Why Medical Bills Are Killing
Us," *Time,* April 3, 2013; Damien Cave, "Doctors Remove 6 Organs, Then
Cut Out a Tumor," *New York Times,* March 25, 2008; Denise Grady, "'I Had
Never Faced the Reality of Death': A Surgeon Becomes a Patient," *New
York Times,* June 3, 2021; Denise Grady, "Cancer Patient Dies Despite Dar-
ing Surgery," *New York Times,* April 26, 2010; Denise Grady, "Beating the
Odds, and a Storm, to Get a Transplant," *New York Times,* November 26,
2012; Ryan D'Agostino, "Dr. Tomoaki Kato," *Esquire,* November 22, 2010;
"Amazing Things: Heather McNamara," NewYork-Presbyterian, Feb-
ruary 17, 2017; "Inside the Successful Separation Surgery of Conjoined
Twins," NewYork-Presbyterian, November 23, 2021; Siddhartha Mukher-
jee, "What the Coronavirus Crisis Reveals About American Medicine,"
New Yorker, April 27, 2020.

Chapter 3

Interviews: Elizabeth Oelsner, Lindsay Lief, Nathaniel Hupert, David
Berlin, Matt McCarthy, Jaclyn Mucaria, Melissa Harvey, Arthur Evans,
Jeffrey Shaman, Joan Steitz, Liz Squadron, Dina Lichtman, Jake Lief,
and Judith Cherry. Articles and books: Melissa Chan, "This Doctor
Was Vilified After Contracting Ebola. Now He Sees History Repeat-
ing Itself with Coronavirus," *Time,* February 4, 2020; David Oshinsky,
Bellevue (New York: Doubleday, 2016); "Reasons to Love New York
2014," *New York,* December 14, 2014; text message provided by

Nathaniel Hupert; "Naming the Coronavirus Disease (COVID-19) and the Virus That Causes It," World Health Organization, February 11, 2020; Scott Gottlieb, *Uncontrolled Spread* (New York: HarperCollins, 2021); Elian Peltier, "France Confirms First Death in Europe from Coronavirus," *New York Times,* February 15, 2020; Eric Lipton et al., "He Could Have Seen What Was Coming: Behind Trump's Failure on the Virus," *New York Times,* April 11, 2020; Matt McCarthy, *Odd Man Out* (New York: Viking Adult, 2009); Matt McCarthy, *The Real Doctor Will See You Shortly* (New York: Crown, 2015); Matt McCarthy, *Superbugs* (New York: Avery, 2019); Matt McCarthy, "Where Does Ebola Hide?" *Slate,* October 22, 2014; "Part 1: Coronavirus Strikes Iran," United States Institute of Peace, February 24, 2020; "Coronavirus: First Brazil Death 'Earlier than Thought,'" BBC News, May 12, 2020; Caroline Chen et al., "Internal Emails Show How Chaos at the CDC Slowed the Early Response to Coronavirus," ProPublica, March 26, 2020; Jeneen Interlandi, "Inside the C.D.C.'s Pandemic 'Weather Service,'" *New York Times,* November 22, 2021.

Chapter 4

Interviews: Laura Forese, Yoko Furuya, Jay Varma, Michael Fosina, Nathaniel Hupert, Matt McCarthy, Mark Apfelbaum, Andrew Amaranto, Arthur Evans, Julia Iyasere, Elizabeth Oelsner, Anna Podolanczuk, Sarah Maslin Nir, Xenia Frisby, Laurie Ann Walsh, Gregg Rosner, Laureen Hill, Emme Deland, Kate Heilpern, Anthony Hollenberg, and Rudy Tassy. Additional sources: Data retrieved from an e-mail provided by Nathaniel Hupert; e-mails provided by Yoko Furuya; Emily Smith, "Let's Drown Her Before We Burn Her!!! Johnny Rotten," *New York Post,* February 27, 2020; Julia Marsh, et al., "Long Is. Eyes 83 Possible Victims," *New York Post,* February 27, 2020; Leah Asmelash, "The Surgeon General Wants Americans to Stop Buying Face Masks," CNN, March 2, 2020; Kevin Sheehan and Tamar Lapin, "Panicked New York Shoppers Stock Up at Costco amid Coronavirus Fears," *New York Post,* March 1, 2020; Scott Gottlieb, *Uncontrolled Spread* (New York: HarperCollins, 2021); Charles Ornstein, "New York Hospital to Pay $2.2 Million Over Unauthorized Filming of 2 Patients," *New York Times,* April 21, 2016; Charles Ornstein, "Dying in the E.R., and on TV Without His Family's Consent," *New York*

Times, January 2, 2015; e-mail provided by Matt McCarthy; Bill de Blasio, "We Can Officially Confirm Some More Information on the Second Coronavirus Case Connected to New York City," Twitter, March 3, 2020; Matt McCarthy, *The Real Doctor Will See You Shortly* (New York: Crown, 2015); D. T. Max, "The Public-Shaming Pandemic," *New Yorker,* September 21, 2020; Tom Elliott, "NYC 'Health Commissioner' Oxiris Barbot on Feb. 7th: 'We're Telling New Yorkers, Go About Your Lives,'" Twitter, March 27, 2020; "Transcript: Mayor de Blasio, Governor Cuomo Hold Media Availability on the First Confirmed Case of Coronavirus in NYS," NYC.gov, March 2, 2020; Amanda Woods, "NYC Doctor Has to 'Plead' with Health Department to Test for Coronavirus," *New York Post,* March 2, 2020; Denise Grady, "Chicago Woman Is Second Patient in U.S. with Wuhan Coronavirus," *New York Times,* January 24, 2020; Roni Caryn Rabin, "Lost Sense of Smell May Be Peculiar Clue to Coronavirus Infection," *New York Times,* March 22, 2020; Nolan Hicks and Aaron Feis, "Ex-NYC Health Chief Speaks Out on de Blasio's Handling of Pandemic in New Doc," *New York Post,* March 8, 2021; Joseph Goldstein and Sharon Otterman, "What New York Got Wrong About the Pandemic, and What It Got Right," *New York Times,* March 17, 2022; Lawrence Wright, *The Plague Year* (New York: Alfred A. Knopf, 2021).

Chapter 5

Interviews: Xenia Frisby, Susie Bibi, Reuben Bibi, Manish Sharma, Rahul Sharma, Suzanne Pugh, Roy Gulick, Lindsay Lief, Arthur Evans, Nathaniel Hupert, Tomoaki Kato, Bradley Hayward, Kirana Gudi, Amir Jaffer, Laura Forese, Karen Bacon, Elizabeth Oelsner, Kapil Rajwani, Fernando Martinez, Felix Khusid, Mark Apfelbaum, Jessica Forman, Judith Cherry, Kevin Roth, Daniel Brodie, Anthony Pucillo, and Laureen Hill. Additional sources: Michael S. Schmidt, "Obstruction Inquiry Shows Trump's Struggle to Keep Grip on Russia Investigation," *New York Times,* January 4, 2018; e-mail from Lindsay Lief; information from Nathaniel Hupert's modeling; James Mauro, *Twilight at the World of Tomorrow* (New York: Ballantine, 2010).

Chapter 6

Interviews: Rosanne Raso, Noah Ginsberg, Kerry Kennedy Meltzer, Jay Varma, Kirana Gudi, Laureen Hill, Stephen Rush, Suzanne Pugh, Manish Sharma, Steven Corwin, Bradley Hayward, Nathaniel Hupert, Ken Raske, Daniel Barchi, Laura Forese, Steven Miller, Angela Mills, Corey Feist, Craig Smith, Arthur Evans, Matt McCarthy, Ellen Corwin, Harjot Singh, Lindsay Lief, and Tomoaki Kato. Articles: Kevin Freking, "Trump Defends His Rhetoric in 1st TV Town Hall of 2020," Associated Press, March 5, 2020; "Rush Limbaugh: Coronavirus Is Like the Common Cold, and 'All of This Panic Is Just Not Warranted,'" Media Matters for America, March 11, 2020; Nina Strochlic and Riley D. Champine, "How They Flattened the Curve During the 1918 Spanish Flu Pandemic," *National Geographic*, March 27, 2020; Ian MacDougall, "How McKinsey Is Making $100 Million (and Counting) Advising on the Government's Bumbling Coronavirus Response," ProPublica, July 15, 2020; Maureen O'Connor, "A Doctor's Emergency," *Vanity Fair*, September 17, 2020.

Chapter 7

Interviews: Joe Ienuso, Rosanne Raso, Lindsay Lief, Steven Corwin, Ellen Corwin, Rahul Sharma, Peter Fleischut, Rob Glaser, and Anand Joshi. References: Daniel Goldman, *Morning Joe*, March 16, 2020; Steven Corwin, *Morning Joe*, March 17, 2020; Daniel Goldman, "Let's Be Very Clear: Unless You Have Pneumonia and Traveled to One of 5 High-Risk Countries Recently, You Can NOT Get a #COVID19 Test in New York City," Twitter, March 11, 2020; "Read Democratic Counsel Daniel Goldman's Opening Statement," *Politico*, December 9, 2019; "Keeping Emergency Hospital Staff Safe in Face of Coronavirus," *Morning Joe*, MSNBC, March 17, 2020; Lawrence Wright, *The Plague Year* (New York: Alfred A. Knopf, 2021); Jordan Fabian, "Trump Outbid Governors on Coronavirus Supplies After Telling Them to Buy Their Own," *Fortune*, March 19, 2020; Vincent Barone, "New England Patriots Deliver 300K Face Masks to NYC for Coronavirus Relief," *New York Post*, April 3, 2020; Usha Lee McFarling, "A 'Duty to Warn': An ER Doctor, Shaped by War and Hardship, Chronicles the Searing Realities of Covid-19," *STAT*, December 21, 2020.

Chapter 8

Interviews: Nathaniel Hupert, Ken Raske, Michael Schmidt, Denise Walcott, Xenia Frisby, Fernando Martinez, Jeanne Rizzuto, Lindsay Lief,

Bradley Hayward, Beth Hochman, Karen Bacon, Kerry Kennedy Meltzer, Cleavon Gilman, Rosanne Raso, Jessica Forman, Anthony Pucillo, Mark Apfelbaum, Tomoaki Kato, Gregg Rosner, Anna Podolanczuk, Julia Iyasere, Elizabeth Oelsner, Hadi Halazun, Amir Jaffer, Suzanne Pugh, Manisha Sharma, Jaclyn Mucaria, Angela Mills, Michael Breslin, Marjorie Walcott, Peter Liou, Craig Smith, Anand Joshi, and Jim Malatras. Articles and books: Kerry Kennedy Meltzer, "I'm Treating Too Many Young People for the Coronavirus," *Atlantic*, March 26, 2020; Julia Marsh and Vincent Barone, "Coronavirus Killing People in New York City at Rate of One Every 17 Minutes," *New York Post*, March 27, 2020; Andrew Cuomo, *American Crisis* (New York: Crown, 2020); Matt Richtel, "Frightened Doctors Face Off with Hospitals over Rules on Protective Gear," *New York Times*, March 31, 2020; Usha Lee McFarling, "A 'Duty to Warn': An ER Doctor, Shaped by War and Hardship, Chronicles the Searing Realities of Covid-19," *Stat*, December 21, 2020; Hadi Halazun, "'Today, We Are All Covid-19 Doctors,'" *New York Times*, April 6, 2020; Lawrence Wright, *The Plague Year* (New York: Alfred A. Knopf, 2021).

Chapter 9

Interviews: Jessica Forman, Kenneth Prager, Xenia Frisby, Anthony Pucillo, Joseph Fins, Rick Evans, Bradley Hayward, Kapil Rajwani, Lindsay Lief, Steven Corwin, and Felix Khusid. Other sources: Matt McCarthy, *Superbugs* (New York: Penguin Random House, 2019); Ashwaq Masoodi, "Make Your Wishes Known," *Atlantic*, July 10, 2013; Brendan J. Lyons, "Top Health Officials Told to Prioritize COVID Testing for Cuomo's Relatives," *Times-Union*, March 24, 2021.

Chapter 10

Interviews: Bradley Hayward, Anthony Hollenberg, Fernando Martinez, Lindsay Lief, and Jake Lief. Any quotations or thoughts attributed to characters in the text are taken from interviews with the author. Articles: Julia Marsh et al., "Bedlam," *New York Post*, March 28, 2020; Bernadette Hogan and Aaron Feis, "New York's Coronavirus Death Toll Jumps 100 in Just One Day to 385," *New York Post*, March 26, 2020; "Governor Andrew

Cuomo New York Coronavirus Press Conference Transcript," Rev.com, March 26, 2020.

Chapter 11

Interviews: Steven Corwin and Laura Forese. Other sources: "Top Earners at NewYork-Presbyterian Hospital and NYP Brooklyn Methodist Hospital," *Crain's Health Plus Extra,* June 23, 2020; Carl Campanile, "NYC Paramedic Says Coronavirus Patients Brought to Hospitals 'to Die,'" *New York Post,* March 31, 2020; "Transcript: Mayor de Blasio Appears Live on NBC's *The Today Show,*" NYC.gov, March 31, 2020.

Chapter 12

Interviews: Kerry Kennedy Meltzer and Stephanie Pagliuca. Articles: Peter Hermann, "Kennedy Mother and Son, Swept Away in Chesapeake Bay, Are Mourned by Family," *Washington Post,* April 4, 2020; Kathleen Kennedy Townsend et al., "RFK Jr. Is Our Brother and Uncle. He's Tragically Wrong About Vaccines," *Politico,* May 8, 2019.

Chapter 13

Interviews: Nathan Stern, Craig Smith, and Steven Miller. Article: Ben Cohen, "The Pandemic's Most Powerful Writer Is a Surgeon," *Wall Street Journal,* April 1, 2020.

Chapter 14

Interviews: Anand Joshi, Cleavon Gilman, Susie Bibi, Reuben Bibi, Kapil Rajwani, and Lisa Stoia. Gabriel Sherman, "'This Is Spiraling Out of Control': Allies Panic About Trump's Hospital Stay as White House Deflects," *Vanity Fair,* October 3, 2020.

Chapter 15

Interviews: Andrew Knapp, Victor Holness, Craig Smith, Jay Varma, Kenneth Prager, Bradley Hayward, Katherine Fischkoff, Steven Miller, Laureen Hill, Felix Khusid, Victor Holness, and Gabrielle Clarke. Articles: Tia Powell et al., "Allocation of Ventilators in a Public Health Disaster," *Disaster Medicine and Public Health Preparedness* 2, no. 1 (March 2008);

Cornelia Dean, "Guidelines for Epidemics: Who Gets a Ventilator?" *New York Times*, March 25, 2008.

Chapter 16

Interviews: Nathaniel Hupert and Fernando Martinez. Articles: Dareh Gregorian, "'I Operate on the Data and on the Numbers': Cuomo Responds to Trump Ventilator Claims," NBC News, March 27, 2020; Brian M. Rosenthal, "This Hospital Cost $52 Million. It Treated 79 Virus Patients," *New York Times*, July 21, 2020.

Chapter 17

Interviews: Angela Mills and Corey Feist. Articles: Corina Knoll et al., "'I Couldn't Do Anything': The Virus and an E.R. Doctor's Suicide," *New York Times*, July 11, 2020; Maureen O'Connor, "A Doctor's Emergency," *Vanity Fair*, September 17, 2020.

Chapter 18

Interviews: Tomoaki Kato and Peter Liou.

Chapter 19

Interviews: Fernando Martinez, Hasina Outtz Reed, Robert Kampel, and Felix Khusid. Articles: Kevin Menes et al., "How One Las Vegas ED Saved Hundreds of Lives After the Worst Mass Shooting in U.S. History," *Emergency Physicians Monthly*, November 3, 2017; Brian M. Rosenthal et al., "'The Other Option Is Death': New York Starts Sharing of Ventilators," *New York Times*, March 26, 2020; "Archive: Governor Andrew Cuomo, 'Our Single Greatest Challenge Is Ventilators,'" Twitter, March 25, 2020.

Chapter 20

Interviews: Laura Forese. Articles: David Begnaud, "2 Weeks Ago Some Back Office Staff at @nyphospital Told Execs They Feared Going to Work in a Pandemic," Twitter, April 10, 2020; "Medical Community Battles Pandemic Despite Mounting Fear and Deaths," *CBS This Morning*, April 10, 2020.

Chapter 21

Interviews: Perry Cook. Article: William J. Broad and Dan Levin, "Trump Muses About Light as Remedy, but Also Disinfectant, Which Is Dangerous," *New York Times,* April 24, 2020.

Chapter 22

Source: Craig Smith, letter, May 6, 2020.

Chapter 23

Interviews: Benedict Harvey, Ben-Gary Harvey, Reuben Bibi, Susie Bibi, Bradley Hayward, Lindsay Lief, Fernando Martinez, Hasina Outtz Reed, David Berlin, Steven Corwin, Veronica Roye, Monica Nelson-Kone, and Nicole Golden. Article: "NewYork-Presbyterian Launches Dalio Center for Health Justice," NewYork-Presbyterian, October 13, 2020.

Chapter 24

Interviews: Lindsay Lief, Robert Kampel, Bradley Hayward, Samantha "Sam" Sportiello, Judith Cherry, and Jake Lief.

Chapter 25

Interviews: Robert Kampel, Bradley Hayward, and Judith Cherry.

Chapter 26

Interviews: Cleavon Gilman, Perry Cook, and Ellen and Steven Corwin. Other sources: J. David Goodman et al., "Cuomo Set to Receive $5.1 Million from Pandemic Book Deal," *New York Times,* May 17, 2021; Noam Scheiber and Brian M. Rosenthal, "Nurses and Doctors Speaking Out on Safety Now Risk Their Job," *New York Times,* April 9, 2020; Jane C. Timm, "Fact Check: Trump Needs 'Miracle' to Be Right About Rosy Vaccine Timeline, Experts Say," NBC News, May 15, 2020; Michael Dowling and Charles Kenney, *Leading Through a Pandemic* (Simon and Schuster, 2020); Andrea Salcedo, "An Arizona Doctor Went Viral Decrying a Lack of ICU Beds. Then He Says His Hospital Shut Him Out," *Washington Post,* December 11, 2020; Perry Cook, "We Have a Lifesaving Treatment for Covid-19. Why Is It So Hard to Get?" *New York Times,* March 31, 2021.

Chapter 27

Interviews: David Scales, Arthur Evans, and David Weir. Books and articles: Rebecca Solnit, *A Paradise Built in Hell* (New York: Penguin, 2020); Brian M. Rosenthal et al., "Why Surviving the Virus Might Come Down to Which Hospital Admits You," *New York Times,* July 1, 2020; Michael Barbaro et al., "The Mistakes New York Made," *The Daily* podcast, July 27, 2020; Sameer S. Kadri et al., "Association Between Caseload Surge and COVID-19 Survival in 558 U.S. Hospitals, March to August 2020," *Annals of Internal Medicine,* 174, no. 9 (September 2021).

Chapter 28

Interviews: Nathaniel Hupert, Pierre Saldinger, Jessica Forman, JoAnn Difede, Laura Forese, Rahul Sharma, Bradley Hayward, Tomoaki Kato, Veronica Roye, Chris Belardi, and Jay Varma. Articles: "'He's a Miracle': A Beloved Physician Walks Out of the Hospital After Battling COVID-19 for 164 Days," NewYork-Presbyterian, September 16, 2020; Dan Diamond, "Trump Officials Interfered with CDC Reports on Covid-19," *Politico,* September 11, 2020; Noah Weiland, "'Like a Hand Grasping': Trump Appointees Describe the Crushing of the C.D.C.," *New York Times,* December 16, 2020; Sharon LaFraniere, "Trump Health Aide Pushes Bizarre Conspiracies and Warns of Armed Revolt," *New York Times,* September 14, 2020.

Chapter 29

Interviews: Judith Cherry and Susie and Reuben Bibi.

Chapter 30

Interviews: Kerry Kennedy Meltzer and Fernando Martine. Article: Keziah Weir, "How Robert F. Kennedy Jr. Became the Anti-Vaxxer Icon of America's Nightmares," *Vanity Fair,* May 13, 2021.

Chapter 31

Interviews: Randy Subramany and Fernando Fernandez. Article: Campbell Robertson, Amy Harmon, and Mitch Smith, "'Healing Is Coming': U.S. Vaccinations Begin," *New York Times,* December 15, 2020.

Chapter 32

Interviews: Ellen and Steven Corwin.

Chapter 33

Interviews: Veronica Roye, Matt McCarthy, Elizabeth Oelsner, Anna Podolanczuk, and Xenia Frisby. Article: Kerry Kennedy Meltzer, "Vaccines Are Safe, No Matter What Robert Kennedy Jr. Says," *New York Times,* December 30, 2020.

Epilogue

Interviews: Steven Corwin, Emme Deland, Xenia Frisby, Veronica Roye, Laureen Hill, Laura Forese, Henry Murray, Lindsay Lief, Hilary Shaw, Rick Evans, Kate Heilpern, Nathaniel Hupert, Jim Malatras, Matt McCarthy, and Susie and Reuben Bibi. Books and articles: Brian Rosenthal, "The Largest Hospital System in New York Sued 2,500 Patients for Unpaid Medical Bills After the Pandemic Hit," *New York Times,* January 6, 2021; Ed Yong, "Why Health-Care Workers Are Quitting in Droves," *Atlantic,* November 16, 2021; B. H. Kean, *M.D.* (New York: Ballantine, 1990); David Gelles, "The C.E.O. at the Center of New York's Coronavirus Crisis," *New York Times,* May 1, 2020; Albert Camus, *The Plague,* translated by Stuart Gilbert (New York: Vintage, 1991).

Bibliography

The following works were helpful to me as source material.

Awdish, Rana. *In Shock: My Journey from Death to Recovery and the Redemptive Power of Hope*. New York: St. Martin's Press, 2017.

Barlett, Donald L., and James B. Steele. *Critical Condition: How Health Care in America Became Big Business—and Bad Medicine*. New York: Doubleday, 2004.

Barry, John M. *The Great Influenza: The Story of the Deadliest Pandemic in History*. New York: Viking, 2004.

Belkin, Lisa. *First, Do No Harm: The Dramatic Story of Real Doctors and Patients Making Impossible Choices at a Big-City Hospital*. New York: Simon and Schuster, 1993.

Brill, Steven. *America's Bitter Pill: Money, Politics, Backroom Deals, and the Fight to Fix Our Broken Healthcare System*. New York: Random House, 2015.

Bryson, Bill. *The Body: A Guide for Occupants*. New York: Doubleday, 2019.

Camus, Albert. *The Plague*. Translated by Stuart Gilbert. New York: Vintage, 1991.

Caro, Robert A. *The Power Broker: Robert Moses and the Fall of New York*. New York: Vintage Books, 1974.

Clarke, Rachel. *Breathtaking: Inside the NHS in a Time of Pandemic*. New York: Little, Brown, 2021.

Cuomo, Andrew. *American Crisis: Leadership Lessons from the COVID-19 Pandemic*. New York: Crown, 2020.

Dowling, Michael, and Charles Kenney. *Leading Through a Pandemic: The Inside Story of Humanity, Innovation, and Lessons Learned During the COVID-19 Crisis.* New York: Skyhorse Publishing, 2020.

Finch, Charles. *What Just Happened: Notes on a Long Year.* New York: Alfred A. Knopf, 2021.

Gottlieb, Scott. *Uncontrolled Spread: Why COVID-19 Crushed Us and How We Can Defeat the Next Pandemic.* New York: Harper, 2021.

Gotto, Antonio M., Jr., and Jennifer Moon. *Weill Cornell Medicine: A History of Cornell's Medical School.* New York: Cornell University Press, 2016.

Heineman, Matthew. *The First Wave.* New York: National Geographic Documentary Films, 2021.

Larson, Erik. *The Splendid and the Vile: A Sage of Churchill, Family, and Defiance During the Blitz.* New York: Crown, 2020.

Leonnig, Carol, and Philip Rucker. *I Alone Can Fix It: Donald J. Trump's Catastrophic Final Year.* New York: Penguin Press, 2021.

Lerner, Barron H. *The Good Doctor: A Father, a Son, and the Evolution of Medical Ethics.* Boston: Beacon Press, 2014.

———. *When Illness Goes Public: Celebrity Patients and How We Look at Medicine.* Baltimore: The Johns Hopkins University Press, 2006.

Lévy, Bernard-Henri. *The Virus in the Age of Madness.* New Haven: Yale University Press, 2020.

Lewis, Michael. *The Premonition: A Pandemic Story.* New York: W. W. Norton and Company Inc., 2021.

Mauro, James. *Twilight at the World of Tomorrow: Genius, Madness, Murder, and the 1939 World's Fair on the Brink of War.* New York: Ballantine, 2010.

McCarthy, Matt. *Odd Man Out: A Year on the Mound with a Minor League Misfit.* New York: Viking, 2009.

———. *The Real Doctor Will See You Shortly: A Physician's First Year.* New York: Crown Publishers, 2015.

———. *Superbugs: The Race to Stop an Epidemic.* New York: Avery, 2019.

Morgan, Matt. *Critical: Science and Stories from the Brink of Human Life.* New York: Simon and Schuster, 2019.

Morris, Charles R. *The Surgeons: Life and Death in a Top Heart Center.* New York: W. W. Norton and Company Inc., 2007.

Ofri, Danielle. *What Doctors Feel: How Emotions Affect the Practice of Medicine.* Boston: Beacon Press, 2013.

Oshinsky, David. *Bellevue: Three Centuries of Medicine and Mayhem at America's Most Storied Hospital.* New York: Doubleday, 2016.

———. *Polio: An American Story.* New York: Oxford University Press, 2005.

Picoult, Jodi. *Wish You Were Here: A Novel.* New York: Ballantine Books, 2021.

Roberts, Andrew. *Napoleon: A Life.* New York: Viking, 2014.

Rothman, David J. *Strangers at the Bedside: A History of How Law and Bioethics Transformed Medical Decision Making.* New York: Basic Books, 1991.

Sacks, Oliver. *Hallucinations.* New York: Alfred A. Knopf, 2012.

Salamon, Julie. *Hospital: Man, Woman, Birth, Death, Infinity, Plus Red Tape, Bad Behavior, Money, God, and Diversity on Steroids.* New York: Penguin Press, 2008.

Slavitt, Andy. *Preventable: The Inside Story of How Leadership Failures, Politics, and Selfishness Doomed the U.S. Coronavirus Response.* New York: St. Martin's Press, 2021.

Solnit, Rebecca. *A Paradise Built in Hell: The Extraordinary Communities That Arise in Disaster.* New York: Viking, 2009.

Snyder, Timothy. *Our Malady: Lessons in Liberty from a Hospital Diary.* New York: Crown, 2020.

Swartz, Mimi. *Ticker: The Quest to Create an Artificial Heart.* New York: Crown, 2018.

Washington, Harriet A. *Medical Apartheid: The Dark History of Medical Experimentation on Black Americans from Colonial Times to the Present.* New York: Doubleday, 2006.

Wright, Lawrence. *The Plague Year: America in the Time of Covid.* New York: Alfred A. Knopf, 2021.

About the Author

Marie Brenner is the author of eight books and writer at large for *Vanity Fair*. She has been a staff writer at *The New Yorker*, a contributing editor at *New York*, and has won numerous awards for her reporting around the world. Her exposé of the tobacco industry was the basis for the 1999 movie *The Insider*, which was nominated for seven Academy Awards, including Best Picture; her story on war reporter Marie Colvin became the 2018 film *A Private War*, starring Rosamund Pike; and her profile of Richard Jewell, falsely accused of attacking the 1996 Olympics, became the basis for Clint Eastwood's 2019 film of the same name. She lives in New York City.